Tales
of Old
New England

Compiled by **FRANK OPPEL**

CASTLE

Tales of Old New England

TABLE
OF
CONTENTS

1
Nantucket

SCRIBNER'S MONTHLY.

VOL. VI. AUGUST, 1873. No. 4.

NANTUCKET.

THE ARRIVAL—NANTUCKET WHARF.

IT sometimes happens to a town built upon the banks of the Mississippi, in consequence of a sudden alteration in the course of the river, to be unexpectedly cut off from the waters upon which its prosperity depended, and to be transformed into an inland settlement with useless wharves and warehouses. What the crevasse does in the case of the unfortunate Western town has been accomplished for the renowned whaling port of Nantucket by the freaks of commerce. Let no traveler visit it with the expectation of witnessing the marks of a flourishing trade, such as its enterprising citizens pursued while the various species of whale abounded in the neighborhood of our Atlantic coasts, or even after those monsters of the deep had been driven into the distant Pacific. Of the great fleet of ships which dotted every sea, scarcely a vestige remains. Two vessels were indeed still abroad at the time of our visit, but they had met with poor success, and were more likely to be sold than to return with cargoes of the precious oil. The solitary brig "Amy" lay rotting at the wharf, waiting for some purchaser to take her away and turn her to some more profitable use.

But if Nantucket has few attractions to offer such as arise from present prosperity, there is scarcely a seaboard town in America so quaint and so interesting on account of the reminiscences of the past which one constantly meets in every ramble.

If the reader will cast his eye upon any good map of the Eastern States, he will discover a group of islands of various forms and

A NANTUCKET FROLIC.

—when about to die, allowed his three daughters to choose for themselves among his possessions. The eldest, Elizabeth, for some not very evident reason, fixed her preference upon the islands, which accordingly took her name. Sensible Martha had the next choice, and did not hesitate to appropriate the "Vineyard." Alas! for poor Nancy, the youngest, nothing remained but a desolate heap of sand scarce rising above the ocean's waves. But necessity knows no laws, and so "*Nan tuk' it.*" It is a pity to spoil so good a story, in whose accuracy many an islander implicitly believes, but it is reasonably certain that Nantucket was an old Indian name, while Martha's Vineyard (called by the Indians *Capawock*) and the Elizabeth Islands, each of which still retains the aboriginal name, received their present appellations from the discoverer, Captain Bartholomew Gosnold, who, in 1602, made upon one of the latter the first attempt at colonization in New England. Good Queen Bess was certainly intended to be honored in the designation of the smaller group. What fancy led Gosnold in naming the largest island is un-

sizes lying off the southern shore of Massachusetts. First and nearest the mainland, a chain of small islands, jutting out from the south-western corner of the peninsula of Cape Cod, helps to inclose the sheet of water known by the ill-chosen name of Buzzard's Bay. These are the Elizabeth Islands. Further to the south-east, and a little more distant from the continent, is the somewhat triangularly shaped Martha's Vineyard, with its off-lying islet, No-Man's Land. Still further in the Ocean, and just south of the hooked projection of Cape Cod, lies Nantucket, with three or four smaller islands no less singular in the names they have received. Indeed, so puzzling is the origin of the appellations of the larger members of the group themselves, that the inhabitants have been driven to a fanciful derivation which can scarcely be admitted to the honors of undoubted history. A father—so the story runs

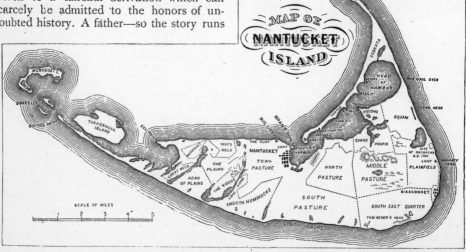

MAP OF NANTUCKET ISLAND

SCALE OF MILES

certain, and it is worthy of note that for years the name fluctuated between Martha's and *Martin's* Vineyard.

The island of Nantucket is a crescent, of which the two horns project far to the north and north-west. The town of Nantucket lies on the inner face of the crescent, protected from the violence of the ocean's waves by these two great natural breakwaters. The sole communication with the mainland is by the good steamer Island Home, in which we not long since left the little station of Hyannis, on the Cape Cod Railroad. The sail of about thirty miles consumed a little more than two hours, and a part of the time we were almost out of sight of land. At last

from this port, the custom was to relieve the heavily-laden ships on their return outside of the bar by means of lighters, or when stormy weather interfered with the operation they were compelled to take refuge in the haven of Edgartown, on Martha's Vineyard. A few years before the necessity for such a relief was obviated by the total decay of commerce, an ingenious contrivance was introduced. The *camels*, as they were called, were two immense caissons which were placed on either side of the whaler, with three great iron chains passing under its hull. From these caissons the water was then pumped until the vessel rose sufficiently out of water to escape the bottom of the bar.

THE AUCTION.

the white spires of the town began to show themselves on the horizon, while the great projections on the right and left, like gigantic arms, seemed to extend to take us into the embrace of that hospitality for which the island is justly famous. Gradually the houses, rising one above another, came distinctly in view. It was, however, no easy matter to enter port; for the difficulties of the sailor increase as he approaches. A bar of sand stretches completely across the entrance, which the ingenuity of man has been taxed in vain to remove. The tides in a few days fill up any excavations which may be made, and a vessel drawing over nine feet can enter only at rare intervals. When whalers were fitted out in large numbers

Nothing remained but to tow the whaler into the harbor.

Once successfully over, our steamer began slowly to thread the narrow channel, and finally, rounding the lighthouse on Brant Point, drew up at one of the four or five wharves upon which the active commerce of the place once displayed itself. A goodly part of the population was awaiting our arrival; for the advent of the steamer with the passengers and mails from the mainland is the most exciting event that disturbs the monotony of the daily routine of existence. As varied as was the assemblage about us were the carriages that stood ready for the reception of any stray passenger. There was the unavoidable hack, of course, to accommodate the fashionable visitor and carry him to one or the other of the hotels ; and a few carry-alls of foreign construction. But the majority of the vehicles were those peculiar wagons which the old-fashioned Nantucketer clings to with fond affection and styles his *carts.* The more modern cart has four wheels, and resembles nothing more than it does an ordinary coal-wagon. As the high sides, made to protect the feet effectually from the winter winds which sweep with terrific force across the level plains, make it difficult to clamber in between the closely-set wheels, the step is placed behind, and one must pass over the seats to his place. The genuine cart is different, for it has but two wheels, and is altogether destitute of permanent seats. If the whole family ride, each member, instead of standing, will be provided with a wooden chair taken from the kitchen. We can bear witness, after trial, that this mode of riding—"barring," that is to say, the danger of a sudden tipping back of the chair from some sudden jolt—is not unpleasant. It is in these "jaunting-cars" that the natives of Nantucket are particularly fond of indulging in their country frolics. Indeed, the young gallants are said to like nothing better than to collect in the cart a goodly number of their female acquaintance, and then, having reached some convenient spot, slyly unfasten the hooks that retain the

THE TOWN-CRIER.

body of the cart in its horizontal position, and suffer their screaming companions to slide out upon the soft sand.

If the crescent-like island is unique in shape, the appearance of the town itself is not less singular. The houses, especially in the southern part, rise one above the other, somewhat after the fashion of Quebec. The shingled sides and small-paned windows are sufficient marks of their age. Crowded together, with little room between and none in front, they testify to the social tastes of their original builders, and to the fact that those ancient residents cared little for the bit of green grass, or the patch of gay flowering plants, which elsewhere lend a peculiar grace even to the cottage of the lowly. Nearness to one's neighbor, far from being a drawback, was evidently regarded as an advantage. When the husbands and fathers were far off on the ocean, on cruises that occupied many months or even years, the wives and daughters were glad that their homes were huddled together in one corner of the island, instead of being scattered over its entire extent. The most palpable relic of the time of the whale-fishery, however, is found in the many "*walks*," as they are styled, which are even yet preserved. Of old no whale-fisherman thought of inhabiting a house from whose roof he could not obtain an easy and pleasant outlook upon the harbor, or at least gather some idea of the prospects of the weather, and the probable return of the sailing craft of the place. Much more than the half of the walks have been taken down as useless ; but from a single point we have counted thirty in sight. The platform is small or large, built around a single chimney and barely accommodating two or three persons at a time, or running the entire length of the roof, and with room for the whole family to congregate on a pleasant evening ; and the balustrade surrounding it is as plain or as ornamental as the taste or means of the occupant may have dictated.

Whatever the pretensions of the house, however, upon it or upon some adjoining barn, the seafaring taste of the former occupants is likely to be visible in a vane, which, instead of taking the form of a weather-cock, is rudely shaped to represent a whale or other monster of the deep.

There are other reminders of the olden time not less odd than the external appearance of the houses. We were scarcely comfortably domiciled before our ears were greeted with the jingling of a bell in the street, and the voice of the town-crier was

NANTUCKET HARBOR, FROM THE CHURCH TOWER.

heard. Nantucket can, it is true, boast of a weekly journal with its columns of advertisements, but these reach few persons compared with those intrusted to the town-crier. Two or three times a day he perambulates the streets, each time with one or more new announcements. It would be a vain attempt to represent on paper his tremulous inflections of voice. For the town-crier is an "institution," and whether he cries a "Concert in the Church" or a "meat auction," his singularly comical tones command instant attention. There are those indeed who will have it that this notable character is not altogether of sound mind, alleging in proof the circumstance that, having enlisted for a bounty during the late war, he soon reappeared as a civilian, and could give no better reason for his speedy return than that he had been discharged "because they said that he was '*noncompous*,' or something of the kind;" —an allegation in no wise credible, in view of the apt retorts he has been known to make. For instance, to a somewhat forward young lady, who from the steps of a boarding-house inquired of him where he had obtained the bell he was ringing, he instantly rejoined: "From the same foundry, ma'am, where you got your brass."

Ascending the tower of one of the churches, we find that from this elevated situation we can obtain a commanding view not only of the town, but of nearly the entire island. Almost at our feet the harbor is stretched out, with its deserted wharves and warehouses. Directly opposite Brant Point, and leaving a gap of little over half a mile— the passage through which we entered port— we see the long and narrow peninsula that still bears its old Indian name of *Coatue*. Sheltered by this tongue of land there is a broad bay reaching five miles or more, a placid sheet of water, which is the favorite sailing-ground for pleasure-parties, and upon whose shores are held *squantums*, or picnics, that constitute the chief diversion of the islanders in the pleasant season of the year.

And here we may as well say that Nantucket, besides retaining aboriginal appellations for almost all her districts, capes and ponds, has admitted a number of words from the same source into her spoken vocabulary, of which the *squantum* may serve as the type. In fact, the inhabitants, proud of their barren island, and by no means ashamed of any dialectic peculiarities, were accustomed, a few years ago—and probably the usage is not yet quite extinct—to designate all the inhabitants of the mainland, but more particularly their dangerous rivals, the fishermen of Cape Cod, by the somewhat opprobrious name of *Coufs*, which was, we presume, a part of their inheritance from the savages who for so many years lived upon the island with them.

A short distance from the town the eye takes in the principal bathing-ground, whose

RESIDENCE AND STUDIO OF EASTMAN JOHNSON.

been experimenting, but thus far with little success.

In the town, whose tortuous streets, with their old-fashioned unpainted houses, are mapped out below us, there are few buildings of special interest. The churches are modern and not essentially different from those of many other retired towns in New England, with the exception of this peculiarity —that, having been built for a growing place of about 10,000 inhabitants, they are much too large for a steadily diminishing one, whose population does not exceed 4,300. The "Coffin School," a brick structure which we see in a by-street, is chiefly interesting because it is a monument to the patriotism and munificence of a native of Boston, Admiral Sir Isaac Coffin, who, after attaining distinction and wealth on the other side of the Atlantic, returned to America to visit the birthplace of his ancestors, and to acquaint himself with the numerous descendants of Tristram Coffin, one of the original twenty pro-

growing attractions draw strangers hither from all parts of the country, and contribute somewhat to replenish the scanty purses of the discouraged tradesmen. Safety, quiet and delicious temperature, such are its characteristics, and nowhere can they be found in greater perfection. Those who love the rough surf need but to drive three miles to the southern side of the island, or to take up their abode in the fishing village at its eastern end; but the majority who shun the perils of the "under-tow" can ask for nothing better than what they can find just out of town at the Cliff, whither a fast-sailing pleasure sloop is constantly in readiness to take them. In fact, the high ground just above this beach, and commanding a magnificent sweep of the ocean, is the spot which ought to be occupied by cottages and hotels. The artist, Eastman Johnson, has shown his usual fine taste in taking up his summer residence here, and has transformed two or three old houses that stood on the site into a home, a convenient studio, etc.

As we turn our eyes over the narrowest part of the island, our attention is drawn to a feature of Nantucket that gives it quite a European aspect. It is the *windmills*, which, in the total absence of water-power, have from time immemorial ground all the corn the island produces. Once there was a long line of them along the top of the rising ground; but there now remain only two of the old familiar pattern, to which must be added a mill with horizontal vanes, upon which some inventive mechanic has for some years

THE OLD MILL.

prietors of Nantucket, and first magistrate of the island. The school was intended exclusively for those who could trace their origin back directly to this ancient worthy, but this in itself included no small part of the islanders, for so closely are they connected by successive intermarriages, that it was difficult to tell who was not entitled to its privileges. At present all are permitted to attend on payment of a small fee.

The active business of the place is almost confined to a single broad street, which, if it does not wear that thriving look which characterized it when Nantucket was the great whaling port of the world, still is lively enough at times even now. Near the water the fish-dealers sit at the proper hour of the day, with their article of merchandise before them upon a table—respectable and intelligent elderly persons, who to a man have "followed the sea for a living," and are full to overflowing with strange stories of outlandish places. And further up the street the auctions are held, at which a goodly portion of the population is wont to congregate for the purchase even of those articles of daily consumption which elsewhere are mostly sold over the counter.

One of our first excursions was to the small village of Siasconset, commonly abbreviated into 'Sconset. The ride thither was one of seven or eight miles. Emerging from the sinuosities of Orange street, we soon passed the few fenced fields, and came to the open country. Of roads, properly speaking, there were now none; but in every direction tracks diverged, making it difficult to take the bearings. The tracks consisted of the deep ruts, into which the wheels of our carriage plunged at times up to the hubs. Between them a single wider piece of sand, destitute of grass, marked the path of the horse. For a two-horse vehicle it is impossible to travel on the country roads, unless the horses are harnessed tandem. Once engaged upon a particular track, it was out of the question to leave it until we reached a "soft spot," without serious danger of upsetting or damaging the vehicle. And now we began to understand the traditional barrenness of Nantucket. When, just before the outbreak of the Revolution, the British Government contemplated coercing the inhabitants of New England into submission by the "Massachusetts Bay Restraining Bill," which would

A FRUITLESS EXPERIMENT.

have excluded them from trading elsewhere than with Great Britain and Ireland and the English West Indies, or from fishing on the banks of Newfoundland, the Society of English Friends made a plea of extreme poverty for Nantucket, which we cannot but regard as sufficiently forcible. "A great number of innocent persons," they urged, "particularly in the island of Nantucket, would by the prohibitory bill be reduced to extreme distress. The inhabitants of this island amount to between five and six thousand in number; the soil of it is so barren that, though fifteen miles in length and three in breadth, *its produce is scarce sufficient for the maintenance of twenty families.*" With the customary recklessness of the first settlers in New England, the colonists of Nantucket cut away the luxuriant forests which are said to have clothed it when first discovered by the whites, and their children followed their example, until now not a single tree of the original growth remains. It was not until some twenty-five years ago that the essential step of replanting the island was begun, and now there are thousands of acres of young but thrifty pines. Meantime the severe winds that swept over the denuded island blew away much of the light soil, and the improvident farmers made no attempt to enrich the ground which they drained of its richness, until now there is scarcely a pretense of cultivating the greater part of the surface. A more unproductive tract can rare-

THE OLD FISH DEALER.

parts of the island, where there were stated religious services, conducted by native preachers. Almost from the very first the colonists perceived the danger to which the impulsive and excitable Indian was subject from the introduction of ardent spirits, and among the earliest enactments made by the general court which had jurisdiction over both Nantucket and Martha's Vineyard was a law that punished any one who furnished them "wine or strong drink other than beer" by a fine of five shillings for every pint thus given. To tell the truth, the law was dictated scarcely less by prudence than by humanity; for many years the red men were far more numerous than the whites,—in 1675 not less than 500 or 600 against 30 whites capable of bearing arms. Nearly a century later, there were still 358 Indians; but a strange pestilence which visited the island, entirely confining its ravages to them, in a single year (1763) swept away all but 136 of their number. The last of the Nantucket Indians was one Abraham Api Quady, or Quary, who died in 1854, at the age of 82 years. Many of the inhabitants remember him as a venerable, inoffensive old man, living by himself in a comfortable house of his own not far from town, and supporting himself principally by selling the berries which he

ly be met with, and the old myth does not seem so utterly absurd "that Nantucket arose from the ashes from the pipe of the Indian deity, who, when tobacco was scarce, after borrowing all he could, filled his pipe with sand, and when his smoke was ended emptied the pipe into the sea!"

The village of Siasconset has quite merged its character of a fishing village into that of a watering-place. The rude cottages have been modified as far as possible to accommodate the new visitors, and numbers of houses in the town of Nantucket have been taken down and removed to Siasconset. Rough and inconvenient as are the quarters, we were told that every room was engaged for the ensuing year.

As the name indicates, there was once an Indian village at or near this spot. All vestiges of the aborigines, however, have now disappeared. When Nantucket was first discovered, there is said to have been a considerable native population, although it was variously stated from 700 to nearly twice that number. The colonists treated the Indians with greater kindness than the savages received elsewhere. They bought their lands from each of the four sachems by whom the island was governed, giving them in the aggregate far more than they paid to the English grantees from whom they bought their claims. Not only so, but they permitted the Indians to retain for cultivation as much land as they actually needed. They also undertook in good earnest to Christianize them, and the Mayhews were especially successful in this good work. For a long time there were four meeting-houses on different

THE "COFFIN SCHOOL."

picked on the commons. He had seen his wife and all his children die before him, and for a long time appeared to be himself awaiting the tardy summons to follow them. In his youth, like most of his red brothers, he was a fisherman, and no one was a more faithful hand upon the whaling ship. Later he was the prince of Nantucket caterers, and without his assistance no evening entertainment was deemed complete. An oil painting by Madam Dassel in the Athenæum Library is said to reproduce faithfully the melancholy and somewhat severe features of this last representative of the Indian race.

Since Abraham Quady's death the excursions which used to be made to his humble cottage have taken another direction. For want of better material for romance, the lonely huts of two white men, voluntary recluses, have of late become places of resort. Old Fred Parker, as he is familiarly called, is the better known of the two "hermits." His lonely residence is in the extreme eastern part of the island, at Quidnit, near the sea, and not far north of Sankati Light. Here, dressed in the rudest of costumes, with clothes originally far too small for his great height, and now patched to such an extent as to render recognition of their pristine shape and material difficult or impossible, the solitary man lives from year to year. His sole diversion is reading; his means of subsistence the scanty product of his fishing, eked out by the few copper coins which he obtains from visitors on the plea of using the pieces of metal to nail to the floor of his cabin and form the initials of their names. His rival in the art of solitary living, David Coffin by name, lives, or lived, in the vicinity of Maddequet, in the western side of the island, an object of equal interest, according to those who have visited him.

The eastern and southern shores of Nantucket offer peculiar dangers to the foreign commerce of the country. Most of the coasting vessels cling to the mainland; passing between this island and the southern shore of Cape Cod. Vessels from abroad, however, are apt to find Nantucket directly in their way. For their protection the United States Government has built a lighthouse on Sankati Head, a mile or two north of Siasconset, the flash from whose revolving light we have been assured by careful captains they have seen when full forty miles distant upon the ocean. The French mechanism by which this result is effected is of splendid workmanship, and well deserves a visit to inspect it. About thirty miles very

ABRAHAM QUADY, THE LAST INDIAN.

nearly south, a light-ship marks the eastern extremity of the too famous Nantucket Shoals. Notwithstanding every precaution, however, the number of shipwrecks is still very great. In rare cases, a sloop or schooner getting aground in calm weather can be hauled off by the aid of a steamer. During our stay upon the island, this occurred to a small craft that allowed itself to venture too near Great Point in broad daylight. But usually the sand closes in about the keel so firmly as to defy the puny efforts of man. Such was the case of the brig Poinsett, which ran upon the South Shore, on the first of September, 1870. All Nantucket streamed across the island to see the stranded vessel, and not a device was left untried to save it. It was a magnificent sight, for the waves that dashed upon it were high and strong. One only needs to compare the two views taken by photography, of the Poinsett when she first came ashore, and again of the scanty remains of the same ship that alone were to be seen embedded in the sand two days later, to form some idea of the terrible energy of the angry sea.

The loss of life is happily far less frequent than the destruction of property,—a circumstance that is due perhaps chiefly to the absence of rocky headlands. An incident that happened in the depth of the cold winter 1870-1, nearly proved fatal, and furnished a fine opportunity for the display of that latent heroism which is so large an ingredient in the character of all seafaring men. Just as one of the most severe storms of the season was setting in, on Sunday morning, February 5th, 1871, the announcement was made in town that a schooner was aground upon the bar outside, and indeed a strong glass revealed not only the vessel, but the sailors, some five in number. The Island Home was in port, and there was no lack of volunteers to go out with her to the rescue. Meantime the thermometer was at or below zero. Before the steamer had gone half-way, the ice had formed so strong a barrier that she could neither advance nor return. But one hope remained, and that was, that the crust of ice which had been forming out from shore to the scene of the wreck, might prove firm enough to permit the advance of a rescuing party from some point of the shore. Night had again closed in, and darkness added to the perils of the undertaking. But there were those who were willing to make the venture in order to save the lives which the sea and the cold already claimed as their own. "At about ten o'clock," writes the Nantucket *Inquirer and Mirror* of the next Saturday, "a party of eight men, provided with two dories and several long boards, pushed out from the Cliff Shore, feeling their way cautiously towards the distressed vessel. The night was beautifully clear, but the air was stinging cold, and the ice, in some places, unfit to bear the weight of the dories. At such places, the boards came into play; and in two instances they were obliged to take to the dories and pull for it. Thus, altering the different means of locomotion to suit the circumstances, the party of heroes toiled on for some two hours and a half in passing a distance estimated by them at two miles." They found the captain and crew alive but exhausted and well-nigh frozen; but the rescuers had not forgotten to bring extra clothing and such other comforts as they could carry about their persons. With but little delay both the crew and their deliverers set off on their return, which proved to be easier than the passage out, as every hour had added to the firmness of the ice. The whole party landed about three o'clock on Monday morning, we are told, safe and sound except some frostbites, but nearly worn out with

PORTRAIT OF ADMIRAL COFFIN.

cold and exhaustion. The names of the gallant men who imperiled their lives in the gallant exploit—and these include some representatives of old and honored Nantucket families — were Isaac Hamblen, George A. Veeder, Alexander Fanning, James A. Holmes, Joseph P. Gardner, William E. Bates, Stephen E. Keyes and Henry C. Coffin. They richly merited the medal which each of them received as a recognition of his bravery. The remains of the vessel from which the sailors were rescued may still be seen advancing with every storm, and gradually nearing the "Cliff" bathing-ground, where they will probably soon join the other wreck which forms so picturesque a feature of the neighborhood.

The insular character of Nantucket, and its comparative distance from the mainland, have conferred upon its natives a number of peculiarities that render society here quite different from almost anywhere else. The great majority of the islanders are descendants of the "twenty first proprietors"—of whom we shall shortly have occasion to speak—and bear their names. The Coffins, the Folgers, the Starbucks, the Macys, the Barnards, the Swains, are each to be counted by hundreds. By intermarriages almost the whole island is bound together. The interests of all are the same and their tastes similar. Much of this community of feeling arises from the extent to which the islanders are thrown upon their own resources during the inclement portion of the year. The summer visitor has little conception of the seclusion of Nantucket in winter. Even now, it often happens that all communication with the mainland is cut off by stormy weather for a week or ten days ; but before the days of steam it was common enough, a Nantucket writer says, for a month or two to pass without news from abroad. "The month of February was especially known as 'trumpery month,' for the reason that we, or our ancestors, had nothing to discourse about but such as transpired in our midst. As lately as the winter of 1856–7, a vessel approached the East end of the island, and landed *twenty-four* mails at one time !" Indeed, the story is currently reported as being the sober truth, that a few years ago, the first news received from the "States," after a considerable interval of time, reached Nantucket *via* London, having been carried across the Atlantic, printed in the English papers, and brought here by a British vessel that touched at one of the "points" for water and provisions.

The poet Whittier, who sings loud praises of the hospitality of Nantucket, has immortalized the incidents of its first colonization in "The Exiles," some of the stanzas of which deserve a place among the finest our countryman has written. The island, after its discovery by Gosnold, was granted by the crown of Great Britain to the Plymouth Company, and by them to the Earl of Stirling. In 1641, the Earl's agent for the sale of all the islands between Cape Cod and the Hudson River, James Forrett, sold Nantucket to Thomas Mayhew and his son, merchants of Watertown, Massachusetts, for £40. To fortify his title to Martha's Vineyard and the neighboring islands, Mayhew had taken the precaution to obtain deeds also from Sir Ferdinando Gorges, Proprietor of Maine, whose claim covered part of the same territory. But not only did the island remain pretty much unoccupied, but the neighboring colonies seemed in little haste to appropriate such distant and apparently worthless property. After being under the nominal jurisdiction of Massachusetts Bay for a few years, the authorities, apparently unwilling to be troubled with the outlying islands any longer, voted them to be without their limits, and the islands became for a time practically independent. It was under these circumstances that some inhabitants of the little town of Salisbury, dissatisfied with the intolerant legislation of the Bay Colony, turned their eyes towards a spot where they might be freed from the operation of the hated laws. Mayhew, who valued Martha's Vineyard more highly than the barren island east of it, was easily brought to consent to part with his exclusive right to Nantucket. The deed is yet extant, in which, in July, 1659, he sold Nantucket to Tristram Coffin, Thomas Macy, Christopher Hussey, Rich-

THE HERMIT OF QUIDNIT (FROM A PAINTING BY GEO. B. WOOD).

ard Swayne, Thomas Bernard, Peter Coffin, Stephen Greenleaf, John Swayne and William Pike, "for Thirty Pounds Current Pay ... *and also two Beaver Hatts, one for myselfe and one for my wife !*" Mayhew reserved himself an equal interest with each of the new proprietors. Early in the next year, each of the ten was empowered to take to himself a partner, and thus was formed the body of the "Twenty First Purchasers."

Meantime, the event occurred which induced the first actual settlement of the island. Thomas Macy and his wife had rendered themselves liable to severe penalties for harboring three or four Quakers, one of whom, at least, was afterward sent to the gallows for his faith. Excuse their fault as they might,— and Macy did apologize for his violation of the law, as his preserved letter shows, in a much humbler tone than the poet would lead us to suppose,—Massachusetts was no longer a comfortable abode. And so one autumnal day, the young couple, with but a single companion, Edward Starbuck, started in an open boat upon their dangerous trip. But the winds and the waves were propitious—

    "On passed the bark in safety
      Round isle and headland steep—
    No tempest broke above them,
      No fog-cloud veiled the deep.

    "Far round the bleak and stormy Cape
      The venturous Macy passed,
    And on Nantucket's naked isle,
      Drew up his boat at last.

*   *   *   *   *   *   *

WRECK OF THE POINSETT.

    "And yet that isle remaineth
      A refuge of the free,
    As when true-hearted Macy
      Beheld it from the sea.

    "Free as the winds that winnow
      Her shrubless hills of sand—
    Free as the waves that batter
      Along the yielding land.

    "God bless the sea-beat island !
      And grant for evermore,
    That charity and freedom dwell
    As now upon her shore."

The spot which Macy selected for the site of the town was on the western side, a tract now called Maddequet, and since then deserted. Here the party wintered, and then Starbuck went back to Salisbury, where his good report induced others to follow him to Nantucket. The twenty proprietors became twenty-seven, by the addition of a few others whose acquaintance with some art or trade rendered them useful acquisitions to the community. One of these was Peter Foulger or Folger, the only person among them all who had any claim to literary attainments. The principal interest attaching to his name arises from the fact that his daughter was the mother of the immortal Benjamin Franklin. So implicit was the confidence reposed in his accuracy and integrity, that his associates not only made him one of the five commissioners for laying out their respective shares, but, when making three of them a quorum, provided that Peter Folger should be one of the three. A curious poem of his is still to be found, with the characteristic title : "A Looking-glass for the Times, or the Former Spirit of New England revived in this Generation." The poetic merits of the piece, it must be confessed, are not great. It is an attempt to account for the misery of the times, resulting from war :—

    "New England for these many years
      Hath had both rest and peace,
    But now the case is otherwise ;
      Our troubles *doth increase.*"

The "plague of war" was now begun :

    "Our women also they have took,
      And children very small.
    Great cruelty they have used
      To some, though not to all."

From this poem we learn that the majority of the first settlers of Nantucket were Anabaptists, in whose persecution the poet finds the "crying sin" that called for the anger of Heaven :

SANKATI LIGHT-HOUSE.

"The cause of this their suffering
   Was not for any sin,
But for the witness that they bare
   Against babes' sprinkling."

It is interesting to notice that for a considerable part of the seventeenth century, the islands which Massachusetts Bay so cavalierly refused to recognize as dependencies formed part of the colony of New York. Martha's Vineyard and Nantucket were both incorporated in the appanage given by Charles the Second to his brother James, Duke of York. Governor Lovelace, however, did not hesitate to recognize the authority previously conferred upon Mayhew over both islands, upon due acknowledgment of the Duke's paramount jurisdiction. Accordingly we read in an old patent the somewhat amusing condition of the *quasi* independence the islanders were to enjoy, by "ye said Patentees and their Associates. . . . rendering and paying yearly and every Yeare, unto his Royall Highness ye Duke of Yorke, his Heyres and Assigns, or to such Governor or Governors as from Time to Time shall be by him constituted and appointed, as an Acknowledgment, *foure Barrells of good merchantable Codfish*, to be delivered at ye Bridge in this City " (New York).

The settlers early directed their attention to the admirable fishing in which the neighborhood of Nantucket abounded. Soon the pursuit of the whale became the favorite employment of the whites, who found able assistants in the Indians. So numerous were the whales in the neighboring ocean, that almost every storm stranded some upon the beach. In one case *eleven* were thus counted. Indeed the Indians made such account of this source of gain, that in their deeds of the land they were accustomed expressly to reserve the right to have *one-half of all the drift whales*. It was not until 1765 that the supply of whales in the immediate vicinity grew so small that the practice of going out from the shore to pursue them was entirely abandoned. Meanwhile, however, the enterprise of the islanders had been aroused, and ships were built to cruise in search of the retreating prey. By the middle of the century, the Nantucket whalemen had penetrated Davis's Straits and Baffin's Bay. Within about ten years from that time they visited the Guinea Coast, and a dozen years later they used the harpoon off Brazil.

The Revolutionary War almost annihilated the single branch of industry upon which Nantucket depended for existence. It is true that the inhabitants, being now in great part Quakers, took no active part in the hostilities; but for their known sympathy with the patriotic party they were permitted to suffer the misfortunes to which their peculiar geographical position naturally exposed them. It was not until a year or two before the return of peace that they received permits to resume the whale-fishery. Even then they had lost 134 vessels, captured by the English.

Still the indomitable perseverance of the whalemen soon restored them to comparative prosperity. It may be doubted, however, whether the enterprise has on the whole proved a remunerative one. When the disastrous results of the two wars with Great Britain are taken into account, and to these are added the losses consequent upon an extremely hazardous fishery, and an article of commerce subject to violent fluctuations in price, it may readily be comprehended that the returns have been far less than those which would have been obtained had the

Obverse.

Reverse.
MEDAL OF THE HUMANE SOCIETY.

same capital, labor and energy been embarked in the ordinary pursuits of agriculture or trade. Not rarely a ship well equipped, and furnished with the greatest care, met with such reverses that after being absent three or four years, she returned only to exhibit a considerable positive loss of money to her·owners, officers and men, each one of whom took a certain proportionate interest in the undertaking. Happily in the majority of cases it was otherwise. The largest sum we have ever heard of a single voyage netting was $108,000, of which about two-thirds went to the owners. It required but few spermaceti whales, such as that of which the jaw has recently been placed in the Nantucket Athenæum, to fill even the largest whaler. We say *the* jaw; for it is well known to naturalists that the spermaceti whale has teeth only upon the lower jaw, while the upper is provided with sockets into which these fit. The ponderous jaw we speak of weighs some 800 lbs. and is about 17 feet long, while the marine monster to which it belonged measured not less than 87 feet in length, and produced for its fortunate captors

110 barrels of oil. Some idea of its magnitude may be derived from the circumstance that a barrel of pure oil was extracted from the cavity of each half jaw which is shown in the accompanying illustration.

But the day of the whale-fishery, and with it that of the prosperity of Nantucket, have passed away, apparently forever. The first serious blow at the town's commercial importance was struck in the month of July, 1846, when a conflagration consumed most of the business portion of the place. Similar disasters, but on a smaller scale, had previously visited the place; but from one of such magnitude Nantucket could not recover. The fire was followed, two or three years later, by the discovery of gold in California, and by the consequent exodus of a very large number of the most active and promising young men, carrying with them no small part of the capital and enterprise of the town. More fatal than either of these causes was the rapid decrease in the number of whales. In vain did the fishermen explore the frozen regions of the north, or penetrate the most remote gulfs of the Pacific Ocean, directing their attention indifferently to "spermaceti," "right" or "fin-back" whales; and consenting to spend weary years in distant navigation. The number of whales captured was small, and few vessels returned with more than half their complement of oil. Unfortunately for Nantucket, though fortunately for the world at large, the diminution in the supply was not compensated by the rise in the price of the commodity. The oil-wells of Pennsylvania began to yield an oil so abundant and so well adapted for illuminating purposes, that whale oil came to be employed to a much more limited extent than previously. The few remnants of the Nantucket whale-fishery gradually drifted to the city of New Bedford, otherwise possessing many natural advantages. One of the last whales whose capture delighted the hearts of the inhabitants was a single individual of the "fin-back" species, which was killed four or five years ago at a short distance out, and was towed into port to be cut up and "tried." It was but a small fish, compared with those with which the whalemen were accustomed to do battle in the open seas.

Before leaving Nantucket, it was necessary, of course, to visit the different cemeteries, of which almost every Christian denomination has one. Except the Friends' burying-ground, with its unmarked graves, all furnish their full proportion of curious

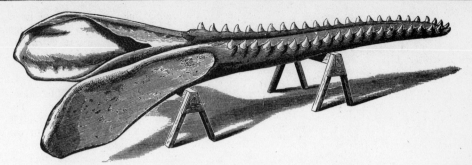

JAW OF A SPERMACETI WHALE (IN THE MUSEUM OF THE ATHENÆUM).

epitaphs. Here are two or three. One laconic inscription reads thus :—

"Father *gorn* home !"

The grammar of the second is not perfect :

"As you pass by, pray cast an eye,
For as you *am,* so once was I.
As I am now, so you must be ;
Prepare for death, and follow me."

But we doubt whether "ould Ireland" itself can surpass the following blundering verses over the tomb in which one not over-bright genius *intended* that his wife should rest. It is to be found in the "South" bury-ing-ground. His wife's relations, thinking it only right that after supporting her, and probably the husband too, during their entire married life, they should have the choice of her last place of repose, had insisted upon laying her remains in the "North" grounds. Which state of affairs the widower thus records :—

"Here lies the body of my wife.
Though very dear, *she's not laid here.*
Some private grief was her disease,
Laid to the North, her friends to please."

Our return to the mainland was relieved of monotony by a characteristic incident. Early in the morning, the captain of the Island Home was notified by the Com-missioner of Wrecks, who at Nantucket holds an important position, that his steamer would be held in requisition to go to the relief of a schooner which from the South Tower had been observed to be fast upon the small sand-spit called the Handker-chief. In such cases there is no option left, for, according to law and custom, the wreck must be first attended to, irre-spective of mail-connections and the con-venience of passengers. In truth, the captain and sailors were nothing loath to take the wrecking crew on board, anticipating a hand-some return for their additional trouble. The adventure turned out better than we feared. The schooner proved to have got aground through singular carelessness in neglecting to observe the position of the neighboring light-ship ; but the tide was rising, and our steamer, having soon succeeded in drawing her into deeper water, was able to resume her course without serious delay.

PRIMITIVE FISH-CART.

2
Ice

ICE.

ICE and frozen snow were known as luxuries as far back as history records, the latter being mostly in use in the East. The mode of gathering it in winter, and transporting it for use in summer, and the method of preserving it in those intensely hot climates, was truly primitive, and frequently involved great labor and cost. In many portions of Asia the snow was gathered in sacks, far up in the mountains, and transported to the principal cities on the backs of mules, there preserved in cisterns sunk in the earth, and packed carefully between layers of straw. This method still prevails in some sections.

But up to the commencement of the present century, in those climates where the temperature never reaches the freezing point, ice was a luxury that few beyond the wealthiest could indulge in. In India, as also

21

among the ancient Greeks and Romans, artificial ice was produced in small quantities, and within the last half century successful experiments in its manufacture have been made both in this country and Europe.

The natural production, however, of our northern climates, together with the great facility for transportation, has almost entirely superseded the use of this artificial movement. It is astonishing to what an extent an article, once regarded as a simple luxury in non-producing countries, and in the northern latitudes as an article of no computed practical value, has become recognized in the commerce of the world.

One hardly realizes that the frozen lakes and rivers of the North furnish labor for thousands who would otherwise be unemployed during the greater portion of the winter months; that the ice trade employs millions of capital; that in the revenue to the carrying trade of the United States, both foreign and coastwise, it ranks next to cotton and grain, and frequently exceeds the latter; that the universal practical use to which it is applied in the preservation of meats, fruits, and vegetables, has, within the past thirty years, produced an entire revolution in the system of domestic economy, to say nothing of the blessings it has brought to suffering humanity, in our hospitals, and in our pestilence-stricken cities.

The transportation of ice by sea was not thought of until the commencement of the present century. The world is indebted for the beneficent results that have followed from the introduction of the ice trade, to Frederick Tudor, a wealthy and eccentric citizen of Massachusetts, well known seventy-five years ago for his extensive salt-works at Nahant.

In 1805 the yellow fever raged through the West India Islands, the towns and cities were decimated, and the officers and crews of the European fleets were almost entirely swept off by the disease. The need of ice was very greatly felt throughout the islands. In the winter of that year, Mr. Tudor cut from a small pond, situated on a plantation of his own in Saugus, some two or three hundred tons of ice, hauled it on teams to Charlestown, loaded a portion of it into the brig " Favorite," and sailed with it to the island of Martinique. The venture was regarded by his friends as a wild and visionary one, and he suffered nearly as much ridicule as his contemporary eccentricity, " Lord Timothy Dexter," did when he shipped the warming-pans; but one of Mr. Tu-

dor's prominent points of character, and one exemplified in nearly every act of his long and useful life, was an utter contempt for other people's opinions; he never asked advice of any one, and always turned his back upon all that was offered. The strength of his purpose was generally measured by the amount of opposition he encountered. We were well acquainted with him, and often, when in one of his pleasant moods, he would delight to rehearse his early experience. There was nothing of fancy or mere speculation that induced him to embark in this experiment. He had made the subject a study, and the results of his theories effectually vindicated their soundness.

The first experiment proved a failure in a pecuniary point of view, as Mr. Tudor himself predicted, but it satisfied him as to the future, when he should have had time to work out the problems presented by the experiment.

The English Government was the first to appreciate the advantages likely to accrue to its colonists from the introduction of ice, and ten years after Mr. Tudor's first shipment, or shortly after the close of the war of 1812, he received and accepted overtures that were eminently favorable; the first was the grant of a monopoly of the trade upon conditions that were readily acceded to; the second was the release of certain port dues (then very heavy) to all ships bringing ice.

The Island of Jamaica was then in the zenith of its wealth and commercial prosperity, and the richest colonial possession of Great Britain. Mr. Tudor established his ice-houses at Kingston, the commercial capital of the island. This was the first prominent and *permanent* point,—although this distinction has been accorded by some to Havana, and up to the time of emancipation the trade was quite brisk. Mr. Tudor also secured the monopoly of Havana, with liberal arrangements for the introduction of ice in other ports on the Island of Cuba. The Tudor Company still retain the monopoly of Havana and the Island of Jamaica. All other ports in the West Indies are practically open to competition. Of these, the principal are St. Thomas, Martinique, Barbadoes, Trinidad, Demerara (on the main), Cienfuegos, Santiago de Cuba, Manzanillo. The ice supplied to these ports is shipped exclusively from Boston.

Next in order after the West India ports comes the introduction of ice into our domestic ports by Mr. Tudor. The first cargo was shipped to Charleston, S. C., in 1817. Charleston was then the most important commercial port in the Southern States.

In 1818 Mr. Tudor established a branch of the trade in Savannah, then, as for years afterward, a rival of Charleston. In 1820 he established ice-houses in New Orleans, which city, thirty years later, became the largest consuming city in the United States, south of Philadelphia.

It is a singular fact that the bulk of ice consumed was in foreign and Southern domestic ports. This, however, may be accounted for in this way : Before the introduction of Croton in New York, and Cochituate in Boston, the deep wells in both cities answered the double purpose of supplying cool spring water for drink, and as reservoirs for keeping meats, butter, milk, etc., cool in summer. It is not necessary that one should be very old to remember when we did not have ice-chests in our markets, and refrigerators in our hotels and private residences. The dairyman who brought his butter and milk to market, and the farmer and butcher who slaughtered his beef and mutton during the hottest of the summer months, had his little ice-house, or cellar, containing from ten to fifty tons, which answered every purpose. Now there are delivered and consumed in New York City alone, during the winter months, more tons of ice than were cut, shipped, and consumed, in the United States in a twelvemonth thirty years ago.

In May, 1833, Mr. Tudor, at the request of English and American merchants resident in Calcutta, sent a small cargo of about 200 tons to that port. A Calcutta voyage in those days involved about six months for the passage out. The result, like that of his first shipment to the West Indies, was not a pecuniary success, but it proved that ice brought twenty thousand miles could, with all the attendant waste and losses, successfully compete in prices with that prepared by the natives. The result was the establishment of a trade which has steadily increased in volume and importance, and which enables Boston to hold the key to the rich and extensive commerce between Calcutta and the United States.

In 1834 Mr. Tudor extended his trade in another direction, and sent a cargo to Rio Janeiro. Up to 1836 Mr. Tudor was the ice king of the world. At this remove of time we can easily figure up results, but words are inadequate when one attempts to do justice to the memory of this wonderful man, whose genius and ability have opened up such blessings to the race. He saw the conception of his brain take form and shape ; he nursed it, and watched over it through trials and obstacles that would have disheartened one less confident in his own resources ; he lived to see it at its full maturity, a giant among men and nations. He had succeeded, but this success did not narrow him, and he was willing, if not gratified, in seeing others spring up to share in and increase the trade he had labored so diligently to build up.

In 1842 certain intimations were received from parties in London, which induced a shipment of Boston ice to that city, in the bark "Sharon," by the firm of Gage, Hittinger & Co. Mr. Jacob Hittinger, of this firm, is, by the way, at the present writing, the oldest living representative of the ice trade in the country.

Previous to this the aristocracy and the London clubs had depended for their ice upon small shallow reservoirs or wells, where the water was let in periodically and frozen. These, with the exception of a comparatively large well-shaped reservoir on the summit of Ludgate Hill, constituted all the resources of London in that respect.

At that date fancy drinks were almost unheard of in the clubs, taverns, and gin palaces of London. Mr. Hittinger conceived the idea of introducing these, to show to what extent ice was used in "the States" for this purpose. He, therefore, secured the services of several bar-keepers, whom he had initiated into the mysteries of mixing juleps, smashes, cocktails, and other drinks known only in Yankeeland. His experience, as he relates it himself, is very amusing :

" I went out in the steamer, so as to make arrangements for the arrival of the bark and cargo, delivered my letters, talked with parties, and felt perfectly sure that I had struck a vein. In due time the 'Sharon,' having made a good passage, arrived in the Thames. The thing had been talked over so much, that the cargo of Boston ice was as well advertised as it could have been in the columns of the 'Times.' But, after all, it appeared to them a strange fish that no one dared to touch. My feelings were just about the temperature of my ice, and wasting as rapidly. At last, I was introduced to the Chairman or President of the Fishmongers' Association, an association which I was not long in discovering had the merit of wealth, if not of social position. He was sociable, and seemed to comprehend *my* position if I didn't *his*. Matters were soon arranged; a magnificent hall or saloon had been secured; I ascertained that my bar-keepers, through constant drill, had attained the correct sleight of hand in mixing the drinks. The hour arrived. The hall was long and brilliantly lighted. After the company was seated, the chairman introduced me and the subject matter of the evening's discussion. Now, thought I, I am all right. At a given signal the well-trained waiters appeared, laden with the different drinks. The effect was gorgeous, and I expected an ovation that no Yankee had ever had. But, alas! the first sounds that broke the silence were: 'I say—aw, waitaw, a little 'ot wataw, if you please; I prefer it 'alf 'n' 'alf.' I made

taking passage in a steamer from Boston. His reception was flattering, and the most brilliant inducements and the most sanguine assurances were held out. "Wenham Lake" ice all at once became the talk in London; but, like another bubble that went before, it soon burst. After extravagant outlays, and the almost entire loss of several cargoes, the enterprise was given up, never to be repeated, and England now gets its ice from Norway. And yet to-day Wenham Lake ice is advertised in London. In this connection a story is told by Mr. Thomas Groom, a prominent merchant of Boston, a native of England, who visited London a year or two ago:

"In passing through the fish market, I noticed a sign reading thus: 'Norway,

SCRAPING

a dead rush for the door, next day settled my bills in London, took the train for Liverpool and the steamer for Boston, and counted up a clear loss of $1,200."

This was the story of the first cargo of ice sent from the United States to England. Young Lander of Salem, however, saw fit to discredit the statement of Mr. Hittinger in regard to his loss, and, being wealthily connected, had no difficulty in obtaining the best bankers' letters of introduction, and also others from gentlemen eminent in social life, to parties holding a corresponding position there.

Thus armed, he chartered a ship to carry one thousand tons at $10 per ton freight, and anticipated her arrival in London by

London, and American ice for sale.' I asked the fishmonger which he thought was the best.

"'Oh, the London ice, sir.'

"'Why?'

"'You see,' he replied, 'the American ice and the Norway ice is nothing but congealed water; it is too thick, while, you see, London ice is made in one week; and being only six inches thick, is so much 'arder than the American.'"

The loading of ships at Charlestown is, perhaps, one of the most interesting features connected with the ice trade. Formerly, or in the early days of shipping, ice was loaded on board ships very much in the same manner as common cargo, and it was a tedious process, besides involving a large waste of material. Modern inventions, originated and improved by the large dealers, have made this part of the business comparatively easy. The diagram given below will explain the manner of delivery from the cars to the ship.

PLANING AND RIBBING.

the check lever A; B represents the drum over which the chain runs, holding a gig at each end. As one gig is loaded with a cake of ice to go into the hold, the corresponding gig comes up empty over the rods marked D, which makes the operation almost self-governing. E is the platform for the gig, which, when the ship is loaded, is placed back upon the wharf in readiness for another ship. The average amount of ice loaded on board a ship in one day is three hundred tons, but, upon an emergency, five hundred tons can easily be disposed of.

Some forty cars, containing say two hundred tons, are loaded from the houses at Fresh and Spy ponds and taken to Charlestown. As the cars pass down the track from the main road to the wharf, where the ships are waiting, they are separately weighed; then the car is moved to a position opposite

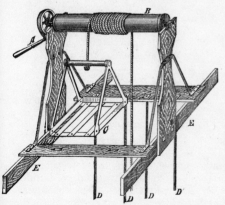

GIG FOR CONVEYING ICE INTO SHIP'S HOLD.

the gangway of the ship; a long platform, rigged with iron or steel rails, is placed between the car and the gangway of the ship. Over this platform the ice is slid from the car door to the ship's rail; there it is received on the "gig" C; the tender holds

Our foreign shipments are now confined to Japan, China, East Indies, South America and the West Indies, with now and then a cargo to the Mediterranean. The bulk of the shipping trade is with Boston and with ports on the Kennebec and Penobscot rivers, supplying all the principal cities south of New York, and frequently the latter city.

The following statistics will give an approximate idea of the extent of the trade at the present time, and of its increase since 1805. The shipments are confined to Boston:

From 1805 to 1856, 230,000 tons.
" 1856 " 1872, 2,768,000 "
In 1805, . . . 130 tons.
" 1856, . . . 146,000 "
" 1872, . . . 225,000 "

The average rate of freight per ton paid ships is $5.

The foreign shipments for 1872, 1873 and 1874 were as follows:

To	1872.	1873.	1874.
St. Thomas, .	1,800 tons.	1,554 tons.	2,600 tons.
Martinique, .	2,000 "	2,300 "	1,400 "
Barbadoes, . .	1,500 "	1,955 "	1,900 "
Trinidad, . .	2,400 "	2,400 "	2,300 "
Demerara, . .	4,500 "	4.500 "	4,300 "
Cienfuegos, . .	1,000 "	735 "	600 "
Santiago de Cuba,	1,000 "	900 "	900 "
Manzanilla, . .	300 "	300 "	300 "
Aspinwall, . .	2,500 "	2,626 "	3,100 "
Rio Janeiro, .	2,500 "	3,100 "	2,400 "

To Calcutta, ports in China, Batavia, Yokohama, and Marseilles, say about fifty thousand tons yearly.

There are no reliable data at hand from which to determine the exact date of the first shipment from Maine, but it was not till some time after the breaking out of the war.

In closing this part of the subject the following incidental facts may not be uninteresting. At a low estimate, the annual consumption in New York, Philadelphia, Baltimore, and Boston is:

New York,	1,000,000 tons.	
Philadelphia,	500,000 "	
Baltimore, .	200,000 "	
Boston, . .	300,000 "	Total, 2,000,000 tons.

The practical cost to consumers, taking a very small average price, would be:

In New York,	$5 to $12 per ton.	
" Philadelphia,	6 " 12	"
" Baltimore, .	6 " 12	"
" Boston, . .	4 " 6	"

about the lesser cities and towns, and one can realize the amount of the ice traffic of the country as reduced to dollars and cents. A large amount of this ice, however, say from one-third to one-half, is wasted in handling and transportation. · When progressive science introduces some method whereby this great margin of waste can be reduced, the benefit will be as much to the producer as the consumer.

The principal points on the Atlantic seaboard where ice is cut are, for New York, Rockland Lake, Hudson River; for Philadelphia, Schuylkill and Delaware Rivers; for Baltimore, the Patapsco and Susquehanna Rivers, for Boston, Fresh Pond, Cambridge; Smith's Pond, and Spy Pond, Arlington, Wenham Lake, Wenham; Sandy Pond, Ayer; Horn Pond, Woburn; Lake Quannapowitt, Wakefield; Haggett's Pond, Andover; Suntang Lake, Lynnfield, and the Kennebec and Penobscot Rivers, in Maine. During the year 1870, when the crop failed south of Boston, the amount cut and shipped from Maine was quite large, but recently the trade has fallen off.

Boston, from its commercial position, as well as its close proximity by rail to all the principal points of production, must be the advantageous port for shipment. An order for a cargo of ice from that port can be filled at a few hours' notice. It is seldom, if ever, without the requisite tonnage; and

GROOVING.

And, reduced to round numbers, the cost of ice to consumers in these four cities is twenty millions of dollars. Add to this amount all that is consumed in the other large cities of the Union, to say nothing

the appointment of the railroads bringing the ice to East Boston and Charlestown are so perfect, that from one hundred to five hundred cars can be placed at once.

But the ice trade is to day in its infancy;

every year it is attracting more attention. It must soon outgrow the means of individual enterprise, and powerful corporations must follow. Steamships, with air-tight compartments and built for great speed, must take the place of sailing ships, the saving by which, in the one item of waste, would suffice to build such steamers. Again, as the new ports of the East are being opened up to American commerce, the Pacific coast will have to supply the ice for India, China, Japan, etc. Already parties are prospecting for that region, and it would not be surprising to see, before the close of another decade, spacious ice-houses established in Alaska, Oregon, and California.

Let us now see what modern improvements have effected in reducing the cutting, housing, and shipping of ice to a system.

to the shore. These buildings were of wood, *battened* from the base, and were double-walled, the space between the inner and outer being filled with tan or sawdust. These were capable of holding from three to ten thousand tons each.

The next progressive move was in the direction of cutting. When the entire crop hardly exceeded five thousand tons per annum, the original method of scraping the pond answered well enough; so did the method of "shaving" the ice and sawing it into blocks. The scraper was a rudely constructed machine moved by hand; the shaving off of the porous or snow ice was done with broad axes; the cutting was done by means of a common cross-cut saw, one handle being taken off. One can imagine the laborious work thus entailed.

SAWING, CALKING AND BREAKING OFF.

Fresh Pond, in the city of Cambridge, has been selected for the illustrations, for many reasons, principal among which is the fact that here the cutting of ice for commercial purposes first commenced, and that to-day it and its near neighbor, Spy Pond, represent the standard of pure ice as merchantably quoted.

A little more than forty years ago, Mr. Tudor employed as his foreman Mr. Nathaniel Wyeth, of Cambridge, a man of remarkable ability. Up to this time (no reliable data are at hand to fix the year) ice was housed in subterranean vaults, generally excavated on the slope of the bank and removed some distance from the shores of the pond. Mr. Wyeth conceived the idea of erecting buildings without cellars and handy

Mr. Wyeth at once put his ingenuity to work and produced the tools that are now in use throughout the country, and which have reduced the cost of cutting to a mere nominal figure. Under the old process, one season would not suffice to secure a year's supply. Now, the cutting and housing seldom occupy more than three weeks, and the average daily work by one concern of housing six thousand tons is not considered remarkable.

It is seldom that clear ice is secured, that is, ice without a fall of snow upon it. With the modern improvements, this coating of snow is not regarded as detrimental. In fact, the thin layer of snow ice is regarded as a preservative of the clear ice.

As soon as the pond is completely closed

the ice, with the atmosphere at a temperature of ten degrees above zero, forms very rapidly. If, after it has attained the thickness of say three or four inches, capable of bearing a man, a fall of two or three inches of snow follows, then the workmen begin to "sink the pond," as it is termed. This is done by cutting holes an inch or two in diameter, and at three or four feet apart, thus admitting the water to the surface and submerging the snow, which forms the snow ice. With a steady temperature of ten degrees above zero for a week or ten days, the ice will have formed to the desirable thickness, say an average thickness of fifteen inches. We say average, because on many ponds— Fresh Pond, for instance, which is fed by warm springs—the freezing differs. The thickness is ascertained by boring holes with a two-inch auger. If, after the ice has formed sufficiently to bear horses, snow falls, then the scraping process begins, and continues with each fall of snow till the ice is thick enough to cut.

A space on the pond, say six hundred feet in width, is marked out and the snow is scraped from either side toward the center, forming what is called "the dump." Some seasons these dumps will rise to a great height, and then, through their immense weight, sink to a level. The process of scraping the snow into "dumps" is not only expensive, but wastes a great deal of ice, as only that cleared off can be cut. When the ice is twelve inches thick it will yield about a thousand tons to the acre, but so much is wasted by scraping snow, high winds, and various other causes, that it is only in exceptionally "good years" that more than half the average of a pond can be cut and stored.

After the snow is scraped off, the lining of the pond, so called, begins. This is done by taking two sights as in common railroad engineering. The targets are set, representing the line between two supposed points, say A and B. A straight edge is then run by means of a common plank between the points A and B, then striking from the angle B, it runs at right angles with the line A. Only two lines are necessary, one from A to B, and the other from B to an indefinite point.

The liner proceeds with a double instrument, or what is called a "guide and marker;" the guide is a smooth-edged blade that runs in the groove made by the square edge; the marker is a part of the same instrument and runs over the grooved lines laid out with

the cutter. As soon as the machine reaches the objective point, it is turned over by an ingenious arrangement, so that returning, the guide runs in the freshly cut groove, and the marker cuts another groove forty-four inches distant. In this way the machine goes over the whole field, running one way, the last groove it cuts forming the boundary of the second side; then, commencing on this boundary line, it runs at right angles with the first, and goes over the entire field, cutting the ice into blocks of the required dimensions. The marker cuts a groove two inches in depth. Following the marker come the cutters or plows with sharp teeth measuring from two inches in length to ten or twelve, and used according to the thickness of the ice. Then comes the snow-ice plane, which shaves off the porous or snow ice, it first being determined by auger-boring how many inches of snow ice there are. The ice is now ready for gathering. It is broken off into broad rafts, then sawed into lesser ones, then barred off in sections and floated into the canal. The calking operation consists in filling the groove lines or interstices with ice chips to prevent the water from entering and freezing; this is only necessary in very cold weather. The rafts or sheets of cakes are generally thirty cakes long by twelve wide, frequently longer. The ends have to be sawed, but every twelfth groove running lengthwise of the raft or sheet is cut deeper than the other, so that one or two men can, with one motion of the bar, separate it into strips ready for the elevator canal.

As the ice enters upon the van it is cut into single cakes of forty-four inches square. The process of elevating the ice has been reduced to almost scientific perfection. It is done by means of an endless chain fitted with buckets, and the hoisting power is a steam-engine. The ice-houses contain from three to five vaults or bins, corresponding to the several stories in a warehouse. A single range of buildings will contain five or more The elevator is arranged so that one flat or story containing these five bins or vaults can be filled simultaneously; that is, as the ice leaves the elevator and is passed off on the wooden tramway of the platform, a man stand at the entrance of each vault to turn the cakes of ice in, the first cake from the elevato going to the farthest opening, and then in regular rotation till the first or lower flat in the range is filled. When the blocks are taken from the houses and loaded on board car for shipment, they are reduced to twenty-tw inches by a similar process of grooving and burring.

None but the most experienced workmen are employed in storing the ice, as this requires a quick eye, a steady hand, and good judgment.

As each flat or story is completed, the openings at either end are securely and tightly closed, and when the whole building is filled up to the bed-plate, the space between that and the hip of the roof is filled with hay, thus providing a sure protection against waste by shrinkage, which seldom exceeds one foot during the season.

3
Montpelier, Vermont

THE VERMONT STATE HOUSE.

MONTPELIER, VERMONT.

By Hiram A. Huse.

THE towns of Massachusetts (except some in that part which in 1820 became the State of Maine), Connecticut and Rhode Island were settled before the American Revolution. This holds true of a large number of towns in the southern and western part of New Hampshire and of a less number in the southern part of Vermont. Although Fort Dummer, in the southeastern part of Brattleboro, marked the first remembered settlement of English speaking inhabitants within the borders of Vermont and fixed the date as 1724, there may have been a few years before some families from western Massachusetts in what is now Vernon, the southeast town of Vermont; and one hundred and fifty years ago there had come to

be a few families leading a precarious existence a few miles farther up along the west bank of the Connecticut.

In 1749 Benning Wentworth, governor of the Province of New Hampshire, granted the town of Bennington; and within two or three years thereafter Halifax and Westminster were also granted by him. These three pioneers of those grants that were permanent were followed slowly by other grants, but not by settlement for some years. The fall of Quebec in 1759, followed by the known approach of peace, gave an impetus to Governor Wentworth's granting quill, and at the end of 1764 he had given grants of some one hundred and twenty-five towns in what is now Vermont territory, or of about half of the

To the Honorable Assembly of the State
of Vermont

The Petition of the Inhabitants of the
Town of Montpelier in the County of Orange
Humbly sheweth; that your Petitioners are
greatly embarrassed in bringing forward the
settlement of sd Town for the want of a
Bridge over Onion River and the little
North branch so called, and also a Road down
Onion River, which will lead to and from
Market, Therefore Your Petitioners Humbly
pray that your Honours would grant a tax
of Two pence on each acre of Land in sd Town
Publick rights excepted, and in some other
way enable your Petitioners to compleat sd
Bridges and Road, and as in duty bound
shall ever pray

Montpelier Octr 17th 1788   Jacob Davis
           Davd King Junr
                              Ebenezer Upham &c
      Clark Stevens   Parley Davis

                              Parker Burnham
                              Saml Upham Junr
                              Zeba Woodworth
                              Levi Humphrey
                              Hiram Peck
                              Nathaniel Peck
                              Isaac Putnam
                              Benjamin Tucker Junr
                              Theophilus H
                                   brook

JONATHAN PECKHAM MILLER.

"The New Hampshire Grants, in particular, a country unpeopled in the last war, now abounds in the most active and most rebellious race of the continent, and hangs like a gathering storm on my left."

This is not the place to tell of the contention on the part of New York that her eastern boundary, north of Massachusetts, extended to the Connecticut river, nor of the many grants made by the governors of the Province of New York; nor of the "judgment seats" erected and the "beech seals" used by Ethan Allen, Seth Warner, Remember Baker (all cousins from Connecticut), and their fellows of the "Bennington Mob" in resisting New York authority to regrant lands, already granted by New Hampshire; nor of the evolution from the "Bennington Mob" of the Green Mountain Boys and the later growth of hostility to New York control even of lands ungranted by New Hampshire. No territory in Montpelier was ever granted by New Hampshire, but the New York grants of Newbrook and Kingsborough, the

two hundred and forty-six organized towns and cities now in the State.* The virtual close of the French and Indian war brought, beginning in Bennington in 1761, swift settlement of many of the lands so granted. Hence, and from the inborn strength and courage of the settlers, enlarged and disciplined by the conquest from Nature of a wilderness and by the defense of their new-made homes from the aggressions of a powerful adjoining province, came it that a decade and a half later Burgoyne wrote to England, four days after the battle of Bennington:

SAMUEL PRENTISS.

*Wentworth granted west of the Connecticut river 1 town in 1749; 1 town in 1750; 2 towns in 1752; 7 in 1753; 3 in 1754; 1 town in 1760; 60 towns in 1761; 10 in 1762; 34 in 1763, and 3 in 1764: and probably a few more that escaped observation in making this count, which is, however, accurate enough to mark his years of special activity in this business. These grants or charters curiously conserved education, religion and "thrift, thrift, Horatio!" They gave: "One whole share for the Incorporated Society for the Propagation of the Gospel in Foreign Parts. One Share for the first settled Minister of the Gospel. One Share for a Glebe for the Church of England as by Law Established, and one Share for the benefit of a School in said Town;" and to "His Excellency Benning Wentworth, Esqr., a Tract of Land to Contain Five Hundred Acres, as marked B. W. in the Plan." But in many cases if there was in the granted town any land bad enough to be of man and God forsaken, the guileless grantees so managed that that very land turned out to be "the Governor's Right."

TIMOTHY P. REDFIELD.

former made June 13, 1770, and the latter made June 25, 1770, covered at least in part Montpelier territory. Neither of these New York grants was ever settled by people claiming ownership under them; but it is told that "in 1772, Ira Allen drove off Samuel Gale and his surveying party, who were running lines of New York grants; or, rather, Gale and his party fled before Allen, of whose approach they had heard, appeared.

that he had five thousand acres in Kingsborough surveyed in 1767 and lotted out for settlement in 1771, situated partly in Wildersburg (now Barre) and partly in "Mountpalier." If Kelly was right in his statement, more was done within Montpelier bounds under New York grants than has ever been told by any historian of the town; but it is a little curious that the survey in Kingsborough should have been three

STATE STREET.

Rear Admiral Dewey was born on the spot now occupied by his brother's home, the second house on the left.

The surveyors' camp, from which they so disappeared upon the advance of Allen and his friends, was located in the northeast part of the old town of Montpelier, and, therefore, in the northeast part of the present town of East Montpelier."

The petition of John Kelly, who was to 1775 a Yorker and afterwards a Tory (but never a member of Tammany), presented to the Vermont Legislature in 1787 shows how difficult it is to make all statements of the olden time fit each other; for Kelly says

years before the grant, and what he speaks of as happening in 1771 may very well be the same undertaking that was broken up by Ira Allen.

The towns on the east side of the state settled from 1761 to the breaking out of the Revolution were along the west bank of the Connecticut as far up as Newbury (with a very few families as far north as Lunenburg, Guildhall and Maidstone); on the west side of the state some towns as far north as Addison (and some towns in Chittenden county abandoned when the war

MAIN STREET, SHOWING PART OF THE BUSINESS SECTION.

The Kellogg-Hubbard Library on the extreme left.

broke out); and various others in the south and south central part of what is now Vermont, Royalton being perhaps as far north as any of these more central towns. Some seventy of the towns granted by New Hampshire had been settled before the Revolution. From these last came the Green Mountain Boys, who under Ethan Allen took Fort Ticonderoga May 10, 1775, and those who under Seth Warner later constituted a part of the army which invaded Canada, and those who still later in the Continental Army under Warner fought under St. Clair in defeat at Hubbardton, and a few weeks afterwards under Stark in victory at Bennington, and

THE POST OFFICE AND COURT HOUSE.

THE HEATON HOSPITAL.

who remained for several years in the Continental service.

A convention of members chosen by the several towns on the New Hampshire grants at Westminster, January 16, 1777, declared the territory comprehending these grants "a free and independent jurisdiction or state; to be forever hereafter called, known and distinguished by the name of New Connecticut." It has been generally stated that the declaration read: "New Connecticut, *alias* Vermont"; but there was no Vermont about it then—it was just plain New Connecticut. Dr. Thomas Young, a friend of Ethan Allen, the next April suggested the Pennsylvania constitution as a model for the constitution of the new state and Vermont as an appropriate name; and the next summer a constitution much like that of Pennsylvania, and

the name of Vermont were adopted.

But the name first, though far from forever, used was significant of the origin of the new commonwealth. The majority of its inhabitants were from Connecticut, though a good many were from Massachusetts. They found here conditions other than those existing in the colonies from which they came. Many of them had fought in the French and Indian war. The younger were those of most adventurous spirit in the communities

THE SEMINARY.

whence they emigrated. Coming here in reliance on the grants of the governor of a royal province issued in the name of George the Second or George the Third, "by the Grace of God of Great Britain, France and Ireland, King, Defender of the Faith, etc.," they found the governor of another and greater province in the name of the king regranting their lands to other people. Out of their defense of their rights against great odds they got that discipline and growth that made them the men whom Burgoyne described. They were Connecticut and Massachusetts born, but so environed and "the elements so mix'd" in them that they became Green Mountain Boys; just how perhaps is hard to explain.

Vermont began to make grants in 1778. During the Revolution settlements were begun in ten towns so granted. Two towns, Bradford and Royalton, settled before the Revolution, continued their landed proprietorships under New York grants. In 1780, Barnard, just north of Woodstock and about forty miles south of what is now Montpelier, was the most northerly of the New Hampshire grants that were settled; northeast of Barnard and adjoining it, Royalton, a New York grant, had quite a number of inhabitants; to the west of Royalton, Bethel, a Vermont grant, had a few families; and to the north of these last towns, in Randolph and Brookfield, that same year granted by Vermont, there were also a few families. From Randolph and Brookfield to Montpelier, a distance of some twenty miles, there were no inhabitants.

Monday, October 16, 1780, came the "Burning of Royalton," famous in tradition through the early days of

Vermont, and kept more clearly in mind in later years because of the account written by Zadock Steele, or some one for him, and published here in Montpelier in 1818. The attacking party consisted of about three hundred Indians from Canada commanded by an Englishman named Horton. They went up the Winooski through the valley where Montpelier City now lies, thence up Stevens Branch and through what are now

THE NATIONAL LIFE INSURANCE COMPANY'S BUILDING.

Washington and Chelsea and through Tunbridge to Royalton, where they killed Thomas Pember and Elias Button. During the day of their depredations they took twenty-five prisoners, burned more than twenty houses and killed all the live stock in sight. Returning they went through Randolph, where early on the morning of the 17th they took Zadock Steele prisoner, and thus made certain that their raid would be long talked of at Vermont firesides. The evening of the 17th they camped at the mouth of Dog river, on the Berlin side of the Winooski and opposite the spot where,

MONTPELIER FROM BERLIN HILL.

UPPER MAIN STREET.

nearly six years later, the first white settler in Montpelier located, and on the 18th resumed their journey back to Canada. On Saturday of the same week, October 21, 1780, the General Assembly of Vermont, at a session held in Bennington, made a grant of the town of Montpelier to Timothy Bigelow and his associates. Vermont towns as a rule were six miles square, and Montpelier, like most of the rest, was supposed to contain 23,040 acres; but the listers' books now show East Montpelier to contain 17,814 acres and the city of Montpelier 4,419 acres, so that the supposed original acreage in some way fell short.

The grant of Montpelier was followed by a formal charter issued by Governor Thomas Chittenden, August 14, 1781. It continued as a town on paper only for five years, when Joel Frizzel, a trapper and hunter, with his wife, Mary, who is said to have been a little red-haired French woman from Canada, began living in the southwest corner of the town near the bank of the river. Frizzel has not been given until lately the credit of being the real first white settler; but he remained here at least until January 11, 1794, when he finally deeded away the hundred-acre lot on which he lived.

Colonel Jacob Davis came and had most of the town surveyed in the summer of 1786, but he found Frizzel living here and Frizzel helped in the survey.

It is to Colonel Jacob Davis that the town owes its name. How the name of the French city of Montpelier came to take the fancy of Colonel Davis is not known; but Daniel P. Thompson, the Montpelier historian and Vermont novelist, gives as his authority for saying that Colonel Davis had the name Montpelier inserted in the grant, George Worthington, who married Colonel Davis's youngest daughter, Clarissa, who was the first child born in the new town.

Jacob Davis was from Charlton, Worcester County, Massachusetts, had served in the Revolutionary army,

WORCESTER MOUNTAINS FROM
SEMINARY HILL.

that at the time of the grant Jacob Davis, Jr., was but twelve years of age, and Thomas Davis but eight years of age.

Colonel Davis early in 1787 moved his family from Charlton to Brookfield, Vermont, and May 3, 1787, came with his hired man and his nephew, Parley Davis, by way of Williamstown Heights and by Berlin Pond to the Winooski river, which his party waded about twenty rods above where Dog river joins it and thence went down to the

and was evidently interested in Vermont lands about the year of Montpelier's charter, for he was one of the original grantees of Calais, of which the General Assembly gave a grant on the same day that Montpelier was granted, and one of the original grantees of Salem, which was granted November 7, 1780. In 1783 the Colonel was for a time actively engaged in the survey of the town of Calais, which lies north of Montpelier. Of the sixty or more grantees of Montpelier, Colonel Davis and his sons, Jacob, Jr., and Thomas, appear to have been the only ones who settled in the town; and it is worthy of remark

BENJAMIN'S FALLS IN WINTER.

THE WINOOSKI RIVER AT LOWER STATE STREET.

house of Seth Putnam in Middlesex, about a mile below their crossing. May 4, 1787, from which the settlement of Montpelier, other than by Frizzel and his wife, dates, the Colonel and his two companions cut a bridle path from Putnam's along the bank of the river to the Montpelier line, and thence a mile or more still farther up to where the North Branch empties into the main river, and thence forty or fifty rods up the North Branch to a hunters' camp near where the jail now is. To this camp they brought their horse and luggage the same day and the next went to clearing land. Colonel Davis built a log house which stood three years, when it gave place as his residence to a large frame house, which was moved in 1858 farther up Elm street and is still standing. The Colonel settled in what was for years called Montpelier Hollow and is the site of the present city. His nephew, Parley Davis, following the more common custom of early days, settled on the hill where Montpelier Center now is. The rest of Colonel Davis's

family, his wife and four daughters, were brought to their new home in March, 1788; and the petition to the General Assembly which is given in this article shows that in that year quite a settlement had been formed.

When Jacob and Parley Davis came up from Putnam's on that fourth of May, 1787, on reaching the Montpelier line they faced up the Winooski, or as they called it the Onion, river as it flowed to the west along the southern boundary of the town. The lands of Montpelier were north of the river, and about a mile from the west line the North Branch, or, as it is now more commonly called, Worcester Branch, flowing to the south almost parallel with the west line of the town, emptied into the Winooski. Near the southeast part of the town there is such a bend in the Winooski that its course is not far away from the town's east line. Between the North Branch and that part of the Winooski which flows near the eastern line of the township was found a body of excellent farming land that placed the town in the front rank of agricultural communities.

It has been seen that the paper existence of the town began in the days of the Revolution, but its settlement was post-Revolutionary. The greater number of early settlers were Massachusetts men, but several were from Connecticut. Many were men who had seen military service i n t h e war then three or four years closed. The new community w a s simply a Massachusetts or Connecticut neighborhood m o v e d further north and into ruder surroundings that brought the hardships of pioneer life that had been in large measure modified or done away with for nearly a century in the towns of southern New England. The settlers of Montpelier were not "Green Mountain Boys"; they were not the men who had founded the new state, but were those who from their Massachusetts and Connecticut f a r m s and v i l l a g e s, when the news of Lexington and Concord came, went to Bunker Hill and the siege of Boston instead of to Fort Ticonderoga. The same holds true of half the towns of the state, and newcomers from southern New England came swiftly after the Revolution into towns par-

STATUE OF ETHAN ALLEN, IN THE PORCH OF THE STATE HOUSE.

Designed by Larkin G. Mead.

tially settled before it began. But newcomers and old were of the same blood and pretty much the same kind of folks and worked in unison for the good of the new commonwealth.

The first school was kept by Jacob Davis, Jr., in 1789, near the Middlesex line; and after Colonel Davis built his large frame house in 1790 David Wing, Jr., kept in a part of it the first school in the village. In 1794 six school districts were established. T h e first "March meeting," as Vermont town meetings are called, was held at the house of Colonel Davis March 29, 1791, and twenty-seven voters were present. The first "Freemen's Meeting" was held at the house of Parley Davis at the Center on the first Tuesday of September, 1792; and the Center was thereafter t h e place of holding town and freemen's meetings for the old town of Montpelier until its division in 1848 into the two towns of Montpelier and East Montpelier, and is yet the place of such meetings in the town of East Montpelier, which contains four-fifths in area of the old town, including the excellent hill farms and many along the banks of the Winooski.

It has been heretofore stated that Montpelier's population at the taking

THE WINOOSKI RIVER, "CAMEL'S HUMP" IN THE DISTANCE.

of the first United States census in 1791 was 113, but as will be seen, it was 118. In 1800 it had increased to 890. The census taken in 1791, while not as full in statistics or in names of persons as the enumerations taken since, is quite a mine of information as to the status of communities and the location of persons who were householders at that time; and it is a mine that has been very little worked for the information it can furnish. For instance, it, as well as the town records of deeds, refutes the old statement that Montpelier's first settler only remained in town two or three years, and shows that he and his wife were both here at least five years. It shows that Colonel Davis's house was the home, either temporary or permanent, of a number of people not of his immediate family; and it shows in the house of the Quaker Prince Stevens almost as many people as in Colonel Davis's house, — one of its inmates doubtless being that noble man Clark

BERLIN POND.

Stevens, the ancestor of Mrs. Anna S. Robinson, wife of Rowland E. Robinson of Ferrisburg, whose word-pictures of Vermont and her people, whether in history or fiction, are the delight of thousands who read his books.

These returns of the 1791 census as they now exist in Washington are in the form shown in the following transcript of that portion of them containing the Montpelier statistics.*

PICTURESQUE STREETS.

The table shows seventeen households in the town four years after its settlement.

POPULATION OF MONTPELIER, VT., AUG. 16, 1791.

	A.	B.	C.	D.
Theophilus Brooks............	3	1	3	7
Allen Carpenter..............	1	2	4	7
Jonathan Cutler..............	5	3	2	10
Jacob Davis.................	12	..	5	17
Perley Davis................	2	..	..	2
Solomon Dodge..............	3	2	2	7
Joel Frizzle.........	1	..	1	2
James Hawkins..............	2	3	3	8
Josiah Hurlbutt.............	2	2	3	7
James Morey................	1	..	5	6
Nathaniel Peck..............	2	..	..	2
Ebenezer Putnam...........:	1	2	4	7
Jonathan Snow..............	3	..	1	4
Prince Stevens..............	8	1	4	13
John Templeton.............	3	2	3	8
Jerathmel B. Wheeler.......	4	1	4	9
Ziba Woodworth............	2	..	..	2
Total................	55	19	44	118

A. Free White Males over 16 years, including head of family. B. Males Under 16. C. Free White Females, including head of family. D. Total.

Imprisonment for debt prevailed in Vermont and did not go off her statute books until 1839, although the liberties of the jail yard were at times very great. It was the duty of the judges of the several county courts to set out yards for the liberty of prisoners in their respective jails; and the judges became so liberal in this behalf that in 1813 a law was passed, providing that these judges, within two months from the passage of the act, should cause the extent of the liberties of the jail to be so set out and limited that no prisoner's yard should equal more than four square miles. Debtors imprisoned in cases on contract, whether on *mesne* process or execution, could be admitted to the liberties of the jail yard by giving bonds to the sheriff of the county, conditioned that they should remain within the limits of the jail yard without committing any escape therefrom; so that a contract debtor, if he could get some one to go on his bond, could live anywhere within a distance of a mile from the

*The above statistics were furnished the writer by Capt. Dwight H. Kelton, U. S. A., who copied it from the original Census Returns now on file in Washington, D. C. Captain Kelton made an effort to have these first census returns published by the Government. He says that the returns for New England are still in a fair condition, while the returns of many states are missing. Captain Kelton's effort for the publication of the census returns for 1791 ought to be successful. He first saw their value to the local historian and in tracing family history by the location of families in the very first years of the Union.

jail. It is told that Judge Kinne of Plainfield, who used to practice early in the County Court in Montpelier, but who, not being a member of the bar, had to address the jury from without the bar, was once defending a suit on one of these bonds. The plaintiff claimed that the debtor had been beyond the limits of the jail yard, in which case, of course, the bond was forfeited, and to establish his claim put on witnesses to prove that just about daylight the debtor, whose family was living a couple of miles from the jail on the road to East Montpelier, had been seen on the dead run down hill and towards the jail only about a rod inside the mile limit. Of course it was very evident that the man had made a visit home, and had not got back to safe ground under cover of darkness; but Judge Kinne offered no evidence and his address to the jury was very brief: "Gentlemen of the Jury, the plaintiff in this case has taken every method to prove my client within the limits of the jail yard, and I shall take no manner of means to prove him out." The defendant had the verdict.

About the year 1800 Colonel Davis fell into financial difficulty; and in one case a large judgment was obtained against him, so unjust in his estimate and in that of his family, that he made up his mind never to pay it. The execution so issued that the place for his commitment was the jail in Burlington in Chittenden County. He had conveyed his property to his sons and sons-in-law, and when about to be committed he moved his wife and younger children to Burlington within

the limits of Chittenden County jail yard and quietly lived in Burlington a dozen years or more, keeping always, of course, within the liberties of the jail. He rejected all offers of compromise made by the plaintiffs, until in 1814, the plaintiffs virtually abandoning their claim and offering to settle for a nominal sum, he accepted their proposition and was going to return to Montpelier. He was taken sick, however, before removing to his old home and died in Burlington, April 9, 1814, at the age of about seventy-five years.

Montpelier has been from the start a business town. Its merchants, manufacturers, bankers, and managers of insurance companies have, by conservative and successful methods, given it a well deserved reputation for reliability and soundness in financial matters. But it has never forgotten the church and the school. Two of the men who came very early, Ziba

ALONG THE WINOOSKI.

REAR ADMIRAL DEWEY.

mont he was one of the founders of the old Leicester Academy.

In the days of Stevens and Woodworth there came, beginning in 1795, a Methodist preacher; and in 1805 Rev. Clark Brown came for the Congregationalists. The first Congregational Church in Montpelier was organized July 20, 1808, with seventeen members, and Rev. Chester Wright, who was ordained August 16, 1809, and dismissed December 22, 1830, became the first pastor. There were admitted during his pastorate four hundred and twenty-eight members, and the "Old Brick Church" was erected in 1820. Rev. Samuel Hopkins was pastor from 1831 to 1835; Rev. Buel W. Smith from 1836 to 1840; and Rev. John Gridley from 1841 to 1846. Then followed the long pastorate of Rev. William H. Lord, D. D., extending over thirty years. The present large church known as Bethany Church was built after Mr. Lord had been here about twenty years. Mr. Lord died in 1877 and was succeeded by Rev. J. H. Hincks, who was followed by Rev. Mr. Gallagher. For some years Rev. Norman Seaver, D. D., has been pastor of this church

Woodworth, who had been a soldier in the Revolution, and Clark Stevens, were zealous preachers of the Gospel — Woodworth a Baptist and Stevens a Quaker. By just what forms and ceremonies they were ordained to their work is not clear, but they were in good standing in their denominations, and in their work had apostolic success if not succession. It has been said that Jacob Davis, Jr., and David Wing, Jr., were the first school teachers, and Mr. Wing was a scholarly man, later becoming secretary of state and a leader in educational matters. Colonel Davis himself, while of great business activity, was, as may be seen by the old bridge petition of October 7, 1788, the body of which is in his handwriting, a man who could wield the pen as well as the axe. Before his coming to Ver-

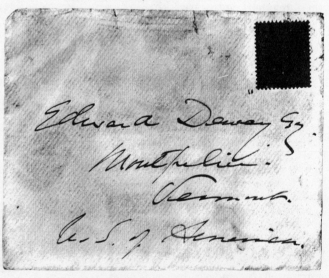

Fac-simile of an envelope sent by Rear Admiral Dewey from Manila, containing the letter reproduced on the following page.

"Olympia".
Manila Bay
9th July /98

Dear Brother Edward
+ + + + + + + +
Your letter con-
gratulating me on
our late victory
gave me much
pleasure -
+ + + + + + + +
As soon as
there is a "lot up"
in business I shall
try and answer
some of the hund-
reds of letters I
have received
What a given world
it is! I expect
the blockading will have
drive her before
the Spanish Squa-
dron now at Port
land can possibly
get out, in which case
I think they will be
sorry they came.
Tell ... be hav-
ing an experience
off Santiago -
+ + + + + +
Your affectionate brother
George Dewey

and has kept its pulpit to the high standard of its past. The Methodists, who had held meetings for many years, in 1826 built a meeting-house at the Center, and in 1837 one in the village. Trinity Methodist Church built its present house of worship about thirty years ago, and the present pastor, earnest and eloquent, is Rev. Andrew Gillies. Beginning with Elder Ziba Woodworth the Free Will Baptists had several preachers during the seventy-five years succeeding the settlement of the town. In 1865 the Baptist Church of Montpelier was organized, and its present church building, on School street, begun in 1870, was dedicated in 1873. Rev. W. A. Davison is the pastor. A second Congregational Church was organized in 1835, which built for a house of worship the structure on State street, afterwards long known as Village Hall. Rev. Sherman Kellogg was for some years the pastor, but in 1848 this church dissolved, some of its members going back to the First Congregational Church and some going to the Methodist Church. The Universalists early organized a society at the Center and in 1831 one in the village. Later they organized a third society, which still exists, in East Montpelier village. In 1865, under Rev. C. A. Allen, a church was organized in the village by the Unitarians and Universalists. It is known as the "Church of the Messiah," and its pastor since 1869 has been Rev. J. Edward Wright, a grandson of Rev. Chester Wright. So for the greater part of this century Montpelier has had the good of earnest and effective work in the Christian ministry by a "Parson Wright"—the grandfather and the grandson, the orthodox and the liberal; and both in turn have had the respect and love of the community. In 1842 a Protestant Episcopal Church was organized. Its first church edifice was built where the "Riverside" is, but from 1868 Christ Church Parish has occupied the church built thirty years ago opposite the Court House. Rev. George B. Manser was the first rector, and those following him have been Rev. E. F. Putnam, 1850-3; Rev. F. W. Shelton, 1854-65; Rev. D. C. Roberts, 1866-8; Rev. William J. Harris, 1869-70; Rev. Andrew Hull, 1871-9; Rev. H. F. Hill, 1879-89; Rev. James C. Flanders, 1889-91; and Rev. A. N. Lewis, the present rector, who has just completed seven years of most faithful and valuable work in the parish. The Roman Catholics since 1850 have held regular church services in Montpelier. Their church is known as St. Augustine's, and has the largest congregation in the city. They are building, to take the place of their brick church on Court street a new granite church on Barre street, and their present priest, Rev. William J. O'Sullivan, has been the moving spirit in this undertaking, which for years he has untiringly pushed with the energy and power that mark his pastorate.

While the pursuit of business enterprises has been the characteristic of Montpelier, it has all its days cared for education. Montpelier Academy was chartered in 1800, and soon work was begun by it. Instruction other than in the district schools was also given by Joshua Y. Vail in 1807. Mr. Vail's select school and the early academical instruction were followed in 1813 by changing the Academy charter to the charter of Washington County Grammar School. This school had its home on upper Main street for many years. The bridge that crosses Worcester Branch near its site is still known as the Academy Bridge, and it has no other material monument. The Grammar School and the district schools were in 1859 united under the name of the Union School. A large building was then erected at the head of School street for the combined educational institution, and in 1800 a large addition was made to this building. Mr. Southmayd's name is one of those remembered from the old academy or grammar school days, and D. D. Gorham gave the Union School a good name in the early years of its exist-

ence. From 1885 to 1889 Joseph A. De Boer was the principal, and under him the school came to be highly efficient as an educational power in the state. Mr. De Boer resigned to take the place of actuary in the National Life Insurance Company, of which he is now secretary and actuary. Mr. S. J. Blanpied, who died in March, 1897, while principal of the school, had conducted it with success for some years. Mr. N. J. Whitehill, who taught for several years at West Randolph, or as it is now named, Randolph, has been for somewhat more than a year the principal. St. Michael's School is a largely patronized parochial school maintained by the Catholic Church. Newbury Seminary, founded in 1833, was the leading Academy under conduct of the Methodists for many years. A more central location was desired, and in 1868 its home was changed to Montpelier. It is now Montpelier Seminary, and its buildings stand upon Seminary Hill. Rev. William M. Newton is the principal. The seminary has the good will and support of the Methodists of almost the entire state, and well deserves their favor.

From the days of Philip Vincent and Rebecca Peabody, who healed the sick in the eighteenth century, to those of J. E. Macomber and Dean G. Kemp, Montpelier has had the great good fortune to have physicians whom neither summer's heat nor winter's cold, nor storm nor night could keep away from the bed-side of the suffering. Doctor Macomber and Doctor Kemp were the last of the long line to "die in harness" — the former in 1896 and the latter September 3, 1898. Dr. Edward Lamb, in the typhus fever epidemics of 1806 and 1813 and in the spotted fever epidemic of 1811, did work that still lingers in tradition. Other physicians of note were James Spalding, Julius Y. Dewey, F. W. Adams (who mended bodies and made books and violins), and in late years Sumner Putnam, G. N. Brigham, J. H. Woodward, C. M. Chandler, J. M.

BAPTIST.

UNITARIAN.　　　EPISCOPAL.　　METHODIST.

CONGREGATIONAL.

SOME OF MONTPELIER'S CHURCHES.

Templeton and Drs. Macomber and Kemp. The doctors now in practice are A. B. Bisbee, C. E. Chandler, J. G. Dequoy, H. A. Fiske, W. L. Goodell, C. N. Hunt, M. F. McGuire and Minnie S. Marshall, representing the "old school;" H. S. Boardman, I. H. Fiske, Homœopathists; H. E. Templeton and P. L. Templeton of the Eclectic school; and E. E. Beeman and W. W. Brock of the school of Osteopathy. It is possible that there are others and the above classification may not be absolutely correct.

Charles Bulkley was the first lawyer, and Cyrus Ware, who came here in 1799, was the second. Judge Ware's youngest daughter, Mrs. Joel Foster, is still living and resides in Montpelier. Mr. Ware was the Montpelier representative in the general assembly in 1805, and to his efforts, seconded by those of David Wing, Jr., then Secretary of State, was due the passage of the act making Montpelier the capital of the state. Up to this time the road to Burlington went where Court street and the present State House now are. Soon after the passage of the act, what is now State street was laid out and the old State House and old Pavilion were built, the old State House being to the northwest of the site of the Pavilion Hotel. A new State House of granite on the present site was begun in 1832 and first occupied in 1836. This was burned January 6, 1857, and the present State House was erected within the next few years and first occupied in 1859. In 1885-6 an annex was built which contains the State Library, the rooms of the Vermont Historical Society and the Supreme Court room.

The first tavern was built for Colonel Davis by James Hawkins in 1793. It stood on the site of the old Union House and where the Church of the Messiah now stands at the corner of Main and School streets. The second tavern was on the westerly side of Main street about opposite the beginning of Barre street and was built in 1800. It was first called the "Hutchins Tavern," and afterwards for many years was known as the "Shepard Tavern." The old Pavilion was built so as to be in readiness for the first session of the Legislature held here in 1808. Daniel P. Thompson, then a boy, was present on that first "Election Day," which in other states would be called "Inauguration Day," and has given a very graphic description of it in his History of Montpelier. The present Pavilion Hotel was built in 1875 and opened in February, 1876.

In 1810 a new county by the name of Jefferson was incorporated, with Montpelier as its shire town. The name was changed in 1813 to Washington County. The first court in the new county was held Monday, December 2, 1811, in the old State House.

In the days of the first Court, Col. James H. Langdon was the leading merchant. Colonel Langdon died in 1831 at the age of fifty-seven years. His son, James Robbins Langdon, who died in Montpelier, September 20, 1895, was during his whole business life the leading man in Montpelier in financial matters, being largely interested in railroads and in banking. Whatever at various times was the corporate name of the bank of which he was president, it was always known as the "Langdon Bank."

Samuel Prentiss, the third Montpelier lawyer, born in Stonington, Connecticut, March 31, 1782, grew up in Northfield, Massachusetts, where he began the study of law which he finished in Brattleboro. He came to Montpelier in May, 1803, and married Lucretia Houghton of Northfield, Massachusetts, October 3, 1804. There were twelve children of this marriage. Mr. and Mrs. Prentiss were alike an honor to Montpelier. In 1825 Mr. Prentiss became a member of the Supreme Court and in 1829 chief judge of that court. From March 4, 1831, to 1842, he was a United States Senator from Vermont, and in the last named year was appointed judge of the United States District Court, which office he held to his death, January 15, 1857.

William Upham, whose parents lived on a farm near Montpelier Center, was admitted to the bar of this county, December term, 1812. He became a famous jury lawyer and was a member of the United States Senate from March 4, 1843, to January 14, 1853, when he died in Washington. Lucius B. Peck as well as Mr. Upham read law with Mr. Prentiss and was for a third of a century the leader of the bar of Washington County. He was a member of Congress from 1847 to 1851. Stoddard B. Colby, of the firm of Peck and Colby, read law with Mr. Upham and was a lawyer of great power with juries. Mr. Peck said of him: "Give him a case with neither law nor fact on his side, and he would win where another man would never dream of trying it."

Isaac Fletcher Redfield, though never a member of the bar of Washington County, lived in Montpelier for eleven years after he was elected a judge of the Supreme Court. He was on the Supreme Bench twenty-five years, the last eight of which he was chief judge.

Timothy Parker Redfield, a

younger brother of Isaac F. Redfield, with whom he read law, was admitted to the bar in Orleans County, and in 1848 moved to Montpelier, where he practiced until his election as a judge of the Supreme Court in 1870. He declined a reëlection in 1884, and in 1888 died in Chicago, whence he was brought to Montpelier for burial.

Jonathan Peckham Miller, who practiced law in Montpelier from May term, 1831, to his death, February 17, 1847, was a knight errant of the olden time projected into the nineteenth century. He was born in Randolph, Vermont, February 24, 1797, went in the Randolph company to the battle of Plattsburgh in 1814, and in 1817 enlisted in the regular army, in which he served two years. He then fitted for college and was still a student at Burlington when the college buildings burned May 24, 1824. He sailed for Greece, August 21, 1824, and became a colonel in the Greek service. Fear was unknown to him. After his return to Vermont he went back to Greece to distribute a shipload donation to the suffering women, children, old men and non-combatants. This service he performed with skill and courage and returned to Montpelier in 1828. Colonel Miller was a good lawyer, but so much a man of affairs that he did not devote his entire time to his profession. He was an earnest abolitionist, and by his personal courage once prevented a mob from maltreating Samuel J. May.

Charles W. Willard, able lawyer and editor, was a member of congress from 1869 to 1875, and died lamented in 1880. Charles Reed, Charles H. Heath, Joseph A. Wing and Stephen C. Shurtleff are well remembered for their excellence in their profession as are Timothy Merrill, F. F. Merrill and others of an older time.

The newspapers of Montpelier, from the first one in 1806 to the present time, have maintained a high place in the press of the state. Among the editors of note were the elder Walton, E. P. Walton, Jr., who was member of congress from 1857 to 1863, Charles W. Willard, Joseph Poland, Hiram Atkins and others. The present newspapers are the *Vermont Watchman*, the *Argus and Patriot*, published weekly; the *Evening Argus* and *Montpelier Record*, evening dailies; and the daily morning issue of the *Watchman*.

The Bank of Montpelier was founded in 1826 and the Vermont Bank in 1849. During the War of the Rebellion they were succeeded by the Montpelier National Bank and First National Bank of Montpelier. James R. Langdon was president of the Montpelier National Bank until his death in 1895, since when Albert Tuttle has been its president. The president of the First National Bank is Charles Dewey. The Montpelier Savings Bank & Trust Company was founded in 1870, and Homer W. Heaton has been president from its organization. The Capital Savings Bank and Trust Company was chartered in 1890, and of this T. J. Deavitt is president.

Montpelier has been a center of well conducted insurance business for many years. In 1828 the Vermont Mutual Fire Insurance Company was organized of which Col. Fred E. Smith is now president. The Union Mutual Fire Insurance Company was chartered in 1874. Its president is James W. Brock. The National Life Insurance Company was founded fifty years ago by Dr. Julius Y. Dewey. Charles Dewey is its president.

The city has an excellent system of water works, the water being taken from a reservoir fed from Berlin Pond, or Mirror Lake. Not only is water supplied for public and domestic purposes, but the overplus is used in affording power for manufacturing establishments.

The oldest and best known manufacturing establishment is that of the Lane Manufacturing Company, which sends out saw-mills and other woodworking machinery not only to various states of the Union, but to South America, the eastern continent, and Australia. This company was established some thirty years ago by Gen. P. P. Pitkin, Dennis Lane and James W. Brock, and first did business as a partnership under the name of Lane, Pitkin & Brock. The Colton Manufacturing Company, on the Berlin side, employs many hands; and the development of the granite quarries in Barre within the last eighteen years has not only built up the city of Barre but has brought to Montpelier many firms and corporations engaged in cutting granite work. It is probable that the granite industry to-day employs more hands in Montpelier than any other business.

The post office building, which also contains a court room for the accommodation of the United States Courts, was built in 1885. The courts for Washington County were held in the old State House until 1818, when a county court house was built to the north of the Pavilion. This court house was given up and a new one built in 1842. The new one so built was soon burned, and its successor was enlarged in 1879. It was partially burned in 1880 and was repaired the same year, constituting the court house as it now stands. It has occupied its present site at the corner of State and Elm streets for fifty-six years.

A circulating library was begun in Montpelier in 1794. About 1814 another library was established. In 1885 the Montpelier Public Library Association was formed, and still exists. In 1894 the building of the Kellogg-Hubbard Library was begun and this new library was completed and opened in 1895. The cost of the grounds and building was about $60,-000. The library is one of the best in the state. The Kellogg-Hubbard Library is incorporated and holds its property in trust for the inhabitants of Montpelier.

In 1895 Thomas W. Wood, a native of Montpelier and president of the National Academy of Design, established an art gallery in Montpelier in connection with the Young Men's Christian Association and the Montpelier Public Library Association.

Homer W. Heaton in 1895 and 1896 erected a hospital building on the northern part of Seminary Hill, and deeded the property to trustees who were incorporated in 1896 as the Heaton Hospital. A new wing has been added to the hospital building during the present year and its cost defrayed by Mr. Heaton. The city appropriates $2,000 annually to the hospital. Mr. Heaton is the oldest member of the Washington County bar. He was born in Berlin, August 25, 1811; studied law with J. P. Miller and was admitted to the bar in November, 1835.

The Apollo Club is the leading association organized in the city for social objects.

The first railroad train to run into Montpelier came over the Vermont Central line June 20, 1849. About 1873 the Montpelier and Wells River Railroad was completed, and branches have been since built from Montpelier to Barre by both the Central and Wells River roads, the Central branch extending now to Williamstown and the Wells River branch connecting with a railroad that makes a circle among the granite quarries.

Since in 1886 the use of gas for street lights was abandoned, electric lights have been used instead. There are now two electric plants, that of the Consolidated Lighting Company, whose power is furnished by the Winooski at the Pioneer Mills, supplemented by steam; and that of J. S. Viles, who has built very substantial electric works at Middlesex, the power being supplied from the waters of the Winooski at his dam in Middlesex Narrows. The Consolidated Company is about to put in a dam and an extensive plant at Bolton Falls some eighteen miles below Montpelier and twelve miles below Middlesex.

In 1897-8 was constructed the Barre and Montpelier Street Railway. Its cars began running regularly about July 1, 1898, and the number of passengers carried has exceeded expectation.

Montpelier furnished its full share of soldiers in the war for the Union and the hall of Brooks Post of the Grand Army is a place for frequent reunions of the veterans. Company H of the First Regiment of Vermont Volunteers is just back from Camp Thomas at Chickamauga for muster out. Col. O. D. Clark of the First Regiment and Adjutant A. G. Eaton were Montpelier men.

The division of the old town of Montpelier into the two towns of Montpelier and East Montpelier took place in 1848, and the town of Montpelier was chartered as a city at the legislative session of 1894. This city charter went into effect March 1, 1895, George W. Wing being the first mayor. John H. Senter is mayor at the present time. The city's last representative, William A. Lord, was speaker of the House in 1896 and Harlan W. Kemp is the present representative of Montpelier in the general assembly.

It is a far cry back to that Thanksgiving night in 1791 when Theophilus Wilson Brooks of Montpelier, and Betsey Hobart of Berlin, were drowned in the Onion river after the Thanksgiving ball held at the house of Colonel Davis; but in all the intervening days the town has gone forward, as is the habit of most New England towns, to better conditions and with retention, in somewhat modified form but in real substance, of the old New England characteristics and virtues. That same river by the way, some sixty years after the tragic night of December, 1791, came near drowning a Montpelier lad, then in his teens, whose name was George Dewey.

Simeon Dewey, William Dewey and Israel Dewey from Hanover, N. H., were early settlers in Berlin, their farms being near Dog river, two or three miles up from its mouth. It was

with Israel Dewey, his brother-in-law, that Daniel Baldwin in 1803, a boy of eleven years, was living; and Daniel's home-going from a neighbor's of an evening was the cause of the famous Berlin wolf-hunt. The neighbor gave Daniel a fire-brand in part to light his way and in part to keep off the wolves. The wolves sure enough began to howl and come, and Daniel waved his fire-brand and used his legs and came to his destination in safety, but in alarming proximity to the fierce beasts, who had only been kept from him by the fear of his fire-brand. The men of the town turned out in a day or two and by concerted action corralled and killed most of the wolves. Daniel lived to be one of Montpelier's most honored citizens, one of the founders of the Vermont Mutual Insurance Company and its president for many years, but to the day of his death, in 1881, he never forgot his race with the wolves on the banks of Dog river.

Julius Yemans Dewey, a son of Simeon, was born in Berlin, studied medicine, settled in Montpelier and was, until about fifty years of age, in active practice. He then founded the National Life Insurance Company and devoted his energies to its success. By his first wife, Mary Perrin, he left three sons and a daughter, Charles, Edward, George and Mary, now Mrs. Mary P. Greeley, three of these now living in Montpelier and the other in the United States as to be bounded.

George Dewey was born in Montpelier, December 26, 1837, in a house now moved farther down State street, but which then stood where Edward Dewey now resides, directly opposite the State House. He went to school here in Montpelier, then to Morrisville Academy and then for two years he attended Norwich University, a military school which has been of great value to the good name of Vermont in war. In 1854 he went to the Naval Academy at Annapolis, where he graduated in 1858. In the Civil War he saw much service, a good share of it under Farragut. After the war for nearly a third of a century his service was of the usual kind that falls to the lot of a naval officer, promotion coming step by step.

He married October 24, 1867, Susan B. Goodwin, a daughter of Ex-Governor Ichabod Goodwin of New Hampshire. They had one son, George Goodwin Dewey, born at Newport, R. I., December 23, 1872, who is now with the firm of Joy, Langdon & Co., of New York. Mrs. Dewey died at Newport, R. I., December 28, 1872. George Dewey was an energetic boy and not of Quaker habit. After the Rebellion was over he used the long years of peace in preparing himself for further service in war if war should come again. This year the opportunity came and the man was ready,—brave, cool, chary of words, but certain in deeds. The battle of Manila Bay, with its intermission for breakfast, was not a mushroom growth of the night before, but the fruit of a lifetime of faithful preparation for the performance of a high duty for which the time might or might not come. Study and foresight and care so brought result that on the evening of the first Sunday in May, whose morning opened the gates of the Orient to the republic of the Occident, good Parson Lewis in the Commodore's home church read the collect of thanksgiving for victory at sea. Montpelier counts too as one of her sons, this one by adoption, Captain Charles E. Clark, of the *Oregon*.

Vain genealogies are an abomination and a nuisance and all genealogies are a burden to the searcher; but running the line of descent of an old New England family down from its first comer from England in many cases gives an epitome of the course of settlement of a large part of New England. This is true of the line of George Dewey's New England ancestry. His is the ninth generation from the first settler, and the generations are these:

1. Thomas Dewey came under Rev. John Warham from Sandwich in Kent, England, to Dorchester, Mass., in 1633. Two or three years later he moved with others of the congregation to Windsor, Conn. There he married widow Frances Clark, had five children, died, and was buried April 27, 1648.

2. Sergeant Josiah Dewey, born at Windsor, baptized October 10, 1641; married November 6, 1662, Hepsibah Lyman; lived at Northampton and Westfield, Mass., and died at Lebanon, Conn., September 7, 1732.

3. Josiah Dewey, Jr., born at Northampton, Mass., December 24, 1666; married January 15, 1690, Mehitable Miller; died at Lebanon, Conn.

4. William Dewey, born at Westfield, Mass., January, 1691; married July 2, 1713, Mercy Bailey; died November 10, 1759.

5. Simeon Dewey, born at Lebanon, Conn., May 1, 1718; married March 29, 1739, Anna Phelps; died at Lebanon, Conn., March 2, 1751.

6. William Dewey, born at Lebanon, Conn., January 11, 1745; married in 1768, Rebecca Carrier; died at Hanover, N. H., June 10, 1813.

7. Capt. Simeon Dewey, born at Hebron, Conn., August 20, 1770; married February 27, 1794, Prudence Yemans; died at Berlin, Vt., January 11, 1863.

8. Julius Yemans Dewey, born at Berlin, Vt., August 22, 1801; married June 9, 1825, Mary Perrin; died at Montpelier, Vt., May 29, 1877. Dr. Dewey after the decease of his first wife married August 3, 1845, Susan Edson Tarbox and after her decease married March 9, 1855, Susan E. G. Lilley.

9. George Dewey, born in Montpelier, Vt., December 26, 1837.

It is worthy of note that within the "palisado" of Windsor, upon the lot next south of the northeast corner lot, lived Matthew Grant, the recorder or first town clerk of Windsor, while upon the first lot north of this corner lot and without the palisado lived Thomas Dewey. So that for ten or eleven years before Thomas Dewey's death, in 1648, Matthew and Thomas lived about ten rods from each other. Matthew came from England and General Grant was one of his descendants.

Dr. Stiles in his History of Windsor explains the "palisado" thus: "Upon the breaking out of the Pequot war, in 1637, the Windsor people, as a precaution against surprisal by the Indians, surrounded their dwellings with a fortification or palisado"; and elsewhere he says: "The Palisado Green, the veritable shrine of Windsor history and romance. Very pleasant it is as we see it now in the warm sunset light of a summer day, lined with noble trees, behind whose waving tracery neat and elegant dwellings assert the presence of happy homes. On this spot, more than two centuries ago, our fathers dwelt. Here protected by the rude log defense which their own hands had thrown up, they slept secure from savage foe. Here stood the meeting-house wherein the gentle Warham and the earnest Huit preached and prayed. Here, too, was the little village graveyard close under the palisado wall, where, one by one, they put off life's toils and cares and laid them down to an eternal rest."

Old Windsor is one of the very great grandmothers of Montpelier, and the lines of descent of the little city encompassed about by the green hills of Vermont run back to many another old town of Puritan New England. Montpelier is a place of thrift, of progress and of happy homes. Those who dwell within her borders love her, and hope that she will keep in the future, as she has kept in the past, fairly true to the virtues of her old New England ancestry, and when her sons and daughters are done with the duties and pleasures and the happy homes of life, there remains for the mortal part of one and all her "Eden of the Dead," Green Mount Cemetery, which her poet Eastman called:

"This fairest spot of hill and glade,
  Where blooms the flower and waves the tree,
And silver streams delight the shade."

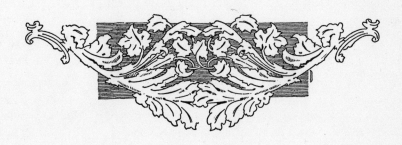

4
Hanover, New Hampshire
Dartmouth

Beautiful
New England

OVERLOOKING THE CONNECTICUT RIVER, HANOVER, NEW HAMPSHIRE

The Bema, Hanover, New Hampshire

The Tower, Hanover, New Hampshire

ROLLINS CHAPEL, HANOVER, NEW HAMPSHIRE

65

THE OLD PINE, HANOVER, NEW HAMPSHIRE

View of Main Street, Hanover, New Hampshire

Ex-president William J. Tucker of Dartmouth College

NEW ENGLAND MAGAZINE

VOL. XLI.   JANUARY, 1910   NUMBER 5

THE NEW DARTMOUTH

By MELVIN O. ADAMS, A.M., '71
and WILLIAM T. ATWOOD, '09

WHEN Dr. Earnest Fox Nichols assumed the presidency of Dartmouth College last October, he undertook the administration of an institution so different from that to which his predecessor, Dr. Tucker, succeeded sixteen years ago, that it has sometimes been designated as the "New Dartmouth." A word of explanation is perhaps necessary in this connection, for the term "new" has carried to many the idea of a breaking down of the old traditions—a conclusion which they strive to prove by pointing to the increase in numbers of the student body, the change from a local into a national college, the comfortable and even luxurious accommodations so different from the Spartan life experienced by the older alumni. These things, they say, must have changed the standards of the college and reduced the traditions to empty tales.

But the "New Dartmouth" is not the result of revolution, but of evolution. The old traditions have not been broken down, but have adapted themselves to modern requirements. No institution can stand still and succeed, and the policy of even Dartmouth has been ever progressive, alive to the present needs. Indeed, it was the knowledge of present need that prompted Eleazer Wheelock to plunge into the wilderness and found his little log college for the education of the Indians.

The alarmists are so assiduous in gathering statistics, and so zealous in spreading the results of their investigations, that it is eminently fitting now at the end of the splendid administration of Dr. Tucker, who, above all men, is responsible for the New Dartmouth, that we discuss the college in its new position, and question whether the change has been other than a healthy growth. The conclusion will be, we believe, that the splendid traditions of democracy and loyalty which make up the famous "Dartmouth Spirit" have never been stronger than they are at present.

A comparison of the College in 1893, when Dr. Tucker assumed the presidency, and now is most interesting. The external appearance shows it to be far from the "little college" it was at that time, although it was then vastly larger than when the phrase was made famous.

Massachusetts, Sanborn, Crosby, New Hubbard, Wheeler, Richardson, the three Fayerweathers, and New Hampshire Halls, all dormitories and housing over seven hundred students, have been erected during the administration of Dr. Tucker. With three exceptions they are constructed of brick. Several houses have also been remodeled into dormitories. Besides the dormitories, Webster Hall, a magnificent auditorium, the Tuck School of Administration and Finance, Butterfield Hall, the biological laboratory, and Wilder Hall, the physics laboratory, have been built. Even historic college yard has had its changes, for New Dartmouth Hall was completed in 1905, and while it is a replica of Old Dartmouth, occupying the same site and burned in February, 1904, it is of brick instead of wood. An important addition which must not be omitted is College Hall, containing the Commons and rooms of the College Club, the social center of the institution. And now the new gymnasium is under construction.

The architecture of the college is varied, but most of the buildings, especially the newer ones, are of colonial type.

In Webster and Dartmouth Halls the colonial scheme is used in the interior, mahogany and white enamel being used for woodwork in both cases. The lecture room in Dartmouth Hall is said to be the most beautiful room for that purpose in the country.

In 1898 the central heating plant was built, from which the entire college it heated. An electric lighting plant was installed in 1905.

The fraternities have prospered and increased, and their fine chapter houses form no mean addition to the beauty of the town.

As the number of students has grown, their character has changed. It is no longer the college of the New England farmer's son—all honor to him—who earned his way by alternate terms as country schoolmaster, boarded 'round and

"Sang songs, and told us what befalls
In classic Dartmouth's college halls."

Dartmouth has become a city man's

MASSACHUSETTS HALL

PRESIDENT EARNEST FOX NICHOLS

college. Neither is it longer a poor man's college, in the sense that the students do not come from wealthy homes, but it decidedly is the college for a poor man in the sense of social equality of rich and poor. The snob is not tolerated in Hanover, and any attempt to display superiority results in ostracism or a visit to the horse-trough.

In distribution of students, Dartmouth is probably more representative than any college except Yale. Every state is represented in its catalogs, a large number coming from the Middle West.

All the foregoing facts the pessimist collects, gravely tells us that the Dartmouth spirit, outgrowth of a small community of sturdy New Englanders, poor and simple living, cannot exist under present conditions that are the very opposite. His deductions seem sound, too, and it is rather more difficult to prove on paper that the Dartmouth

WEBSTER HALL

spirit does still exist, than it is to prove that by all logical reasoning it should not. However, one only needs to know a few Dartmouth men, to see how firmly they stand by each other, to realize that the famous spirit still exists. When one hears how a whole college turned out at two in the morning, walked a mile over roads ankle deep in slush and ice, with a cold, heavy rain falling, just to cheer a team returning from defeat, one does not question the existence of the Dartmouth spirit.

One of the most potent factors in the keeping up of the old spirit is the alumni and the alumni associations. It has been said that a Dartmouth man can talk on no other subject than Dartmouth. While a few men, Webster and Choate, for instance, could talk intelligently and forcefully on one or two other subjects, it is true that the favorite theme of every alumnus is his

Alma Mater. The alumni do inestimable work in arousing an interest in the prospective student. He knows from them the traditions of democracy and loyalty before he starts for Hanover, nor does he have the traditions from word only, but sees them in practice.

When he is graduated, the older alumni help him in securing a position. In every city of any considerable size in the country there is a Dartmouth Club—a club that is working every minute for Dartmouth.

The second cause of the preservation of the Dartmouth spirit is the isolation of Hanover. Away from the diversions of large cities, the students are forced to seek the companionship of their fellows. Tennis, golf, snowshoeing, skiing, all call for companions, and offer the most favorable opportunities for promoting close friendships. A man soon falls into that *cameraderie* with his fellows which lasts throughout life and when he becomes an alumnus extends to all Dartmouth men.

The dormitory system, too, has much to do with the development of democracy, since the rooms are so arranged that students of varying pecuniary ability may room in the same building.

In 1901 College Hall was erected. The first floor is occupied by the rooms of the College Club, composed of the entire student body. The apartments are furnished with all the appointments of a prosperous club, and form the center of social activities in the college. Here the fellows gather to sing college songs and discuss college events. Here, in the great Commons dining room adjoining, are held the Saturday evening smoke talks, during the winter and spring. Speakers like General Miles, Elbert Hubbard, and Norman Hapgood are secured. The result is that the students are constantly together. How can democracy fail to flourish?

A man's college course is passed during the most sentimental period of his life, and it is not strange that in such a place as Hanover, at such a time of life, and with the old traditions constantly repeated about him, and the names of the great sons of the "little college" who were not ashamed to declare their love for it, daily words,—it is not strange that he, too, should absorb and pass on their love and veneration for the "Mother of Men."

The town of Hanover itself is well suited to the perpetuation of romantic traditions. Its elm-lined streets, the high hills that surround it, the placid river, its steep banks, pine covered or stretching away in rolling meadow, have been the haunts of Webster, Choate, and Thayer; by that road Wentworth, royal governor, came to the first commencement, there by the bridge Ledyard landed his canoe; and as we pass the shady streets, or gaze out over the valleys to the purple

NEW DARTMOUTH HALL.

DARTMOUTH COLLEGE FROM THE TOWER

hills, or walk beside the quiet waters, like the exiled duke, we find sermons in stones, and tongues in the trees, and they all proclaim the glory, past and future, of Dartmouth.

Can you be surprised at the loyalty of the Dartmouth man?

But besides all this, the student since 1893 has had the privilege of intercourse with the man who has made the New Dartmouth possible, through whose skillful hands, by whose unwearied work, the college was piloted

student body in the incident of two or three years ago, when the entire baseball team was charged with summer ball playing and prohibited playing on the college team for the rest of their course. It will be remembered that the decision was never questioned, even by the suspended players.

Whatever is pure and manly Dr. Tucker stood for. At Sunday vespers he preached much against littleness and nastiness. A most forceful speaker, what he said will be long remembered

LIVING ROOM—COLLEGE CLUB

through the transition from old to new, whose enthusiasm and zeal have not for a moment relaxed, yet have been tempered by wise conservatism that has made the change an evolution and not a revolution.

It is doubtful if there was ever a college president more beloved by his students than Dr. Tucker. He was, and is, the ideal of all that is manly and honorable. His decisions are never questioned, witness the attitude of the

by his hearers, and the lessons of purity and simplicity which he taught from the pulpit of Rollins Chapel will shape many a man's life.

A Boston paper recently spoke with some wonder of Dr. Tucker's practice of raising his hat to the students, but to one who knew him it is not difficult to picture him as at any time other than a gentleman—kindly, considerate, courteous, and unassuming.

When he retired from the presi-

THE COLLEGE CHURCH

dency, Dr. Tucker built a house in Hanover, a house strong and simple, like the man himself, where he will continue to live. Although not actively concerned with the college, his advice will doubtless often be sought and his example will, for many years to come, be open to the entering students, who, knowing him, will declare: "He is a man. Take him for all in all, we shall not look upon his like again."

The great work of Dr. Tucker is but the beginning. He has changed a little college into a large one, a provincial college into one of national scope and territory, a simple collegiate life into one far more complex; yet he has accomplished this without diminution of the democracy and loyalty which made the Dartmouth of yesterday famous.

"Founded by Wheelock, saved by Webster, refounded by Tucker." With such men as these ever ready to give their aid, men of Dartmouth have no need to "set a watch, lest the old traditions fail," whatever changes of growth or life may come.

Dr. Tucker has never spared himself when the good of the college was his end.

One of the trustees, speaking before the Dartmouth Lunch Club of Springfield when the choice of Dr. Tucker's successor was being considered, told of a visit of the Doctor's to Cleveland a year or so before. He was scheduled to speak at several places in the interest of the college and had fulfilled all but one of the engagements, although suffering from a severe cold. On the way to the final lecture, the car on which he was riding was disabled and no carriage being available there, he started to walk through a blinding snow storm to the hall, over a mile away. The gentlemen of his party urged him to return lest the exposure should bring on serious illness. Dr. Tucker replied, "I feel that I am but executing one of the duties of the presidency. I trust that my successor, whoever he may be, will feel as I do in this matter."

It is to such a man that the New Dartmouth is due. May his retirement be as pleasant and peaceful as his long term of energetic usefulness and self-sacrificing devotion to Dartmouth has deserved.

Last October Dr. Earnest Fox Nichols, of Columbia University, was chosen to take the place of Dr. Tucker. Although not a graduate of Dartmouth, his several years' experience as a teacher in the college has made him thoroughly familiar with its spirit and traditions, and familiarity in this case, far from breeding contempt, begets the most sincere admiration.

There is not an alumnus who does not look forward to his administration with the greatest confidence, trusting that the policy of conservative expansion, which his predecessor has established, will be carried out and developed. The seed of a greatness far beyond the present has been planted; it is for him to till the soil and show the world that the ideal college may exist with unchanged standards despite all the vicissitudes that time may bring. How great a change awaits Hanover if in the next sixteen years Dartmouth increases as it has in the sixteen years just passed! Even now there is no room left around the campus for college buildings. The dormitories must push farther and farther away from the recitation halls. This is an important problem that faces the engineers. The new "cut-system"—a very important consideration in an isolated college—must be tried out. At the present rate of growth, Rollins Chapel will soon be inadequate, in spite of the addition completed within the past year. Thanks to Dr. Bowler and the generosity of students and alumni, the new gymnasium, the largest in the country, will be completed within a year. This means a great stimulus to athletics of all kinds, having, as it does, a baseball diamond, a gridiron, a long dirt track, besides the regular gymnasium equipment, all under cover, where the teams may practice during the long Hanover winter. All these things bear directly or indirectly upon the future of the college. All mean changed conditions which must be carefully considered by those in administration. But into their hands we unhesitatingly commit the college, knowing that the Dartmouth spirit, which they possess, will not suffer the Dartmouth spirit to be lost, nor let the voice crying in the wilderness call in vain.

A century hence the college will be thrilled by the speeches of Dartmouth

BUTTERFIELD MUSEUM

night, with the same love of Alma Mater as it is to-day, and the Seniors will crowd about the Old Pine stump to smoke the final peace-pipe with the same reverence for tradition as they have since college record began.

And the spirit of the Old Dartmouth shall be in the New Dartmouth, strong as the granite rocks that tower above her, deep as the silent river that flows past her, beautiful as the sunset on the Norwich hills.

PEACE PIPE AT THE OLD PINE STUMP

5
From Light to Light

FROM LIGHT TO LIGHT

A CRUISE OF THE ARMERIA, SUPPLY-SHIP

By Kirk Munroe

OT one of the white squadron! Not a war-ship! What is she then? She is certainly a Government vessel of some kind."

Such are some of the remarks likely to be overheard at the Maine coast resorts, upon the appearance in the harbor of the United States steamship Armeria. Nor is it any wonder that the big white steamer, with her yellow funnel, many boats, gleaming brass work, and uniformed officers and crew, should be mistaken for a war-ship, or that she should at once suggest pleasing visions of receptions, hops, and the various interesting possibilities of a naval vessel in times of peace. But the Armeria is not a man-of-war, nor does she belong to the Navy. She is merely the largest and most important of the great fleet of Government vessels controlled by the Treasury Department, and devoted to the peaceful service of commerce. She is the lighthouse supply-ship, the only one of her kind owned by the United States, and the finest of her class in the world. Her duty is to pay an annual visit to every light station on the Atlantic and Gulf coasts of the United States, from Calais, Me., to Point Isabel, Tex., and to deliver at each a year's supply of oil and the other articles necessary for the maintenance of its light. In addition to visiting the coast lights, she supplies the numerous post lights of the Connecticut, Hudson, Delaware, Potomac, James, Cape Fear, Savannah, St. John's, and Indian Rivers, shipping the re-quired stores by rail, or by river steamers, to those points that her draught, of thirteen feet, will not permit her to reach. In thus making her annual rounds the Armeria visits about 700, and supplies about 850, light stations.

The supply-ship was built on the Delaware by John Dialogue in 1890, and went into commission the following year. From June 30, 1891, to the same date in 1892, she steamed 14,000 miles, and delivered at light stations 250,000 gallons of mineral oil, 220 tons of paints and paint oils, 3,735 boxes of lamp-chimneys, and 10,735 packages of miscellaneous supplies.

Prior to 1860 all light stations were supplied with sperm-oil from New Bedford, by a contractor named Howland. When sperm was superseded by lard-oil, the business reverted to the general Government, and the old customs station at Tompkinsville, on Staten Island, being transferred to the Lighthouse Department, became the central supply station for the entire country. From here the eastern coast lights, which at that time were practically the only ones in existence, were supplied by the schooners Pharos and Guthrie, the latter of which was commanded by Captain William Wright, the present master of the Armeria. In those days the lard-oil was carried in great casks, from which it was pumped through a line of hose into the light-house tanks; and many a thrilling tale of hardship, adventure, and narrow escape is told concerning the landing of those unwieldy casks, through the breakers of the rock-bound New England coast, or the combing surf of

Southern beaches. Innumerable are the records of overturned boats and of brave swimmers battling with the waves, while painfully pushing the heavy oil-casks through them to the beach. On such occasions the broadside of a cask would be presented to an inflowing sea that might help it along, and then it would be quickly turned so as to present an end to the reflux waters. Oftentimes it was found necessary to carry surf-lines to the beach, becket the casks, and thus with infinite labor drag them ashore one at a time.

In 1876 lard began to give place to mineral oil, and the schooners Pharos and Guthrie, the former of which is still in the service as a tender attached to the sixth district, were replaced by the supply-steamer Fern, with Captain Wright as master. The Fern had a capacity for 30,000 gallons of oil, and the business of supplying lights, while steadily increasing in volume with the rapid establishment of new stations, was greatly simplified by the introduction of the new illuminant, which is carried and delivered in small cases. For fifteen years the Fern performed her important duties with unbroken regularity, but at the end of that period the demands of the service had so far exceeded her ability to meet them, that a new and much larger ship was an imperative need. So the present supply-ship was built, and named, as all but eight of the forty-four lighthouse tenders now in the service are, after a flower. The Armeria is the only one of the floral fleet to which is given a botanical name and but few persons would recognize the common sea-pink or thrift under its more learned appellation. Armeria is also the Latin name for Sweet William. It was a somewhat unfortunate choice, as Armeria so nearly resembles America that the ship is often reported under the latter name, while she sometimes figures in the papers as the "Amelia," or the "Armaria," much to her cap-

Portland Head, Me.

Landing Supplies at West Quoddy, Me.   Extreme Eastern light in United States.

tain's disgust. However, Armeria she is, and the device on her bows is a lighthouse surrounded by sprays of her name-flower in gilded carving.

All the light stations of the United States are grouped in sixteen inspection districts, to each of which is assigned an Army officer as engineer, and an officer of the Navy as Inspector. Eight of these districts are allotted to the Atlantic and Gulf coasts; the ninth, tenth, and eleventh cover the Great Lakes; the twelfth and thirteenth extend from southern California to Alaska; while the remaining three embrace all navigable waters of the Mississippi Valley, on which are displayed some 1,400 stake or post lights. There are about 150 light stations on the Pacific coast, about 265 on the Great Lakes, and about 850 in the eastern districts; or between 2,600 and 2,700 in all. It is impossible to state the exact number, as new stations are constantly being established. Of all these the oldest is Boston Light, on Little Brewster Island, in Boston Harbor, which was established in 1716 and last rebuilt in 1859. The next oldest is on Brant Point, at the entrance to Nantucket Harbor, which was established in 1746 and last rebuilt in 1856; while the third in point of age is the Gurnet, off Plymouth, established in 1769.

For the Pacific coast light stations all supplies are shipped from Staten Island in sailing-vessels around the Horn to San Francisco, whence they are distributed by the tenders belonging to the twelfth and thirteenth districts. For the Great Lakes and Mississippi Valley districts, oil is purchased in the West, but all other supplies are

Heron's Rock, Penobscot Bay, Me.

furnished from Staten Island; while to the eight eastern districts everything necessary to the maintenance of lights is supplied by the Armeria.

In order to pay an annual visit to every light station along this vast extent of coast, the supply-ship must make three trips during each year. The first, or eastern cruise, which covers the territory between Staten Island and Calais, in Maine, is undertaken in the summer and occupies the greater part of August and September. Upon its completion two months are allowed for cleaning, overhauling, repairs, and reloading, before the winter cruise, which is from Cape Lookout in North Carolina to the mouth of the Rio Grande, is begun. Coming north in April, the ship is immediately reloaded for her spring or middle cruise, which is from Cape Lookout to New York. After this cruise she is again docked and overhauled. From the dry dock in Brooklyn she steams across to Staten Island glistening in fresh paint, with her bottom freed from every trace of the barnacles and grass accumulated during her long Southern trips, and begins to take in supplies for her forthcoming cruise along the New England coast.

Now nearly, or quite, 100,000 gallons of the best refined petroleum, that has successfully passed the 170° flash-test of the lighthouse proving-room, are stored in her hold. This oil is contained in five-gallon tins, each protected by a stout wooden case, to which is affixed a strong bail or handle. While this most important item of lighthouse supply is being snugly stowed below, the great storehouse of the station is being drawn upon for as miscellaneous an assortment of articles as would furnish a country store.

As these multifarious supplies are received on board the Armeria, they find their allotted places in the capacious store-rooms that occupy the after-parts of the maindeck and hold. Here they are under the supervision of a chief clerk, an assistant clerk, and a yeoman.

The Armeria carries a crew of forty-one officers and men, or rather, forty-two all told; for it would never do to omit from the list the captain's wife, who accompanies him on all his cruises and shares many of his anxious watches on the bridge in seasons of fog and storm.

Captain Wright himself is a typical American shipmaster; ruddy-faced, deep-chested, with a voice to be heard above the roar of a gale, cool and self-possessed in times when these qualities are most needed. He has been master of lighthouse supply-ships for twenty-five years, and is probably the only man living who is a pilot to every harbor on the Atlantic and Gulf coasts of the United States. Not only this, but he knows and remembers the location of every lighthouse, lightship, beacon, and buoy, from Maine to Texas.

As the white ship sets forth from Staten Island on her summer's cruise to the perilous New England coast, she is deeply laden with supplies for the three hundred and odd light stations she is to visit before her return, for the tenders of the several Eastern districts, and for a number of buoy stations. She does not begin her work

The Landing at Egg Rock in Frenchman's Bay, Me.—Mount Desert in the distance.

United States Lighthouse Supply-Steamer Armeria.

at New York, but proceeds directly to the Maine coast, making her first stop at Portland. Even after leaving that point she passes, without notice, the lights of Portland Head, Half-way Rock, Seguin, at the mouth of the Kennebec, Pemmaquid, Monhegan, far out at sea, which held the first white settlement made in Maine, Marshall's Point, Tennant's Harbor, and half a dozen more, until Whitehead light, at the extreme western point of Penobscot Bay, is reached.

As the Armeria approaches Whitehead she is welcomed by a hoarse salute from its deep-toned, steam fog-horn, and the few inmates of the lighthouse gather on the rocks to witness this most interesting arrival of the year. She rounds the bold headland into a haven of glassy, forest-bordered waters, and her ponderous anchor rushes to the bottom, with a deafening roar of chain. Almost at the same moment the capacious freight-boat in which the supplies are to be carried ashore is lowered from the forward davits, and dropped back to an open port opposite the main

hatch, from which the cases of oil are passed by a dozen members of the crew clad in working suits of brown canvas.

As Whitehead is a third-order light, it is entitled to 275 gallons of mineral oil, with 40 more for use in the keeper's dwelling, or 63 cases in all. Besides these, the boat receives a miscellaneous freight of paints, cases of lubricating oil, cans of tallow, brooms, mats, shovels, hoes and rakes, lamps, boxes of chimneys, one of window-glass, and another of soap, and last of all a good-sized tin chest known as the "supply-box," and filled to overflowing with the linen, stationery, brushes, cleaning materials, and numerous other minor articles of supply. Down the rope side-ladder, into the boat, slide the second and third mates, the assistant clerk, the yeoman, and a crew of eight or ten stalwart Scandinavian sailors. If there is a favorable breeze a lug-sail is hoisted, if not the boat moves off under the impulse of lusty oars. A long experience has taught the mate, who holds the tiller-ropes, where to find the best landing. He

Pumpkin Island, Penobscot Bay, Me.

steers straight for it, and in another minute, to the sharp orders of " Way enough ! In oars ! Stand by with the boat-hook ! " the boat shoots into a basin between two low ledges, bow and stern lines are made fast, and a plank is run ashore. The light-keeper in full uniform, hastily donned at the first intimation of the Armeria's approach, stands at the water's edge, to give these welcome visitors a hearty greeting, and lend them what assistance he may. He reports the amount of oil that he has still on hand, and the number of empty cases to be returned. Possessed of this information, the second mate directs the third to deliver such a number of full cases as will stock the little isolated brick oil-house with a thirteen months' supply. Then in company with the keeper he visits the latter's house, whither the assistant clerk and the yeoman, bearing the supply-box between them, have preceded him.

The grounds about the neat dwelling-house are in perfect order, its exterior is bright with fresh paint and whitewash, and every inch of its interior is as scrupulously clean as soap, water, and persistent effort can make it. The assistant keepers appear in uniform, the women, if there are any, show to advantage in fresh calicoes, and the bashful faces of the children, dressed in their Sunday best, shine above clean collars as though they too had been polished for the occasion. In the best room of the house, the walls of which are decorated with the keeper's marriage certificate, or honorable discharge from the army, in a neat frame, with photographs of light-houses or brilliant marine lithographs, the mate and clerk, pens in hand, seat themselves at a table and unfold portentous-looking papers. At the same time the yeoman opens his supply-box on the floor, and displays its treasures as a pedler would those of his pack.

The mate's paper is a voluminous form filled in by the keeper with a list of articles remaining on hand from the supplies of the preceding year. The clerk's is a blank form of the same character, in which he will note the articles delivered on the present occasion. "One broom, give three," says the mate. "Two linen towels, give ten. One sponge, give two. Sandpaper, none, give twelve." This is continued through page after page of the long lists, while the yeoman places the articles to be delivered on one side of his box and those to be returned to the ship storeroom on the other. As the box gradually becomes emptied, and the floor covered with its varied treasures of linen, glass, cutlery, brushes, stationery, etc., the yeoman's resemblance to a pedler displaying his wares becomes stronger than ever. At one side sits the keeper, nervously fingering his cap and hoping that he has made no mistake in his list. His wife also hovers near, determined that he shall not be allowed to forget the old hand-lamp that leaks, and which she means to have exchanged for a new one ; while the bashful children, whispering excitedly to each other, crowd the open doorway. When the lists are finished, and an extra one of articles to be procured from the boat has been made out, the keeper is called upon to produce all his worn-out brooms, brushes, mops, and broken tools, decrepit lamps, or dust-pans, which must be gathered up and taken to the boat before they can be replaced by new utensils of the same character. Eventually these worn-out articles are thrown overboard when the lighthouse from which they came has been left so far behind that there is no chance of their drifting back to it, and being picked up to be again offered in evidence the following year.   While this

The Portland Breakwater.

portion of the supply business is being transacted at the dwelling, the boat's crew is carrying oil, two cases at a time, up over the slippery rocks to the oil-house. Each of the men is provided with a wooden shoulder-yoke, such as are used by farmers for carrying milk-pails. From each end of the yoke depends a chain terminating in an iron hook. These hooks catch on to the stout wire bails of the oil cases, and thus a man is enabled to carry two cases, or about 120 pounds, at a trip. On his return from the oil-house he brings two "empties," which are ultimately returned to Staten Island to be refilled. To each of these is attached a tag bearing the name of the light station, the date on which the case was emptied, and a note as to its condition signed by the light-keeper.

During these proceedings the captain's gig has come ashore, bringing the member of the Lighthouse Board who happens to be making this particular cruise. He is received with due deference by the keeper, and conducted through the buildings to the top of the tower, where he carefully examines the mechanism of the light, and into the engine-room of the fog signal. He listens attentively to the keeper's complaints or suggestions, and makes a note of them. He is so affable and expresses such a lively interest in all that he sees, that even the keeper's wife plucks up courage to enter a plea for a new porch over her front door as a protection against the driving storms of winter, or an addition to the dwelling to meet the needs of her growing family, all of which is readily promised, provided the appropriation holds out —which it rarely does.

After supplying Whitehead, the ship lies quietly at anchor all night, but if the weather be favorable she is off for Matinicus Rock, 18 miles out at sea, by early daylight. At six o'clock, with the sun an hour high, she is at anchor on the inner side of the grim rock-pile that stands as outer sentry to Penobscot

Saddleback Rock, Maine.

Bay. It is a bleak and rugged place, cleft with deep fissures and piled high with huge bowlders, but supporting in sheltered nooks a few acres of rich grass that afford pasturage to a lonely cow. Its two light towers are of gray granite as grim and forbidding as the Rock itself, while the principal keeper's house, nestled at the foot of one of them, is of the same sombre but substantial material. The engine-house for the steam fog-signal, standing in front of the same tower, is a low building of granite and brick, with immensely thick walls, founded on the everlasting rock, fifty feet above the mean water-level, and apparently able to withstand any natural force short of an earthquake shock. Yet, a few years ago, during a furious winter gale from the southeast the huge seas uplifted themselves until they were hurled with irresistible force over every portion of the island, sweeping away everything movable, and shattering the stout outer wall of the engine-house as though it were but a wooden shell. Huge bowlders, weighing many tons, were rolled hither and thither; while one great cube of granite, measuring $20 \times 8 \times 6$ feet, was tossed from the base nearly to the summit of the Rock. In the midst of this wild war of elements, the keeper's little daughter, seeing a coop containing her two pet chickens about to be washed away, ran out and brought them back in safety to the tower in which she and her parents had taken refuge. Captain Isaac Grant, who was then the principal keeper, and who in his seafaring years commanded thirty-four different vessels, declares that he never witnessed another gale of equal fury, and hopes never to again. He is now a hale veteran of ninety, and only recently resigned his position as keeper in favor of one of his sons. Now three generations of Grants contentedly occupy this little granite dwelling, and call this bit of storm-swept rock in the open sea their home. One advantage possessed by Matinicus is its great natural rock cistern, which receives a large portion of the island's rainfall and thus stores an ample supply for use in the boilers of the fog-signal.

On the inner side of the island stands a little slanting boat-house, from which stout timber-ways, well greased for the sliding of boats, extend down over the rocks into the restless waters. The freight-boat from the supply-ship, coming in on the top of a long roller, is headed to a nicety for these, a stout cable that runs to a winch in the boat-house is hooked on the instant she touches, and in a minute more the heavily laden boat is drawn clear of the water, and half-way up the ways, where its unloading is a matter of comparative simplicity. When the supplying of the station is finished, the crew tumbles into the boat, the cable is cast off, and she slides down the greased incline into the water with the exciting rush of a toboggan.

The supplying of Matinicus is hardly completed before a sea-fog begins to roll in, and the captain is glad to turn his ship's head landward toward the inshore stations that the fog may not yet have reached. So the lonely rock is quickly lost to sight, and only the hoarse booming of its ten-inch fog-whistle, uttering a warning note every half-minute, gives proof of its existence. The course now laid is for Heron Neck, on the most southerly of the Fox Islands, from which granite has been quarried for half the public buildings of the country. As this is a fifth-order light, and only requires twenty cases of oil, its supplying is quickly accomplished, and the Armeria is headed for Saddleback Ledge, within three miles of the highlands of the Isle au Haut. Saddleback Ledge, as seen last summer, was a bare rock absolutely devoid of vegetation, save for three sickly pea-vines, two hills of potatoes, and a dozen spears of oats, which, with a longing to look upon something green, the keeper had coaxed into life in his trash heap, though with the certain knowledge that the first heavy gale would sweep them away.

At this station the rocks rise so abruptly, and the break of the sea upon them is so constant, that an anchor is dropped over the stern of the freight-boat, a line from her bows is made fast ashore by the light-keepers, and, as she lies thus, moored in tossing white waters, within a few feet of the sullen coast, her cargo is transferred to the Ledge by means of a stout iron derrick, securely planted in the solid rock high above her.

This is one of the wildest and bleakest of light stations of that savage region, and, according to a story told there, it was once the scene of a remarkably plucky adherence to duty on the part of a fifteen-year-old boy. He was the son of the keeper, and on this occasion was left alone in the tower while his father went ashore for provisions in their only boat. Before the latter could return a violent storm arose, and for the next three weeks there was no time in which the keeper's boat could have lived for a moment in the wild seas that raged about the lonely rock. Still the light was kept burning by that fifteen-year-old boy, who had little to eat and but scant time to sleep. Night after night, for three weeks, its steady gleam shone through the blackness of the pitiless storm and gladdened the father's straining eyes. When the ordeal was ended the boy was so weak from exhaustion as to be barely able to speak. At the same time there was no prouder father, nor happier young light-keeper on the Maine coast, than those who met on the storm-swept Ledge of Saddleback that day.

After supplying several smaller lights the Armeria is again headed seaward toward Mount Desert Rock, twenty miles southward from the nearest point of Mount Desert Island. So truly does the white ship steer for this distant bit of rock, barely four acres in all, that when the solemn tolling of its fog-bell comes to the ears of the anxious listeners on board, it is dead ahead. In another moment the Rock looms grimly out of the fog, not half a dozen lengths away, the great anchor plunges overboard and the ship becomes motionless amid a fleet of bobbing buoys that mark the location of the keeper's lobster pots and trawls.

Here, as at Matinicus, the freight-boat, borne in on the swell of a long roller, is run high up on the boat-house ways before the task of unloading can be undertaken. Her arrival is greeted with vociferous barkings of a fine dog, who even plunges into the water to welcome the new-comers and afterward frisks about them in a state of the wildest excitement. For years this dog has kept the station supplied with drift firewood dragged out on the rocks from the surrounding waters. One pleasant summer afternoon the keeper's only child, a little five-year-old boy, played outside the house while his mother was busy within. Unnoticed he wandered away. Half an hour later the mother's attention was attracted by the dog, which bounded into the house barking, whining, and trying in every way to tell her of what he had just done. He was wet, and the woman, thinking he had only captured another bit of driftwood, ordered him out to dry in the sun. He went, but in another minute returned and laid her child's hat, draggled and water-soaked, at the mother's feet. Taking instant alarm, she ran from the house and followed the excited animal, until he led her to the place where her little one lay, cold, wet, and unconscious. He had evidently fallen into the sea and the dog had plunged in after him. The child's clothing was torn to shreds by the dog's teeth and the sharp rocks over which he had been dragged, and the tender body was bruised from head to foot. Otherwise he was uninjured, and he soon recovered from the effects of the accident that had so nearly turned the lonely light station into a place of mourning.

On Mount Desert Rock there is no soil, save such as has been brought, with great labor, in barrels from the mainland. With this a tiny flower-garden has been made in a sheltered corner. In it, and in a number of boxes, a few hardy plants bloom brightly, and afford a new source of joy with each opening bud. In the windows, too, as is the case at nearly all the light stations on the coast, a few pots of flowers receive assiduous care. The tiny garden is carefully fenced in to protect it from the flock of fowls that constitute the sole live stock of this rocky farm. Having no soil in which to scratch, these poor birds have struggled with the unyielding rocks until their scratching apparatus is entirely worn away, and there is every prospect that the situation will sooner or later evolve a breed of toeless chickens. A number of tame gulls, and a stately heron, live peacefully with the barnyard fowls, and in the house many cages are filled with song sparrows, robins, and other land birds that have been picked up exhausted or with broken wings on the rocks, after nights of storm and intense darkness. Besides these, dead birds of all descriptions, including hundreds of ducks and geese during the migratory seasons, have been found at the foot of the tower, against the glowing lantern of which they have dashed themselves during bewildered night flights. Some of the best specimens of these have been skilfully mounted, and now adorn the keeper's parlor; for even in a lighthouse far out at sea, and remote from a possibility of formal visits, the New England parlor or "best room" is a sacred and carefully guarded institution.

At Mount Desert Rock the Armeria's crew is always allowed an hour for fishing, with the result that a score of lines over the sides, baited with herring, serve to fill any number of tubs with cod, hake, haddock, pollock, and cusk; while dogfish and sculpins cumber the deck in every direction. At the end of the fishing hour, the anchor is again lifted, and with a parting salute to the fog-bound rock, the supply-ship starts on a sixty-mile run through the impenetrable mist banks for Moose Peak light, on Mistake Island, which marks the western entrance to the Bay of Fundy.

In these fog runs the captain and first mate strain their eyes and ears from opposite ends of the bridge; the second mate is stationed in the foremast crosstrees; the third and one of the crew peer anxiously ahead and listen for breakers, whistles, or bells from the point of the bows; and the quartermaster at the wheel steers the designated course to a nicety. The silence is only broken by the hissing swash of parted seas from the ship's sides, the deep tones of the steamwhistle blown at two minute intervals, occasional answering notes from some-

where, far away, and the sharp stroke of the ship's bell announcing, with startling distinctness, the passage of hours and half-hours. On top of the pilot-house, ready to the captain's hand, lies his own book of sailing directions, compiled during former cruises of the Armeria or Fern, containing all the courses, and the time occupied in running from light to light, and from buoy to buoy, at both full and half speed, along the entire Atlantic coast. By a glance at this he knows just how long he ought to run before picking up the whistling buoy off Moose Peak. He also knows the exact course to be steered, and by frequent glances at the bridge compass he detects the slightest carelessness of the quartermaster at the wheel. Thus when he calls out to the various persons on watch to keep a sharp ear open for the whistling buoy, they know for a certainty that it must be close at hand. Yes! there it is! One of the forward lookouts has detected a faint moaning sound coming from the sea almost dead ahead, and reports it. "How does it bear?" demands the captain. "A point on the port bow, sir," answers the man, at the same time pointing in the direction thus indicated. All at once the abrupt moanings of the restless buoy are heard by all hands, then the swaying beacon itself emerges from the fog and glides by, not a biscuit toss away. Instantly the course is changed, and in a few minutes the clanging of a hand-bell, rung from Moose Peak light, comes clearly through the heavy atmosphere. Directly afterward the ghostly form of a white tower, and a wall of black rocks fringed with dashing spray, loom into view so close at hand that one catches his breath at the sight; then, as the ship rounds an abrupt point and glides in to a safe anchorage behind it, the fog seems suddenly to tire of its efforts at bewilderment and destruction. It draws back and hangs in sullen folds just outside, leaving the Armeria and her immediate surroundings in pleasant sunlight.

Moose Peak is a second-order light, and as such demands one hundred and forty cases, or seven hundred gallons, of oil. As the rocks here are very slippery and very steep, the task of transporting the supplies from the wave-tossed freight-boat at their base to their summit, and thence to the distant oil-house, is so great that it occupies two full hours. Several of the crew slip on the kelp-covered rocks and roll, with their burdens, into gullies or salt-water pools. In these mishaps a case or two of oil is broken and the contents spilled; but beyónd a few bruises and cuts, which no one seems to mind, the men are uninjured, and the ship finally receives all hands safely on board again. Once more she plunges into the fog, this time for a twenty-five mile run to the light station of Little River. Now there is another whistling buoy to be listened for and picked up, but when it is found the heavy, machine-rung bell of the Little River station is plainly heard at the same time. Slowly, but surely and safely, the white ship makes her way through a narrow, rock-bound entrance into an exquisitely beautiful harbor. Here, as at Moose Peak, the fog rolls sullenly back after the haven is reached, and leaves the anchorage bathed in the crimson and gold of an undimmed sunset. It is dark by the time the supplying of the station is finished, and so the Armeria remains in this pleasant place for the night in company with a fog-bound fleet of yachts and fishermen.

The following day is Sunday, when no work that can be avoided is done on board the supply-ship. Even the fog has retired from business, and the day is of that dazzling beauty known only to a northern sea-coast in summer-time. The officers of the ship appear in their newest uniforms, and the brown canvas working-suits of the crew are replaced by the natty blue shirts, trousers, and hats, and the black silk neckerchiefs of men-of-war's men. Although the business of supplying light stations is interrupted by the day, the sunlight on that wild coast is too precious to be wasted. So about noon the white ship steams out of the harbor and, still headed eastward, passes West Quoddy Head, on which is located the most easterly coast light station of the United States, skirts the outer shores of the Canadian island

of Campobello, and rounds East Quoddy, where, from the light station, she is saluted by a dipping British ensign, into Passamaquoddy Bay.

Stretching far into the bay from either shore are scores of fish-weirs from which millions of small herring are taken during the summer season for the supply of Eastport sardine (?) factories. Leaving Eastport on the left the ship sturdily breasts the outrushing flood of an ebb-tide that will fall twenty feet before turning, and enters the mouth of the St. Croix River. This broad waterway forms the boundary-line between Maine and New Brunswick, and on it, just below Calais, nearly ten miles up, is the stake light that marks the most easterly station of the United States Lighthouse Department. The light is only a lantern hung to a tree; but it must be supplied with oil as regularly as the Dochet Island lighthouse, five miles below, which is the most easterly of the lighthouse establishments.

The next six days are like the boy's diary, in which every entry for a week was "Same as yesterday;" for when the great Fundy fog mill gets well to work it continues to grind out fog until the supply of raw material is exhausted. In spite of the fog, guided by the roar of breakers on unseen rocks and dripping ledges, the ship slowly retraces her way, as though by instinct, along the perilous coast.

Fogs of this character, trying as they are to visitors, are little minded by the light-keepers of that enshrouded region. One of them, in fact, reported, with evident pride, that his steam fog-horn had been in uninterrupted operation for twenty-seven days, and declared that he dreaded the silence which would come with clear weather. The fog is as nothing when compared with the wild storms of winter, that cut off their communications with the mainland. Then, indeed, the dreary monotony of the light-keeper's life on one of the outlying Maine islands becomes well-nigh unbearable. For weeks at a time he is confined to his isolated rock, or tiny islet, as absolutely as a prisoner to his cell. He receives no tidings from the world, no letters nor papers, and he reads his few books over and over until he knows them by heart. He cannot go fishing, for, even if the weather would permit, the fish have sought deeper and warmer waters. His children are away at school on the mainland, and, of the many visitors, whose coming and going through the summer has created a constant ripple of excitement, not one is left. Even the light-house tender does not visit him more than once or twice during the winter. So, compared with such a condition of affairs, a mere fog, which does not interrupt the fishing, nor keep visitors away, nor even delay the mail-boat to any great extent, is a very minor evil.

As the ship creeps down the coast the saturated solution of humidity may be precipitated in a downpour of rain that partially clears the heavy atmosphere, and enables her to proceed at full speed through a bewildering maze of ledges, sheep-covered islands, and jagged rocks resonant with the shrill screams of countless sea-fowl, to Moose-a-Bec Reach, on which is located the straggling, fish-scented town of Jonesport, and a lighthouse.

After leaving Moose-a-Bec, another seaward plunge into the invisible is taken for a run out to 'Tit (Petit) Manan. But for its powerful steam fog-signal, 'Tit Manan would be hard to find; for when the Armeria anchors within a biscuit toss of its snarling rocks, its tower still is hidden from the deck.

There is no safe anchorage for any length of time near 'Tit Manan, and a haven for the night must be found. Prospect Harbor, only ten miles away, is the nearest, but the way to it is so narrow and so beset with deadly ledges, that to attempt the run seems little short of suicidal. Nevertheless, by proceeding with infinite caution, and bringing into play every detail of his absolute knowledge of the coast, Captain Wright successfully accomplished the feat, and after two hours of the most anxious and delicate work, anchored his ship in the exact centre of the Prospect Harbor inner basin. This bit of seamanship draws forth the hearty plaudits of a group of weather-beaten Yankee coasting skippers, whose schooners are fog-bound in the harbor. One of them declares there wasn't "airy

nuther cap'n would have dared tackle the job, or could have put it through ef he had," and this is the unanimous verdict of the assemblage.

Prospect Harbor light station is supplied without being seen from the ship, which lies but two hundred yards away, and with this the week's labor ends. Only nine lights supplied in eight days beats the record for slow work since the business was undertaken by a steamer.

But there is a limit even to Fundy fogs, and one morning the sun rises in the teeth of a snapping northwest breeze such as no fog can withstand for a minute. Two hours later, under the bluest of skies and ploughing the most sparkling of waters, the white Armeria, having already visited the lights at Winter Harbor and Egg Rock, was saluting the white warships anchored off Bar Harbor and steaming toward the head of Frenchman's Bay, to supply Crabtree Ledge light on Hancock Point, the station that all Mount Deserters know so well.

That same night finds her on the other side of the island, anchored in Southwest Harbor, with the stations on Baker's and Great Duck Islands supplied and left behind. From this point, as the swift steamer speeds from light to light, she seems to feel the exhilarating influence of glorious weather as keenly as do any of her crew. Bear Island is supplied at daylight, and Bass Harbor Head, the last of the Mount Desert lights, by sunrise. Then comes the station of Blue Hill Bay, and a run amid the exquisite scenery of Eggemoggin Reach, past great coasting schooners loading with ice or granite, dashing yachts, and flying fishermen, past tiny islets, each with its crown of evergreens, and bald headlands, past Sedgwick on the mainland, and Isleboro on Deer Island. At the western end of the Reach she lies off and on for an hour before Pumpkin Island light station, and its cluster of pretty cottages owned by Keeper Babson, which forms a summer rendezvous for one of the brightest and jolliest circles of emancipated school-teachers to be found on the New England coast. The next stop is at Eagle Island, where the lighthouse, perched on a lofty height, commands the most superb view of any in the district. From it the course is again inshore to Dice's Head, at the entrance to Castine Harbor, and thence still farther up Penobscot Bay to the mouth of the river, where the Fort Point light stands in front of a great summer hotel, the guests from which always flock to the beach to witness the unlading of the freight-boat. Down the island-dotted bay again goes the busy steamer, to where the white tower on Grindel's Point, sharply outlined against the dark green of a spruce forest and looking like a toy structure, shines in the full glory of sunset. From here a quick run through the long shadows of the Camden Mountains takes her to Negro Island, where the laden freight-boat is dropped ; and then, slowing down as though weary with her day's work, the Armeria swings into the beautiful harbor of Camden and anchors for the night. The light station on Negro Island is the ninth supplied since daybreak, and thus the record for this one day is the same as for the whole of the preceding week.

So the white ship moves on from light to light, her coming always anticipated with pleasure, and her arrival always warmly welcomed, until the circuit of her Eastern trip is complete, and she is again moored off the Staten Island station, making ready for her long winter cruise to the southward.

While on the Maine coast she leaves at the Seguin station 2,200 gallons of oil for use in its light, which is of the first order, and the first of its class to be encountered on the Atlantic coast. At Thatcher's Island, off the point of Cape Ann, in Massachusetts, she leaves double that quantity of oil ; for here are shown two lights of the first order. Fortunately, first-order lights are not nearly so numerous as is popularly supposed, for if they were, several Armerias would be kept busy supplying their needs. From Maine to Texas they number but forty, all told, and are the lights of Seguin, Cape Elizabeth, Thatcher's Island, Cape Cod (Highland light), Gay Head, Block Island, Montauk, Shinnecock, Fire Island, Nave-

sink, Barnegat, Absecom, Cape May, Cape Henlopen, Assateague, Capes Charles and Henry, Currituck Beach, Body's Island, Hatteras, Cape Lookout, Cape Romaine, Charleston, and Tybee ; the eleven East Florida coast lights, extending from St. Augustine (Anastasia Island) to the Tortugas (Loggerhead Key), Pensacola, and two at the mouths of the Mississippi. For their annual supply and that of their keepers' dwellings, these forty powerful lamps demand very nearly one hundred thousand gallons of oil.

Of all the light stations visited by the Armeria, that at Jupiter Inlet, well down on the eastern coast of Florida, is the hardest to supply, for here the work must be done on an open beach, where a heavy surf is always encountered. In it the freight-boat is frequently overturned, and its contents are scattered far and wide. If the inlet is closed, which often happens, the supplies must be landed on the beach, carried across a high and wide ridge of loose sand, then shipped into other boats to be taken across the inner lagoon, and finally carried to the top of the high bluff on which the lighthouse stands. Here, too, must be delivered all supplies for the twenty-six post lights on the Indian River.

Another difficult station to supply is that of the Highland Light, on Cape Cod, which is perched on the edge of a sheer cliff, one hundred and forty-two feet above water-level. It being thus inaccessible from the sea, its supplies are landed on the bay, or inner side of the Cape, and carried across the intervening country in carts. The price paid for this work is five cents a case, or fifty cents per load, and so eager are the natives to obtain the job, that the moment the Armeria heaves in sight the two-wheeled Cape carts are to be seen racing toward her landing-place from every direction, and as the deeply laden freight-boat nears the beach, the rival competitors for her cargo drive into the water until their ponies are almost at swimming depth, and urge their claims to be employed with excited gesticulations and a confusion of cries rich in Yankee dialect.

Thus the great work of lighthouse

supply goes on from year's end to year's end. Its details are varied according to circumstances, but never shirked, and with the succession of the seasons the white Armeria voyages from the lights of Maine to those of Texas, and from the lights of Texas back to those of Maine, with the changeless regularity of the migratory birds that follow in her wake.

6
The City of Providence

THE

NEW ENGLAND MAGAZINE

AND

BAY STATE MONTHLY.

Vol. V. No. 6.   APRIL–MAY, 1887.   Whole No. 30.

NEW ENGLAND CITIES AND TOWNS.

— THE CITY OF PROVIDENCE.

BY FREDERIC N. LUTHER.

THE singularity with which the name of Providence stands out in the list of American municipalities is, in no mere fanciful sense, borne out by what may be called the individuality of its history. Founded under most exceptional circumstances, and by a man whose strongly marked personality was at once his highest worth and his greatest defect, it has retained, throughout the two hundred and fifty years of its development as village, town, and city, much of that unique character which was impressed upon it at the beginning.

THE BETSEY WILLIAMS HOUSE.

Its history, therefore, beyond that of many American cities, is worth examination. It has not been, like Boston, New York, or Philadelphia, the scene of important events in the nation's annals; its early years were not, like those of Baltimore or New Orleans, brightened with the warm colors of romance; nor has it been, like Chicago, Minneapolis, or San Francisco, marked by the rapidity of its growth, the bustling energy of its people; but the story of its life is at times picturesque, frequently instructive, and always unique.

The men who have shaped its development have been almost without exception marked by striking peculiarities of thought and motive; the strength of their mental fibre has been inwrought into the constitution of Providence life; and throughout each period of its evolution the intellectual has dominated the physical. It would almost seem, indeed, that in a greater degree than elsewhere, mind, thought, and invention have shaped material progress. Although,

THE ABBOTT HOUSE.

too, the people of Providence, from Roger Williams down, have shown a curious disposition to think, so to say, in tangents, nevertheless the catholicity, as well as the vigor, of its mental life is among its most striking characteristics. Its growth from a cluster of rude houses to a city second in size to but one in New England, and surpassed in wealth by none in the United States of equal population, has not been merely a material growth. Its outward physical development has been but the shell of an expanding idea.

So it happens that, for these and other reasons which may not be here referred to, the history of Providence has an individuality of its own. In aims, methods, and scope of effort it finds a parallel in no other city.

This would the more clearly appear were it the object of the present paper to trace the subtle causes and underlying forces which have made Providence what it is, or had choice been made of that method which concerns itself less with the sequence of outward events than with what the French historians call the *vie intime*. That, however, falls without the scope of the present purpose. At this time it is only proposed to give in as compact and readable a form as possible the salient points in the city's history. The ground has already been gone over again and again, but it is still difficult for the busy reader to get in a reasonable time an ade-

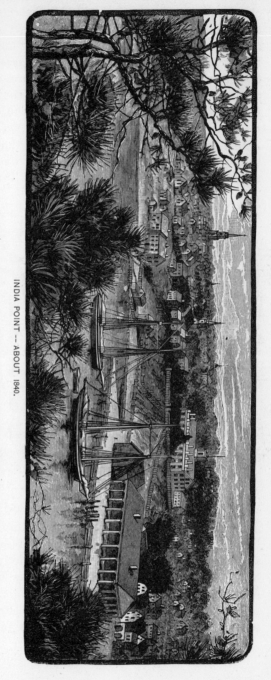

INDIA POINT — ABOUT 1840.

quate conception of the totality of that history or of the regular
sequence of its successive periods.   To get at the bare facts and,
to the ordinary mind, the most important incidents, one must
burrow through a great mass of more or less uninteresting details,
or wander for days in the maze of the purely personal speculations
of over-curious antiquaries.   It will be the present object, therefore, to give in the briefest time what the hurried but inquiring
reader most needs, to present in a not wholly disconnected way
events selected either for their inherent importance or their picturesque qualities, and to give them, too, not without regard for
the historical perspective.

BROWN UNIVERSITY HALL. BUILT IN 1770.

At the very outset of Providence history mooted questions are
encountered which offer the temptation for much digression.   The
life and character of Roger Williams, for example, have been the
subjects of a heated discussion which is not yet closed.   Questions
have been raised as to his birth, parentage, education, and early
life before coming to America ; and though it is claimed that the
recent researches of a local antiquarian have done much to settle
them, they can hardly be regarded as yet answered with complete
satisfaction.   Nor, indeed, are these questions as to mere dates and
minor facts of much importance save as affording subjects for the

annalists to enjoy themselves in disputing about. It is enough to know that Roger Williams was a Welshman by birth, a Cambridge man by education, a clergyman of the Church of England by ordi-nation, and subsequently a dissen-ter from that body by choice; that he arrived in Boston in 1631, and settled in Salem as pastor of the church there; and that finally, in 1636, he was forced to flee from the jurisdiction of the Colony of Massachusetts Bay, in order to avoid the execution of a threat on the part of the authori-ties to transport him back to Eng-land.

BOARD OF TRADE BUILDING.

Here, again, arises a much con-tested question as to the exact causes of the difficulty between Williams and the Puritan hierarchy. In the words of the for-mal sentence pronounced against him, he was said to have "broached and dyvulged dyvers new and dangerous opinions against the au-thoritie of mag-istrates." But exactly what these opinions were one cannot be altogether sure. Rhode Isl-and historians have naturally been inclined to insist that he was banished, because he had

OLD TOWN HOUSE.

definitely asserted that broad doctrine of the entire separation of church and state which subsequently became identified with his name. It must be said, however, in all candidness, that such was not probably the fact. It is undoubtedly true that the first faint

PROVIDENCE IN 1808.

conception of the great principle of religious liberty was already taking shape in his mind, but that its affirmation was the sole or the chief cause of his banishment could be readily disproved by the testimony of his own writings. The truth of the matter seems to be that Roger Williams was a rash, impolitic young man, over-fond of opposition and dispute, and tortured by a hundred vague new thoughts, hardly one of which had yet crystallized into a firmly held principle. He threw himself, with his eyes wide open, against one of the most compact and despotic

HOUSE BUILT BY JOSEPH, SON OF ROGER WILLIAMS, ABOUT 1680.
[Formerly standing opposite Roger Williams Park. Demolished May, 1886.]

forms of social order that the world has ever seen, and he should have counted himself fortunate that he escaped with so mild a sentence as banishment, when others, less obnoxious to the Puritan theocracy than he, were scourged and hanged.

Fleeing from Salem in January, 1636, after a toilsome and hazardous winter journey through an unfamiliar, if not a trackless country, he began late in the month of April a settlement on the east bank of the Seekonk River within the limits of the present town of East Providence. His land was obtained by a grant from Massasoit, sachem of the Wampanoags; and he was soon joined in his new home by his wife and family, and also by Thomas Angell, John Smith, Francis Wickes, William Harris, and Joshua Verin, and possibly by others. Scarcely, however, were their crops in, than a friendly intimation came from the Plymouth authorities that the new settlement was within the limits of their jurisdiction, and it was recommended that it be removed across the river. Roger Williams cheerfully obeyed. Once more he set out in search of a home. There is an accepted tradition that when the canoe in which he and his five companions had embarked first touched the opposite bank, and came within the limits of what is now the city of Providence, a group of Indians greeted them with the friendly salutation, "What Cheer, Netop," and that the voyagers disembarked for a moment on the broad Slate Rock which is still pointed out by the people of Providence as the landing place of Roger Williams. It was not there, however, that the little voyage was to end. Rounding the two points to the southward which now bear the name of India and Fox, they turned again to the north, and ascended the next arm of Narragansett Bay, the stream that has since taken the name of the city that grew up on its banks, but which in earlier days

THE FIREMAN'S STATUE.
[North Burial Ground.]

was known as the Great Salt River. A short distance up the stream, near the point where the Moshassuck and Woonasquatucket rivers united in the broad cove whose much contracted self still forms a feature of Providence topography, they found a spring of water, and there they made their final landing. The exact spot was a little to the south and west of the site on North

Main Street where, in its somewhat English appearance, the venerable St. John's Episcopal Church now stands.

Here the building of the new colony was begun, and, to quote from Professor Diman's eloquent and scholarly eulogy on Roger Williams, "in grateful recognition of the guiding hand which he never doubted had led him all his way, he named the place Provi-

RHODE ISLAND HISTORICAL SOCIETY'S CABINET.

dence. The dreamy, mystical, unworldly temper of Roger Williams is nowhere made more evident than in this unique designation which he selected for his infant settlement." The exact date of the foundation is a matter of doubt and dispute, but it is known to have been in the last days of June, and probably about the twenty-third or twenty-fourth of the month.

It was one of Williams's firmly held principles, which, too, sharply distinguished him from his neighbors of Plymouth and the Bay,

that he recognized the full rights of the Indians to the land they
occupied.   The territory, therefore, within which the new settlement was begun, had been previously obtained by a verbal grant
from Canonicus and Miantonomi, sachem and co-sachem of the
Narragansetts.   Subsequently this grant was confirmed by a
formal deed which, in a somewhat mutilated state, is still preserved
among the treasured archives of Providence.   The land so obtained
was apportioned among the original proprietors, and soon the first

houses began to
be erected along
a road called "the
towne   street
which was laid
out parallel to the
river bank in the
general course in
which North and
South   Main
streets now run."
But by far the
most important
and   interesting
fact   connected
with the first set-
tlement is the
unique govern-
mental principle
on which the
town based itself.
The written in-
strument which
was drawn up as

ROGER WILLIAMS MONUMENT.

[Roger Williams Park.]

the basis of public order pledged its signers, the inhabitants
of Providence, to an active and passive obedience to all orders
made by the majority for the public good, but with the express provision that this obedience should be "only in civil things."
Here, then, for the first time in history, a form of government was
established which made a clear distinction between the temporal
and the spiritual power.   It was not, be it observed, the establishment of mere religious toleration.   That doctrine was far from

THE FRIEND'S SCHOOL.   FOUNDED 1784.

RHODE ISLAND HOSPITAL.

novel, even in the middle of the seventeenth century. It had been taught in England by Sir Thomas More; and in France, in the heat of a period of intense religious fanaticism, it had been urged with almost tearful emphasis by the great Chancellor de l'Hopital; and already in the Maryland charter it had been made an actual practice. But in that colony religious freedom was expressly intended to apply only to those who professed Christianity; those who blasphemed God or denied the Trinity were made punishable with death. The religious freedom which Roger Williams set up was not mere toleration, but true religious liberty. He believed, to quote his own words, that "true civility and Christianity may both flourish in a state or kingdom, notwithstanding the permission of divers and contrary consciences, either of Jews or of Gentiles." Here, in its first completeness, is the great doctrine of liberty of conscience first affirmed. The town of Providence, founded on this theory, stood, therefore, from the very outset, unique among all the nations of

PROVIDENCE ATHENÆUM.

the earth; and the covenant on which it was based well deserves, as the eulogist of the founder has said, a place beside the compact signed by the Pilgrims in the cabin of the *Mayflower*.

The first eight years in the history of the town contains but few things necessary to be considered. The rise of difficulties in the Massachusetts Bay Colony between the Puritan heirarchy on the

OLD ARSENAL.

one hand and the Antinomians and Baptists on the other, led to still further banishments or withdrawals, and many of the exiles sought in Providence or its vicinity an asylum for relief from persecution, thus rapidly swelling the population. The little town soon became quite distinctively a Baptist community, and in 1639, or possibly just before the close of the preceding year, the first Baptist

EXCHANGE PLACE AND UNION DEPOT.

church in America was formed, which was also the second of its
order in the world, and the first of any kind in the colony.   At the

same time, or thereabout, Roger Williams himself received the rite of baptism, by immersion, at the hands of Ezekiel Holyman, and, in turn, administered it to Holyman and ten others. Williams then became for a few months the leader and pastor of the new church, but after a very brief pastorate his ineradicable individuality again asserted itself, and, with two or three others, he seceded and "set up a way of seeking" which he probably followed with much pleasure, if not much profit, for the rest of his life. The church organization which came into being under such peculiar circumstances has survived through all the phases of the history of Providence, and is now justly revered as the First Baptist Church, alike in name and in fact.

In 1640, when the population had become more numerous and varied, it was found that the pure democratic government which had first been established was no longer practicable, and a system of representative government was therefore set up by intrusting the interests of the town to five "disposers," from whom, however, there was a right of appeal to the town meeting. In the same year much trouble, even resulting eventually in riot, began to be experienced with Samuel Gorton, that interesting and much misrepresented figure in early New England history. The chief point of his contention was that Providence was deficient in not having a royal charter as the authority of its existence, and in advocating this idea he made himself obnoxious to the townsmen, and even dangerous to social order. When to this difficulty were added the facts that both Massachusetts and Plymouth were claiming jurisdiction over Providence and its vicinity, and that the Dutch of Manhattan were threatening the colony with war, it became evident that there was a real need for an English charter which all could be made to respect.

Accordingly, in 1643, Williams was sent to England to obtain the formal and chartered patronage of the ruling king. He found, however, on arrival, that in the exigencies of the political situation the management of the colonies was in the hands of a Parliamentary committee, and from it he obtained a charter of unusual liberality, which granted to the people of Providence, Portsmouth, and Newport the full power and authority of self-government. This document was received with great acclamations by the colonists in the fall of 1644. Not, however, till nearly three years later was the government organized under it, and two years after that the freemen of Providence were incorporated into a town under the authority of the colony. From that time until 1660 this charter was the basis of the political organization. The years covered by this period, though not eventless, present nothing that calls for elaboration at this time. There were dangers from Indian wars which Roger Williams happily averted by his pacific influence; there were conflicts of authority with Coddington of Newport; but in general it was a period of quiet growth and development.

When Charles II. ascended the throne in June, 1660, he was prompt to declare null and void all the acts of the Long Parliament. This, of course, left Providence once more without a charter. Again Massachusetts took advantage of the uncertainties of the time to lay claim to Providence territory, and Connecticut, too, asserted jurisdiction; and again, therefore, appeal was made to the English government for protection. Through the agent of the colony, Dr. John Clarke, a new charter was obtained in 1663 from King Charles, which, while re-affirming the old privileges, was much more definite in marking the bounds of the colony and in securing the right to freedom in all matters of religion. In short, it gave to Roger Williams full power and authority to carry on the "lively experiment" he purposed. It was one of the very best charters ever given to an American colony, and for this chiefly among other reasons it was retained as the organic law of Rhode Island long after allegiance to England had been thrown off, even until the middle of the present century.

Of the events which marked the forty years succeeding the arrival of the second charter, all others are dwarfed into insignificance when compared with the terrible catastrophe of King Philip's War. There were, it is true, some local dissensions, semi-political in nature and very violent in tone; and while as yet Providence owned no vessels, it was during this period that the first evidences of a coming commerce began to appear. But controversies and enterprises alike lapsed when Philip of Mount Hope, sachem of the Wampanoags, put into actual execution his determination "not to live till he had no country." The war was declared and opened upon Plymouth Colony, not upon Providence, which remained as yet safe in the friendship of the Narragansetts which Roger Williams had from the first cemented with kindness and good deeds. The Narragansetts, however, soon became allied with the Wampanoags, and though at first the neutrality of Providence was strictly respected, when the army of the United Colonies of New England marched through the town and lured some of its citizens away as volunteers, the Indians naturally lost the power of discriminating between neutrals and combatants and forgot the ancient ties of hospitality and peace. Realizing their danger as the combatants closed in about them, the women, children, and all but about three score of the men of Providence fled from the town. The Indians, then, coming up in the last days of March, 1676, burned the town almost completely. Probably not more than five houses were left standing, two of these being the garrisoned houses in which the men who remained in the town were quartered. These garrisons were not attacked, presumably in consequence of the friendship of the Indians toward Roger Williams who was known to be in one of them. The town records, after being partly burned, were saved by being thrown into the mill-pond, and ever after, in the apt words of Staples, the town's annalist, bore "plenary evidence of the twofold dangers they escaped, and the twofold injury they suffered."

The blow thus dealt to the little town was exceptionally severe, but its recuperative powers proved equal to the emergency. By August the work of rebuilding was well under way. Larger houses, more conveniently arranged, replaced the simple structures which had been burned, and from the date of this disaster, too, there was a tendency to enlarge the town toward the south and west instead of northward, as had previously been the custom. The work of reconstruction seems to have given a general impulse to enterprise. New streets were laid out; a regular ferry established over the Seekonk on the site of the present Red Bridge, to accommodate travel to Boston and Plymouth; and in 1679 the first wharf and warehouse were built.

In the political disturbances of this period, Providence shared the difficulties and disadvantages of the rest of New England. From the accession of James II. and the change of colonial policy consequent upon it, the charter was practically in suspension ; and Providence, even beyond most other towns chafed under the restraints of Joseph Dudley's provisional government, and Sir Edmund Andros's personal rule. It does not appear, however, that the town was made to suffer any exceptional hardship ; but the native independence of its people, and their warm love of local self-government could ill bear the overlordship of an alien. So soon, therefore, as the news came, in 1689, that James had been over-thrown and Andros imprisoned in Boston, the freemen were quick to resume the old charter government, and to ask and obtain from England a confirmation of its power and authority.

By the opening of the eighteenth century, as is shown by the town's proportion of taxation, it had entirely recovered from the impoverishment of the Indian War, and was beginning to enter upon that career of growth as a maritime and commercial centre, which was to be the next phase of its development. Prior to 1700, Providence had been entirely in the chrysalis state. Heated religious discussion, disputes over boundaries and jurisdiction, and experiments in governmental policy had mainly occupied the attention of its inhabitants. For the rest, they were largely engaged in agriculture. The town at that time stretched out broadly over the northern part of what is now Rhode Island, and very nearly coincided with the present limits of Providence County. In the farmhouses scattered over this territory was a population of about eight hundred, while in the limits of the present city were about seven hundred more. Of these latter, too, many carried on farms in the outlying districts.

This condition of affairs, however, was inevitably to be changed. The people could not always remain blind to the opportunities offered by an excellent harbor. The period, then, beginning with 1700, and ending with the opening of the Revolutionary epoch, was pre-eminently the era of commerce. Wharf after wharf was speedily built along the east shore of what is now the Providence River, and storehouses were erected upon them, abutting on the old town street, which, corresponding with the present South Main Street, was even then beginning to be a bustling thoroughfare. Pardon Tillinghast, who built the first wharf in the town, was perhaps the earliest of this new class of merchants, and Gideon Crawford is another name that ranks close after him. The vessels they employed were built at various points along the river and bay, and consisted of sloops and schooners not exceeding sixty tons burden. They were largely engaged in the West India trade, carrying out the ordinary colonial exports, as, for example, lumber, beef, pork, dairy products, Indian corn, etc., and bringing back sugar, molasses, ginger, indigo, and, above all, rum. There was also considerable business done in the slave trade. English goods, too, both woolen and linen, were imported not directly but through the English, French, or Spanish colonies.

Although the maritime phase of Providence history extended, in its later development, somewhat beyond the period now under consideration, it may be better for the sake of clearness to group together at this point the main facts in the rise and fall of its commerce, before taking up the part the town bore in the Revolutionary struggle. The summary must necessarily be brief. It may be said, then, that prior to the Revolution the commerce of Providence was unusually large as compared with other colonial towns. Its people, after 1700, were mostly sailors, shipbuilders, and merchants. The Revolution, of course, was a serious blow to maritime enterprise. Yet as long after its close as 1790 it was stated in the United States Congress that there were more ships belonging in Providence than in New York. Her vessels were known in almost every port in the world; and one of them, the *George Washington*, is said to have been the first to carry the national flag of the new American Union into the ports of China. Among the more prominent names identified with the building up and maintenance of Providence commerce were the houses of Brown & Ives, Samuel Butler & Sons, Edward Carrington, the Nightingales, and the Russells. Almost without exception these men laid the foundation of large fortunes in their maritime ventures; and, in fact, it may even be said that very much of the present wealth of Providence is the result of the judicious investment of capital which originally accrued from the West India trade. But from the first decade of the present century the commercial supremacy of Providence began to decline, although it was not till 1841 that the last Indiaman arrived and cleared at this port. The causes of the decline are not difficult to see. In the natural course of things the foreign commerce of the United States became concentrated at a few ports, like Boston and New York, because at these points there was developed a more direct and speedier railroad communication with the West. The trade of other ports which were not made the termini of the great trunk lines necessarily waned to nothing; and to-day there is not a single ship wholly owned in Providence.

But while foreign trade lasted it brought wealth, prosperity, and growth to the town. By the opening of the Revolutionary epoch the result was plainly apparent in the material changes which had

come over it. Since the beginning of the century the population
had increased more than fourfold. The town had grown to the
westward, the first bridge had been thrown across the river, on the
site where ever since, in the vernacular of Providence, "the bridge"
has stood, and on the west side of the river busy streets were
occupying the old marshes and pastures. A stage line to Boston
had been just established ; packet lines were running to Newport and
New York ; regular postal communication had been established ;
and schools and churches, the first theatre and the first public
library, marked the rising intelligence and taste of the townsmen.
In 1762 the first printing-office was opened, and was quickly followed by the first newspaper, the forerunner of about one hundred
and fifty different periodicals, which have from time to time appeared with a Providence imprint. In all the homes of the town,
at the outbreak of the Revolution, one could have found the
evidences of comfort and prosperity, and, in not a few, the signs
of wealth and luxury. All this material progress was the direct
outgrowth of half a century of commerce and trading.

Upon a community engaged in such pursuits the exactions of
England in the form of taxes and stringent maritime laws fell
with especial severity. It was but natural, therefore, that the
feeling of rebellion should early manifest itself in the town of
Providence, and maintain its strength throughout the long struggle.
Indeed, the first armed contest between the American and British
forces took place almost within the limits of Providence, and the
attacking party was composed of Providence men. In 1772 the
British government had stationed a vessel called the *Gaspee* in
Narragansett Bay in order to enforce the revenue laws. Not only
the purpose for which she was there, but the arrogant manner, too,
in which she performed it, made her especially obnoxious. It
happened that, in chasing a Providence schooner, the Gaspee
grounded a few miles below the city on the point which has since
borne the name of the vessel. The tide was falling, and it was
known that she could not get off until after midnight. Here was
the opportunity which Providence people were longing for. A crier
passed hastily through the streets, calling on all friends of liberty
to meet at Sabin's Tavern. After consultation, enough men were
found, ready for any expedition, to man eight long-boats. The
little fleet was commanded by Abraham Whipple, subsequently a
captain in the Continental navy. The grounded vessel was silently

approached in the darkness, surprised and boarded, her men captured and put on shore, and the hated schooner burned to the water's edge. The British commander, Lieutenant Duddington, was wounded in the attack. The boarding party then returned to the city, and though the British authorities offered a large reward for their apprehension, it was found impossible to get the name of a single participant until long after Providence had passed from British jurisdiction.

In other ways, too, the townsmen gave proof of their patriotism and independence before the war actually began, as, for example, when in March, 1775, they assembled in the market-place and made a bonfire of their tea, pledging themselves to use no more of it until the obnoxious tax should be removed. When it became evident that open hostilities were inevitable, the town ordered breastworks to be thrown up between Field's and Sassafras Points and a battery to be erected on Fox Hill. Arms were prepared, powder secured, and the militia placed in readiness for instant marching. On the second day, therefore, after the attack at Lexington, one thousand men had left Providence for Boston, and more were ready to follow. It is needless to follow the slow progress of the war in detail. The fortunes of the contest never brought the opposing armies very near to Providence; her fortifications of defence were never attacked. But through it all she kept up her preparations and furnished her full share of men and means. Her troops fought bravely and effectively on many a field, and when at last Yorktown fell, the first company to enter the captured city was a Providence company, commanded by Captain Stephen Olney.

But no sooner had the war closed than Providence found itself confronted with two new difficulties. In the first place, in common with the rest of Rhode Island, the town was afflicted with an unusually poor form of paper money, and it had depreciated to such an extent as seriously to interfere with business stability. The effort to get rid of this incubus and to restore the unflated values to their proper state gave rise to some very curious phenomena in economics and jurisprudence, and, especially as resulting in the famous case of Trevett *v.* Weeden, is of surpassing interest to economists and publicists. But there is nothing about it of popular interest. In the second place, much hostility of opinion arose between Providence and the country towns. The inhabitants of the latter, engaged still in agriculture, had retained and intensified their rock-ribbed conservatism, while the people of Providence, having been brought into contact with the quicker movements of commercial life, had become more enterprising and progressive. On these lines a country party and a town party sprung up in the State, and each held the other in great contempt. It was the existence of these two parties which prevented Rhode Island from sharing in the framing of the United States Constitution and made the State the last of the original thirteen to accept it as the law of the land. The town people were almost from the first in favor of ratifying the document, but the country people, from ignorance, prejudice, and jealousy, were opposed. The controversy was long and bitter, and once came near to bloodshed; but ultimately sound sense triumphed, and in 1790 Providence dragged the rest of Rhode Island into the American Union.

Meanwhile a marked change had begun to come over the business life of the town. As has been seen, Providence remained, in greater or less degree, a maritime centre, far down into the present century. But already in the early years of the new nation a tendency set in toward an era of manufacturing. The war had destroyed many of the town's finest vessels, and, for the moment at least, foreign trade was seriously impaired. In this crisis the people proved their native wisdom, sagacity, and versatility, by turning from the broad bay to the narrow, tumbling streams and utilizing these for industrial purposes. Ever since 1783 attempts had been made in Providence to spin cotton and wool by power. Little, however, of practical value was accomplished until Samuel Slater came into the vicinity, bringing from England a thorough practical knowledge of the Arkwright spinning machinery. At first the development of local manufacturing enterprises was slow, but the movement was immensely quickened by the War of 1812, which made still more clear the desirability of developing home industries. From that time up to the present day new forms of manufacturing have been every year added to the resources of the town and city, until now no municipality of its size has so varied a list of industries. Since the middle of the present century at least, Providence has ceased to be a commercial port, and become entirely a manufacturing community.

Of the events which marked the town's growth during the first third of this century, few are of any general interest. Physically, the most notable changes were made on the west side of the river. Westminster, Weybosset, and Broad streets were well built up even at the opening of this period, and soon the cross-streets began to multiply and teem with life, as gradually the centre of the town's business moved westward. A public school system was established in 1800, and by that time, also, Brown University had been long enough established in Providence to be of some indirect service to the people. In 1805 the streets were for the first time authoritatively named; in 1810 the public whipping-post was removed from the market-place; and in 1815 a terrific September gale raised the waters of the river twelve feet above the spring tide-mark, drove ships through buildings, carried away bridges, overturned churches and dwellings, and, in the aggregate, caused an immense amount of damage. But this disaster was not without its compensations. It opened the way for new and broader streets, and was made the occasion of erecting more substantial and elegant structures. In 1828 the Blackstone canal to Worcester was opened, and

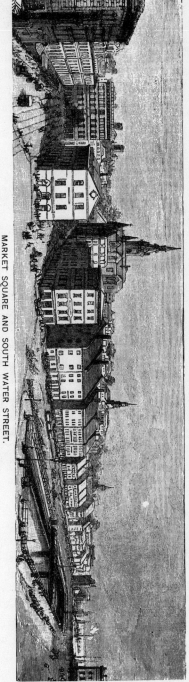

MARKET SQUARE AND SOUTH WATER STREET.

Showing Board of Trade and What Cheer Buildings, and the County Court-House.

thereafter maintained in unprofitable existence until ruined by the railroad; and in the same year one of the most unique land-marks of the present city was completed — the old Arcade, a curious granite structure with a central court lighted from above and flanked by three tiers of stores, the upper two being also furnished with galleries. It is a building somewhat suggestive of the foreign in its appearance, and never fails to strike the stranger's eye.

HIGH SCHOOL.

Meanwhile, in this period of quiet growth, the necessity for transforming the town into a city began to be apparent. The change was undoubtedly precipitated by a serious riot in 1831, which originated with some sailors spending a night ashore, but ultimately developed into such proportions as to last three days and necessitate calling out the militia. This incident was deemed sufficient proof of the weakness of the town government to administer the affairs of so large a community; and after due deliberation, the freemen voted to accept from the General Assembly a charter for the incorporation of the city of Providence. Accordingly, on the first Monday in June, 1832, the new city government was organized, with Samuel W. Bridgham as the first mayor.

The remaining history of the city may be passed over very briefly. In very few respects does it present events of unusual importance, and a mere chronology would be profitless and uninteresting. With the organization of the city government began also the era of railroad development. The Boston and Providence line was the first to be completed, and this was followed at not wide intervals by the others. With regard to the agitation for

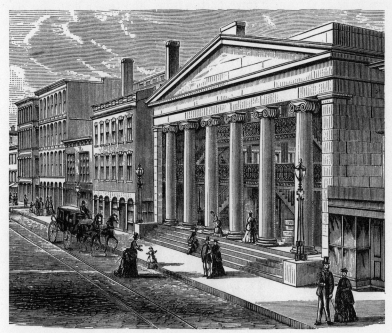

THE ARCADE.

an enlarged suffrage and a new constitution in place of the old charter which had served so long, and with regard, also, to that instructive and heroic little rebellion, the Dorr War, which resulted from that agitation, it can only be said that Providence was the scene of some of the chief events of that stirring time; for it is really a matter that pertains to the history of the State, not the city. It may be added, however, that, as is usually the case, time has proved that it was the rebels who were right in principle, if rash in action.

In the matter of growth, progress was steady, and still in the line of manufactures. To the cotton and woollen mills of the preceding period were added machine shops, foundries, and jewelry manufactories. Once or twice, as in 1856, financial crises temporarily checked the accumulation of wealth. But in general there was constant and steady progress in all classes of society.

On the share which Providence bore in the war to preserve the Union, it is unnecessary to enlarge. Her record was a noble one, but not essentially other than that of hundreds of northern cities. Her troops were quick to reach the front, and throughout the long

STATE HOUSE.

contest they were, as individuals and as regiments, conspicuous for gallantry and intelligent work on many critical fields. Although this four years' struggle could but diminish the productive capacity of the city, yet from 1860 to 1865 the population increased from 50,666 to 54,595, and the valuation from $58,000,000 to $80,000,000.

So soon as the war was over, there came an energetic renewal of industrial effort, and new enterprises were everywhere projected. As a result the period which has elapsed since 1865 has been a period of most rapid growth in wealth and population. The latter has considerably more than doubled, and the city's valuation shows a proportionately large increase. It has been, too, the era of modern improvements in municipal affairs. Better and larger schoolhouses have been built; public water, with an attendant sewerage system, introduced; a public park, given to the city by a lineal descendant

WEYBOSSET STREET,
Looking toward Westminster, with Custom House and Post Office Building on the right.

of Roger Williams, has been accepted and improved; a new City Hall and a modern high school building have been erected; and a public library founded. In area, too, the city has been growing. Several square miles have been taken back from the towns which were themselves carved out of the original territory of the town of Providence; and the six wards with which the city began in 1832 have gr wn to ten. Of the men who have shaped and guided this exceptional era of progress, many might be deservedly named. But the one who has been the most thoroughly identified with recent phases of Providence history — the late Thomas A. Doyle — is elsewhere in this magazine separately discussed.

CITY HALL.

As for the future of the city, nothing but a degenerate public spirit can make it less bright than the past. Well started in the race, with an infinity of industrial resources, with a geographical position that gives the combined advantages of a railroad centre and a maritime port, and with a long and honorable past to serve as a standard and as stimulus to continued activity, it only needs vigilance, ambition, and public spirit on the part of her individual citizens to keep her where she has so far always been, in wealth, intelligence, and sagacity among the foremost of American municipalities.

SOLDIERS' AND SAILORS' MONUMENT.

7
The Making
of Yale

The Making of Yale

By Edwin Oviatt

THE Bi-Centennial celebrated by Yale in October commemorated the culmination of an epoch in American university education quite as much as it did the close of the first two hundred years of Yale's history. After an evolution of two centuries, marked by earnest purpose, by brave advances and by an ever present conservatism of method, Yale finds herself in 1901 a factor in the national life of the utmost importance. That evolution has not been without its crises, nor has it been crowned with success without self sacrifice; but that it has come, and is of so great a promise for the future, is a cause for national thanksgiving. Dignified in its intellectual features, jubilant in its spectacular, the Bi-Centennial of October, 1901, was a most notable affair. One had only to shift his eyes from the plain brick pile of South Middle to the magnificent stone palace of Vanderbilt to be impressed with the marvelous development that the two centuries have brought, or only to gaze upon the splendid procession of American University leaders to understand the pow-

er of education in the country. It was not simply a Yale birthday, it was as well, the Jubilee of American higher culture.

While the making of Yale was the cause for that brilliant occasion, the spirit of modern America was no less conspicuous in its celebration. For Yale, perhaps, more than any other of our Universities, has shared in the broadening of the horizon of national culture and education, and has herself been more influenced by it. She has preserved less of Colonial self-esteem, and has been nearer to the people than her elder sister. In the early days she sent her sons into the pulpit and public life and later into the law, politics and education. The spread of the colleges westward has been due largely to the missionary spirit of the Yale training. But if Yale has been the "Mother of Colleges"—in the 19th century one hundred American college presidents were Yale graduates— the embodiment of the thought of the people, and the pioneer among universities in nationalism, she has perhaps, in her strenuous character building, lost something more subtle in the

131

From a photograph copyrighted 1897, by H. O. Andrews.

WHERE YALE COLLEGE WAS FOUNDED

character of her work. Yale has been less than Harvard a place for the finer culture, for the more delicate ideals of the literary life. Yet this very fact has made her what she is, hardworking, democratic, nearer to the everyday purposes of the people.

Democracy, high purpose and vigor of intellectual life have, from the beginning, been constant characteristics of Yale's upbuilding. Perhaps her poverty has had something to do with her democracy, the stern orthodoxy of the early days with her high purpose, and a rigid curriculum and hard discipline with her intellectual vigor. Yale's curriculum has been iron clad; her culture vigorous. If it has been less ideal, it has been more strenuous; if less fine, more rugged; if less cultured, more democratic. The sum-total of Yale's characteristics has been force. If thus far Yale has lost something more intangible than a working education, she has plenty of time in which to make it up.

The making of Yale has been in the main due to two things—her fine line of intellectual leaders, and her quick grasp of opportunities. The names of the men who have fashioned Yale are known and honored throughout the whole country. They are those of theologians, scholars, public servants and public benefactors. Her opportunities have been those which the development of the nation has laid at her feet—colonial staunchness, national republicanism, theological orthodoxy, national expansion, and the demand for educated leaders of the people. It has been her chief pride that the college and the university have responded to these opportunities and have each time given the best of what was asked.

If one were to choose the several influences that have been most constant in their presence in Yale's life he might speak of theology, with its attendant conservatism, scientific investigation, sympathy with the genius of the country, and expansion. But any exclusive selection of one of the

THREE VOLUMES PRESENTED AT THE FOUNDING OF YALE COLLEGE

main tendencies of the two hundred years that have gone to the making of the institution would be abitrary. Yet in the main I am of the opinion that it has been these several threads that have run through Yale's life to which she is most indebted. With each came its intellectual leaders, with each its opportunities. It may be possible to trace the rise of the university through these several currents of her development.

Puritan protest against the ascendancy of the English Church lies far back in the dim beginnings of the college at New Haven. When Rev. John Davenport and Theophilus Eaton brought their band of earnest Puritan worshippers to the new land at the mouth of the Quinnipiack River, it was one of the first ambitions of those

eminent men to found a college in the new colony of old England. All through the sixty years following the founding of New Haven in 1638 attempts were made to carry out the plans of Davenport and Eaton. Financial embarrassments hindered the undertaking. It was not until 1697 when Davenport had disappeared from the scene and Rev. James Pierpont had succeeded him, that definite steps were taken to establish a collegiate school in Connecticut.

The opportunity and the man arose together. In 1700 Harvard college was the only American school for higher education to which wealthy colonists could send their sons, and there was no place to which the poor man might go without great expense of travel and accommodation. So

ELIHU YALE

Proposalls for Erecting An UNIVERSITY,
in the Renowned Colony of Connecticut:

Humbly Offered by an Hearty (tho' unknown) Well-wisher to the Welfare of that Religious Colony.

I. Let there be called a SYNOD of all the Consociated Churches in this Colony.

The Synod, (or Council of Elders and Messengers from the Churches,) may as yett be Called by the Civil Government, upon the Motion of some Eminent Pastors.

Or, if that Way should fail, Why may not as many of the Pastors as can come together, modestly write a Circular Letter unto the Churches, intimateing their desire, of their Sending their Deleyates unto a Synod (att a proper Time and Place agreed on) upon this great Occesion of Settling an UNIVERSITY, for the propagation of Literature and Religion among them;

II. The SYNOD being Assembled, Let the Wark of that Venerable Assembly be, To resolve upon an UNIVERSITY, that shall be, The School of the Churches: and upon the LAWS, by which the said University shall be Governed.

Let these LAWS declare, What shall be the Qualifications of them that shall be admitted into the Society;

What shall be the Studies therein followed, & how Managed!

What shall be the Manners of ye Students, and how Re-warded, or Censured:

And upon what Accomplishments the Persons there Edu-cated, shall go forth, with Ample Testimonials, Recommending them to the Acceptance of the World:

III. Wee cannot presume to give Degrees, Pro: more Academiarum in Angliâ, — nor are the Degrees of Bachelour of Arts, and Master of Arts, in the Forms they are now Ordinarily given, much more than Empty Titles.

A Diploma, or, Testimonial, (Signed by the Presidont, & the Tutors of the University, and by Three of the Inspecors,) Aserting the Qualifications of him, that Recieves it, will be as Good as a Degree, in the Honourable Thoughts of Reysonable Men. And, it is hoped, A Society of Such Persons, thus founded and formed, may

with-out

135

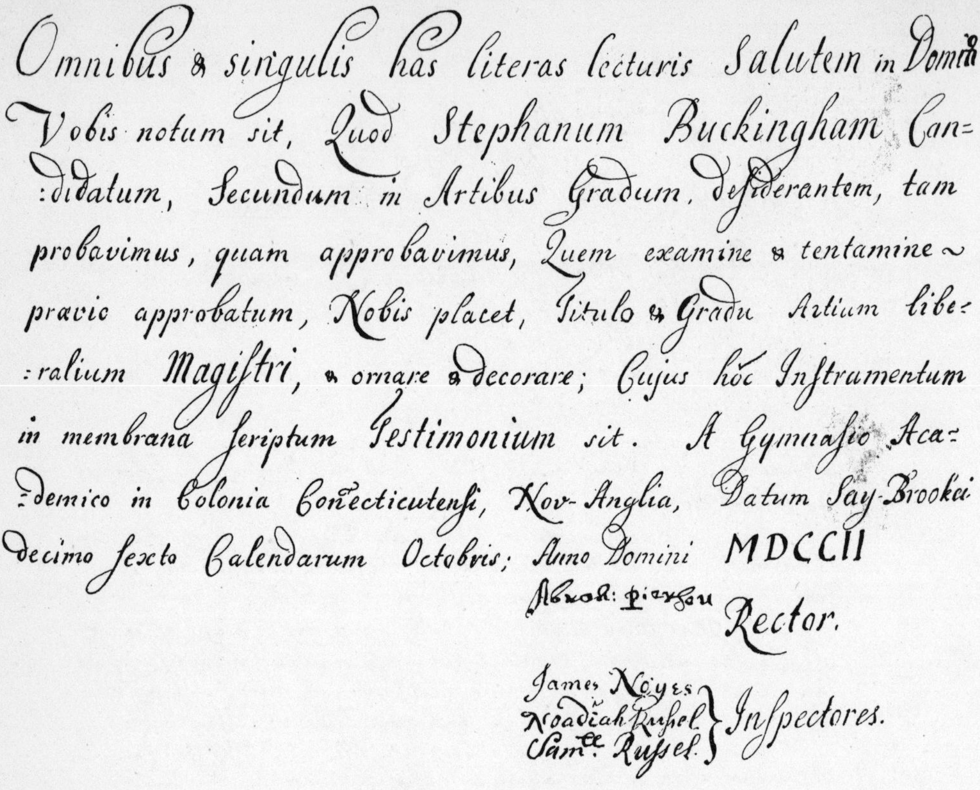

Omnibus & singulis has literas lecturis Salutem in Domⁿᵒ Vobis notum sit, Quod Stephanum Buckingham Can=:didatum, Secundum in Artibus Gradum, desiderantem, tam probavimus, quam approbavimus, Quem examine & tentamine pravio approbatum, Nobis placet, Titulo & Gradu Artium libe:ralium Magistri, & ornare & decorare; Cujus hóc Instrumentum in membrana scriptum Testimonium sit. A Gymnasio Aca=:demico in Colonia Conecticutensi, Nov-Anglia, Datum Say-Brookæ decimo sexto Calendarum Octobris; Anno Domini MDCCII

Abrah: Pierson

Rector.

James Noyes
Noadiah Russel } *Inspectores.*
Samᵉˡ Russel.

FACSIMILE OF AN EARLY DIPLOMA

that, when in 1697 James Pierpont again broached the scheme for a new college he found the economic conditions ready for him. Not only did the personal question of economy enter into the situation, but there was an urgent call from all sides for a collegiate school that would teach a sounder theology than the brilliant Harvard did, and where a young man might prepare for the ministry untrammeled by conflicts of dogma. Harvard's liberal tendencies had awakened distrust in many quarters and had especially roused the ire of Cotton Mather of Boston, who figured largely in the establishment of the new institution. The ferment and disturbances of Eastern Massachusetts towards the end of the 17th century were powerful stimulants to the new school enterprise. Connecticut shared but little in the intellectual storms centering about Massachusetts, and Boston especially, at that period. The conflict between the Orthodox and the Unitarian found little sustenance in Connecticut, where the difficulties were social and political rather than religious and intellectual. If Harvard was too far advanced for the majority of the country to follow, the Collegiate School of Connecticut offered a safe harborage for the distrustful. In 1700 Pierpont's endeavors took effect in the attempt of a Synod of Churches to establish a school. This failed, but the religious

PRESIDENT EZRA STILES

Jeremiah Dummer, Connecticut's agent at London, in its behalf. Dummer in turn placed the situation before a number of wealthy patrons of literature in London, with the result that Elihu Yale, sometime Governor of Madras, and a rich man, became interested. Governor Yale sent to the college in 1714 and again in 1718 a number of books and a consignment of East India merchandise from the proceeds of which the trustees were enabled to erect a college building. This building was completed in time for the Commencement in 1718 and so overjoyed were the trustees that they named it "Yale College," thus at once and forever associating the name of the chief benefactor up to that time with the institution. Governor Yale's interest was the more notable in that he could hardly have heard of the Connecticut college before Dummer's introduction of it to his notice, and because the goods that he sent to New Haven were originally

impetus given by it matured immediately afterwards in the gathering of ten orthodox ministers in Branford, in response to Pierpont's "Proposals for a Collegiate School," and in the founding then and there of the new college. There was no doubt about the spirit of the enterprise when the charter was obtained in 1701, for it clearly stated the object of the undertaking: that "Youth may be instructed in the Arts and Sciences who through the blessings of Almighty God may be fitted for Publick Employment both in the Church and Civil State."

At first the new school, founded on orthodox principles, threatened to decline. But during the Saybrook period there had been three influences at work to infuse new life into the struggling institution. Cotton Mather, whom we have seen to be a friend to Harvard's new rival, watched the college closely, and in 1714 secured the services of

PRESIDENT JEREMIAH DAY

138

Apr 28. F. Dispute. I opened the federal Court with Prayer Judges Iredell & Law present
29. Read Judge Sullivans Hist. of Province of Main
30. Rec'd a Letter & Hist. of Moravian Missions from the Director at Bethlem Pensylva. attended Professor Mays Lecture. Rec'd Lett. from Mr Woodward N York & he say it was shipwreckt on one of the Bahamas, lost every thing, over saved, in an open Boat only, & nine days in getting to Havanna in great Distress
May 1. q: Began the pub Exam of the Classes. Seniors this day. Rector Williams Portrait copied from Smibert, by Mr Moultrope, finished. Francis Murray & Eddy for N.Y. here
2. Proceeded with the Jun Class
3. Lds dy. No Chapel. I attended at Dr Edwds AM. I heard him & attended with my Wife at his Communion — present about 50 Communicants. P.M. at Dr Danas — Contribution for Missionaries. Read Paget Ansr. to Stinfn. 1618
4. Proceeded in Exam. Rec'd Lett. fr Camb. Children no better
5. Finished Exam & announced Adjudication.
6. Vacation begins. Deans Examd. Marsh Elected.
Last Week I was visited by Capt George Smith, born in Scotland & from Æt. 10 follows the Seas — now Ships Æt 40. — He sailed from Boston in N Engld, & was 1785 taken by the Algerines, & confined in Captivity at Algiers, 9 years. Then redeemed — went to Egypt, & Joppa, & fr. Joppa travelled inland 18 M. into the holy Land to within 8 M. of Jerusm which he saw at a Dist. but did not visit it. Thence to Cyprus, Candia, Morea, all Italy & Germany.

REPRODUCTION OF ONE OF PRESIDENT STILES' MANUSCRIPTS

intended for an endowment of Oxford University. Elihu Yale will always be regarded as one of the greatest benefactors of Yale. His gift of £562 seems small enough in these days of million dollar endowments, but it was large then and assured Yale for the first time of financial support. He was followed later by Bishop Berkeley, who, though an Episcopalian, was generous enough to give largely to the struggling college.

It was Orthodoxy that inspired the founding of Yale. And Yale has been orthodox ever since. For a hundred years Yale educated ministers and public men almost exclusively. When the "New Light" furore swept the country in 1740 President Clap was drawn into the dispute, and triumphantly passed through the crisis, bringing the college solidly over to the popular side. President Stiles indeed abolished the stiff doctrinal tests that

PRESIDENT THEODORE T. WOOLSEY

But theology at Yale has also had a most beneficial influence in several important particulars. It may have trammeled the early days with a hard and fast educational system, but it produced a Jonathan Edwards and, later, a Horace Bushnell. These two men exemplify what was old and what is new in Yale's theology. In Edwards, Yale sent out a brilliant but old school thinker, who impressed his time mightily, but whose influence has long been waning; in Bushnell Yale graduated a theologian of the new school, who has exerted a tremendous influence for broad thinking and Christian living. Yale's theology may have had its weak places, but it has worked to wonderful advantage in giving of late years a splendid impetus to broad mindedness.

The main characteristic that has

his predecessor had formulated for the orthodoxy of the tutors, but clung to the Saybrook Platform, which, in a minor degree, insisted upon the adherence of the teachers of the college to the tenets of the Congregational Creed. The Saybrook Platform had a long and tried service, and it determined the theological atmosphere of the institution rigidly until as late a date as 1823, when President Day and the scientific movement caused its removal. Clergymen have from the first formed the mainstay of the corporation. Theological training has until very lately formed a part of the college curriculum. If Theology has been a central thread through all of Yale's development it has at times had a retarding influence. The curriculum was, until President Woolsey's reign, strongly dogmatic in character; until President Dwight's day it was rigid and unbending; it is only just emerging from comparative narrowness into what President Hadley intends that it shall be.

PRESIDENT TIMOTHY DWIGHT

grown out of Yale's theology has been its conservatism. Yale has ever been slow in stepping out into new fields. Not until President Dwight Hitchcock, the Divinity School its Nathaniel Taylor, but these schools grew up apart and it was not until 1899 that they were fully brought together.

Perhaps the most marked result of the old time theological atmosphere has been its repression of broad studies. The purely literary, and I mean by that all impetus to seek ideal-

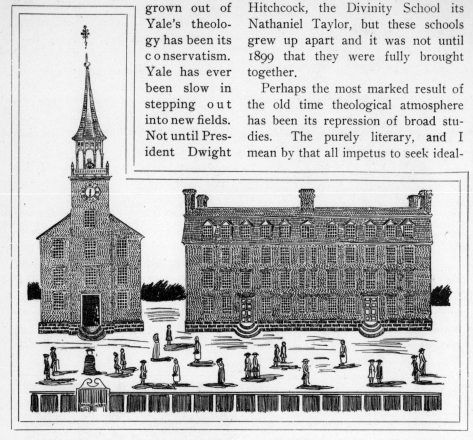

AN EARLY VIEW OF YALE COLLEGE

was inaugurated in 1795 did the college curriculum and the teaching force partake of the modernity that characterized other institutions. The strength of her traditions and the fact that she has had no extraneous literary center, such as Harvard had in Boston, upon which to draw, hindered the development of the university idea. The professional schools up to 1887 were loosely grouped together about the college, and the various departments had very little interest in each other. The Medical School had had its Nathan Smith, the Law School its Samuel ism, has suffered through the preëminence until lately given to a rigorous curriculum. Yale has striven to give a complete education; in early times for a special class and in later times for leaders in every branch of life. She has thus far been slow in imparting the finer subtleties. It was during President's Dwight's term that the only literary movement in her history took place at Yale. In the school of the "Hartford Wits," which a distinguished professor among "our friends the enemy" has stated to have been "the highest literary activity of the latter 18th century in America,"

THE ONLY BUILDING OF OLD BRICK ROW NOW STANDING

Yale has its only remarkable contribution to the literature of the country. There have been sporadic bursts of poetic fire at Yale since that day, and there has been constant undergraduate literary activity, but with the exception of such occasional poets as Percival, Edward Rowland Sill and Stedman, Yale has produced no marked literary men.

But more characteristic, and of much greater influence in the development of the institution was the scientific movement inaugurated by the first Timothy Dwight, again a proof of the commanding importance of that President in the making of Yale. When we speak of the first Timothy Dwight we name a man who above all others of his generation helped to make Yale. He was a broadminded,

rounded man; with a far eye for the future, and not afraid to bring innovations into the college faculty and curriculum. On his entrance upon the control of affairs Yale sprang at once from a Colonial school to a modern college. Up to 1800 the chief end and aim of the college had been to train young men for the ministry and the state. The curriculum had been very narrow, with plenty of theology and mathematics, and little of everyday learning. The teaching had been disciplinary rather than helpful to the students and the college laws were a species of grinding down the undergraduates. With Dwight these things at once changed. He came to his high office at an opportune time, for the country was just entering upon a period of tremendous growth,

THE OLD LABORATORY

where there was strong need for broadly educated men to take the lead. A more generous conception of a college's duty to the nation was demanded by the state and this President Dwight fully realized. His first step showed the change which he later carried fully out. He called to tutorships and professorships young men of talent who were not necessarily clergymen. Previous to Dwight the teaching force was made up mostly of ministers, young and old, but with Dwight there began that splendid line of professional scholars and investigators that has had so many truly great names on its roll. He gathered about him Jeremiah Day, Benjamin Silliman and James L. Kingsley, all men who made their mark on the college. Before the first Dwight had finished his course he had, for that day, shaped the curriculum on really broad lines, and had greatly added to the revenues of the college and increased its attendance. His administration was an immense benefit to the institution.

Naturally dividing itself into two movements, the scientific school that began under the elder Dwight may be regarded as the most important single tendency in the later development of the college. When the elder Silliman took the chair of Chemistry, Mineralogy and Geology in 1802 he had to go to Scotland to prepare himself to teach. So little scientific knowledge had

COLLEGE STREET

reached this country that when Silliman found a box of minerals in the Yale buildings he had to go to Philadelphia to find a man who could name them for him. Astounding has been the progress made since that day. Under President Day came Olmsted, the truth seeking, patient investigator, whose study of the meteoric showers of 1833 made him famous. Woolsey added to the movement, though he was essentially not a scientific man, by appointing several young men of promise to scientific chairs:—Elias Loomis, the chainer of the storms; Silliman, Jr.; Newton, the astronomer; James D. Dana, the geologist; Josiah W. Gibbs, the student of physics. This great coterie of scientists advanced the cause, not only at Yale but in America, and to them is due

much of the accumulating impetus that Yale received in the middle of the century. The beginnings made under Woolsey produced the Scientific School—through the generosity of Joseph E. Sheffield—which was regarded at the time as "the most important educational movement in the century in America."

A long line of distinguished scientists have followed in Dana, Silliman, and Loomis; men like Othniel C. Marsh in paleontology and original proof of Darwin's theories; like William H. Brewer in exploration and agriculture; like Chauvenet in science; like Ebenezer Mason in astronomy; Percival, the Connecticut, and Whitney, the California geologist; S. F. B. Morse, the electrician, and a score of others. The scientific movement

PHELPS HALL

VANDERBILT HALL

brought new ideals to the college, introduced new aims in the curriculum and new ambitions to the students. No one event in her history has had more important consequences.

It has been a characteristic of Yale, and a part of her making, that she has kept in close touch with the country since her early days. She was as republican under Ezra Stiles in the Revolution as she was patriotic under Woolsey in the Civil war. She was as much in touch with the people in the Constitutional Convention of 1788 as in the antislavery movement of 1861. She sent her sons to the front at both times in great numbers, and each time sympathized with the country's resultant momentary retrogression. When the nation began its constructive period in 1781 the college grew with it, and expanded under Dwight and Day as the country expanded. The call for educated leaders has from the first been answered by the college, as witness her Sherman, Clay and Evarts, Fuller, Brewer, Brown, Taft, White, Choate and a score of others.

It has been sympathy with the country at large that has brought to Yale her peculiar characteristic of a national institution. Her democracy has also helped to make this. Comparatively poor in resources, with no place for the man who would not work, she has from the beginning of the last century been the poor man's college. It has not only been the growing paternalism in the administration that has made the place one of attractive prospects for the student without money, but it has also been the inherent spirit of the undergraduate body, which has always asked of a man that he succeed at something in his college course, and has ignored his ancestry and his bank account. It is this as much as anything that has made Yale a national institution.

It was natural perhaps that full development should come late. The sum total of the first century of progress has since then been often surpassed in a single decade. Yale was a small country academy in almost every respect until the first Dwight's administration. Then it suddenly bloomed. President Day, a smaller man than Dwight, carried on the expansion, building the last of the Brick Row, and the library, and extending the influence of the college westward. Theodore T. Woolsey, in a period of unprecedented prosperity for every branch of the college, built deeper and broader still, adding Peabody Museum, the Medical School, and the Observatory to Yale's buildings, organizing the Graduate School and beginning the Sheffield Scientific School department.

Woolsey, with Dwight, may be said to stand at the head of the list of Yale's Makers. He was eminently an expansionist, far sighted and courage-

ous, believing in the gathering of the various schools about the original college, and it was he who first breathed the possibility of a University. The old and narrow curriculum passed away under Woolsey and a modern course, with traces it is true of the old, took its place. He laid the foundation for the wonderful progress of the next two administrations. Noah Porter continued the work of expansion; but the greatest progress was during the administration of Timothy Dwight the second.

President Dwight concludes the brief survey which has been attempted of the upbuilding of Yale. A theologian, and yet a business man; a scholar, and yet an administrator; retiring, and yet a man of affairs, Timothy Dwight the second accomplished in thirteen short years more actual advancement for

PRESIDENT ARTHUR T. HADLEY

the institution than all of his predecessors had before him. The opportunity was there, and he was the man of the hour. He found the institution crudely made up of four or five departments; the buildings inadequate, the attendance small, the curriculum narrower than the times demanded. When he laid aside his "diadem," which old Ezra Stiles likened to a "crown of thorns," he had in every way immensely benefitted the institution. He had found it a college and he left it a University. He had found it poor and he left it rich. He had found the teaching force small, he left it immensely added to. He more than doubled the attendance of the Academical department, just doubled the Scientific School, multiplied the Medical School five fold, the Graduate School four fold, and doubled the body of instructors. In 1889 Yale graduated more students than had left her halls during the whole first sixty years of her history. He added fifteen magnificent buildings, exactly the same number that had been built in all the college's previous history. But the greatest success of President Dwight's great régime was the fashioning of a University. The woof and the warp were there, but it took a weaver to work them into the finished fabric. When he retired from office in 1899 after thirteen years of unprecedented progress in every department of university life, the praise of the great army of Yale graduates went after him. He, with the first Dwight, and with Woolsey, stand at the head of Yale's great makers.

Now again an opportunity faces Yale. President Hadley, loved and trusted by every alumnus, and by his faculties and students, has the best wishes of every Yale man. It would be presumptuous to outline the opportunities before him, as no man understands them better than does this young president himself. Is it not enough to say that with this fine history behind him and this great promise before, he will be equal to the burden?

8
The Fisherman
of Gloucester

Gloucester Harbor.

THE FISHERMEN OF GLOUCESTER

By VICTOR J. SLOCUM

PHOTOGRAPHS BY ARTHUR HEWITT

THERE are two Gloucesters. One is the Gloucester that has forgotten the rigor of its traditions, when hardy men from England made fishing voyages to the coast of Maine, and cruised as far South as Cape Ann, in 1623. She is ashamed of the smell of gurry, grown into a false estheticism, and generated into cheap politics like many another city.

The other Gloucester is an honor to manhood, and crowned by a galaxy of beautiful vessels, America's famous fishing fleet. There

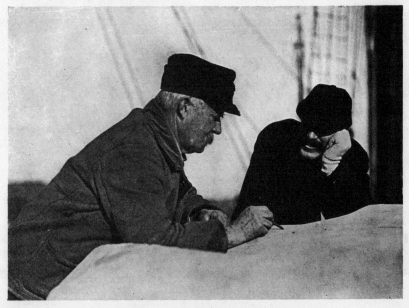

Figuring Out the Profits of the Catch.

151

Old Hulks, High on the Shore.

"The big fellows come swinging out of the hold by the tail."

From the Sea to a Barrel.

are three or four hundred sail in this fleet. The most modern of them are modeled somewhat after the type of the Burgess idea when yachts were yet healthy. In fact, Edward Burgess designed several "fishermen" besides defending the *America* Cup three times, and it was quickly discovered that the innovation brought in fares ahead of the old-timers. The vessels are superior to yachts as real ships, and in point of beauty are above comparison.

Many yachtsmen with real sailor blood in their veins have felt proud to beat one of these flyers under a cloud of canvas, and one was even known to build a vessel just to hold his own in general sailing qualities when he met a certain fisherman off shore.

See a fleet in the open harbor ready for sea! The topmasts that float so much coquettish muslin to the amorous summer air are stowed ashore, and their absence gives the vessel a long, rakish look. These vessels are "bankers" and sail for cod and halibut, to be found where icebergs tell them to go no farther north, and where the ice floe may catch them on the coasts of Labrador or Newfoundland. The sharp, high bow is not yet covered by ice, as it soon

will be while the ship is riding at anchor on the fishing grounds, to her immense manilla cable, now coiled down abaft the windlass. They wait for their crew. Some dark forms are seen crossing to her in a boat, and, although the wind is strong enough to blow down fish-houses, they peak up the white sail without thinking of a reef, set the head sails, and stand out with lee rails awash, out by Norman's Woe and around the whistling buoy that makes its faithful moan off Eastern Point. The seagulls scream a warning that speak of frozen rigging, and of the stark corpse adrift in the dory. But what care they for warnings! There are mouths ashore to feed, and bread must be gotten out of the sea.

* * * * *

All the fishing is done in dories, flat bottomed boats, peculiar to Gloucester, about eighteen to twenty feet long. A good-sized schooner carries ten or twelve dories, lashed down to the deck in two nests, piled upon each other like saucers.

When the fishing grounds are reached and the weather is suitable, the crew are told off in pairs to man the dories and lay out the trawls. This is the French way of fishing, and before its general introduction each man would go on his own hook and fish over the side, account being taken of the exact number of fish caught by each. Now, the fare is lumped together and shares are taken from the general stock. A trawl is a long warp fastened at either end to the ground and to it, at short intervals, are attached cod lines about a fathom long, each ganged with a hook. The dory starts out at one end of the warp that runs over a roller at the bow, and the men simply haul ahead, pick off the fish, and rebait the hooks as they go along. When the end of the line is reached they haul back again, and repeat the process until the dory is full to the gunwales. No danger arises from filling a dory this way, for the mucus that envelopes

Long Lines of Fish Drying.

On Shore—Between Cruises.

Sometimes a voyage of despair brings them to some rocky coast, and their little world is startled by a tale of exposure; again they may be picked up when it is too late and the sea tragedy is complete; but most often they are never heard of again. A greater percentage of men are lost in this calling than in any other, not excepting the profession of arms; so there is truth in the saying that the history of Gloucester fisheries is written in tears.

Next to fog fishermen fear the liner. It is bad enough when the weather is clear, but when it is so thick that the end of the bowsprit is out of sight, the lone lookout keeps an anxious ear open for the throbbing machinery, and the rush of water hurled from a thirty thousand horse-power machine on its flying mission. According to international law, ships must slow down to moderate speed in a fog, but fishermen know too well how this is evaded, for they can tell a twenty-knot from a ten-knot gait in spite of all the log-book red tape. But they sleep soundly in their bunks and, if the steel cutwater sends them to an icy death, no one is the wiser except the officer on the bridge and a few others who know how to keep their mouths shut. The sea *is* cruel when one has n't the upper hand.

The men who sail out of Gloucester are sure that a third of their lost vessels go in this way.

In early times, on the shores of Europe from France to Italy, people went down on the quay to chant a vesper for their toilers on the sea. This custom was, no doubt, brought over by the early fishermen who first found cod near the shores of Newfoundland; so now we find the tradition exemplified in Gloucester when once a year little orphans scatter flowers on the sea for the unburied dead.

When men leave their port to go to sea there is no demonstration on the part of mothers, sisters, or wives. That is all done in the little home and is not to be seen. These

the fish causes them to form a jelly-like mass, and the sea rolls right over them without interfering with the stability of the load, so the fishermen sit in the center of their catch and load until they are practically in a decked boat. Perhaps this is the reason why they don't eat much fish at the table. They go a whole cruise without so much as seeing one on the bill of fare; and yet people ashore who cannot get fresh fish even for money, will envy them.

Men working together are called dory mates, and peril breeds the attachment common to all men who face danger together, whether on land or sea. In the little boats they see some of the greatest perils of their calling. They are seldom capsized; but a sudden fog bank sometimes shuts off the schooner. Then there is a long, hopeless drift about, until by mere chance some other vessel picks them up and brings them into port. Sometimes men have been on the wharf to see their own schooner come in with flag at half mast for them. Thus they would literally attend their own funeral.

Straight to Market.

homes are never squalid, though their tastes may be a little crude. In many homes you will see an upright piano of the very latest garnish, but never a token of the dangerous calling, no models of fishing craft or festoons of netting, and seldom any painting of them on the walls, but rather a characterless chromo of no particular subject.

It is strange to see so little mark of character amid the surroundings of men who have

In From a Cruise.

"While the vessel is being fitted up again."

so much of the real thing. In the crooked streets along the water front, where the real Gloucester breathes, one meets these men, dressed in oilskins and sou'wester', hands encased in huge white mittens (blue ones bring bad luck), wet with gurry. They may have just landed the fare, have the sea noises yet in their heads, and still a contempt for the solid soil, that the strong, clumsy gait denotes. It does one good to meet men so perfectly in touch with the elemental forces. They throw around them such an atmosphere of delightful freshness. Their eyes look straight to yours with the beautiful honesty they learn from being prime producers. They need none of the garnish of culture to make them men, and if the page of knowledge that is so rich with the spoils of time is seldom unrolled before them, the

secrets of real life and nature are focused on them stronger than they know, and they reap an unconscious benefit from her teachings. It is one of the glories of the sea that she has always a page that is still unread. The advancements of science and the encroachments of heroism make this page more of a mystery instead of less, for it is a secret that grows the more by the very forces we use to unlock it. Men brought close to it by the prosaic demands of mere bread and butter are strangely loth to leave it, and many never can. They often swear by all the prongs of the Trident of Neptune, and by his Nereids to boot, never to face it again; but a few weeks of shore monotony tells them that their resolution was a mere sophistry.

Fishermen often perform feats of heroism

Laying Up Alongside the Wharf.

and self-sacrifice without just compensation. One was known some time ago to render aid to a steamer on the Newfoundland coast and gave up a five-thousand dollar fare to do it. Another case called to my attention was the rescue of the crew of a British steamer. The skipper told me that neither he nor his men got the customary allowance of gold awarded for these occasions; "But they sent me a letter!" "It was writ on a kind of paper that was thick as the fore staysail, big enough to make trouser seats for all hands, and there was a lion and a unicorn on it. Yes, sir, I kept it five years and then burnt it up, for it was a regular nuisance looking at it."

"Yes, sir; I was out in the gale of '62, off Prince Edward Island, and there was a slew of vessels lost then. It was my first year master. I was twenty-two then. Fifteen sail lost at one clip. One hundred and twenty lives lost, and there were seventy widows and a hundred and forty orphans made in just that one blow. No, we don't

mind a flag at half mast any more than that it is part of the business; that one you see over there had the captain and one man washed overboard. Never saw them after she shipped a heavy sea. These craft they have nowadays never lift the lee rail, and they just smother her down into it when they have a fare, and don't think much of reefing either.

"I'll tell you how many of them are lost," said he, drawing a diagram on a sail that was hauled over some fish casks. "They often sink each other when they drag their anchors. You see, on the grounds one vessel will anchor about here, and another about there, and another one there, and so on, about three cable lengths apart. Now, when it comes on to blow and kicks up a rip we all try to hold on as long as we can, and if this one drags why she will drift into that one, and they will both sink, and sometimes that happens to almost a whole fleet. The proper thing to do is to cut and set a jib and risk it; that is your only chance.

"I had a close shave once," he continued. "We started to drag on another fellow, and I got the ax out to cut, and there I was between those men and their lives, and the owner's interest, for a cable costs about four hundred dollars, and I hated to cut it. The sea was standing right on end, and we came closer and closer, and I got the fore staystail on and hauled it over, and, by gracious, we dragged by without even touching him, and I saved the crew, the vessel, and the cable."

The most interesting vessels of the fleet in the winter are the halibut trawlers. As some halibut weigh three hundred pounds, it is regarded as quite a feat to get one of them over the side of the little dory without capsizing her. They are killed by a few good whacks with a club before being hauled aboard, and I heard one amusing account of a halibut that "came to" after being hauled. The man got right down and held it flat in his arms in the bottom of the dory to prevent its leaping overboard, The arrival of one of these vessels at the wharf is the signal for a gathering of the people who know about fish, and who like to see the big fellows come swinging out of the hold by the tail.

The crew unload their own fare in about two hours—it took a month to get it—and then rig up in shore togs to look at the town and recreate for a week or ten days, while the vessel is being fitted up again. All of this work is done by the owners, who engage professional riggers and mechanics to put the craft in perfect shape and to bend the sails, so that all the crew have to do is to set sail, bait the trawls, and be off for the fishing banks. In the summer these halibuters make voyages to Iceland, where they find larger fish than on the home grounds.

Gloucester has many nationalities, but they are all one type, honest, strong, manly fellows; untutored in the wiles of general civilization. Most of them are from the British Provinces. A large percentage are Scandinavians; there are many Portuguese from the Western Islands, Italians and Greeks; there is even a Japanese on record from this port.

As a general thing fishermen are quite prosperous, and most of them have snug bank accounts as soon as they get over the little debt at the outfit store that started them out with proper clothes, oilskins, and sea boots.

One of the Fleet.

9
A National Breathing Spot

The Maine Coast

There are few finer beaches to be found in America than on the Maine coast.

A NATIONAL BREATHING SPOT

BY DAY ALLEN WILLEY

ILLUSTRATED BY PHOTOGRAPHS

"They seek for happier shores in vain
Who leave the summer isles of Maine."

READ Whittier from end to end and you could not find more truthful lines than these. Yet it is saying much when we remember the multitude of spots which Nature has prepared for playgrounds—for old as well as young. But in creating the place the nation knows as "Down East," she apparently included everything that the average man or woman wants for healthful, reasonable enjoyment. The good old poet wrote these words many years ago—long before the summer and winter resort became a national fad and before the casino and the merry-go-round were known; but to-day, as then, the shores of these "summer isles" are so attractive to the seeker of rest and recreation that each year finds island and mainland more and more a Mecca for the tourist—not merely from the near-by states but from the other end of the country as well. Yes, Maine is not only a national breathing spot but one of the nation's great recreation parks, because here the people in whatever walk of life can satisfy the craving of body and mind for that which is strengthening and renewing.

All over the United States you find the sons of Maine, but the *Wanderlust* has never made them forget the old place. Their remembrance of the verdure-clad islands, the rock-bound shores, the forest-lined rivers is as vivid as their recollection of Old Agamenticus and Mount Desert and Penobscot Bay. Whether as children they played on the smooth white sands of Kennebunk beach or hunted for arrow heads on the Ogunquit, they know that it is still

"Down East" and that they can go back and find the one-time playgrounds little changed. Nature has taken care of that. Although "Down East" has become one of the world's great summer resorts, the visitor sees the same beautiful vistas upon which the Indians gazed centuries before the pioneer from the Old World set foot on the Western shore. Man may increase the comforts and luxuries of life here but he can never mar the picturesque wildness of the region—the wildness which those born amid it learned to know and to love.

If you consider the great woodland that covers so many thousands of miles of the interior, the five thousand streams which flow through it and the one thousand five hundred lakes concealed amid the trees, you will concede Maine to be the recreation ground of America; for over twenty thousand square miles of it comprise what we miscall wilderness, where the summer days may be made a continual pleasure for the hunter, the fisherman, the man of science who would reveal the secrets of botany, geology and natural history and the plain nature lover. With canoe and boat one can travel hundreds of miles through some of the most alluring scenery in America. Deer, even bear, await the patience and skill of the big-game seeker. The mountaineer has a challenge in Katahdin, Pisgah and other peaks which, while not reaching above the snow line, are sufficiently steep and rugged to test his endurance and climbing ability. And there are corners of this region as yet practically unknown to the white man—some, scores of miles distant from even the hut of the half-breed trapper, and to reach which the adventurer must go a hundred miles from the sound of the locomotive whistle. It seems strange to talk about exploring, to

Portland Head Light.

use such expressions as "pioneering" in a state which is a part of the birthplace of the Republic; but we have heard so much and read so much of the "Great West" and other parts of the country that we may have forgotten that this corner of our states is as large as the rest of New England put together.

Put the rule on the map of Maine's coast, and as the arrow flies it measures about two hundred and twenty-five miles; but the land is so fissured with rivers and bays, and, when the world was made, so many islands came up out of the ocean, that the real coast is about two thousand five hundred miles long. The shores of the mainland and of most of the islands rise picturesquely out of the clear blue and green of the sea, some in sheer bluffs, some in gentle hills crowned with trees, shrubs and greensward, others in great masses of rock hundreds of feet in height. Mount Desert well merits its gloomy name, as it is an island mountain range ascending skyward over one thousand five hundred feet above the level of the sea. Here and there, to be

sure, are unbroken stretches of coast; frequently, indeed, the land slopes seaward so gently and the waves have made the surface of these beaches so smooth and hard that the chauffeur or horseman ·may use them as admirable speeding courses. On some of them you can take an after-breakfast stroll of a half-dozen miles without turning back. As clean as the polished floor, they present an animated picture during the hours when people most enjoy a dip in the surf or a promenade. One may see a sand stretch alive with ten thousand people, old and young, on an August morning. For when the fresh air and sunshine, full of the tonic of the sea, have cast a spell, father and grandfather are children for the hour, content to dig their feet in the warm white sand, perhaps even joining the youngsters in throwing it over each other. The shore shelves so gently that even the little folks can wade in safety, while to the expert swimmer the white-crested waves offer a strong temptation to mingle with them.

True, bathing and beach-napping are

popular pastimes, but these are only a few of the ways of letting life drift with the hours. You can see an actual illustration of this on the Kennebunk, Saco and other rivers. Go out into the stream when the tide is coming in. With oar or paddle steer your craft into the moving waters; then let the current take you along without a stroke of your own. Wait until the tide recedes and float with it. Is there a lazier way of spending the July hours? But tide drifting is so popular that you may have a flotilla of a hundred boats keeping you company. The state is a boating paradise, for the water lover can find a cruising ground adapted to the fragile canoe as well as to the fifty-ton yacht or the motor boat; the lover of the racing shell has his choice of many stretches on river and bay so well protected from wind and sea that they are as peaceful as a mill pond.

When Nature sprinkled these islands so plentifully in this northern sea and cut into Maine's rocky frontier with the numberless bays and inlets, she formed a cruising ground for the yachtsman that is unexcelled. In the clear deep water a fifty- or a hundred-ton cutter can be run so close to the land that the crew might leap from deck to shore in some places. Indeed most of the narrowest sounds and other passages that separate island from island, or island from mainland, can be safely navigated if the man at the wheel keeps his nerve and his fellows at the sheet are quick to handle them. Literally, the yachtsman can lay out a route of a thousand miles or more between Portland and Bar Harbor by guiding his craft among this labyrinth of channels —yet cover every mile under canvas.

Not only is yachting one of the most enjoyable and popular pastimes for the people who have red blood in them, but it is inexpensive, strange as this may seem. The party who are willing to keep away from the hotels and spend their nights in cabin or camp and who relish coffee made in the open and know how to cook over the fagots, can get a week or month of this life and feel like Nature's noblemen, though it may cost each less than half the expense of the "resort." There are plenty of places where the fat clams or "quahogs" are waiting to be dug out of their beds. Then

Bald Head Cliff, York, Me.

remember that Down East you are among white folk. If some potatoes are wanted to go with the roast quahog on the shell, just put out a line at one of the little wharves you see along shore. Any of the country folk will give you a peck for a pair of dimes—if they let you pay them. A quart of milk and a dozen eggs go for a quarter. Another quarter gives you the fat pullet which can be grilled on the coals at the next stop for dinner. It seems to be in the air to be kindly and hospitable and

the thousands. Generally speaking these islands are huge masses of rock, which seem to have been originally placed here by the Creator to furnish fitting antagonists for the restless, angry waters of the Atlantic just as they are found off New England and the Provinces; to give the waves, as it were, something to wreak their fury upon. They are of every shape and size, from the bit of bare rock lifting its gray-brown head presumptuously out of the midst of the waters, to areas of

Sailboats are plentiful and the sport of the best.

you remember it whenever you think of that run to the Junk of Pork, the Devil's Cut, Pulpit Harbor or Blacksnake Ledge.

Mount Desert is the monarch, in size, of the Maine islands, but it is only one of a literal archipelago. A mere glance at the map shows how the mainland from Portland away up to the St. Croix River is edged with islands, how every bay and even inlet is crowded so thickly with them that it is difficult to tell them as islands. There are so many that they actually run into

sloping plains and hillsides miles in extent. Occasionally towns or villages are found upon them, but most of them are small, and rise from the sea at distances ranging from a few rods to two miles or more from the coast of the mainland. Their surface is usually more or less thickly covered with a coating of earth, which, during the warm months, is bright with verdure and often studded with the tree growth of the region. Winding between the islands are the deep-water channels leading to the ports along the shores, and forming highways for shipping. When the islands are arrayed in the fresh green of early summer, and the warm breezes play over their winding channels, marking all their shores with the daintiest of silver surf-lines, the whole scene is beyond description.

And hundreds await the seeker of the wild, for the only living things which inhabit them are beast, bird and insect. They are as sylvan and as rural as a cen-

of the older days, not only to the student of history but to the man who would know the world of to-day. All the way from Kittery on the west to the shores of the St. Croix, are to be seen old forts and blockhouses as well as other landmarks, some of which are not described in the schoolbooks. Quaint Kittery itself is believed to be the site of the first settlement in Maine, and the appearance of its buildings seems to substantiate this belief. To-day the trolley car hums past the ancient mansion

Picnicking in the woods is a diversion of hotel guests.

tury ago and he who would spend the summer days in the very heart of nature can paddle his canoe to many an islet where for the time he may be supreme. In Casco Bay alone are so many islands that the good people of Portland and those who live upon its shores have a saying that there is an island for every day in the year and two for each Sunday. It is a fact that from the waters of Casco alone rise four hundred of them.

Interesting indeed are the mementoes

at Kittery Point—the home of Sir William Pepperell, who led the King's American soldiers when they sailed to Nova Scotia to capture Louisburg from the French. The throngs of tourists who go to York beach find old York a pleasant place to linger a while, for its jail and garrison houses dating back to the troublous times of the Colonies are still standing. Wells, with its single street lined with old houses, dates back to the time when the Indians concealed themselves in the marshes near-

Nowhere are there such building sites.

by to attack its people. Ogunquit is so curiously named on account of its many Indian traditions. Along the King's Highway which stretches out to Kennebunkport and Kennebunk Beach go buckboard and phaeton. It has become one of the beach boulevards of the Atlantic coast on which the fashionables delight to display their dress and horse flesh. Over two hundred years ago some of the ancestors of this gay throng might have gone cautiously picking their way with weapon in hand to defend themselves from the savage bands which frequently lay in ambush for the settlers who traveled by this route. It is one of the oldest roads in New England and still one sees "rest houses" upon it that date back over a century. Even Old Orchard Beach has its evidences of the past, while Portland, despite its natural beauty and its scenic surroundings, is especially attractive to the visitor because of the quaint structures that form such a contrast to its modernness. In its vicinity are also some of the best-preserved defenses of the old days which well repay the tourist willing to take a day to visit them. The town of Castine, so charmingly situated near the mouth of the Penobscot, brings to mind a mediæval city of Europe with the frowning walls of old Fort George on the hillside above it.

While the smooth white beaches, the clefts in the rocky shores and the islands are the sites of more summer colonies than can probably be found elsewhere in the United States, some of these resorts have a reputation that is peculiarly their own. For instance, Bar Harbor boasts of being the most exclusive resort in America—whatever that may mean. The class of people who make this their home are not only very wealthy but they belong to the highest "social sets" in the places from which they come.

We might think Mount Desert of small consequence without Bar Harbor, but as a matter of fact the social colony occupies but an insignificant bit of this island which is truly an ideal place for the wooer of nature. No scenery on the coast is grander or more impressive than that of Mount Desert. An island fourteen miles long and a dozen broad, embracing a hundred square miles, it is actually traversed from end to end by mountains. As the

mountains bar the way to the southern shores, you must often make a long detour to reach a given point, or else commit yourself to the guidance of a deer-path or the dry bed of some mountain torrent. In summer or in autumn, with a little knowledge of woodcraft, a well-adjusted pocket compass and a stout staff, it is practicable to enter the hills and make your way as the red huntsmen were of old accustomed to do. Southwest Harbor is usually the stranger's first introduction to Mount Desert. Its neighborhood is less wild and picturesque than the eastern shores of the island, but Long Lake and the western ranges of mountains are conveniently accessible from it, while, by crossing or ascending Somes sound, which resembles a Norwegian fjord, and which nearly cuts the island in parts, avenues are opened in every direction to the surpassing charms of this favored corner of New England.

Nature has played some strange pranks with the geography of this part of the world. It is a fact that Mount Desert was once a part of the mainland detached in the course of time by the action of the sea waters. Indeed, it is so near the coast that an artificial bridge has for many years united the two, and the Maine Central Railroad runs trains to a terminus practically within the very limits of the island. Of all the Atlantic islands this is the highest, being made up largely of mountains of solid granite. In many of the valleys between these mountains are found ponds of fresh water. The southwestern section of the island constitutes a fairly level plateau, while at Bar Harbor level lands of considerable extent are found. In other sections the mountains come down to the water's edge. The man who would be in the great outdoors can be contented by a sojourn here, for he is as isolated in the interior as if no human being were within a hundred miles of him.

Have you ever "hit the trail," as they say in the West? Whether you have or not you can do it down in old Maine and get a taste of the real joys of outdoor life. It may be on rugged Mount Desert or some smaller island or it may be in the woodlands of the mainland. Where, makes little difference. One can do as did the Redmen in the former years and tread the narrow paths that lead into the heart of the wilderness with pack on back. In a party, the luggage can be so divided that a month's outfit can be easily "toted" without even the aid of a pony. Heavy-soled shoes and puttees or boots should cover the feet and legs, but banish the "boiled shirt" with its collar and tie, and wear the rough and ready sweater or flannel shirt with trousers of khaki or some other weatherproof cloth. The old slouch hat protects from the sun's rays and is as good as an umbrella in the rain. Thus you can hit the trail day by day, sleep with only the canvas roof between you and the stars, and constantly breathe the air laden with the balsam of the pine and often the ozone of the sea. Nature has here made every thing sweet, healthful and pure, and for a mere trifle compared with the bill of the summer "resort" the whole family may get what is real recreation and with it plenty of enjoyment.

Yes, Maine is an ideal camping ground, the center of a pastime of which we as a nation know too little, for we have been pampered far too much with the luxuries of the modern watering place. Here the cost of the vacation can be reduced to a mere fraction by the family who are not afraid to don the garb of the adventurer and experience the delight of really "roughing it."

To the many men to whom time is golden in the sense that work means fortune, this part of "Down East" is appealing, for one can quickly place himself where he can forget the click of the tape wheel and clatter of the typewriter—if he wants to forget them. It is not necessary to spend two or three days in a Pullman or to "stage it" hour after hour from noon to sunset. The pathfinders have been busily at work and either by land or water most of the islands and coast-clefts can be reached in a few hours from the near-by cities. A night's run from the Metropolis places the rest seeker at his favorite "beach" in time for the morning meal and surface bath—with not an hour of his day wasted in travel. If he would go further, say to Bar Harbor or Eastport, a few hours more bring him to his destination, for the steel way has been laid along the coast line so that it winds in and out, following the shore of the numberless inlets; and thus the traveler has a whiff of the ocean breeze and many a glimpse of its waves long before his journey ends. Thanks to the channels that connect the coast with the sea, the tourist who prefers to travel by water may leave Boston or New York and in twenty-four hours take his grip and go down the gang plank, for a fleet of steamers, little and big, are now needed to aid in carrying the multitude of pleasure seekers to this breathing spot of the country.

The old lobsterman.

10
Woodstock, Vermont

WOODSTOCK VERMONT
BY HENRY BOYNTON

ABOUT the year 1765 a young man by the name of Timothy Knox, a member of Harvard College, came into the woods and made his home on the spot which is now the town of Woodstock. Whether he found in this wilderness a compensation for the loss of the maiden whose love he could not win, no record has ever told; but among the many lovers of sound learning who have made a home in Woodstock all have been proud to remember that her first settler was a graduate of the oldest college in America.

The first settlers of Woodstock experienced the struggles and privations which were incident to the settlement of most of the towns on our New England frontier. Those men who pushed their way into the dense woods, made clearings and built themselves homes, were brave, strong and steadfast. Without any reservation, they gave their whole energies, soul and body, to the work they had undertaken. As the material elements out of which those homes were built were fresh and strong, if, indeed, a little rough, so those early home-makers filled their homes with an atmosphere permeated with high purposes and noble aims, and made them clean and sweet with domestic purity and Christian simplicity. To-day a few outlining foundation stones, and hard by an old well, alone remain to mark the spots where once thriving and prosperous families lived; but the men who were reared there will be found in every land on the globe, making the world better by the lives they are living.

One fortunate circumstance attended the early settlers of Woodstock—they never suffered from Indian raids. The trails by which the Canadian savages swept down through the country lay either to the north or the south of the Ottauquechee valley, where Woodstock nestles, surrounded by her clustering hills. At first the energies of these

MONUMENT TO AARON HUTCHINSON.

where the marketable products of the farm were exchanged for goods which had been boated up the Connecticut and hauled overland to their various points of trade.

While these first years in the life of the town were necessarily given to the work of grappling with the forests and the soil, while yet only the germinal elements of society could be found, there was great need of educated men, men capable of devising and effectually executing such measures as would prove the sure foundation for the good order of a well-established society. In due time such men appeared, and each in his own way did his chosen work so well that it would be difficult to conceive how it could have been better done.

Among these the most commanding figure is that of Rev. Aaron Hutchinson, who settled just outside the town line in Pomfret, but gave Woodstock the benefit of his great influence.

pioneers were employed in making the necessary clearings and cultivating the crops needful for the support of the family. Then followed road making and bridge building. Soon the shops of the rude artisans appeared, with the log meeting-house and the school-house, and the community passed from a state of existence where each family was an independent unit to the more complex life of an organized township.

These preliminaries filled up the years from 1767 to 1773, when the town was organized according to the king's patent issued under the great seal of the State of New York. After its organization the town received a new impetus, and for the next decade and a half made a rapid growth. Good frame houses began to take the places of the first log buildings; the roads began to receive attention; mills were built; and at the cross-roads stores were opened,

This man was a great scholar, the peer of any in Harvard College at that day. Seldom taking either hymn book or Bible into his pulpit, he repeated from memory the hymn and chapter he wanted. Had the whole New Testament been lost, it was said he could have reproduced it from memory in the original Greek. Finding in the woods no council to ordain him and no one to ask about his theology, this man was content to teach his neighbors to deal justly, to love mercy, and to walk humbly with their God. But if any man loving controversy pushed him into theological debate he was always ready and well equipped for the stoutest foe — and no one ever cared to engage him in a second encounter. In the winter he preached in barns,

TITUS HUTCHINSON.

and in the summer in the open woods. He took an active part in all the interests of the town, held his own plow with his own hands, and fitted for college the young men who drove his oxen. He had the first Boston newspaper ever seen in the valley, and used to read it to his neighbors gathered round his door. When he was invited to preach before Ethan Allen at Bennington, such was the effect of his powerful personality upon that old hero, that those who witnessed it said it reminded them of what the scene must have been when John Knox preached before Queen Mary. This man lived and labored and died here in the woods, and to this day all through these valleys harvests are being gathered from the seed he scattered.

It was more than fortunate for the struggling town that not long after Mr. Hutchinson cast in his lot here another man, his equal in ability and in devotion to the best interests of the people, came and made Woodstock

CHARLES MARSH.

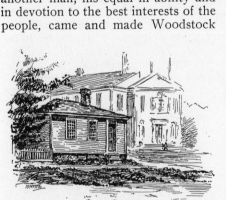

CHARLES MARSH'S OFFICE.

his home. This man was Charles Marsh. He settled here in 1788, practised law for sixty years and one, and then died. Like Mr. Hutchinson, Mr. Marsh possessed abilities which would have secured for him eminence in any of the older communities of New England, had he chosen to live and work there. Yet these two men gave great abilities to the woodland community and spent their lives in helping others to make Woodstock a village where law and order should prevail, where the principles of the Christian religion should be reverenced, and high ideals of social life be maintained. Mr. Marsh was a gentleman in the fullest sense of the word, and he built and maintained a gentleman's home. In that home were always seen simple but courtly manners. Its doors were always open to noted visitors to the state, and never closed to the poor in the neighborhood. The elevating and inspiring influences that went out from that home made a deep and abiding impression upon the young and growing town. Much of the charm which has always been felt in the social

THE FIRST MEETING-HOUSE.

THE OLD EAGLE HOTEL AND BARKER'S TAVERN.

Medical College in the town of his adoption.

In 1786 Woodstock became the shire town of Windsor County, and therefore the business center of the surrounding country. This was an event of as much importance at that time as the establishing of the terminus of a great railroad would be to-day. Hence Woodstock became an attractive point not only for professional men but for strong and energetic characters in every enterprise then opening in the new town. Among these men were such as Capt.

life of Woodstock village has been largely due to the old Marsh homestead on the hill. Mr. Marsh did much for his profession both locally and in the state, much for the cause of education during his forty years' service as a trustee of Dartmouth College; but he did more for the people among whom he lived and with whom, when life was done, he rested.

In the person of Dr. Stephen Powers the town early enjoyed the services of a typical old-time New England doctor. Strong in all his leading characteristics, his influence was always for the best interests of the community, and he left a descendant whose career is to be hereafter noticed.

Dr. Joseph A. Gallup, the first man to whom Dartmouth College gave a medical diploma, came and settled here. He became a noted teacher of medicine in the state, and an author, one of whose works is still an authority, and was one of the leaders in the work of establishing the Vermont

WIDOW DAY'S PINE.

Israel Richardson, Jesse Williams, Jesse Safford, Joel English, Benjamin Emmons, Lieut. Ransom, and Julius Bennett, all distinguished for their business ability and sound integrity. These men formed not only the bone and muscle of the growing town but infused into it a spirit of enterprise, a love of law and order and a regard for stable government.

With these ends in view, they did

character of the elements which entered into, controlled and vitalized the town of Woodstock during its formation period, from 1771 to the close of the century.

Exultant in the freshness and vigor of its youth, thus equipped and thus trained, with self-confidence and courage, Woodstock was ready and eager to slip from the last years of the old into the first of the new century and

WOODSTOCK AND MOUNT TOM.

not overlook the religious and educational interests of the place they had chosen for their home. Bringing with them a high regard for the Sabbath and Sabbath ordinances, they built meeting-houses and engaged able ministers, and soon there were here more communicants than in any other town within a hundred miles. Before the close of the century, the town had been divided into districts, and as good schools were maintained as the times could furnish. Such was the

enter upon the work of its development. Responsive to the intellectual stimulus which had been breathed into the town by those leading spirits who shaped her destiny, the opening of the new century was inaugurated by the establishment of a select school, under written contract on the part of some of its leading citizens. Thus early did the town learn to appreciate the value of educational advantages which should secure better results for the youth than could be had elsewhere.

This enterprise was followed by others in the same line for the next sixty years. Select schools were taught in stable-lofts, in corn cribs, and in underground rooms. In some of these were teachers who in after years won wide and enviable reputations in this and other states, and among the pupils were some who made brilliant records in after life.

As in the period of its youth, so in the years of its later growth, from time to time just such men appeared as were needed to uphold and carry forward the plans already entered upon,

second in his class, studied law, was admitted to the bar, returned to the scenes of his boyhood, opened an office in Woodstock, and was ready for professional work at the very beginning of the new century. In settling here he also gave evidence of the faith that was in him. Charles Marsh was here several years before him, and was already securing a strong foothold and a wide influence in the community. Mr. Marsh had already proved himself a man of fine natural endowment, a scholar of broad general culture, and a lawyer equipped with a

THE SQUARE.

whose object was to make Woodstock a business center of high character, and a field for broad professional activity. The first in this list was Titus Hutchinson, a son of the renowned Aaron. Titus Hutchinson proved the quality of his material when, in 1792, being fitted to enter the Junior class of Dartmouth College, the trustees would not receive him unless he would pay full tuition for four years. Being unable to meet this demand, he mounted a horse and, with a few dollars in his pocket and his scanty supply of clothes in his saddle bags, started for Princeton College, New Jersey. In due time he graduated,

good knowledge of the law and an inexhaustible magazine of wit and sarcasm. Nothing daunted, Titus Hutchinson sat down by his side, and soon Mr. Marsh found that he had a worthy competitor in the field. Mr. Hutchinson was successful as a lawyer and highly honored as a citizen. The town sent him five times to the legislature. In 1813 President Madison appointed him district attorney for the state of Vermont. In 1825 he was made judge of the supreme court, and served the state four years as chief justice. He died in 1857, ending a life full of honors.

During the fifteen years next after

THE JOHNSON HOUSE.

lage. They were active in laying out streets, building houses, aiding the struggling churches, and in building up the schools. It is pleasant, in this day of hustling and selfish activities, when men bend their whole energies to the advancement of their private fortunes, to think of such men as these, laboring for the highest good of the community, while apparently thinking little of their private affairs.

In remembering what they accomplished, it is well not to overlook the wide contrast between the means at their hands and those with which professional men work to-day. They had no magazines, giving the current facts and thought of the day, and few books; but they did not consider their equipment com-

Mr. Hutchinson settled in Woodstock, four other young men opened law offices here, Job Lyman, Norman Williams, David Pierce and Isaac N. Cushman, all college-bred men and all admirably equipped to aid in maintaining the high intellectual standard already set up

THE CONGREGATIONAL CHURCH.

by Marsh and Hutchinson. For the first thirty years of the century those men did much to establish the high repute which the bar of Windsor County gained in their day and which lasted for many years after their active labors ended. Their homes, and especially that of Mr. Williams, were always centers of intellectual culture and social refinement. They entered heartily into whatever enterprises were undertaken for the advancement of the vil-

THE NORMAN WILLIAMS MEMORIAL LIBRARY.

plete till they knew what those few
contained. They studied them till
their contents soaked into their consciousness. They *knew* the law;
it became a part of themselves.
Their limitations for professional
knowledge were not more narrow
than for general literature; but their
limited field was exceedingly well cultivated. It was high and ennobling
in its aims, pure and strong in its quality. What few works of literature
these men had, they made their own,
as they did the contents of their works
of law, and so they became masters of
strong, clean speech. Their profession first and the interests of their village next, occupied their time and absorbed their energies; and they were
tormented with no dreams of outside
unprofessional pursuits which promised larger and more speedy pecuniary
gains.

The first fifteen years of this century
were times of great religious excitement in Woodstock. After many
trials and some failures, at the end of
about twenty years four religious organizations became permanently established at the "Green"—as the village had then begun to be called—
the Congregational, the Universalist,
the Methodist, and the Christian, and
to these in 1826 was added the Episcopalian. The labors of some very able
and noted men went into the building
of these societies. These religious
organizations have met the wants of
the community until recently, when a
beautiful Roman Catholic church
has been added.

At the end of the first third of
the present century the town
had a population of three thousand. Thirteen physicians were in
readiness to attend upon the sick,
while ten lawyers stood by to aid them
in collecting their bills. Eight ministers instructed the people in things
spiritual; and nine printers were busy
in keeping the community supplied
with the news of the day and in giving
instruction for its political and social
well-being. Artisans in every trade
then known in the country were found
here, and all were in a flourishing con-

THE VALLEY OF THE OTTAUQUECHEE.

ROUND ABOUT WOODSTOCK.

dition. Nearly a score of societies for reading, debating or general improvement sprang into existence, flourished each its own little day, and then expired.

At this point it is well to notice a little more in detail the fortunes of two Woodstock boys, whose lives prove that sometimes the descendants of famous men become even more famous than their sires. While not a few Woodstock men gained enviable state reputations, and one at least lasting national renown, it remained for George P. Marsh and Hiram Powers

to achieve each an eminence which has made them known to the world.

To such as acknowledge the workings of the laws of heredity it is evident that Mr. Marsh was largely indebted to his father for his mental endowment. Mr. Charles Marsh was a man of a high order of intellectual ability; and hence George had the advantage of being well born. He also found himself born into an intellectual environment. Books were his early companions, and from the dawn of his mental activity he breathed an intellectual atmosphere. When once settled in the profession of the law at Burlington he readily secured a place by the side of the brightest and ablest men of the Vermont bar; and while maintaining his place there he found in himself much surplus energy and this he devoted to the study of English philology. Here he laid the foundation for his astonishing achievements in this department of learning in the later years of his life. He gave but little attention to the law after the fortieth year of his life, being at that time called into the field of politics. He was in the House of Representatives at Washington for six years, and in 1849 was appointed minister resident of the United States at Constantinople. In 1853 he was sent on a special mission to Greece; and in 1861 was appointed minister to Italy, in which office he continued till his death in 1882. In the discharge of his duties in this high office he not only rendered eminent service to our country but endeared himself to Victor Emanuel as a wise counsellor in the many trying conditions in which he found himself during the first years of his new kingdom. In the streets of Rome to-day the traveler will find many common men who knew "Mr. Marsh, the American." But great as he was as a diplomatist, it was in the field of literature that he won his highest fame. However much his duties pressed upon him, he always found time for his favorite pursuits. The result was that he came to be acknowledged as one of the learned men of the world. His acquisitions were wide and thorough in many departments of human learning, and his contributions to the stock of the world's knowledge were very large.

When the court of Victor Emanuel was held at Turin, Matthew Arnold met Mr. Marsh there, and, writing to a friend, spoke of him as a "tall, stout, homely man redeemed from Yankeeism by a long European residence"; and then he adds: "Mr. Marsh is a *savant*, and has written an excellent work on the English language." Still again: "When you find that *rara avis*, a well bred and well trained American, you feel the bond of race driectly." Mr. Marsh died in 1882, in the vale of Vallombrosa. His valuable library is now the property of the University of Vermont, having been given by a citizen of Woodstock hereafter to be referred to.

HIRAM POWERS.

Unlike Charles Marsh, the father of Hiram Powers was not a man of any marked intellectual endowment. If it seems plain that Mr. Marsh inherited much from his father, it seems equally plain that Mr. Powers inherited nothing. Unlike Mr. Marsh also, Mr. Powers was not born into an intellectual environment. The implements of husbandry to be found on a common New England farm, and not books, were his earliest companions, and he knew all the limitations then usually met in a Vermont farm household. Armed only with the simplest rudiments of knowledge, when a mere lad he was taken to the then wild country of Ohio. In Cincinnati he did what he could find to do to earn his bread. At length finding himself in a clock-maker's shop, he there discovered his mechanical and inventive powers; for he not only repaired the deranged clocks but made improvements in them. Next he modeled some automaton figures attached to an organ which he had fitted up to be run by clockwork. At the age of twenty-five he saw for the first time in his life a piece of work done in marble—Canova's bust of Washington. This was to him both a revelation and an inspiration; it revealed to him his personal genius and inspired him thenceforward to follow his guidance. He at once began to visit the studio

GEORGE P. MARSH.

of the celebrated artist, Echstine, each visit only intensifying the passion which had been aroused by the sight of the Washington bust. From that time on he gave the entire energies of his being to his chosen work—rather, to the art which had chosen him. He soon went to Washington, where a friend secured for him as patrons President Jackson and some of the leading statesmen of the time. Here the character of his genius quickly showed itself, and the work he produced proved him to be no common artist. Other friends gathered around him; and soon it was made possible by them for young Powers to go to Italy to perfect himself in his art. So at the age of thirty he found himself settled in Florence, where he lived till his death, in 1873. Circumstances compelled him to earn his daily bread; and as he could do this most easily by making busts, this branch of work absorbed most of his time and energy, while it was in ideal work that his genius showed itself most clearly,—works like the Fisher Boy, Eve, and the Greek Slave. The last two particularly attracted the attention and won the admiration of Thorwaldsen, and he published his estimate of them. Immediately Powers took his place among the great sculptors of his time. After this his studio in Florence became the resort of all Americans visiting Italy. Hawthorne said that all the travel from both Europe and

BIRTHPLACE OF HIRAM POWERS.

JACOB COLLAMER.

SOLOMON WOODWARD.

ANDREW TRACY.

P. S. WASHBURNE.

America flowed through it. In his Italian Note-Book, the great master of romance gives ten pages to Powers. He had not so much to say of any other one person in all Italy—not even the Pope. Hawthorne said of Powers: "I hardly ever before felt an impulse to write down a man's conversation, as I do that of Powers. The reason may be because I find it possible to do it, because his ideas are square, solid and tangible, readily grasped and easily retained." George S. Hilliard said of him: "No one could meet him, even casually, without feeling that he was a superior man."

With eyes undimmed and spirits unabated, George P. Marsh and Hiram Powers worked till the end came, and at the close of long and eventful lives, around which the halos of glory had clustered, these two men, who as barefoot boys had played together among the stumps in the streets of Woodstock, side by side, laid down for their final rest in the sunny soil of Italy.

During the years which make up the second third of the present century Woodstock reached the fullness of her life. The elements which were then blended no longer exist. Other forces have come in and are working out results which some other observer will report.

One of the most noticeable results of that energy was the establishment of the Vermont Medical College. This institution flourished for a quarter of a century, graduating half a thousand physicians, a large majority of whom have done creditable work in their profession.

In the days of its prosperity, the faculty in this medical school was acknowledged to be second to none in New England. At its head was H. H. Childs, president of the medical college at Pittsfield, Mass. Then there was Alonzo Clark, afterwards president of the College of Physicians and Surgeons in New York, Elisha Bartlett, of wide fame as an author, whose rare refinement as a gentleman was only equaled by his great learning, and, not

less notable than these, E. M. Moore, Chester Dewey, and B. R. Palmer, — a Woodstock boy, acknowledged to be the equal of any man in the country as a teacher of anatomy. These were all strong men and did thorough work. What there was to be known of medicine and surgery at that day the graduates of this school *had* to know. Into the founding of the school went the best energies of Dr. Powers, Dr. Gallup and Dr. David Palmer, and their names, equally with those mentioned, will be held in grateful remembrance as long as there is any man to remember the Woodstock of those days.

It is a notable fact that, as in the first years of the first third of the century there came four able men to take part in the activities of the new town, so early in the second third

THE BILLINGS HOUSE.
RESIDENCE OF F. S. MACKENSIE.

there came four other men, who ably carried on the work begun by the first comers, heartily blending their energies and their fortunes with those of Woodstock in the days of her highest prosperity. These men were O. P. Chandler, Andrew Tracy, Julius Converse,

more convention in 1840, and had he chosen the political field he could have had any place in the gift of the state. In his fibre Mr. Chandler was of the very finest grain. In manner always gentle and urbane, he never willingly wounded the feelings of any man. He was always in love with what is best in literature and delighted in keeping abreast with the advanced thought of his day. Strong in his friendships, he never deserted those who trusted in him. In intellectual keenness he never grew old, and at the end of eight and eighty years his mind was as fresh and vigorous as in the dew of youth.

In 1838 another lawyer came to Woodstock. He was tall, thin and angular, and looked like a consumptive well on the road towards the end of life's journey. His head was well formed, and a pair of cold, piercing gray eyes lighted up a face which was pale and cadaverous, never showing the least color except under excitement. This man was Andrew Tracy,

and Jacob Collamer, all lawyers. Mr. Chandler began his professional life here; all the others had won for themselves a good professional reputation in other places.

In coming to the bar of Windsor County, Mr. Chandler met men equal in ability and technical skill to any in the state; yet he soon proved that he was able to take and hold a position which brought him a good business and secured the respect of his professional brethren. The town told what it thought of him by sending him to the Constitutional convention in 1835, five times to the House, and three times to the State Senate. He was sent to the Balti-

probably the greatest jury lawyer the state had then produced. Quick in perception, swift in applying legal principles to facts, expert in sifting the essential from the non-essential elements of a case, gifted with a nervous eloquence of terrific power, he could handle a jury as few men ever could. Their sympathies and their indignation

QUECHEE GORGE.

seemed alike at his command. In the use of sarcasm the state never had his equal, and it is doubtful if he ever had a superior. His will power seemed without limit. It kept his body alive many years after, judged by all ordinary human experiences, it should have been dead. On one occasion, when his physician told him he could not get well, he peremptorily sent him out of his house, never afterwards had anything to do with doctors, and continued to live on another quarter of a century, dying at the age of seventy-one.

Julius Converse came to Woodstock in 1840, and the law firm of Tracy & Converse was formed.

THE WOODSTOCK INN.

In 1849 the firm was further strengthened by the admission of James Barrett, who remained till he was chosen to the supreme bench, where he served the state as an able judge for nearly a quarter of a century. He is now enjoying the fruits of a serene old age at Rutland. In every line of professional labor Mr. Converse was an able lawyer; but he did his finest work in cross-examinations. He served the state two years as lieutenant-governor, and in 1872 was chosen governor. He died at the age of eighty-seven.

The name of Jacob Collamer is known in every part of the land; his fame is national. Mr. Collamer had already been three years on the bench of the Supreme Court when he fixed his residence in Woodstock, in 1836. He had at that time taken his place in the front rank of the lawyers of the state. If ever there was a man of whom it could be said that he knew the principles of law by intuition, that man was Jacob Collamer. What most men discover only after long and wearisome study, he *saw*. Where others had sight, he had insight. Every legal fact stood out to his vision not only with a clearly defined individuality, but also in its true relations to all associated facts; and through them all he saw the true end of law, and never lost sight of it. If possible, his moral vision was clearer than his mental insight. What justice and equity called for was never obscured by the demands of the law.

THE PARK—TOWN HALL AND WOODSTOCK INN AT THE LEFT.

When he found himself in Congress, Judge Collamer was fifty-three years old, and opened his eyes upon an entirely new field of labor. Taking for his guide that broad common sense which had never failed him, he discharged his duties in the House so satisfactorily that at the end of six years he was invited to a seat in President Taylor's cabinet. But it was during his ten years' service in the United States Senate that the true greatness of his character as a statesman was seen. Lincoln early chose him as a confidential friend and counsellor, and as such retained him till his death. But better than the astute lawyer, more to be honored than the honorable judge, higher than the wise and trusted statesman, was Jacob Collamer the man. Those who knew him in all those relations are still asking: "When will the man be found who can take up and becomingly wear the mantle Judge Collamer let fall?"

In 1844 still another addition was made to the strong legal force already established in Woodstock—the firm of Washburne & Marsh. This was the rival and successful competitor for business of the firm of Tracy & Converse. Both these men proved themselves able lawyers, and worked in singular harmony till the death of the senior partner in 1870. Though Mr. Washburne gained and maintained a high professional reputation, it is for the splendid services he rendered the state during the civil war that Vermont honored him and will remember him. Some years previous to 1861, Mr. Washburne had organized a military company, and when the war opened he had under his command a company of finely drilled men. The Sunday morning after President Lincoln called for troops to defend the capital, in April, 1861, Mr. Washburne marched his company into the old white meeting-house, where all joined in the solemn service of prayer and praise, and the next day started for Washington. He was made lieutenant-colonel of the first regiment of Vermont troops, and afterwards promoted to the colonelcy, returning at the end of three months' service. Soon after his return he was appointed adjutant-general of the state, in which office he served with unexampled efficiency, and as the result Vermont enjoys the reputation of having furnished the fullest and most accurate returns of her soldiers in the war of any state in the Union. General Washburne was chosen governor of the state in 1869, and died in office in February, 1870.

The story of Vermont in the war has been well told elsewhere, and Woodstock is there given her full credit; but it may not be known to every one that a Woodstock man, in the person of Dr. Stephen Powers, served as surgeon at the battle of Bunker Hill, that five others served in the Revolutionary war, all becoming officers and one a colonel, that ten marched with General William Henry Harrison in his Tippecanoe campaign, and that two Woodstock boys hauled down the Mexican flag that floated over the castle of Chapultepec.

Her professional men, brilliant as they were, did not do all the work in the making of Woodstock. The names of a score of men laboring in workshops, in stores and on farms could be given who, in their devotion to the highest good of their town, never fell behind any one of those already named.

When Vermont concluded to establish a state bank, it found here men to whose management its affairs were entrusted. When this institution ended, another bank was established here by the citizens of Woodstock, which for more than three-score years has been so managed that its stock has never been below par or any deposit when called for, ever refused.

When the state, in the year 1800, was looking for a man whom it could trust as her treasurer, it found such an one here in the person of Benjamin Swan. Mr. Swan managed the finances of the state so successfully that he was elected for thirty-two consecutive years; and when the state settled with him, not one dollar entrusted to his keeping had ever been lost. This man lived such a life that when he died every poor man in the town mourned for him, because "Major Swan" had been his personal friend.

The largest single impulse ever imparted to the industrial interests of Woodstock was given by Solomon Woodward, when in 1847 he came here, bringing with him eleven families, any one of which would have been an addition to the social life of any town of that day. Mr. Woodward turned the powers of the Quechee river

to making cloth, and for thirty years did a successful business, making and scattering with a lavish hand throughout the community hundreds of thousands of dollars. The town has sadly felt the loss of the industry which Mr. Woodward established and which was ended with his life.

One industry was originated in Woodstock whose full development required more than town or state domain.

The first "express" line ever established in the country ran from Woodstock to Windsor, Vt. This line was started and managed by Alvin Adams, a young man who had served a term of years as stable boy at Robert

WOODSTOCK CHURCHES.

Barker's tavern. What the Adams Express Company has since become everybody knows.

Conservative, dignified, proud of the fame of her public men and of the ability and enterprise of her men of affairs, Woodstock was calm in her consciousness that the state could show no spot where a richer life could be found. There was no noise or foam in the fullness of that life. Her quiet streets were shaded by wide-branching elms, and her green lawns rested in their freshness and peace. The houses of the poor stood by the side of the homes of those not so poor, and in both in the morning young women baked bread and in the evening entertained learned men and intelligent women. Professional and industrial life shaded so naturally into each other that no irritating line of demarcation was seen or felt. No microbe had entered that peaceful life, and no father or mother was allowed by their neighbors to watch alone by the side of a dying child. The self-assertiveness of modern money was not known there; neither was there any miasm of idleness, breeding the pestilent mildew of rural discontent. Other towns could point to their mechanical productions; Woodstock was content with the men she produced and the life she enjoyed.

The changes which have come over Woodstock in the years of this last third of the century have mainly been like those experienced in many New England towns during the same period. Steam and the electric wire have produced their harvest, but with no more thistles than in the general fruitage of those prolific seeds. The evidences of thrift are everywhere seen. Three miles of concrete sidewalks make neighboring gossiping easy even in mud times, and in the evening the incandescent lamp sheds its cheerful radiance through every street, while an abundant supply of the purest water responds to every one's call. As of old, in the center of the Green, the shaded park smiles in quiet repose and invites the weary to rest. Without the stimulus of any Village Improvement Society, the citizens in recent years have voluntarily adopted a thorough system of out-door housekeeping, so that in point of cleanliness and little touches of local attractiveness the most fastidious eye of the new-comer would find little to suggest.

On the spot where once stood the refined and hospitable home of Norman Williams, his son, Dr. E. H. Williams, of Philadelphia, has erected a library. In architectural beauty and completeness and in fine and fit appointments it has no rival in the state. With ample endowment to keep its shelves always supplied with new books, with its doors wide open to all comers, itself an inspiration to all who look upon it, it stands, with the uplifting and refining influence of its treasures, to abide forever.

Among the changes which have been made in the immediate vicinity of Woodstock village, the greatest are those which have been wrought by Mr. Frederick Billings, on the old Marsh homestead. Taking the old mansion house, built in the early years of the century, Mr. Billings reconstructed and enlarged it into an elegant modern structure, suited to its commanding situation and the beautiful scenery which surrounds it. The original farm of two hundred and fifty acres has been enlarged by additions from time to time till the estate now contains about fifteen hundred acres. In this estate is included the whole of Mount Tom, which rises abruptly just west of the village, and from whose top one looks down six hundred feet directly into the village streets. Leading to the very summit of this mountain, through gorges and deeply shaded groves, wind fifteen miles of smooth, well kept carriage roads. Through the kindness of Mr. Billings, these magnificent drives are open to the public at all times except Sundays. It was Mr. Billings who presented the choice library of George P. Marsh to the University of Vermont; and he also gave to the same institution its beautiful and costly library building.

Fronting directly on the park stands the Woodstock Inn with its accommodations for two hundred guests. This house came into existence in answer to the desire of many tourists who had seen some of the beauties of the Ottauquechee valley and urged that a summer hotel should be built here suited to such surroundings. In its structure, furnishings and appointments this inn is regarded as equal to any country house in New England. It proves a most desirable resting place for parties wishing to seek the country before the mountain houses are open, and also to enjoy the glorious autumn scenery after those houses are closed. Woodstock Inn has already established a reputation as a charming winter resort. Dwellers in Montreal have found here a snugger winter home than their frozen zone affords, and lovers of snow-shoeing resort here from the Atlantic cities to revel amid the beauties of Woodstock's winter scenery.

Radiating from Woodstock are fifty miles of practically level roads unsurpassed for smoothness and freedom from sand and stones. Here is a paradise for bicycles. These roads lead along the river banks or follow the winding of the mountain brooks, where at every turn a new surprise is met, a suddenly opening vista, or a restful, shady nook, under wide branching trees. If one is a lover of mountain scenery, let him drive to Mount Garvin and drink his fill. To the north is a tumultuous ocean of mountain tops stretching away till land and sky meet in a far-off misty line. On the eastern horizon stands Belknap mountain, shepherding his flock of three hundred islands in Lake Winnipiseogee; while in the far southeast, "Cæsar of his leafy Rome," rises the sharp summit of grand Monadnock. Along the entire western horizon sweeps the rugged wall of the Green Mountain range, whose outlines on the evening sky form one of the grandest sights in all New England.

Thus planted by nature and cultivated and beautified by art, all who visit this mountain town will carry away a picture which will not soon fade. But, as the green on the grass of November when the glories of summer have fled, as the fragrance of roses where the footsteps of beauty have passed, so will linger the memories of Woodstock in the hearts of all those who have lived in the midst of her beauties and drunk in the richness of her life.

11
Old Roads of
New Hampshire

OLD ROADS IN NEW HAMPSHIRE.

By William H. Stone.

Illustrated from photographs made along the old roads.

THE dew had not gone from the grass nor the fragrance and freshness from the bright May morning when I turned into the old road. It had been located a hundred and twenty-one years before.

"Then Laid out by the Proprietors Committee a Certain Highway on the East Side the Mountain Beginning at the South Line of the Town a Little South of the Dweling House of Benajah Taylor in the Third Range Leading North West wardly by trees marked with four Noches and Leading to and by the House of Josiah Kilburn in the Second Range thence Northwardly by trees Marked till it falls in the Dividint Line of the Second and third Ranges and then to be one Moyety on the one Side and the other Moyety on the other Side Sd. Line till it Coms to the North Side of the Sixty acre Lotts Said Highway is Laid four Rods Wide and to be and Remain an oppen and Publick Highway."

It became the principal highway of the town, a part of the old "County Road." But now a little stream issuing from a spring in the hillside meandered down the oozy roadway at its own sweet will, undisturbed by the roadmaster; and a little farther on slender poles, weather-stained and with thin bark hanging in strips, stretching across the roadway between tall mortised posts, said plainly, "No thoroughfare." Apple trees, masses of pink and white, were arched overhead; and through the bordering trees, over a stone wall on one side and a brush fence on the other, I could see the white bloom in the orchards. As the road began to ascend the hill, rough, gray stones protruded among the grass and gravel; and beyond the bars the wall had fallen in places, leaving the road open to a pasture that, set with young pines mottled by the light new growth at the ends of the branches, stretched upwards to a wood radiantly golden as the morning sun

streamed through the young foliage. On the other side was a green-gray pasture slope with noble sugar maples and young pines, its farther part outlined against the clear spring sky, on which a low wild growth was projected in brown. A brook of sparkling water crossed the road with a cheerful gurgle, the stones in its bed varnished by the clear water. A little island was populous with blue violets, and the bank of the stream was gay with tiny bluets, white violets, and dandelion blossoms. Swamp maples near by were great masses of red, the winged fruits quite overpowering the green of the leaves.

So I wandered along the old grass-grown road, by damp spots where the dark soil was deep-trodden by cattle, and along cow-paths which here and there were worn through the grass at the side of the road-way, and then the road ran steeply up through a little valley in whose bottom a stream babbled musically, which I could see coming over the rocks farther up, with a cool and pleasant sound. There was a luxuriant wood on the upper side of the road. Close at hand were great rocks sparkling with bits of mica or trickling streams of water, or speckled dark with lichens and deeply shaded by the forest. How sweet was the wild-wood fragrance, how tender the green of the grass, all starred with strawberry blossoms, how shining the leaves of the white-stemmed birches! How the birds sang!

Soon the road entered a damp, shady wood sprouting with rolled-up woolly osmunda ferns, and rank with vegetation, where birches and maples crowded upon the hemlocks, and where herbaceous plants battened on the remains of former growths. The thickets had begun to press close upon the narrowed roadway before it turned a little to the left and, now high upon the hills, again infringed upon the pasture lands. I could see for twenty miles to the south, over the great valley to the misty hills, which, clothed in perpetual forests, rose shadowy to meet an overhanging band of warm, gray-white clouds.

The brook that I had followed up the valley came laughing from the shady pine-carpeted wood, and I left its music with regret. The grass-grown road ran along beside a stone wall whose quartz stones gleamed clean and white among gray, weather-stained ones; and after a time hemlocks and sprouting swamp-maples pressed so close upon it as to leave only a narrow path among them. Here the grass could not grow, and

Above the gay, mottled forest, across a wide intervening valley, was a range of dark hills, and above the hills miles away a stern and mighty mountain dominating all the scene. Its pasture lands and forests and barren summit were but faint variations of color, as seen through the morning haze. There was little perspective to its slope, and it seemed to rise a mighty, sheer, gray wall against the whitish fog clouds beyond. Farther to the right, over and through the noble

the leaves lay thick and brown and crisp along the path. The stone wall now gave place to a straggling fence made with poles running between stakes driven in the ground and crossed; and this fence seemed to run across the indistinct path, and beyond was so dense a growth of pine-saplings that I feared I should not be able to trace the old road farther.

There were, however, faint traces of a road running by a maple orchard and over the brow of the hill that had been to the west of the valley through which I had ascended. So climbing the fence I followed the ill-defined track to the brow of the hill. Before me a forest scarcely broken by woodmen's clearings was variegated by all the tints of May. In the forest, dark-green, almost black, spruces rose tall and symmetrical. Then there were the lighter greens of the pines and dashes of red from the maples and through all the golden gleam of ashes and oaks.

sugar maples that stood adown the slope, great rounded masses of cleanest verdure, I could see the spreading white heads of the apple trees set among the greens. Still farther to the right I saw the roofs of buildings shining in the sun, in the valley below, and then more apple bloom; beyond, down on the plain that lay stretched out long and wide, houses and trees and green meadows were basking in the sunshine; and still beyond were more mountains in the haze. Soft, foaming clouds were along the horizon above the mountains. Nearer on the slope of the pasture the leaves

rustled on the trees as the elated wind swept up the hillside.

A rock pasture it was, all set with gray boulders and mottled with grass

and ferns. As I turned my eyes from the abounding luxuriance of nature that was spread before me, I was surprised to see but a few rods down the slope what seemed to be a grave-stone set in the rough pasture, the grass growing quite to its b a s e; and there seemed to be other stones overthrown near by. Going to the stone over the y i e l d i n g turfs where the dried grass sounded crisp beneath my feet, I found a weather-worn stone of dark slate flecked with yellow and green lichens. The stone inclined edgewise very much, and a conventional weeping branch was at the top. I could read the inscription, and date, 1791. Some long spears of grass pressed close against it, as if to shield it from the ruin that had overthrown the other stones that were scattered about de-

faced and broken. Another stone had at the top "Memento Mori" and a face with wings in place of ears, an abbreviated angel apparently. The inscription was: "In Memory of Revnd Josiah Kilbourn who w a s Minister of Chesterfield in ye Bay State he D e c d Sept. ye 24th, 1781, in ye 29th year of his Age;" and below: "He who cheapens life abates the fear of Death." A part of the inscription could be made out only with difficulty. A third stone was broken off near the base and leaned against another whose inscription was not legible. Upon it I read: "In Memory of Mrs. Jemima

Kilbourn ye Wife of Mr. Ebenr Kilbourn. She Decd June ye 25th 1765 in ye 21st year of her Age." Fragments of other stones protruded from the sod, and others or portions of them lay flat on the ground. On one

wilderness to look over the ground. Here the agent of a land speculator got them bewildered in the woods, and kept them wandering for several days over the level land that lies along the river. Upon returning to Connecticut they reported to Mr. Kilbourn that the township was very level and free from stones. Influenced by this report, the elder Kilbourn joined with others in the purchase of eighteen thousand acres of land in this region. This was in 1761. In the fall of the next year, or earlier, he came to his purchase with his son Ebenezer; and they spent the next winter and the summer following in clearing the land, building a barn and preparing a cabin for their families. The next winter they were in Connecticut, but in the spring of 1764 returned with their families — Ebenezer and Jemima Ford having been recently mar-

stone in large characters, within an elaborate border, was the maker's name and the price of the stone, seven dollars.

The earliest date upon the stone carried my thoughts back to a time when the hills about were part of a royal province, when the primeval forest that then covered them had only just begun to fall before the settlers' axe. Who was this Jemima Kilbourn, who was laid here in a solitary grave so many years ago? Neglected as is her last resting place, something of her history is still preserved. Jemima Ford, afterward Jemima Kilbourn, belonged, it is said, to one of the wealthiest families in Connecticut — from which colony many of the early settlers of southwestern New Hampshire came. Her future husband's father, in business with her grandfather, had there acquired considerable wealth. Desirous of becoming a large landed proprietor, he sent men up here into what was then a

ried — and with a large number of cattle and sheep and several horses. They are supposed to have been the first settlers in the town. A grant of the township had several years before been made to residents of Massachusetts; but, principally because of danger of Indian attacks during the French and Indian war, which ended only a year or two before the Kilbourns began to clear their land, none of the grantees had settled upon the land conveyed. The Kilbourns' cabin, sheltered by the hills and near

a little brook, stood in the valley that lies just below the old burying-ground. On the plain a few miles to the south of it the monotony of the wild forest was broken by scanty clearings; to the north a sea of wilderness stretched away, tossed into huge billows of interminable greens. There are traditions of hardships endured by the Kilbourns during their frontier life.

During the first winter when the two men lived alone in the wilderness, they are said to have come short of provisions and to have been in danger of starvation. Ebenezer Kilbourn's young wife was not able long to endure the exposures of her new home. She died only a little more than a year after her marriage; and on one June day when on the forest around the tender adolescence of spring had just passed into the maturity of summer, she was laid in a lonely grave in a forest clearing on the ragged edge of the wilderness.

A few years after removing from Connecticut the Kilbourns built a frame house, the first in town, a little way from the cabin and only a few rods from the entrance to the old road up which I had come. Ebenezer served as lieutenant in the Revolutionary army. He had married again; and his wife was left at the house with four young children, a blind girl, her husband's father, now a helpless old man, and a large number of cattle and sheep to care for, with only the help of two large dogs, which had been

its original location, then in use as a sugar house. The frame of huge oak timbers was visible and showed the shape of the rooms and the immense size of the chimney.

Once more I looked over the forest, green and golden, the blooming orchards, the grassy fields and the hazy mountains, and then resumed my wanderings. Decrepit apple trees, not too old, however, to bloom in May,

trained to drive cattle and which were a protection against wild beasts. It is said that, on being suddenly ordered to march, Lieutenant Kilbourn's company gathered at his house. Having found that many of his men had not necessary provisions, he put two bushels of flour into kneading troughs, heated two large brick ovens, and started fires in all the fireplaces. His wife prepared the bread, and what she could not bake in the ovens she set around the fireplace. In a short time the men ate hurriedly from long tables in the yard, and, taking in their knapsacks what was left, marched away. A part of the house could have been seen a few years ago near

were a little way from the sadly neglected burying ground, and there seemed to be the ruins of a house near them; but on getting to the spot I found that little besides a depression in the ground and a confused heap of stones was left of what was once a home. Not a scrap of timber was to be seen, and only a few bricks were to be found, and they were mostly buried in the sod. What a wealth of shade was in the maple orchard, where the great trees throw their leafy boughs over the greensward dotted with strawberry blossoms and dandelions!

When I got back into the road which I had followed up in the morning, I found it so nearly obliterated by the growth of low pines at the point where I came back to it that I had doubt as to which way I should go. But upon a low hill ahead I saw a clearing set with apple trees, and among them, rising like some monument, a great pile of stones; so I went to the field and up over the velvety greensward, where cool, dark shadows were under the apple trees and beauty upon them. I came first to an old well, now covered; and, peering in, I saw the clouds and sky imprisoned far down in the earth. The pile of stones proved to be a chimney, — and what a chimney it was! Its top had fallen, but at the base it was seven or eight feet square. It was built of rather small, flat stones laid in clay.

Near the chimney were what appeared to have been a walled barnyard, the remains of a barn foundation, and one great mortised beam. There was a walled terrace about the cellar hole, and in the hole, now choked with stones, some low trees and elder-bushes were growing. Just outside the terrace wall there were ancient-looking currant bushes and rhubarb plants, — former dependents of man, now, undefended, sorely pressed by the all-encroaching grass, — and a thicket of raspberry bushes; and between the chimney

One fireplace, its roof supported by a large wooden beam partly burned, was still undisturbed; and on each of two other sides of the chimney there seemed to have been a large fireplace, now ruined and filled with stones.

and the former barnyard were great thrifty beds of smooth, thick-leaved live-for-ever. There were great clean-washed rocks close by; and the fields were free of stones, which had been piled upon the walls or in great heaps,

which are to stand maybe for centuries as memorials of days of tiresome labors.

Once, I doubt not, there was litter enough about this spot. The soil was long vexed by the plow and hoe; and there were unsightly heaps and ragged footpaths in the grass. But left to herself Nature had scoured the rocks and sent up the grass everywhere. She had set about slowly converting the great timber into mould for grass to grow upon, and for the meantime had painted it a soft, unobtrusive gray. She had partly filled the stiff rectangular cellar-hole with picturesque heaps of stones, and cast over it a drapery of graceful shrubbery. How calm and peaceful the old farm lay, flooded with the warm noonday sunshine! For miles and miles along the horizon, to the south and west, the mountains were ranged in gentle undulations or swelled up to noble forms.

Then I went in search of the old road down a grassy lane bordered by birches and an apple tree that was all pink and white buds, with scarcely an expanded flower. Climbing over some half decayed rails at the foot of the lane, I judged from a stone-wall on one side and the vestiges of a fence, now lying flat and half buried in dry leaves and withered ferns, on the other, that I was in the old road again. The road closely pressed by the forest ran beneath the cool shade of hemlocks down into a valley all shut in by the hills. Over the tree-tops I could see a sad wound made ahead in the bright forest by wood-cutters, but beyond were more grass lands and apple bloom. Great thunder-heads were majestically riding over the hill ahead, their snowy fronts glorious in the sunlight as they foamed into the azure. The road, now smooth and grassy, with a well-trodden pathway in it, kept still down and crossed a brook, where the cool, clear water fell over the mossy stones, and climbed a grassy slope beneath pines, where a partridge scurried across the road and where the deep shade was refreshing.

Passing through a kind of gateway where the logs that had continued the fence and crossed the road were thrown to one side, I seemed to be approaching a residence; for the fields

were smooth beyond and the walls were piled high with stones. But when I had climbed to where the house had stood, I found that it had become a fallen ruin. Seating myself on a mortised sill that still remained in place, I could look

spears of grass grew up between and waved over them. Studs and joists, laths and shingles were scattered about in sad confusion.

It is interesting to call to mind the history of one of these old abandoned New Hampshire farms.

For years and years, — who shall say how many, — before white men came to this new world, these valleys had been filled, and these hills covered by the dense primeval forest. To the forest the seasons had come

down the valley and over to the hills far away. A more beautiful afternoon could hardly have been. The leaves and branches were all rustling and waving in the woods around as the refreshing breeze swept up the valley. A yellow butterfly went zigzagging over the emerald grass; and the sun poured through the translucent oak leaves, making trees near by great masses of leafy sunshine. On one hand was a hill with low trees and bushes scattered over its slope, on the other was the beautiful forest. One side of the house lay flat on the grass, its timbers all exposed, like the bleaching skeleton of some great animal. Long

and gone. In spring purling rills ran joyfully down to join the swollen brooks that flowed by leaf-strewn banks or by drifts of melting snow. By the streams alders lengthened their stiff, brown catkins into swaying, tawny pendants. Willows were decked in downy white, and then in gold. Swamp maples became great masses of red flowers. From the varnished buds of aspens the

out; and then the more uniform green of summer was over the forest. In the damp, umbrageous wood old tree-trunks were turning to mould to furnish nourishment for the saplings that struggled upward to the light above. Some were moss-covered, and perchance half hidden by a straggling growth of hobble-bushes. From the white trunks of birches the papery bark hung in great sheets that flapped in the winds. Dead trees crowded out in the race stood ready to fall, or were supported by the arms of sturdier brethren. Huge trunks lay prostrate, with great gaunt arms thrown up as if in agony at their doom. Soft beds of moss and delicate vines were under the trees. By running streams and on rocky ledges, clumps of small mountain maples bore their dense racemes of white flowers.

crimson masses of stamens protruded; and, when these had lengthened and faded, the trees stood in the bare woods like clouds of rising smoke. Then fresh young leaves came on the branches. Birches with delicate foliage were hung with long golden tassels. The leaves grew apace, and imparted to the old forest a variety of tints rivaled only by that of autumn. Dark spruces and golden oaks and ashes, dull aspens and shining bright green birches, dark green pines and hemlocks, and the late coming whitish, woolly leaves of the larger aspen mottled the wilderness. The new leaves darkened as they matured, and the evergreens grew lighter as the new growth came

In swamps were white-blossomed viburnums; and by the margin of ponds that in the wilderness shimmered in the sun of early summer the wild azaleas flamed. Where the forest was darkest, strange corpse plants gleamed among the moulding leaves pale and ghastly for a time, then turned dark and dry. The summer waned, and autumn came, and the wild forest blazed in red and yellow. Then the fires went out, and sombre hues were over all the land. The leaves fell from the trees, floating down in zig-zag courses or borne away by furious winds. Then the winter came; but the winter sun did not look down, as now, on fields of dazzling white, but on sombre-green and gray-brown for-ests. Only on the lofty mountain top, or where the river wound among the trees, or where the marshy meadow or frozen pond was set in the far-spread-ing forest, could you have seen a broad expanse of snowy whiteness.

Thus the ancient forest measured off the years. Silent it was, for the most part, save for the sounds of run-ning water, or the undulating murmur of the wind in the tree-tops. Some-times, had we been there, we might have heard the cry of a jay or the chirping of a squirrel, or the tapping of a woodpecker; sometimes the dry twigs must have snapped when a shaggy bear shuffled through the for-est; sometimes there might have come to our ears the horrible howling of wolves.

Of human inhabitants, in latter times, these hills had few or none; but to the east and south there dwelt In-dian tribes that maintained themselves by hunting and fishing and by a stinted cultivation carried on among dead, girdled trees that rose gaunt and wind-broken in the green wilder-ness. At length Englishmen came from over the sea and settled along the sea-coast, and began to cut down the forest, to burn it, and slowly, very slowly, to drive back the wilderness, destroying the hunting grounds of the Indians. After a time, embittered by the encroachments of the English, the natives closed in fearful warfare with them. Overpowered in this, many of them withdrew away to the north,

there to nourish their hatred for the victors. There, along the great river that flowed from the inland seas, Frenchmen had planted themselves, rivals of the English for the trade with the Indians and for the possession of the country. They gathered the fugi-tive Indians in missions about them and made them allies in war on the English. Urged on by the French, the savages again brought the horrors of Indian warfare upon New England. Accoutred for war, perhaps led by some Frenchman, they filed through the New Hampshire wilderness to pounce from the forest like a panther upon lonely farm-houses and frontier settlements. Fortified houses were assaulted and their inmates slain. Men about their work were shot down or taken captive by skulking Indians; children at play were carried off; cat-tle were killed. Sleeping villagers woke to find themselves the captives of savages, to see their homes burnt, their friends slain. Captives were tor-tured, women and children forced to endure terrible marches through the snow-covered wilderness. The infirm were struck down, children had their brains dashed out before their mothers' eyes.

Troops went out from the English settlements, perhaps to traverse the vast and rugged New Hampshire wil-derness without being able to discover the wily foe, perhaps to destroy some deserted Indian village, perhaps to fall before some Indian ambush, perhaps, besieged on the shore of some lonely pond in the northern wilderness, to fight a desperate battle with savage foes and then, leaving wounded men to die in the unpitying forest, to struggle through weary miles of wil-derness to the settlements, or to fall exhausted by the way.

So, with intervals of peace, nearly three quarters of a century passed. There was little to induce men to leave the less exposed colonies below and make homes in the New Hampshire wilderness. Families that in an inter-val of peace sat down among these hills, on the renewal of hostilities fled, burying such of their property as they could not carry away on horseback or leaving it a prey to the enemy. But at last the decisive struggle for dominion came. Wolfe died victorious; Canada was conquered. Now captives returned and joyfully greeted friends from whom they had been long separated. Now the wilderness might be settled without fear of Indian forays.

Chuk—chuk—chuk! What sounds are these that break the stillness of the forest? Chuk—chuk—crash! Day after day the axe is plied; tree after tree comes crashing down. From some straight trunks the settler built a cabin. Great columns of smoke rose high above the clearings or drifted dense before the wind. At night fitful fires glowed red in the smoky atmosphere, and for weeks the air was heavy with the smell of burning forests. Among the blackened logs and stumps, in holes made in the loose soil and ashes, the settler planted corn; or wheat or rye mixed with grass seed was scattered on the ground. Where the scorched trunks lay scattered over the clearing grass seed was sown alone; and this, springing up, made pasturage. Quick-growing stalks of fireweed sprang up in the burnt lands and were cut down, or, undestroyed, grew to man's height, injuring the crops. Then fields of waving grain grew rank in the accumulated mould, and in turn gave place to mowing. Where the unconsumed trunks lay among the stones and stumps cattle grazed in the lush grass, or lay in the shade of the bordering forest.

So, where the old forest had stood fields of grain and grass spread over the hills. Fences were made, barns raised; orchards were planted; stones gathered into heaps or piled into enduring walls. In place of the log cabin a commodious house was built. Years passed. The royal province of New Hampshire became the State of New Hampshire. The early settlers died; another generation passed and

yet another; but the old house still stood, — yet all deserted now. Old men had died or become too feeble to labor, and there had been none to take their places. It took nearly a century and a half to settle sparsely the hundred miles of wilderness between the old house and the sea. Events have moved faster in the century and a quarter since. Great cities have risen a thousand miles to the west, and the tide of emigration has flowed quite across the continent. Railroads have been built, bringing the products of the deep-soiled prairies to the East; and these old farms, grown sterile, are abandoned now.

For a time the old house stood unrepaired. Its sides grew more weather-beaten; its shingles curled up: its windows became empty of glass. You might have wandered, unannounced and unquestioned, in at vacant doorways and through deserted chambers, meeting none but such as your imagination summoned from the past. Unlatched doors slammed mournfully and sent weird sounds echoing through the empty rooms. Rains beat in; beams rotted. At last, on some fearful winter night, attacked by roving winds, shuddering and groaning, the old house fell.

The road now turned abruptly to the right and ran past a picturesque wood-cutter's shanty with wide, ragged eaves. Dry brush was heaped against the north side, where green boughs had been piled for protection against the winter winds. Soon I opened a high gate, balanced with stones on the end of a long pole and, passing through the door-yard of a farm-house, came into a traveled highway. Soon, however, I found an untraveled road leading through a barred gateway nearly opposite the farm-house and into a young wood that arched overhead, through whose leaves the sun poured richly, mottling the leaf-strewn roadway beneath. After going through a mowing field and through a wood, where there were many drooping, yellow, lily-like blossoms of bellworts and delicate whorl-leaved star-flowers, the road pitched down into a deep valley.

Near the brow of the hill was the spot where the first meeting-house in the town had stood. The town historian, whose researches added much to the pleasure of my walk, says that in this house "the people gathered in time of the Revolution, to form patriotic plans and to enlist for the defence of their country," and that it "was built like an old-fashioned school-room, with seats raised at the back and sides for the singers, and boards laid upon movable blocks below for the rest of the congregation. The men and women sat on opposite sides facing each other." The spot was quite overgrown by the forest. Near what was once the centre of the building, an oak tree had grown until its trunk was about fifteen inches through.

Going down the hill, I could look far ahead and see the road running straight through a shady tunnel beneath a lofty bank of green formed by the interlacing boughs of great sugar maples. At the foot of the hill, on a grassy knoll surrounded by blossoming apple trees, was a one-story wood-colored house, which I could see was vacant. The window-sashes were gone or broken, the roof was sadly sagged, the shingles had risen up, and the clapboards were all awry. The old fireplace still stood, and the rusty crane was swung over the hearth, now littered with brick and mortar. A part of the flooring had dropped into the cellar; but one room was intact, except that some plastering had fallen. Sad disorder reigned through all the rooms. There was a great clump of lilac bushes covered with purple bloom on one side of the grass plot in front of the house, and a wide-spreading maple on the other. It was a pleasant spot, where one could look over the deep valley and high hills beyond to the great mountain where now, as the sun lighted up its sides, the forest could be distinguished from the barren rocks. Near by a little brook

moistened the grass, and everywhere from the spongy turf the blue violets were peering.

The house stood upon a grass-grown road apparently somewhat traveled, running at right angles with the one over which I had come. This road soon crossed a large brook that flowed by with an obtrusive gurgle and then fell with a mimic roar into a large pool among great fallen rocks overhung by trees. The shadows were stretched across the road, which ascended to the south, streaked with grass and wheel-marks. Not before had I found the ever-present apple blossoms so fragrant. Along the damp roadside, willow catkins, shedding their downy seeds, had the appearance of large white blossoms. At the top of the hill, after passing two more spots where homes had once stood, I came upon the remains of two houses that had been taken down not long before, where bricks, boards and timbers were gathered in unpicturesque piles. Great hewn beams still spanned one of the large cellars, supporting the ruin of bricks, boards and plaster.

One unacquainted with the history of the house might have judged that others than plain, hard-working farmer folks had lived here; for near the ruin, besides the lilacs that still bore their wealth of purple bloom, there were down in front thickets of tall rose bushes and copses of spireas, which spread into the grass and thrive and bloom so long after those who set them out are gone, and other shrubs and trees of species unknown to me. One of the houses was indeed somewhat famous in its day and was known as the old "Fish Place." It had stood upon a "minister lot," a part of the share of land set apart by the town's charter for the "first Settled minister of the Gospel." The Rev. Elisha Fish, a graduate of Harvard, who with his wife, a sister of the poet Bryant's mother, had come from Massachusetts, built the house in 1794. Here he lived for many years, and here he died. He was the first minister settled by the town, — in those days the minister was employed by the town and supported by taxes, — and was voted "Fifty Pounds to rise with the levy of s'd town to Sixty pounds lawful money for his annual Salary."

Now about the ruins of the house the grass was growing rank. A tall larch tree supported an aged grape vine whose matted tangles had dragged the lower branches of the tree almost to the ground.

Soon the sun went down behind the western forest on the hill above, and the shadows ran far out into the valley below. That evening my way led over another old, discontinued road that ran for three or four miles through the woods, with here and there an overgrown clearing. Prostrate trees were across the path, and in the dark I could see the cherry blossoms gleaming white in the thickets. A nighthawk fell overhead; whip-poor-wills called to one another, and from the wood came the sweet notes of a thrush.

———

12
Maple Sugaring
in the Northern Woods

MAPLE SUGARING
IN THE NORTHERN WOODS

By HAMILTON PERCIVAL

PHOTOGRAPHS BY E. A. WOLCOTT

THE lengthening hours of sunlight, the blue of the sky, the rosy afternoon flush upon the naked branches of the woodland, the honeycombing snow—all tell to the initiated that the icy bonds of winter will soon be broken, and sounds of joyous labor resound through the snowbound sugar places of the northern woods. Here and there patches of bare brown earth peep through the snow, edged with a fairy lacework wrought by the sun, and the soft rushing of many little rills, formed from the melting snows, sound gently upon the ear as they flow swiftly down the slopes to join the truly brimming river.

This is the sugar season; the gala time of the north.

Although the primitive and romantic fashion of boiling sap in a huge kettle slung over an open fire has passed away with other things of a like nature, yet the sugaring time is still a season of joy and activity to all living within range of the camps. The first step in the manufacture of maple sugar by present-day methods is the preparation of horse-sled roads, which begins as soon as the first heavy snow falls in early winter. A wooden roller, similar to, but of greater diameter than, a land roller, about eight feet in length and with driver's seat on top, is drawn through the woods in given directions. This packs the snow down solid as well as makes a good foundation, and after every heavy fall the process is repeated so that roads are formed that will not slump when heavy loads of sap are drawn in the thawing days of spring.

As the weather becomes warmer in March, buckets and spouts are overhauled, washed and put in order, to be in readiness when wanted. These buckets are usually of tin, holding about fifteen quarts each, and often covered, although many wooden open ones are used by small and less painstaking manufacturers. Loaded upon sleds,

the buckets are drawn out over the prepared roads and distributed among the trees of the orchard. Sometimes this is done when the snow is still so deep as to necessitate snow-shoes, but the wise old sugar makers tell us that sap will not run until the snow thaws away from the base of the trees; and I have known ambitious sugar makers, lured by a few days of spring-like weather, to scatter their buckets and then not be able to find one of them for several weeks, because a big snowstorm had buried them two feet deep or more.

But finally there are some warm, sunny days. The nights continue sharp and frosty, but the sun comes up with a smiling face and the wind is south and mild. This is ideal sap weather, and the whole working force is at once mustered to tap the trees and hang the buckets. Holes from one and one-half to three inches deep are bored on the south side of the tree with a half-inch bit, and into these are driven round tin spouts, with hooks attached on which the buckets are hung. If the sap starts briskly and the day is still, one can stand in the sugar-house door and hear the measured drip, drip, drip, until the bottom of the empty bucket is covered. In the most up-to-date places the sap is gathered each day; the big monitor draw-tub, so called from its resemblance to the celebrated raft, being drawn along the roads and filled by relays of men who collect the sap from tree to tree by big pails slung from a shoulder yoke. When the "monitor" is filled it is drawn to camp and emptied into huge holders having cloth strainers on top to catch any foreign substance which may have fallen into the sap. Where the orchard lies on a slope the sap is frequently conducted to the camp through pipes, and thus much of the hard labor is saved and a part of its picturesqueness lost.

The camps are frame buildings, well roofed and ventilated and boarded, but

Tapping the Trees.

having large front openings for the escape of steam and the admission of plenty of fresh air. In the center of the building stands the evaporator, and this machine marks the difference between the old and the new method of making sugar. No more kettle hung over a fire built on the ground in the open air. No more pan set over a stone or brick arch, but a long, shallow vat with corrugated bottom set upon a long iron stove. Entering this vat through a regulated feeder, the sap flows

In the camp is usually another iron arch, smaller than the one that holds the evaporator, designed to hold a deep pan for sugaring-off purposes. When enough syrup has been made for a batch, it is placed in this deep pan and a fire built under it. Then is the time when the sugar maker has plenty of company, for his message sent around the neighborhood, "We are going to sugar off at two o'clock; come over," finds plenty to respond.

The syrup in the pan is boiling up a

After a Snow Storm.

down one corrugation and back another until it has traversed the entire number, boiling furiously all the time, and is drawn off, a thin, sweet syrup, to be strained through felt and set away to cool. It is possible to evaporate a much larger quantity of sap by this method than by the old way; some of the best machines are guaranteed to evaporate a pailful a minute; and a pailful (fifteen quarts) of sap will make about a pound of sugar. Sap varies in sweetness, however, and a machine is seldom run to its highest limit, as it requires an expert to avoid scorching the syrup.

beautiful golden brown, with a fragrance that makes our mouths water. The ladies stand about with saucers and spoons, and when the sugar is at the consistency that best pleases them they present these saucers to be filled. The men and the boys sit around on the woodpile, each busy with knife and a birch or maple chip, from which they are fashioning paddles, so-called, with a deftness born of much practice, and with evident knowledge that there will be use for them later on. The children (there are always children), snowball each other outside.

Washing the Buckets and Sap Holders.

Gathering Sap with a "Monitor" Draw Tub.

Gathering Sap with Yoke and Pails.

The master of ceremonies stands beside the pan with a bottle of sweet cream and a big dipper. When the bubbling sweetness threatens to overflow, he throws into it a few drops of cream and it immediately retires to its proper place.

The bubbles become larger, form slower, and break with a little spiteful puff. "Will it lay on snow?" chorus several; and the boys bring buckets of snow and some hot sugar is poured over them. It cools without sinking. It will lay on snow. The boys are now on hand with their paddlers, the children come trooping in, and the buckets are surrounded by a noisy, saucy group who speedily clear the snow of any trace of sugar and loudly call for more. The dipperfuls of sugar that are cooled on that snow and then disappear would drive a stingy man frantic. The man at the pan calls for a twig of birch. One is brought him, slender and supple. He ties the end into a loop and dips it into the boiling sugar until he catches a film in the loop, then he carefully blows upon the film, and when he can blow bubbles through the loop the sugar is done. Some test with a sort of thermometer which registers the density, but a good sugar maker can always test with a twig. When this stage is reached, there is much hurrying and several men step forward to help. A crane is fastened on to the handles of the pan and it is swung away from the fire to a platform. The men, the ladies too, gather round, and some stir the mass with huge paddles, others pour it from the big dipper. The more it is agitated while cooling, the whiter and finer-grained it will be. A very popular method of eating the warm sugar is to dip a big paddle into the mass, whirl it quickly around several times in the air to prevent it from dripping, and cool it to waxiness, then scrape it off in mouthfuls with a small paddle. A big snowball is also used in the same manner. The buckets are kept well covered, and each one eats his fill in one way or another.

By and by as the sugar begins to cool it begins to grain, or granulate. It is then turned into tin or wooden pails and left to harden. The company fall to with the paddles and "scrape the pan" of the last remnants ; and then go trooping home, usually rather sticky as to hands and face, and dirty as to clothes, but happy as grigs and with appetites for supper that require instant attention. There is a brisk demand for sour pickles at that meal, and no other time when they taste so good.

Boiling at night, as in the old days, is no longer necessary; but though safely locked and left alone in the darkness of the woods, the camp is not always free from intruders. It is no unusual thing, when not too far from the village, for it to be invaded at night by a merry band of boys and girls armed with lunch baskets. Then hoisted upon the shoulders of a companion, the lightest weight getting in through a window, opens the camp to his party. Soon the fires are replenished, eggs boiled in the sap, ham roasted over the coals and syrup filched from the cans to sweeten the repast. Nothing ever tasted so good in all the world, and the number of eggs that under such conditions even one boy will make away with is amazing. If there be several in a family, the elders are lucky if they succeed in capturing eggs enough at that season to properly clear their coffee.

Sometimes the man who looks after the boiling and camp affairs goes out to help gather sap, leaving the evaporator to tend itself for a time. Usually the last thing he does is to stuff the stove with wood. If he stays beyond the time the syrup needs drawing, a smell of burning sugar will be borne through the air to the man out of place, while over the neighborhood people sniff and remark that somebody is burning his evaporator.

There are other accidents that are not accidental and are fortunately of rare occurrence. A maker sugars off a big batch late in the day and leaves several hundred pounds of sugar and honey locked in the camp, thinking it safe until it can be moved next day. In the night a big light in the woods marks where a camp is burning; but there is no smell of burnt sugar this time in the air.

Sap does not run every day, but only in "sap weather" as described. Sometimes there comes a cold, stormy time, lasting a week or ten days, through which the trees will be frozen and no sap run.

The old sugar makers divide the season into "runs," some of which are characterized as follows: a "robin run," after the robins come ; a "frog run," after the frogs begin their nightly chorus; and a "bud run," after the leaf buds begin to

Sugaring-off Arch, and Pan Swung Off the Fire—Ready for the Scraping.

swell. They also expect a good run every time the moon changes. They sometimes get badly left, but will always explain satisfactorily to themselves, at least, why the sign failed that particular time.

The product of the last, or "bud run," is usually very dark, very high flavored, and will not grain. Dip a paddle into it and begin to wind, and one can wind until the tub is empty, unless one takes considerable pains to break the waxy thread. When there is such a tub of sugar in the house there is usually a paddle or a spoon near at hand, and it is often visited by the

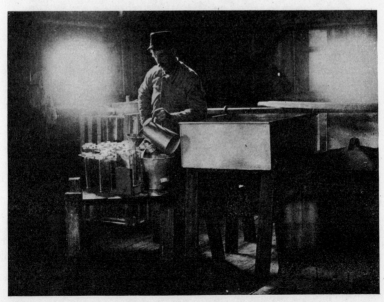

Filling the Cans with Maple Honey.

different members of the family, more particularly the boys. There is little of that quality manufactured nowadays. The seasons have changed largely and there is usually no sap after the robins make their appearance; and none is saved after the buds start. The season's make is nearly uniform in quality, very light in color, and of delicious flavor. It varies in quantity from one to three pounds to a

leaf area and freedom from insect ravages. From two per cent. to four per cent. of the total sugar present is removed during the sugar season by the ordinary method of tapping, though it varies with climatic conditions. If we consider three pounds of sugar the tree a good yield, there must have been about one hundred pounds of sugar present. Maple sap averages, say, three per cent. sugar, so the tree would

Waiting for the Sap to Run.

tree. The first is a small yield, the last a good one. Vermont sugar orchards vary in size from five hundred to two thousand trees, and the season lasts about four weeks. The per cent. of sugar which could be taken from a maple tree, without injury, cannot be definitely stated. It would depend on many conditions, notably whether the previous summer was favorable to growth and consequent storage of starch, from which the sugar is formed,

contain some thirty-three hundred pounds of sap.

As to this—I remember a family living on a farm where there was no sugar place. They had in their yard a mammoth maple tree, whose wide-spreading top drooped its branches over a large area. The woman of the house conceived the idea of cutting the ends from twigs and hanging gourd-shells under them. With the children's help she soon had the old

There are always plenty of helpers at the sugaring off.

tree decorated like a Christmas evergreen, and during the season she made fifty pounds of sugar from that one tree, and the tree none the worse for it that any one could see.

Much of the product is put up in gallon cans as maple honey. It is of a pale amber color, clear as crystal, and of a peculiar flavor that no one who has ever tasted the genuine article will mistake. A large proportion of the "Pure Vermont Maple Honey" put upon the market never saw a Vermont sugar place. In proof of my statement I cite the fact that signs advertising "New Vermont Maple Honey" will be displayed in city grocery windows while Vermont is still buried to her chin in snow and ice. Last year's tub sugar is melted over and largely adulterated with glucose and sold for the real thing.

The sugar output has not been so large as usual for the past three years, owing largely to the damage done the sugar maples by the forest worm; but the worms were not so numerous last year and a good sugar season is predicted for the present season.

Maple sugar making is a more extensive industry than might at first be supposed, the annual output of the country being 51,000,000 pounds, with 3,000,000 gallons of honey; of this Vermont, small though she is, furnishes more than any other State. Over seventeen per cent. of the granulated sugar produced in this country comes from maple sugar.

Scattering Buckets.

13
The Marble Mountains

Drawn by Edwin B. Child.

"FILLING THE PIT WITH BOOMING, ECHOING THUNDER AND FLYING ROCK."

SCRIBNER'S MAGAZINE

VOL. XXXVII   MAY, 1905   NO. 5

THE MARBLE MOUNTAINS

By Edwin B. Child

ILLUSTRATIONS BY THE AUTHOR

"GOIN' to shoot in there. Got about twenty or thirty holes we've got to fire." It was a tall, gaunt Yankee overseer in a mountain marble quarry, and I was asking what the unusual look of things meant. I had hung around this and other quarries for days at a time, and this day was different. The noisy clank of cutters and drills was stilled, and a number of machines had been loaded on cars where the skewy track came elbowing out of the quarry pit, giving somewhat the look of a May moving.

"You ain't goin' to touch 'em all, air ye, Ed?" queried the Blacksmith, who, like all native Yankee quarrymen, always calls the foreman familiarly by his first name, abbreviated. "Got eighteen filled, and I can touch nine. If the other feller's as good as I be, we'll git 'em."

"Guess the fust 'll come pretty near bein' warm before you git round," said the Blacksmith with a grin.

"Ed" looked at him dryly. "Once I touched twenty-two and a 'cotton' alone." A grim twinkle came into a corner of his near eye, and he spit with precision at a chunk of marble. "The fust one *was* pretty nigh burnt when I touched the last, and I wa'n't a hell of a ways out of the quarry when they begun to pop." And he stalked away around a pile of refuse marble— "refuge," Sim Jenkins called it—to another part of the quarry.

So I learned that they were about to blast away a layer of stone that covered a lower pocket of marble in a part of the pit hidden by the buttressed entrance. Before I got in sight of the men who were tamping in the charges there came a sudden sharp explosion, followed by somewhat involved diaconal oaths that belong to Vermonters, and back around the turn came the overseer, running with ashy face, followed by other men, fearful of a premature explosion. Luckily no harm was done, though it had been a close call for young Abe Slocum, lately graduated from water-boy to helper. The scare made "Ed" reminiscent.

"No, nobody ever got hurt blastin' in my time. Once when we was gettin' out a slice up there jest below where you see that derrick"—and he pointed to where a flying buttress of marble seemed to bolster up the mountain at one side of the entrance, a striking piece of natural architecture left by the accident of cutting away the marble each side—"you know we had a way of strippin' back the cotton an inch or so, an' then shakin' out the black paowder. We had about a dozen holes to bust up there, and jest as I had touched two or three, I heard a kind of a 'siss' behind me, an' I sez, 'Gosh, boys, she's in the paowder!' We had to git up about ten or a dozen feet of ladder to git out of that hole, and we didn't stop long. We'd jest got over the edge when the place was pretty well filled with pieces of rock. You can bet I give that feller a combin' thet stripped that cotton. He said they was just goin' down in to find us. They'd heared the blow and didn't see us in the smoke. I told him he'd better git his mind on strippin' his cotton ruther'n goin' down in holes pickin' up pieces of humans. Then we went back and fired the other nine."

Here again our gray is harnessed to a sweep.—Page 517.

In a short time everything was ready. The men were gathered in groups well out of danger, a great shoulder of the mountain protruding itself between us and the charges. The foreman and his helper, Bill Crandall, had gone in with red-hot irons that the blacksmith had been keeping ready, and had come out again on a run, he having touched his nine and one more; for Bill had made but eight. It was a bit thrilling, the explosions following each other irregularly, tearing, wrenching, rending the ledges, filling the pit with booming, echoing thunder and flying rock, some pieces going sky-high and landing far up the mountain in the woods. Dense clouds of smoke and dust followed, against which were silhouetted the foreman's lank figure as he stood with his stocky helper, keeping count, well in advance of the men. As he counted he noted by "That was a good poke" or "Somethin' lifted then" the blasts that were doing what was wanted. "Yes, I kin tell pretty much whether they're liftin' the rock right or jest shootin' off for show. And I caount 'cause it's jest as well to know if all the holes has blowed," he continued. "I

wouldn't want to set down where one was hangin' fire, and it's pretty hard to tell, when two or three go off together, jest how many they be."

"No, 'taint dynamite. We use black paowder: it breaks the rock up better. Dynamite is so sort of sudden: it's apt to crumble everything up into dust in a little hole, and then it's so powerful it strains the hull maountain. It might run a crack right through a good vein of marble, and besides in this quarry we have to look out for the roof of our tunnel."

This quarry of which "Ed" Hooker was the overseer is perched high up on the side of a steep mountain, and reached by a rough road that zigzags its way laboriously through side-hill pastures and sugar-maple woods, past a dingy line of quarrymen's houses, adhering with apparent uncertainty to the steep slope, their front-yard flower-gardens nearly bumping the eaves, and the pig-pens and chicken-yards almost hanging from the cellar walls; then the road curves itself up to where the quarry rears its white cliffs. The open cut is a pit only in part. The marble mountain has been sliced down until, in the rear, the white walls have become precipices from which drop thread-like cables from tall derricks, whose power is steam, or the steady circling of a big gray horse, seeming as unconcerned as a goat or a burro, as he pulls his sweep to the edge of the cliff. Through the pit from the entrance wanders a track, vastly uncertain as to its curves and wilful as to its abrupt changes of grade, carrying single-truck cars on which the blocks are loaded by the far-above derricks and run out to their big plunge down the mountain-side.

Here again our gray is harnessed to a sweep, first to shift the blocks from the small car to the cable, and then to start that car forward to the verge of the incline, where its weight begins to tug at the cable drums with their four great brakes, and the counter-balancing car that is bringing up its load of coal and other supplies. A full mile this incline plunges straight down to the railroad in the valley.

"You can ride if you want to," said Hooker; "I won't charge you no fare, and I won't insure your life. If she should fetch loose she'll go hell bent for 'lection. There won't nothin' stop her this side of Jericho. She never broke but once, and that was after she'd been runnin' seventeen year. It's near seventeen more now, and I shouldn't wonder if somethin' was about due."

In striking contrast to the open cut are the tunnels, where the same veins of marble are reached by burrowing into the heart of

Wide shadowy caves whose narrower entrances are deep-set eye-sockets in the face of the white cliff.—Page 518.

things in wide shadowy caves whose narrower entrances are deep-set eye-sockets in the face of the white cliff. Their wide vaulted roofs are supported by piers and walls of marble, left as the quarrymen drill their way in. They are huge and handsome, but seem too infrequent for safety when one sees the enormous span of the cave roof and considers the weight of mountain overhead.

"There's lots of places in this here tunnel where I wouldn't work, not for tew dollars a day," said the Blacksmith; and he pointed significantly to some large slabs forming a part of the tunnel floor and to the reversed imprint of their shapes overhead. "Bill Jenkins was considerable flatted out a couple of years ago when a ton or tew fell on him—right over there where that broken cog lays. We was comin' out together, I was just a leetle ahead, 'n' he was talkin' 'baout the loose scale, an' he chucked his drill up at it. 'Twas jest enough to start it, an' gosh-fer-a-mighty, but if I wa'n't close! It fanned my hair and ears, an' de'yer know his heart came aout jest like a piece of note-paper. Well, I went off and didn't come to till after they'd got him out. After that they fixed things up some. They knocked off all the loose scale and was pretty keerful for a while; but that don't last long nowheres." By which I saw that the Blacksmith was something of a philosopher.

On rainy and lowery days the work is trying in the tunnels. The steam and smoke thicken and hang heavy, so that the men can with difficulty see each other at arm's reach. It seems uncanny to stand by the half hour within ten feet of a gang of men, your ear assailed by clatter and din of cutters and drills, the hissing of steam, the scraping of shovel and clang of iron bars on stone—hearing the voices of busy contented men, or their united grunts as they heave together, prying at some stubborn stone, but seeing nothing. Look toward the entrance, and the fog lessens a bit; shadowy forms come suddenly out of the gloom walking on fog; a silhoutte of horses, both exactly the same fog color, though one is black and one white in the open. The top of a crane with no base shapes itself out of the smudge, swings a block of fog-colored marble toward some fog-colored men, who guide it to a fog-colored car, on which the foggy horses drag it out into daylight.

With a shift of weather the sun gets the better of the clouds outside, and almost at once the thick smoke and steam are gone. Everything becomes strong, definite, and bold. Powerful lines of natural rock cleavage run riot overhead. In a shadowy corner a torch that was helpless against the fog glows on the men who are mending or adjusting some tool with its aid, and a block of marble that the derrick has lifted from its long sleep of thousands of years comes pearly white from its bed. Close by, outside, is the big dump, its side tumbling down the mountain like rip-rapping on a great river-bank, its top a fine wide level which grows larger with each season's added waste. Here in the summer, overlooking a splendid sweep of the valley that divides the Green Mountains from the Taconic Range, the men from the tunnels, where not even active work prevents the damp chill from penetrating to the bones, come to sun themselves while they eat their dinner. They are not unconscious of the beauty of the place—"Sightly" they call it "Ain't it slick and neat?" said the Blacksmith.

Nearly all of the men at this quarry are Yankees, men whose skill and intelligence are varied and who do not need overmuch bossing; who can, and often do, turn from quarrying to farming or house-building or plumbing or running a river-boat on the Hudson, or even managing a hotel for the unwary summer boarder. Among the young and husky quarrymen old Nathan Weeks looked misplaced. His close-cropped chin-whisker was white, his shoulders narrow, and his movements slow. It seemed that a restful sunny front porch would be a more fitting place for him than a quarry-pit.

"He does move tarnation slow," said the Blacksmith, "but he's the best man in the quarry yet. He don't need no talkin' to nuther. He's alwuz thar an' knows what he's up to, and he can do more'n the best man next, whatever it is. There ain't a man in the caounty can chop as many trees in a day as he can, and every stump he leaves is as slick and smooth as if he'd planed it. It don't make no difference how fast the rest on 'em start, he's alwuz the fust to the top of the maountain, and he never stops to breathe himself before he puts his axe in. I remember seein' him once pullin' a big stone for the underpin-

Drawn by Edwin B. Child.

Powerful lines of natural rock cleavage run riot overhead.

nin' of his barn. He'd yoked up a big pair, weighin' a ton apiece, to the stone, with 'baout fifty foot of chain, and the oxen daown in a mess of brush in a gully, and he'd swing his gad and throw them oxen inter the yoke and stop 'em when she'd slid jest an inch and a quarter. Another quarter would 'a' ripped the whole inside stuffin' out of everything. By gum, you couldn't put a leaf between the stone and the sill he'd drawed to! And he's jest as good anywhere in the quarry. He looks sort of peaked and old, but he's awful tough. Did you ever go to one of his meetin's? You'd oughter have. His father was an old Methody exhorter, an' he kinder inherited it. He used to have meetin's in the school-house over in Spanktown Holler, reg'-lar. But it got so't folks would go to laff jest hearin' him pray and he give it up. Gosh, but Silas Way ketched it once! The old man got up and he sez: 'They's some folks thet don't know any more abaout missions than Brother Silas over thar.' Then Silas he quit goin'."

The Blacksmith threw down the last of the bunch of drills he had been sharp-ening, settled down on a bench near the door, filled his pipe, and went on.

Nathan Weeks.

"'Way up in the end of the Holler, near where them big pot-holes is that you've heared about, Uncle Nate's father used to have a quarry where he an' Nate used to git out a few small blocks the best they could in winter. They didn't have no sech tools as we have nowadays, but they'd manage to split 'em up and smooth 'em down with old pieces of grin'stone and sech like, and bimeby they'd git a bunch of pretty likely lookin' head-stones. Sometimes the old man would set to work and fix up one or two off extra. He'd cut a bunch of leaves with the stems stickin' right out so't you could see 'em jest as plain—or a harp with strings to it. I tell you they was awful slick and neat. Then he'd load 'em up in his wagon and go peddlin'. Sometimes when folks was real healthy he'd git a good ways off, clear to Ohio, 'fore he'd get sold aout.

"Well, one day they found a new vein of marble in the quarry. You know they didn't have no way of corein' the way we do now, an' 'twa'n't easy to tell what was under you. Anyhow, he'd found enough to make him think he was fixed. He wouldn't have to git rich, he could jest sit down an' be rich. So when he got home that night he sez to his wife, 'Miss Weeks,' sez he, 'yer needn't to wear caliker no more. Yer can wear bombazine fer every day naow.' Well, the next mornin' he went back to the quarry an' he found that there'd been a 'slide,' and his quarry an' his tools was under about twenty thousand tons of maountain."

The other old man of the quarry was "Be Num." He was bent and grizzled, and his man-ner of working indicated that he was kept on the job more for what he had been than for any present efficiency. But there was a slight twist in the ends of his moustache that did not belong to Vermont. "Yes, he's French," said the Blacksmith; "a 'Kanuck'. His real name is Alphonse Le Grande, but we all call him 'Be Num' for short. That's French for good man!"

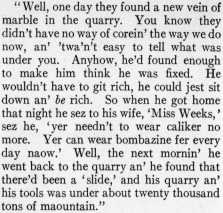

Deeper in the mountain, reached by an unlighted passage dubious to find one's way through, or by a farther out-side opening, partly covered by indiscrimi-nate masses of rock that have from time to time tumbled from the overhanging cliff, is an older tunnel, long since unworked. An irregular squat column of singular charm of color and shape supports the entrance. The interior is richly tinted by time and smoke and water. A shadowy pool fills the back of the cave, reflecting dimly its strange forms and mysterious beauty, the dimness and the mystery deepening until all disappears in veiled shadow that has no boundaries. Figures look unreal like the figures on the low-lighted stage of a great opera. It seems like a dream-setting for some scene from Wagner. A few notes of a Wagner *motif* from a child's treble voice float in high half-echoing vibrations, until they join the mystic shadow. And a

Shadowy forms come suddenly out of the gloom.—Page 518.

bass voice in an answering theme seems to come from and belong to the place. The figures move into the gloom and are still, and, in the silence, comes a beautiful liquid note with its whispered echo as unseen water drips, drips, into the pool whose surface shows no sign.

A line of men formed a long pulsating diagonal across the composition as they heaved rythmically at the end of a rope stretching over the yawning pit. The first man's foot was braced against the lower right-hand corner of my sketch-book, and the last man's straining shoulder smudged against the base of a derrick at the upper left; behind them the open quarry on the edge of which they were working. That was the way it looked as an arrangement. They were replacing a steel guy-rope that the night before had whipped itself loose under the strain of a too heavy load, and savagely lashed the marble within a foot of Cy Cole, the gang foreman, who was now bossing the repair of it, and who was at the moment hanging by a derrick hook half-way down the side of the sheer wall, rigging a block and tackle.

It was at one of the quarries that lie in the open valley, shining with dazzling white in the full glare of the sun, its great pits dropping into dizzying depths, cool, luminous, and clean, where men, looking like flies in a sugar-bucket, slop around in snow-white mud. Far down, black machines, puffing inky smoke from their rust-red stacks, clank heavily to and fro, chiselling deep grooves. Higher up, small battalions of cutters, spurting their criss-crossing jets of white steam, move across tables of rock to the very verge of the lower pits, but never going over. One always expects them to, seeing often no stops at the end of their projecting tracks.

Steam is everywhere, twisting its hot way through endless many-elbowed pipes that creep along ledges, drop into pits, climb dizzy walls, and wander about the quarry in drunken zigzags. It spurts itself out of every loose joint or leaky valve, watching its chances to puff at some unsuspecting bystander with a smother of dirty warm water, and then suddenly with explosive coughs it slams the drills into their grooves. It sputters in spasmodic gasps where the three-legged drills are worrying their way with bull-dog tenacity into the sides of the unsplit blocks, and urges the big pumps with wheezy groan to keep down the incoming water in the lowest levels. It puffs itself out in cloudlets that jump and climb, chased by blue shadows up the cream-white dazzle of sunlit marble walls. It plays little picture games, smothering a figure from view, but leaving his shadow silhouetted beyond. It gathers, on days of heavy cloud and misty rain, from all the machines in a dramatic sweep of white against the angry gray-blue sky and mountain. It screams out of shrill signal whistles; it roars its way out of safety-valves; it hauls endless steel cables on a dozen derricks and coils them snugly around the big drums in the engine-houses; it does a hundred busy things in a hundred busy ways, now with saucy impudence, now with vigorous, forceful emphasis, now with mighty resistless power.

Around the pit, stayed by a clumsy lace-work of guy-ropes, are perched the huge derricks, rearing their powerful arms against the big blue and white and green of sky and cloud and mountain. Its boundaries are piled walls of alabaster, sliced through by railroad tracks, on which snorting locomotives push empty cars up heavy grades for loading, or carefully take them down again with their shining burden.

Such a quarry is in striking contrast to "Ed" Hooker's. It seems more modern, though perhaps it is not. It may be the sensations one gets from creeping in near the heart of a mother mountain, where might be whispered secrets treasured through the ages, giving an element of unreality that disappears here where all is in open day. Differences in ways of working may be due only to differences of conditions; some ways of working will not do where land slopes at an apparent angle of forty-five degrees. One sees modern harvesting-machines—the kind invented in the big flat West—used in the valley farms, but they will not work on "Uncle Nate's" side-hill

"Be Num."

meadows, where to ride an ordinary mowing-machine is dare-devil boys' work. At any rate, it seems more modern. No horses toil around dragging heavy sweeps; no oxen heave their mighty backs straining to start heavy blocks, though even they are still to be seen in some quarries. There are no mysteries of mountain caves. Pictures there are, as are always to be found when sturdy men are doing their days' work.

Here the men are of all sorts—Yankees, French, Italian, Irish, Poles—some having their homes in the near-by farms and villages, where they and their fathers have farmed and quarried and lived the lives of good citizens for generations; others living in bunches in bare, raw, two-roomed boarding-houses, where all the sleeping is done in one room, and the cooking and eating in the other. They all seem to work together in harmony. Indeed, they display wonderful unanimity in dropping sledge or lever, shovel or chain, to start up the long ladders, like ants in unbroken line, when the noon whistle blows.

"Folks always say that these fellows do a lot of loafing," said the foreman, "and some of 'em do seem to stand round a good deal; but quarrying is hard work, and they all earn their day's pay 'fore night comes."

Much of the work is heavy and tiring, but by ten minutes after twelve dinner-pails are out of sight and a lively game of baseball is in progress, played with all the zest of school-boys relieved from several hours over books and whose blood needs stirring.

Back to their work they go at one, and it is a merry crew, full of jibes and horse-play, with now and then a dry Yankee joke slipped in where it will do the most good. There seems always time for a friendly interchange of snowballs, made of marble dust and water, that move with a degree of emphasis that makes clever dodging prudent. Back to the cutters that begin work-

Drawn by Edwin B. Child.

Start up the long ladders, like ants in unbroken line, when the noon whistle blows.

ing their way to and fro, channelling their vertical grooves to the appointed depth. Back to the drills that bore their horizontal holes ready for the splitting. And the splitting of a hundred-and-twenty-ton block of marble is worth watching.

The wedges, carefully greased, are inserted between their half-rounds in the drill holes, which for a horizontal split are neither close together nor very deep, as that is the natural plane of cleavage. Two men with sledges go down the line, giving each wedge a blow, not too hard. It seems at first a play at working, so deliberately is it done,

A bit too much haste, and the marble may split in a sharp diagonal, and what was to have been part of a cornice on a Fifth Avenue palace is ruined and goes to the dump. At last the crack is complete; and now a six-foot Milanese and a swarthy, stocky Yankee—for so the types sometimes run—smash the wedges in and the crack widens. Now the foreman marks certain wedges to be driven home, freeing the rest. For a bit the quiet deliberation has disappeared. With bulging eyes, out-thrust neck, open mouth, each gasping blow is given with all the power a man has, until

Heaved rythmically at the end of a rope.—Page 521.

with an unexplained wait between their turn and the pair following. After two or three rounds there is a longer wait while the foreman and one or two others examine carefully for a sign of a crack. Two more go down the line with steady swing, and in go the wedges a fraction of an inch farther. Now in places the crack begins to show, the rock has begun to lift. Then the foreman himself takes the sledge, and with beautiful precision places his blows, knowing just how much each wedge needs. For the crack must connect from hole to hole, through the entire twenty feet of the split. Carefully he examines the crack, and after a longer wait certain few wedges are chosen for an extra blow or two.

soon the long block is clear and ready to be again split into smaller blocks. For the vertical splitting the holes are drilled much closer and deeper, but the split being comparatively short, it is soon done and a block is free. Now to get the derrick chain with its four-inch links around the block. A steel bar, weighing two, three, or even five hundred pounds, needing a whole gang of men to handle it, is thrust into the crack; a long plank is placed, one end on the ground, the other end on the free end of the pry. Up on this climb the men in a slanting row, and, hugging each other around neck and shoulder, dandle up and down, thereby prying up the marble. Wooden blocks are thrust into the widening crack, and again

Two men with sledges go down the line, giving each wedge a blow.—Page 524.

and again the bar is raised, reset, and forced down by the tetering crew, until a four-inch iron ball can be rolled under the centre of the block. On this the marble mass can roll a bit to the side as the men mount the lever, and at last there is room for the big chain to be carried around the end of the block. The steam derrick does the rest, and soon the chain is adjusted around the centre. Every loose scale is knocked off and thrown down, for it is not pleasant to have loose bits drop off at the wrong moment.

"Where's she going?" asks the signalman. "Right on to the car; you can't better it," is the foreman's answer, and he looks with pride at the big cube. But as the chain tightens, he halts it, and signs to a group of men with busy cutters on a rock-table across the quarry. They shut off steam, and stop their machines' noisy row to hear his word, "Stand from under." The block weighs thirty tons, and is nearly up to the safety limit for this derrick. Up the block goes above the quarry, above the trees, above the line of mountain, and, shining white against the sky, begins to

circle over the pit, where men peer up from safe corners, and over the rock table with its deserted machines. It clears the top of the high wall of refuse blocks bounding the side of the pit, and then, poising a moment, drops gently to a car behind, next the power-house. There it is loaded to start on its journey cityward, to be chiselled and shaped for the cornice, perhaps, of the New York City Library, or to look twenty-three stories down on busy Broadway from a sky-scraper. Its luck, however, may be to tumble off the flat car at a curve of the track, to the disgust of a farmer who objects to having a dozen or more hills of corn ruined, and objects more to the necessity of breaking up what is now only a useless boulder.

We were talking together by the edge of one of the deep pits, the overseer and I (he was not called by his first name in this quarry; that doesn't do from "Guineys" and "Polaks"), looking down to where a gang of laborers were adjusting a derrick chain around a big block, when he suddenly raised his hand in a simple but striking gesture that for the moment had no mean-

Drawn by Edwin B. Child.

Up on this long plank climb the men in a slanting row.

ing to me; but the hoisting-engine, out of sight behind a pile of blocks, stopped as if he had had his hand on the lever. The signal man was far on the other side of the quarry, looking down, the boy who repeated his signals to the engine-house was watching him, but somewhere an eye was on the over-seer, and he had seen something unready that the men nearest had not discovered.

This way in which, amid the everlasting clatter and din of the cutters and drills, where a shout would be lost, the ponderous derricks with their huge chains are con-trolled, blocks are turned, raised, shifted, sixty feet or two inches, all by a slight motion or turn of the hand, is one of the most striking and impressive things in the quarries.

The marble genius is a clean and whole-some sort of spirit. He leaves no dis-figuring trail. Squalor, desolation and dev-astation, dirt and disease, discomfort and hardship, such as follow in the wake of many enterprises of men, are barred by him. His finger-prints are white, and everywhere you find them. He draws a white line down each side of a village green—marble walks for the villagers. He gives white un-derpinning to the houses and barns. White posts form exclamation points at the ends of fences. Cows chew their cuds behind stone walls of white marble. The Mill Brook comes tumbling into the village over a rich arrangement of natural marble steps; bridges cross it supported on piers of marble. Occasionally marble buildings are seen—barns, workshops, and less often houses, mostly old timers. The natural beauty of the stone does not always seem to satisfy. I remember an old one-story marble house that is carefully whitewashed each year. But perhaps many of us try to paint the lily more often than we think.

Clean and wholesome are the lives and work of the men. I know of no disease that comes to the quarrymen from their work. I know no finer air to breathe than comes to them on these mountain slopes. Like Uncle Nate, they grow old and are "awful tough." And I have never seen men more jolly and evidently happy at their work each day to the moment when the night whistle blows and they start for home on foot, or in shackly rigs behind good mares, or on wheels, up the valley road, in a mad, clattery race to the post-office and their daily pa-per, the setting sun making dusty glories around their bent shoulders and their baggy, overalled, pedalling legs.

The abandoned quarries are prodigal in pictures in the key of white, wonderfully varied. Near the base of "Mother Mer-rick" is an impressive one. Sweeping walls and steps of marble, once white, but with rich stainings of time and weather, surround wide-circling pools of water, lying tranquil and inviting, like the bath of some pre-historic king of giants. This in the fore-ground. Across the valley, shining white behind clumps of trees in the pastures, are the dumps of other quarries. High above on the opposite mountain glowing white and lavender blobs of color show the out-cropping of other veins, and over the tops of the mountains bits of cumuli push their nubby tops, repeating the varying notes of white in an aerial chord.

Some lie small and overgrown in deep woods, far from sign of road, some in the open upland, where the only paths are made by cows tracing their devious ways through the "pesky prairie weed." One is a dry, rambling excavation, gray and even black-ish in color, another a deep plunging pit, brilliant and luminous, filled with water of a still vibrant dark blue, rarely ruffled by the wind, reflecting the varicolored walls like a Claude Loraine glass, while in places the moss has massed itself in a fixed waterfall down the sheer side of the opalescent marble.

Up the mountain, on the western face of Owl's Head, are two shallow tunnel quarries whose supporting piers are large, severe, and formal, like something Egyptian. Time and weather seem here to have bleached and whitened, for nowhere is a stain or spot. Walls, roof, and floor are the whitest white, and the pools of colorless water reflect the white as white again.

Still higher, on the southern turn of Green Peak, are more quarries—the "Blue Ledge," "Deef Joe," and "New Opening," the highest of all. "Deef Joe" is on the edge of a precipice—a vast, quiet, open pit, with a majestic entrance where on a cautious ap-proach one may be greeted by the shrill whistle of a scared woodchuck or the angry scream of a red-tailed hawk. On a dead tree by the entrance I one day saw an eagle perched, while clouds were floating below

Drawn by Edwin B. Child.

A gang of laborers were adjusting a derrick chain around a big block.

us, screening the valley. It was here that a young mountain farmer—the very type, in thin-lipped, honest-eyed face and quiet, lithe movement, and even in the old long-barreled muzzle-loader he carried, of the famous Green Mountain boys of early days—told me a strange tale, a tale of a kind of peril not to be imagined among these rock-ribbed mountains.

He was after trout one day last summer, "'way off up in on the maountain," and had fished down a stream a mile or so, when he came to a place where the brook skirted close to an old dump, the scattered blocks fringing one bank. He was moving quietly along over the blocks, with his eye on his line and on a deep pool, where the piled white stone made the water swirl and circle, when his foot slipped, and to catch his balance, he jumped free from the marble to a swampy looking place just behind—wet feet being better than a barked shin. When he landed he went deeper than he had expected, and when he tried to get out he could get no foothold. For a few moments he struggled with no thought of danger, until he realized that he was thigh-deep and helpless. Then it became evident enough what had happened and where he was. The old quarry pit had been filled up by the overflow of the brook, which for years had carried in leaves and sand and dirt, forming a soft, oozy substance, partly overgrown by grass and sedges—looking as harmless as any of the frequent swampy, springy spots that abound on these mountains, but as treacherous as any storied quicksand. He did not know how deep the hole under him might be; it did not seem to matter much. Six feet would settle things as effectually as sixty, and meanwhile he was going steadily deeper. No house nor man was within miles, perhaps no one within sound of gun had he had one. Besides time was getting short.

He began to prod about him with the butt of his fishing-rod, which he still had in his hand, to see if anything solid were near. In a few moments he struck something hard, and pushing the mud and leaves away a bit, he found it was the end of an old plank, but far out of reach, and he more than waist-deep. He reversed his rod, managed to give his line a turn around the end of the plank, and then began gently, cautiously, to

pull. Would it budge? Would this soft, deadly ooze be soft enough to let the plank move? He was pulling every ounce he dared, and it yielded. It came an inch, and if the line held——! An old nail or the edge of the plank might cut it, and he was up to his armpits now. Slowly he gained on it. Gently he nursed it along. A bit freer it moved at last, when it came out of its mud bed, and finally it was within reach of his hand. But his shoulders were almost under, and the real battle was yet to come. For more than a half-hour he struggled, and bit by bit he fought his way out of the slimy clutch of the smiling green hole. He said he did not remember the last of it clearly. He remembered tumbling on the firm earth, but he did not know how long he lay there unconscious. He judged by the sun it must have been an hour. Then he crawled to the brook, got in to let the mud wash off, and after a half-hour in the sun to dry, started home. "No, I didn't say nothin' 'bout it to home; I didn't want mother'n the girls to worry."

On a rock at the top of the clifflike entrance to "Deef Joe," close under the dead birch-tree, where I like to think my eagle perches when I am away, I can look over a vast sweep of mountain region, clothed in wonderful varied verdure from the first tingeing of early spring, through the long weeks of green summer, and I reflect how slight a scratching of this verdant coat brings us to the underlying white.

Ed Hooker's blacksmith started the thought one day when I asked him how far a vein of marble ran. "Clean acrost the valley," he said. "There ain't no end to it. These maountains is all marble." And so it seems. This dotting of white villages, the outcropping white ledges in pastures and woods, the splotches of white where man has uncovered the crystalline stone, the fields bounded often by marble stone walls, make one think that the green coating is only a veneer, that the real mountains are as if the glaciers that covered the region thousands of years ago had in some way stayed, warmed and enduring—a white fairyland, cloaked shyly from the undiscerning by its shifting yearly coat, waiting for some poet to people it and give a new story to the children of the world, a story of the Marble Mountains.

14
Captain Joshua Slocum

At Home on Martha's Vineyard.

CAPTAIN JOSHUA SLOCUM

THE MAN WHO SAILED ALONE AROUND THE WORLD IN A THIRTY-SEVEN-FOOT BOAT

By CLIFTON JOHNSON

PHOTOGRAPHS BY THE AUTHOR

THE *Spray*, as I first saw her, lay gently rocking in a little cove on the Massachusetts coast near Woods Hole. No one could fail to recognize her as an unusual craft at once—such breadth of beam, such homely simplicity, such sturdy strength. Yes, that was the very boat, thirty-seven feet long and fourteen wide, in which Captain Joshua Slocum had sailed around the world. There were other vessels about—catboats, sloops, and yachts, but beside this one they appeared like playthings. The *Spray* could not compete with them in grace and style, yet she had an attractive air of domesticity and was evidently built for a sea home suited to all seasons and all waters and not simply adapted to fair summer weather along shore. It was a pleasure to set foot on her and note her snug appointments. It

was a pleasure to eat with Captain Slocum a rough and ready lunch that he deftly prepared in the little galley, and it was a pleasure when night came to bunk in under a deck awning and sleep on board. But, best of all, was a sail the next morning in "the old *Spray*," as her owner affectionately calls her, from the mainland across to Martha's Vineyard.

On the island at the village of West Tisbury is his home. This is not, however, his native region; for his birthplace was in Nova Scotia. There he began life fifty-eight years ago on a little clay farm overlooking the Bay of Fundy. The sea was two and a half miles distant, but it was in sight, and when the wind was right the boy could hear the waves breaking against the rocky coast. The sea was fascinating to him from the first, and he liked to watch the ships sail up and down the bay. The Slocums were nearly all sailors, and Old Ocean was always beckoning to the lad and claiming him as its own long before he began to cruise on its waters. But as a child he was a farm boy, and Nova Scotia farm life was then only one remove from pioneering. Cabins of logs were still occasionally in use, though they were considered rude and behind the times, and those who dwelt in them were looked on as "low down."

The houses all had big chimneys and depended on open fires for heat and cooking. "Yes," said the captain in relating this to me, "and what good things to eat came from those old fireplaces—oh! those barley cakes and those buckwheat flapjacks—oh!"

Captain Slocum's earliest experience as a navigator was gained on a placid mill pond about a mile down the hill from his home. Here, when he was nine or ten years old, he constructed a raft. It was customary among the farmers to use a knotty spruce log for the bottom rail of the zigzag fences, and three of these with boards nailed across made quite a substantial craft. Joshua rigged up a mast and sail and the rustic vessel carried him many a lagging voyage before the breeze; but he always had to pole back.

Shortly after he built his raft he began to go out on the sea fishing for cod and mackerel in a small schooner with a crew made up among the neighbors. He continued at home working as a desultory fisherman and farm laborer until he was seventeen, when he "slithered off" and started life on his own account in a Yarmouth tannery. He did not, however, find the change congenial and was often down on the wharves nights and Sundays climbing over the vessels. In a few months he had shipped for Dublin as an ordinary seaman and the next four years were spent on the Atlantic. Then he voyaged to California, tried salmon fishing in Oregon, went to China and Australia, and suffered shipwreck on the coast of Borneo. He was not long in becoming an officer and at the age of twenty-three was master of a California coaster. A dozen years later he had command of the *Northern Light*, one of the finest sailing vessels of its time. As a whole he had been remarkably fortunate and prosperous, and presently he bought a ship for himself—the *Aquidneck*—and

engaged in trade on the coast of Brazil. But things now began to go wrong and they culminated in the wreck of the vessel. It was not insured and he lost all he had gained in his long years of voyaging. He had come to consider New England his home, and to return thither with his wife and two boys who had been his companions on the ill-fated *Aquidneck* he concluded to build and navigate his own boat. So he constructed the *Liberdade*, a craft not much larger than a good sized rowboat, and in this the family made one of the most interesting and original voyages ever sailed.

They came safe to port and the captain started life anew. But misfortune dogged his heels and nearly every venture he made, whether on land or sea, turned out a dismal failure. He recalled many times that happy voyage on the *Liberdade*. It seemed as if the only way to be care free was to go on another voyage of that kind. The idea harmonized with his innate love of adventure, and he soon set to work building the *Spray* and at length started off around the world. The project had become known and through the kindness of interested well wishers he left Boston fairly well equipped except in the matter of money. In cash he possessed scarcely ten cents. This financial weakness several times threatened to cut short his voyage in the earlier part of it, but always some one came to his aid in the nick of time. Then he discovered that everywhere he went there was great curiosity with regard to the boat and its owner's adventures and plans. At a number of ports he charged a small admission fee. As a show the *Spray* was very profitable; but it was a severe task to handle the crowds and answer the multitude of questions. "I never worked so hard in my life," he says. "I would be dog-tired at night and drop right down."

To escape this labor he finally, in Tasmania, hired a hall and told his story to an audience, instead of repeating it to individuals on his boat. The lecture was a success and he frequently repeated it as he continued his wanderings. The result was that he returned from his cruise with a bag full of sovereigns and a new vocation. He had hardly set foot on his native soil when he began to get requests to relate his adventures for publication. These

The Lonely Lookout of the *Spray*.

he wrote out one winter living on the *Spray* in the Erie Basin at Brooklyn. He became intensely interested in the work and could do nothing else, often sticking to his task in the tiny cabin of the boat until after midnight.

The story, both in its magazine printing and in book form, was exceptionally successful and won for him a wide reputation. It is not only unique in itself, but it is told in a most engaging way. Its evident

loss of the *Aquidneck* and his subsequent hard luck that made him a writer, and he now declares that his troubles were all good fairies in disguise.

Of late the captain has become a thoroughgoing landsman and has cast anchor on a little Martha's Vineyard farm, where he lives on the outskirts of a rural village with several old sea captains for neighbors. His house is one of the most ancient on the island—an oak-ribbed ark of

The Crew at Breakfast.

faithfulness to the facts, its lucidity, and its never failing vim and humor are charming. The wonder is that a man with such a limited boyhood education, and who had been knocking about the sea nearly ever since, should be able to turn to authorship and express himself so forcibly and fluently. The only hint of a literary turn of mind that showed itself in his youth was a habit he had for a time of copying jokes and anecdotes that pleased him from the newspapers into a blank book. It was the

a dwelling with warped floors and tiny window panes and open fireplaces. Its aspect is at present rather forlorn and naked, but the captain knows how to wield the hammer and the saw, and will soon make it snug. In a single season he has become an enthusiastic agriculturist, is proud of his flourishing garden and would like to own and make fruitful all the land round about. He delights to point out the beauties of the sturdy oak woods which overspread much of the region, the prom-

The Slocums' Pleasure on Shore.

ising condition of the abounding huckleberry bushes, the possibilities of the wet hollows for cranberry culture and of the protected slopes for fruit trees, and he is sure the island water is the sweetest and purest in the world. Martha's Vineyard looks to him like Eden, and it seems likely the sea will know him no more.

So much the better for the rest of us if, as a consequence, we shall see and hear him oftener. The aroma and salt spray of Old Ocean are in his conversation and his writings. He has the power to invigorate and refresh, and the records of that round-the-world-voyage on the *Spray* and of that other long voyage on the *Liberdade* rank among the most enchanting sea narratives ever written.

15
Up in the Berkshires

Photograph by Mrs. H. H. Bergen.

There are, too, real farmers in the Berkshires.

UP IN THE BERKSHIRES

By VANCE THOMPSON

PHOTOGRAPHS BY CLIFTON JOHNSON

THE Berkshires traverse the old commonwealth of Massachusetts, and fall away into foothills in Connecticut on the one side and in New York state on the other. In a general way they run for a breadth of twenty miles through fifty miles of length. It is a pleasant land. And, as the traveler may, I know casually its ancient towns and hills, its lakes and trout-streams, and—what haunts one most of all—the secular pines exhaling an odor of resin.

There are two worlds up yonder in the hills—two races and two civilizations. One of them has got itself widely talked about. It dwells in spacious country-seats and rides the blooded horse—or drives him in a dog-cart; it speeds the French automobile and, indeed, does all those things that people *de haut parage* do world-over in the open places. For it the golf-links are spread. For it life moves in the stately, well-ordered English way. The homes of Lenox, Stockbridge and the lands thereby are rich in comfort and broad dignity; they might be set down in any English county you please and cause no undue measure of criticism. Wide parks and gardens and orchards and lawns, far-stretching avenues of hereditary trees, great stables and kennels, roomy houses, many-featured and time-mellowed; deer-parks and hunting preserves make of this fragment of the Berkshires a kindly and sincere—for imitation is the sincerest flattery—compliment to the Englishman's science of outdoor life. Nature has superadded tumultuous hills, streams that go lawlessly among the rocks, a sky of Alpine purity and forests still savage in their beauty.

The wealth that rolled into the Berkshires in the train of such nature-pioneers as Henry Ward Beecher and Hawthorne, has changed the face of things; the yellow hardback pastures have been turned into lawns and gravelly drives; the homely colonial houses and farm-cottages have bloated out into mansions; the staid villages have become annexes of Fifth Avenue, —jeweler, *modiste* and curio-dealer display their urban wares in the elm-shaded village streets. Enormous, shining in new granite dress, the modern mansions—the stony dreams of architects, mad for modernity and novelty—sprawl on the hillsides. The architectural spoils of Italy and the Lowlands, of Brittany and the Loire are thrown together in the smartest modern confusion. As you drive from Pittsfield to Lenox and on to Stockbridge you will admit—if you are critical and calm—that the landscape has been scarred with many monuments to bad taste. And it strikes you all the more forcibly because there are so many —so very many—old houses and parks upon which time has laid a patina of perfect beauty.

You, perhaps, may like these new mansions and pseudo-Italian gardens; and you may be right. After all, good taste and bad—in architecture as in literature and hats—shifts with the century. Invariably the taste of the epoch immediately preceding our own is bad. I don't know whether you have noticed it, but the rule holds in everything. The bad taste of the time of Pope was Shakespeare; the bad taste of Wordsworth's time was Pope. On the stage or in pictures we find pretty and odd and artistic the costumes and furniture of the early part of the nineteenth century; but the Victorian epoch—the dress and habit, architecture and furniture of the latter part of the nineteenth century—is already abomination. Bad taste, it would seem, is the taste of our fathers; good taste is that of our grandfathers or our own. The mansions that were set up in the Berkshires in the eighties and nineties of the last century seem hideous to our eyes, and we admire the whitish colonnaded houses of an earlier generation; doubtless our sons will admire them. By the same token these sons of ours will sneer at the things we are creating to-day. Our delicious boudoirs, our charming drawing-rooms, our ravishing costumes, our interesting novels, our fascinating plays— oh, oh! how they will be stuffed away into garrets, pulped into paper, tossed to the tides as mere shot rubbish. Our *l'art moderne*, our mission furniture, our *loggie* and Italian balconies—how the next generation will grin at them!

Fortunately more than one generation worked to make the Berkshires beautiful.

I remember one afternoon driving out from Norfolk behind a good bay horse, along a road that went uphill and down through a forest. One might have been miles upon miles from golf-links and casinos and Carnegian libraries. It was a wilderness of woodland. In one place there were faint ruins of an old farmstead—foundations and broken sidewalks overclambered by weeds and moss; notablest of all a little regiment of apple trees holding their own against the forest which had swept down upon the clearing—blotting out pasture and farmlands, blotting out house and barns, dooming the little orchard, which made, so hopelessly, its last stand. I have thought of it a thousand times—this homestead that the settlers of three hundred years ago captured from the immitigable forest now fallen back into its native state. As the good bay horse trotted on, I took off my hat to the gallant little orchard—the forlorn hope of civilization. And an hour brought us into a great, shaded street, sentineled by up-standing elms, behind which, on either side, sat broad, lofty, creamy-white houses, many-windowed, many-pillared stately old houses, they sat like dowagers on the sunny lawns. And this was the good taste of our grandfathers and their fathers. I shall not tell you the name of this old town. No railway goes near it. It lies alone in the hollow of the hills. A broad and gentle stream curves around. Once it was a rival of Hartford as a business center—in the days of stage-coaches. Now, in its ancient dignity, it is nearly deserted; old gentlemen in broadcloth coats and unfamiliar hats walk under the elms and converse; no automobile splits the serenity of the days into discord; no red-jacketed golfers speckle its surrounding hills; and this is a fragment of the Berkshires that I love best—perhaps it is the real incarnation of the Berkshires—perhaps here the spirit of the Berkshires, diffident and aloof, has made its last home, far from the modern cry cf life, the blare of the hunting-horn, the noise of common things. And Great Barrington only seventeen miles away.

Lenox, Stockbridge, Great Barrington, Pittsfield; round them and betwixt and between them, coils and swirls that life which society has created for itself in this part of the world. The "season" is divided as perhaps in no other corner of the pleasure-preempted world. "Society" comes up into the Berkshires the first of June—or, now and then, a bit earlier, when the wild beauty of May is on the woodland ways. And society kilting its petticoats, wanders afield, where the yellow violets are or (by way of change) where the white anemones dance on lithe stalks—so wanders, "going in for nature," making subtle and not immoral friendship with pallid ghost-plants in the moist woods, and—in gayer mood—with certain insolent columbines, that caper, red and gold, across the stony pastures. And so, having seen these things, waited, withal, until the yellow gorse began its riot, society shakes out its petticoats into decorous folds and gets away to Newport (where the sea is) or to Europe. And the great houses yawn emptily, deserted. A little taste of spring and spring's delight. A little of the flush and glory of young summer in the hills. So much fashion approves. In the autumn society comes up to the Berkshires again. It comes in September, when the leaves are turning amber and red; it walks about in the faded purple of the heather. The million-dollar mansions and the broad estates, the hunting preserves and the windy domains are swarmed over by people who are exactly such people as people in good society should be. There is every amusement. He who hunts may hunt; there is shooting—from deer to partridge—for him who shoots; he may golf who will; white, fugacious mobs of girls whirl in the great ballrooms; life, in a word, goes swinging to the tune it likes the best. This is the sort of thing you find in that part of the Berkshires inhabited by the glad race of those who have. It is an opulent existence, colorful and sane. So far as country-life goes in America it is at its best—accomplished, easeful, decorous—in the Berkshires; nowhere else does it reach so fine a height. Acted out, as it is, against a background of patriotic history—for on all these hills and valleys the Revolution laid its mark—and a background, as well, of prettily tamed natural beauty, it is about the best to be found in any country. At once accomplished and simple—at once urban and rural—it is life raised to the *n*th power of comfort and dignity. The mere wayfarer gets pleasure and profit out of it. Nothing so finely feeds the imagination as a drive through these miles of well-kept parks, with all their pretentious grace and emulative charm ; nothing, I say,

you please—to find the true country-side, the red schoolhouse, the girl in the sunbonnet, the lean farmer, trudging at the tail of a plow. A moody man, this farmer of the Berkshires, with darkling views of life. He is dazed by the new things that crowd

Every stream has fish—and eager young fishermen.

except a stroll through those other Berkshires, which are still what nature and the indifferent collaborator, the farmer, made them.

You have to go only a mile or two off the beaten roads of fashion—in any direction

down on him. Sit with him for a while; yonder on the old fence by the cornfield; the sandy road runs left to Pittsfield; on the right it dips down into the valley of Canaan; from the fence on which you sit you can see the far-away Green Mountains

The elm-lined street of a town beloved by city people.

The country store.

What some city people have done.

of Vermont. (Green they are not—only in song; just as the Danube is blue only for waltz purposes.) And the farmer, a calm, lean man, will tell you:

"I was born in the old farmhouse, half a century ago. And my father before me. Do you mark that hill with the pine forest grown clear down to the roots of it? Thirty years ago that was one of the best wheat-fields in the state. What happened? The Western wheat-fields killed our trade in grain; we could not compete with them. Then we turned to cattle. I have seen droves of eight hundred steers go by, driven along the road to New York; but we couldn't compete with the Western pack-ing-houses, so we lost the cattle-trade. What is there left? Well, the women-folk raise chickens for the Lenox market. That doesn't amount to much. Wherever you see a farm that is kept up, you may be sure that the chief crop is summer boarders. Nothing else pays."

And that is true; the summer boarder has descended upon the Berkshires; not yet in his thousands as upon the Catskills; but in numbers that yearly increase. Wher-ever there are a lake and a boat; wher-ever there are hill-climbing and fishing—there he finds his way. As yet he has not got far from the traveled route, but he

forms a very important factor in the life of the Berkshires. Behind the fact is the in-teresting reflection that in time this land of hill and forest will be a rural annex of the great cities. With difficulty the farmer makes a living here; more and more he will have to depend upon urban money; within ten years, or twenty years, or fifty—there is no need of being precise—the Berkshires will be the playground of New York. The big domains have absorbed hundreds of thousands of acres; the Westinghouse place, the Whitney estate and others are colonial in their extent. A wilderness exists un-touched.

I have driven for a day through a coun-try-side where the summer boarder is as rare as the gods; where the wheel of an automobile has never turned. Mile after mile, on either hand the ordered waste of the pine-forests; here and there little farms, quite abandoned, the roof-trees sagging and the barns falling apart, the well overgrown with weeds; a little further on some dogged farmer—perhaps an Italian or a French Ca-nadian or a German—is fighting for a live-lihood against the hardhack and lean soil and the bleak winter. Then the road dips into a valley and there is a stream that once turned a mill; the old mill-wheel is rotting. Follow the road. It broadens into a little

What still remains despite incoming wealth.

village of a hundred houses. Not ten of them are inhabited. Two hundred years ago this was a center of leisurely, comfortable life. The farms that fed it are abandoned. There are scores of such villages as this "Red Rock," I have in mind, quite as deserted. There is not one of them which does not hold its own charm—an idle picturesqueness that fascinates the city-dweller. Here his summer home awaits him—with open door. He may rent it for a song; he may buy it for a negligible cantata. (In the center of the village street is a huge granite rock on which stands a shaft commemorating the founding of the village in Revolutionary—or pre-Revolutionary days —I have forgotten; only with fine village patriotism the few score inhabitants see to it that the rock is painted red, that the name of the settlement may not be lost— Red Rock. It was first reddened in an Indian massacre; every twenty years since the Red Rockers have gone over it with commemorative paint-brushes; and on such great occasions there is speech-making and a lone bugler plays "Yankee Doodle.")

The little village,—it hardly makes a pencil-mark on the empty map of the Berkshires.

Very lightly indeed has the city man touched this land. He has no more than blazed a few fashionable trails through it. There are miles of evergreen forest still as wild and fascinating as when the first Puritans entered. And by the way, wherever the Puritan passed he left a sermon. You may read it in his abandoned farms. Round the desolate wooden buildings the flowers and weeds gather thick and close, nodding their heads as though they whispered, "Man is a poor thing—a poor thing!" Your quick-growing weed is the true symbol of immortality. Beautiful, robust, jocund and strong, it passes in perpetual procession over all that man builds and dreams.

If you think one can wander through this world without being tempted to buy you know not the heart of urban man. I had not been in the Berkshires a month before I determined, like every one else, to buy a farm. It is not so simple a matter as it seems. There are so many of them—each has its peculiar advantage—that to decide on one is as difficult as choosing a ring in a jeweler's window. Hill-climbing is a pretty adjunct to country life. Out Sheffield way there is Mount Washington to be climbed. Beyond Great Barrington the Dorne lifts his broad shoulders—tempting to perch on. You rather think you would like a farm near the Dorne. Then some

The picturesque old village of Canaan-4-Corners.

one tells you of the Boulder Trains. You feel there would be something respectably scientific in owning a bit of the Boulder Trains—though you don't know what they are; so you drive over into New York state and inspect them. You find an antique lane of glacier stones—running from Toy's Hill over to Richmond in Massachusetts, a distance of three miles; monstrous, uncouth, formidably old—indeed a very interesting train of boulders dropped by the frozen river on its way—but you heed them not. You continue to look for that farm.

Now a valley farm tempts you and for a week you call it yours, saying finely "My farm." You and the owner come to terms. Then you hear of a hill-farm. It, in turn, becomes your farm. But you can't decide. Estival nature is getting worn and rusty; autumn is coming up into the Berkshires and you haven't found your farm—the one that appeals implacably to you, that calls to you and insists that it must be your farm. You ride far and wide; you question the natives; from one end of the fifty-mile strip to the other it is known that you want to buy a farm—and every farm in that strip is for sale; but you can't make up your mind.

And then one day——

But why should I lay this adventure at the door of a mythical "you"? It was my experience; I, and no other, am he who wanted to buy that farm; for four months I sought for it; patiently, as a mother going over her child's head, I investigated every square road of the Berkshires; I knew every farm—acreage, price and terms of payment —but I couldn't find what I wanted. Now one day I got a telegram from a city man:

"Am looking for a farm. Do you know of any in the Berkshires? Answer."

I wired him back to come along, that I knew them all, scores and hundreds of them. The next day he came. As one who meant business he had brought his check-book, his camera and his wife. And we drove forth, behind two brown horses, one of which was good.

"There is a farm at Red Rock," I said. "It has been admired."

"Red Rock be it," said the city man.

A road branched up to our left; it climbed sinuously through a leafy tangle of yellowing trees.

"There's one up here we might look at," I suggested.

We turned into the hill road.

"Oh, how beautiful!" cried the city man's wife; "and see that glimpse of the lake in the valley, and oh! those up-going hills. Oh, oh!"

"I don't think you'll like the farm," I said.

The old, low-lying house, the cluster of barns, the old wealth of an orchard, meadow and valley and the lift of hills; indeed the farm looked very tempting; I wished devoutly we had gone on to Red Rock; it came upon me like a flash that this was "my farm," that we were made for each other; that it was what I had been looking for all summer, all my life. I had looked at it a hundred times and never thought so; now I knew. Things happen like that. You never really want a particular heifer, as Mr. Alfred Henry Lewis would say, until you see some one else trying to cut her out of the herd. I poohpoohed that farm to the city man. I told him he wouldn't like it. I tried to drive on.

"How beautiful, how very beautiful!" said the lady, "and the sunlight in the orchard trees."

She sat on the tongue of a broken reaper and looked at the dappled orchard; the city man skipped lightly from hill to hill of the green domain; his enthusiasm sparkled as he went. When he came back to the broken reaper he had an ancient German woman and her husband with him—he had bought the farm and sealed the bargain with a check. My farm! I left them there.

The brown horses, one of which was good, haled me back to the stable they had come from; I packed my trunks and took the train for New York. There was nothing in the Berkshires that I wanted since I had lost "my farm." The broken-hearted girl, when she loses her lover, though at hand are a million or two quite as loverlike, goes dejectedly into a convent. I shall make the foothills of Piedmont or the lowlands of the Loire my convent; and regret eternally the windy uplands of "my farm," the broad, low house, the sinuous road and the glimpse of the lake in the valley. And a regret of that sort is the finest, most comfortable thing one can fare abroad with. The farms we don't buy, like the girls we don't marry, afford the most unvarying satisfaction.

* * * * *

Up in the Berkshires; what' haunting memories you carry down with you into everyday life!

Once in the twilight I came upon a white settlement in the hills. High, square, naked buildings shouldered each other along the lonely road. Far below glimmered the little lights of Lebanon. I went into the furthermost building and found a tranquil society of Shakers. Most of them were infinitely old; they were so faded and calm, so vaguely serene, that they seemed part of another life. Indeed, they were far from this world. Familiar ghosts walked the corridors and stood by their beds at night. And these things they told me in a strange, cheerful way, as simply as a little girl might tell you what she said to her doll, and what her doll said to her. Personally I don't believe in ghosts, I have seen too many of them; but I should not like to rob the Berkshires of anything so picturesque. After all the Shakers may be right; there is mystery in everything; it has always struck me as being very mysterious that two and two should make four, and the more I ponder over it the more mysterious it seems that they don't make something else. Merely for a change.

16
Boating on the Charles River

BOATING ON THE CHARLES RIVER

BY ARTHUR STANWOOD PIER

PHOTOGRAPHS BY T. E. MARR

IGHTY-FIVE miles is the length of the Charles River; for about twenty-five miles it affords perhaps a greater variety of pleasure to a greater number of people than any other river stretch of equal length in America. This aquatic pleasure ground— or water navigable by "mosquito fleets"— is not continuous; it consists of three separate pools, so to speak, each having character of its own. One extends for sixteen miles near Dedham, another for five miles at Riverside, the third for four miles between Boston and Cambridge. On fine spring and summer afternoons these sections of the Charles present spectacles that are probably not paralleled elsewhere in this country.

On the river the life is of two kinds— the life of idle dalliance and the life of strenuous endeavor. You find people dallying all the way along from Natick to West Roxbury—the Dedham section— from Riverside to Waltham—the Riverside section; you find the strenuously employed afloat on the wide stretch above and below Harvard Bridge. The shell is reserved for these lower waters of the Charles; in the upper reaches you see the canoe.

Riverside, ten miles from Boston by rail, is the original canoe resort. There between pleasant wooded shores, kept in trim by a vigilant Park Commission, the river broadens indolently into ponds, incloses low islands, narrows to evade projecting necks of land, and spreads again, more purposeless than before. Along one bank lies Norumbega Park which in the

summer months attracts large crowds; the neighboring boat clubs and public establishments provide on occasions for thousands of canoeists and spectators. The season begins about the first of May and lasts into October; but June and July are the months when the activity is greatest. With a few privileged exceptions, this part of the Charles has been kept free from puff-boats, steam and electric launches. The principal exception is the police patrol.

In the beginning, one must explain the police patrol, for it is a significant feature. Its function is, briefly, that of chaperon. In the case of the inexperienced paddler, the canoe is itself the most competent of chaperons. The authorities, however, finding reason to distrust its efficiency, passed an ordinance limiting canoeists in the attitudes of comfort which they might enjoy, and to enforce the ordinance established the patrol. So a launch in which there are two blue-coated officers, races back and forth continuously between Waltham and Newton Lower Falls, and is reinforced at intervals in its work of espionage by rowboats, manned likewise by special officers. The launch is an explosive little craft and gives warning of its approach from a long distance, so that it is perhaps less effective than the oarsman who, by means of oddly adjusted and jointed oars, has the delusive appearance of rowing away from the object which he is approaching. The device is cunningly adapted for one in whose profession the element of unexpectedness is prized. These officers prowl into sheltered coves and investigate the numerous side issues of the river. They are lonely men and grave, and from the consciousness that the pleasure seekers regard them as an impertinence their faces wear a look of injury.

At night the police patrol is particularly aggressive. The launch darts a searchlight from side to side, explores with it the banks, the interiors of canoes that may be nestling under overhanging boughs, and while one officer sits attentive to the mechanism, the other stands and scrutinizes all that his deadly light reveals. And sometimes he will raise the shout, "Break away there, you! Heads too close together!" and then derisive laughter from masked sources will applaud this heartless exposure of incipient romance. So far as I know, there have been but few persons fined for violating the Park Commission's ordinance, and it was not clear in those cases that any ignominy rested upon the unfortunates. The ordinance is frequently broken. One afternoon a canoe put in ashore as soon as the patrol had passed, and I, coming up a moment later, observed the young man and young woman lying side by side on the cushions—a thing forbidden—and puffing cigarette smoke out in rings—the girl, it appeared, was trying to blow her rings through the man's. Many canoes were passing within a few feet of them, but engrossed in their diversion, they remained quite unconcerned. I do not believe the most determined spoil-sport on the patrol would have haled this couple into court— so clearly innocent, so amiable was their little lapse from what would be prescribed by ordinary good taste.

Massachusetts, however, takes an almost grandmotherly interest in the demeanor of its citizens, and the police patrol has come to Riverside to stay.

Its existence, and possibly the facts which led to its creation, but of which I must plead ignorance, have altered to some degree the character of the crowd which is attracted to Riverside. There are still many persons of an advanced and civilized type who mingle in the throng— members of boat clubs and others for whom access to the Charles is convenient at this point, who enjoy a pleasant sport and a pretty river, and who do not resent the quaintness of the company. But it can hardly be disputed that Riverside has become increasingly the resort of the primitive, the rudimentary.

At Riverside you see the canoe "sport" stripped to a striped and sleeveless jersey, rejoicing in his sunburned and tattooed arms, racing with reckless disregard among the leisurely. There, too, you observe the shirt sleeve and the vest, the suspenders, and the strong cigars. The girl who chews gum and, as she chews, languidly feeds candy to the young man paddling her, is a frequenter of the scene. The laughter seems disproportionately loud for the wit that has provoked it, and there is prevalent an air not merely of audacity but of bluff and rude assertion of the individual, whether it causes annoyance to any one or not. It is a familiar spectacle to see a fleet organize, of a dozen or fifteen canoes massed together, and proceed abreast down the middle of the river, joyously producing panic among the unskilled; at such a time the youth who has invited a girl to share his first experiment in a canoe affords rare sport.

The comments seem perhaps unkind; there is certainly nothing unkindly in the behavior of the crowds at Riverside, even if one must withhold the full measure of approbation. They are rollickingly good-natured. To assure yourself of this, you have but to keep eyes and ears open—see the faces and note the repartee. "Say, old man, this is no obstacle race," will be the protest of one whose canoe is rudely bumped by an embarrassed greenhorn. "Don't mind us; come right in," will be the greeting extended to you by the pair upon whose shady nook under overhanging willows you have unwittingly intruded. "We have no secrets from the world." And when you withdraw you are likely to hear some favorable comment on your tact.

Canoeing seems to breed a pleasurable vacancy of mind which expresses itself upon the countenance. The principal occupation of canoeists is to stare at other canoeists as they pass. It is an odd thing; in trolley cars and on the street convention restrains the most mannerless from indulging in the fixed, persistent stare; the moment one steps into a canoe one adopts a different code of etiquette. The girl lying back on her cushions, the man sitting on the thwart and dabbing with the paddle alike drop into silence and turn their faces toward the passing craft. Always they meet the steady gaze in answer; on neither side is there any flinching; no one is abashed. The boats slowly pass, the heads slowly turn, the eyes slowly move—until the human anatomy can no more; then it is eyes in the boat again and ready for a dispassionate examination of the next that comes.

The canoe is, in fact, but a means to an end; the mere paddling of it, in quiet waters, is not engrossing. And so the occupants of the canoe are really adventurers ready to follow the first distraction

on the bank; two evangelists were passing round copies of the hymns and had lured several hundred persons from the river and the road and were holding others on both river and road in expectancy.

"We will all sing, if you please," said one of the evangelists—they stood together at some little distance from the crowd they had collected—"we will all sing the first hymn on this sheet."

So the two leaders began singing,

"Shall we meet beyond the river?"

Taking their ease.

that offers and seems promising. Hence, perhaps, this absorbed attentiveness to those who pass, hence the popularity of the graphophone, hence the success of small allurements upon the river bank. One Sunday afternoon I saw automobiles gathered upon the stone bridge, canoes crowding together just beyond, and up and down the river other canoes hurrying, they knew not why, to join the throng. Evidently something was happening. It turned out to be an open air hymn-singing

—words appropriately selected for the devotees of Riverside. But no one joined in. All stood and stared, as vacantly, as stolidly, as they stared at one another from the canoes. The evangelists finished the hymn and announced a second—also with beguiling words and the refrain,

"Happy day, happy day,
When Jesus washed my sins away."

The crowd remained unresponsive. In the middle of the singing a young man in a blue and black sweater brought a camera

The scene before a popular clubhouse.

A popular haven.

from his canoe and made a deliberate, careful photograph of the singers.

"Caught 'em with both their mouths wide open," he announced in the pause between two stanzas.

That was the end of the prayer-meeting. Laughing and chattering, the canoeists made for their boats; the automobiles began their racketing, somebody turned on a graphophone, and the disgusted evangelists departed to seek more fertile fields. People who go canoeing at Riverside on a

listens apparently entranced. His attention may be temporarily diverted by small articles of food tossed to him between the bars—but his manner of disposing of these is abrupt; to stand and listen to the music is his real joy.

Not only is the canoeist so casual in his purposes, so amenable to the mild charms of temporary distraction, whether supplied by preachers or bears; he furnishes a spectacle that diverts the loiterer on land. Whenever the river is crowded,

Man is not really necessary.

Sunday afternoon are not urged by a devotional impulse. The big bear in Norumbega Park is more successful than any peripatetic preacher in holding their interest. His cage is on the bank of the river and faces outward upon the stream. Nearly always there is an admiring fleet anchored in front of him; he stands on his hind legs at the bars, holding on with his fore paws, and gravely meets stare with stare. Often he is serenaded with a graphophone; he has a soul for music and

the bridges will be well filled also—the bridges and the floats of the boathouses and the paths along the shore will all be quietly animated with philosophic idlers. They do not expect anything very exciting to repay them for their waiting; an upset is of comparatively rare occurrence, for the canoes let out to the populace are of a substantial nature. It is the procession of recumbent figures and uptilted faces, the snatches of dialogue, the color and movement of the picture that prolong the lingering of the man on the bridge. On the wide stretches of the river, canoes gather into clusters of many mingled colors and then resolve themselves and re-assemble; others glide on independent courses, uninvolved; the movement is all fluent, diverse, gentle and beguiling; the clash that is always imminent seems always just evaded. Green, blue and red, decorated with flags, the canoes shine in the sun, the cushions in them make variegated spots of color, the dresses, the hats of the women and espe-

Then he appreciates the fact that here is a sport in which there is no age limitation. Old men and old women participate in it—passively if not actively; the invalid lies contentedly upon her cushions, the small infant sleeps in its mother's arms. For there are family parties going up the river as well as young persons who are out to enjoy a duet; sometimes they take with them the dog, the graphophone, and their luncheon, and picnic on the bank to music while the dog chases squirrels. The canoe

All the comforts of home.

cially the parasols supply brighter tints—and in all this openwork of brilliant hue one does not single out the occasional sleeveless striped jersey, the useful but homely suspenders, the inappropriate boiled shirt. These trivial blemishes are submerged in the richness of the color, the variety of change, the grace of motion.

After a while the man on the bridge withdraws his attention from the general effect, focuses it on the individual canoes as they pass below him abreast and in procession.

encourages domesticity as well as romance. After all, domesticity—in well-regulated lives—issues out of romance; and the canoe may help to preserve, in domesticity, the romance which perhaps it aided in promoting. At any rate, it is possible to look upon the canoe, not with the cynic eyes of the police patrol, but, in spite of its fragility, as a real bulwark of the home.

On a fine Saturday evening in midsummer, when the sun is about setting, there may be seen picnic parties at frequent

The most popular feature of canoe life on the Charles.

The al fresco luncheon under conditions just right.

intervals on either bank, with their canoes drawn part way up on shore. When the twilight falls and the moon rises, they take to the river again. The boathouses are illuminated, there are strains of band music from a distant pavilion, there are people still dining on the balcony of a clubhouse, lights and lanterns glow among the trees, and are reflected in the water, Caruso sings from a graphophone—and, "Well," says the man who never has had, never will have more than two weeks of vacation in the year and who has his hostages to fortune in the canoe with him —"well, this may not be Venice, but it's pretty nice." And that is the hour for canoeing at Riverside. Then the crudities and the garishness of individuals are not so conspicuous, the chewing-gum girls and the sleeveless young men with the attenuated arms no longer obtrude their failings; only the loud voices of the vulgar, alas, are never subdued by beauty. And everywhere the voices of the vulgar celebrate particularly the vesper hour.

So great has been the development of interest in canoeing in the last few years that now Dedham, farther from Boston than Riverside and possessing a much more extensive stretch of available water, attracts on Saturday and Sunday its multitudes. It began by being a resort mainly for the fastidious, who had abandoned Riverside. Now these poor souls are gazing with dismay at the increasing numbers who have pursued them in their futile attempt to get away from "the crowd." A great public boathouse has been opened, and there are to be seen on the river in that neighborhood all the types that are visible at Riverside. And now they have a police patrol at Dedham. To be sure, he is only one policeman and he patrols only on Sunday in a rowboat; if it is a hot Sunday he takes off his blue coat and in his shirtsleeves is as unofficial and comfortable as possible. But the helmet denotes him; he is a repressive figure—repressive and melancholy, too, poor man, for up and down this crowd of pleasure seekers he must wander lonely "as a cloud." With no colleague to keep him in countenance, what wonder if as he rows by on his tour of inspection, he seems to assume a wistful, a deprecating air?

For some distance along the banks of the river at Dedham there are country estates, houses visible across green lawns and terraces, and roads traversed on Saturdays and Sundays by smart equipages and automobiles; in these respects the view from the Charles here is quite different from that at Riverside. And it is a pretty sight on which the owners of the riparian estates may look down from their piazzas—a pretty sight, but one which irritates as often as it pleases. For the procession of canoes on Sunday is like an interminable street parade—now an interval of noiseless passing and then a noisy brass band—the only difference being that the graphophone is substituted for the band and lasts longer. Every few minutes in the day the graphophone is to be heard, usually with its business end directed at a house on shore; and the unfortunate householder has not the remedy of tossing a few pennies out of the window with the assurance that the music will cease. There is nothing to do but endure; and two young sentimentalists with a well-loaded graphophone do not quickly tire. Often there is to be seen a tedious humorist with a graphophone as his only companion; he arranges a pile of cushions comfortably about one which bears the picture of a red-haired girl, and gazing affectionately at this, he serenades it with love ditties from his musical instrument. In a place of public entertainment there is usually a clown.

Above Dedham the river flows through open country and woodland again, with houses seldom visible, often with no road skirting its shores; and here again it widens out into broad, shallow pools as it does at Riverside, with outlying reedy marshes over which the blackbirds fly, with fields of lily pads and banks of wild rose. From this point on the number of canoes decreases; along the way one passes people who have found a comfortable secluded spot under the trees and are satisfied to remain there, to talk, and to read. The number of persons who go out canoeing to read—or to be read to—is surprising. They carry magazines, novels, and even portentous works of philosophy and history; they read not only anchored in the shade but reclining under parasols while the paddler guides them up the pleasant stream. It used to be a theory among the undergraduates of Harvard that the best way to grind for an examination was to go off with another fellow in a canoe; the theory still holds; and any one who visits Dedham in the month of June will find the youth of Harvard languidly prosecuting their studies, while they drift with the stream.

Twelve miles above Dedham is Natick, another but smaller center of the canoeing industry. And all the way along the river even to its source, beyond Populatic Pond, there are occasional canoes to be seen. It

side, and finally along the four-mile stretch between Cambridge and Boston.

There are boat clubs at the foot of the Back Bay, there are rowboats for hire at Harvard Bridge and at the new stone bridge and on the other side of that where the Charles brushes past Charlestown before it enters Boston harbor; there are schoolboy crews and amateur crews and professional oarsmen who practice and race on these waters; but most of the rowing interest and impetus is furnished by

The boys have their fun, too.

is a pretty river and for the most part may easily be descended in a canoe, even by the inexperienced; there are no difficult rapids to render navigation dangerous, unless one sets out at the time of the spring freshets; there are, however, a number of carries which make the continuous descent of the river from its source an undertaking of some tediousness. That which distinguishes the Charles as a boating river from other little streams on which canoes are launched is the life at Dedham, at River-

Harvard University. The Harvard rowing season covers a month or six weeks in the autumn, three months in the spring. During July, August and September the University's contribution to boating is eliminated. There are two or three holiday regattas in these months; they draw a different class of spectators from those who turn out in May to witness the race between Harvard and Cornell. In midsummer the Beacon Street houses, the backs of which overlook the river, are closed; the shades are drawn across the windows from which eager faces peered in spring; the flat roofs of the stables behind the houses are not, as on a race day in spring, decorated with pleasant-looking people sitting in comfortable chairs and gazing through field glasses; the alley between the stables and the river is not, as in spring, thronged with excited, bustling, impatient youth. Straggling lines of spectators assemble on Harvard Bridge and on the river wall, but they exhibit no warm enthusiasm; most of them seem to have been attracted merely by the inexpensive nature of the entertainment. Only near the finish line are grouped the partisans, the sporting men, the connoisseurs; and there one may detect the same thrill that traverses during a college race the long array of friends and sympathizers. The oarsmen row with as much sincerity as do the college men; but for the beholding of their contests no grandstand is ever erected, no yelling mob struggles for place.

The college boating season is inaugurated in the autumn by the bumping races, which cover three days. Each dormitory or group of dormitories is entitled to put out a crew; there are about fifteen crews, which race in two sections. The boats line up in procession, separated from one another by two lengths of open water. The crew that has drawn first place—the crew that is "head of the river"—has only to keep from being bumped, and if successful in this for the three days is regarded as having a record equal to that of any crew with three bumps to its credit. As soon as one crew bumps another, the two boats drop out of the race; the next day the defeated crew has to start one place lower down the river, and by the same process the winning crew moves up one place. The rivalry of two or three dormitories is keen; the partisans of the others take the races less seriously, and accept them mainly as an opportunity for jocose advertisement— ingenious transparencies and noise.

In May are held the class races—an event which awakens much excitement and causes a great outpouring in the Back Bay. The host of undergraduates gathers in the Beacon Street alley opposite the finish line, and begins shouting, class by class, when the crews are still half a mile distant. Along the wall and on Harvard

bridge are other spectators who raise a cheer as the boats pass; but until the finish line is sighted the chief encouragement to the oarsmen comes from the three or four tugs following them and crowded with young men who are brandishing their hats and shouting through megaphones. Sometimes at the finish line three boats are overlapping one another, the fourth less than a length behind; then indeed is there the mingled roar of class numerals from the shore, the agitated tossing of hats and handkerchiefs from roofs and windows, wild whistling from the pursuing tugs, on which the voices of the megaphone-brandishing young men can no longer be heard. And the next moment everything collapses; the noise, the agitation, the movement; the oarsmen droop in their boats, hang limp over their oars. In the alleyway the crowd lingers for a little while, looking at the drifting crews with sympathy or enthusiasm. Excited members of the victorious class rush about shaking hands with one another, declaring their joy in husky voices; those who are of the defeated parties go quietly away. In a few moments the oarsmen are sitting up again; as they start on their last row back to the boathouse, the crowd gives them one last cheer.

That night there is celebration in Boston; many dine magnificently at hotels; the crews break training; the theaters are particularly enlivened.

In May also take place the four-oared races of the school crews, and the 'Varsity race with Cornell. Soon after that event the 'Varsity crew departs for New London to take up its training there, and the undergraduate boating season ends.

It is a rigorous season. So long as the river is free from ice, the crews maintain outdoor practice, sometimes in rain and snow, sometimes in a wintry wind that numbs the fingers and searches through the sweater. Rowing in rough water develops good watermanship—and so on some bitter days, pedestrians buffeting against the gale on Harvard Bridge see a fragile shell tossing in the basin, while from a small launch close by a man shouts instructions to the oarsmen through a megaphone—and stands ready to rescue them in case their boat is swamped. Occasionally a venturesome class crew, unattended by a launch, capsizes, and the oarsmen have to swim ashore, pushing their shell, and then paddle back to their boathouse in freezing garments. Blisters eat into the palms of the hands, the skin cracks and chaps on fingers and knuckles, the sliding seat becomes an instrument of torture—but the oarsman keeps at his work by the hour, day after day. It is a harder test in many ways than football. "I get so restless," said one fellow. "I'd give anything sometimes if I could get out of the boat for a few moments and walk." It is a harder test in other ways. In a game, even though it is only a practice game, there is always the excitement of some contest to illuminate the darkest drudgery. There is also the opportunity for individual display to stimulate individual ambition. In rowing there is neither of these elements to afford relief.

Only in the race is there excitement; at other times the practice is no more thrilling than is a practice round of golf. And in an eight-oared crew individual brilliancy is of no account. Now and then some youth, striving to outdo himself in a race, breaks his oar; and then it is proper for him to jump overboard—a very pretty act when successfully accomplished—but invariably futile. Once the stroke of the crew that was leading in the class races met with this mishap almost at the finish, and did the expected thing promptly and gracefully. But because of the momentary confusion that resulted, his crew was overtaken and beaten, and he himself was ironically congratulated at his class dinner on the heroism with which he had snatched defeat from the very jaws of victory. He had done the best thing he could do in the circumstances — but the undergraduate spirit is not tolerant of anything that suggests the grandstand play. In a crew the grandstand player has no place. He may find his opportunity on the nine or on the eleven. With the crew it is day after day of monotonous hard work, of patient, unrewarded effort, of endless repetition and criticism—and the individual never has any chance to distinguish himself. And the race, of course; the excitement is worth the agony, worth the year's work—even if it ends in a licking.

17
Newport, The Blessed of Sport

Along the polo side lines at the Clubhouse.

NEWPORT, THE BLESSED OF SPORT

BY ROBERT DUNN

PHOTOGRAPHS BY JAMES BURTON

CIVILIZATION has three corners from which the worldly American may see his idea of it pass in review. They may be named: the alcove of the Café de Paris, the cement terrace of the Grand Hotel, Yokohama, and Newport in tennis week. Life gallops past these coigns, not exactly like the dreams on the walls of the Snow Queen's castle, in the Andersen tale, but with enough unreality to make living pleasant as you watch, and persuade you that you comprehend the universe. Old earth is a proposition quite distinct to Englishman, to Lama, to Red Indian; to see its heart, a journey to a separate compass-point for each. For Swami Bath-Mat-Bahama, the greasy splendor of Potala; for Okahocka, moose-guts at the Bella-Bella potlatch; for Sir Cyril Stubbs, any tropic estuary badly mapped, or—his London club window. Americans demand a culture less savage. We are a gregarious people. Common things are novel to us, else to scour the Continent and to girdle the sphere on the grand tour would not be so enlightening. So, Newport.

It has a very bad name. A fair stake could be laid that in mixed conversation anywhere nearer the Mississippi River than Brenton's Reef Lightship, this town is seldom referred to in terms that are meant to flatter. Newport is a by-word for all of which our strong young children of the prairie disapprove. Their scorn they have sucked from the rich boundless soil of the untrammeled West.

You know best what that repute is, with names and dates for your anecdotes, perhaps. A community's reputation is meat for the stranger, but should amuse its householders. Easterners imagine Kansas

281

to be a honeycomb of cyclone cellars, quite a barberless province. Strange, yet having many times crossed the state from end to end, I have never seen a hole in its ground not covered by a house, a windmill, or an oil derrick.

The town is flattered by being told that it is pursuing later Rome's primrose path to the everlasting bonfire, or, rather, the path of Pompeii, Rome's Newport. Now Newport could hardly be soused in volcanic dust, for its Miantonomi Hill is solid puddin'-stone, and you can't burn matches in its fogs. Rome fell, surely. Gibbon, and many a gorgeous historical novel, blushing unread in the department store, have told all about it. Two vices destroyed the town, as I remember history. First, was the habit one emperor had of eating hummingbirds' tongues in a sort of force-meat ball; second, and most disastrous, was everybody's weakness for watching athletes battle in the arena with lions, and Hircanian tigers.

Hummingbirds still reserve a sensation new to Newport, but its sporting likeness to the bad town on the Tiber is alarming. Most of the best skill in the country at racket, saddle, and tiller kneels at the feet of Bellevue Avenue. Not as slaves, not as hirelings, indeed, but Newport solicits nothing, and pays for its field amusement neither in cash nor kind. Why? Because at tiller and in saddle you see the very sons and brothers of these wicked Pompeiians. Why they should be so skillful is of no concern here. But does Newport properly respond in absorption and enthusiasm to this athletic adulation? If you think it does, you do not know your Newport.

Every day there, after our dip at Bailey's, I would ask my young friend with the purple orchid in his buttonhole, what was on the carpet for the afternoon.

"We might drive out and watch the polo if it wouldn't bore you," he would say. "But the play's pretty rotten this year. Always is."

I would remind him that we went to polo two days before. Did we? Why, yes. And hardly any one was there.

"There may be a hunt somewhere this afternoon," he might add. "We could see what it's like, but I guess they go pretty far, and I've got to be back for eight o'clock dinner."

"Nothing else?"

"The polo at the Pier. Dreadfully dead, the Pier now. Deader than Newport this year. Things may be a little livelier over here next week, when the tennis tournament begins. . . . Oh, then there's the horse show at the Casino the week after. Sometimes that's worth looking at—and the Astor Cup races."

Once I winked into the sand, and observed: "You'd think a place like Newport would be better supplied with outdoor amusements, wouldn't you? Nothing doing but these small field events."

That stirred him. "I play court tennis for an hour every day, don't I? And we've ridden everywhere in the machine. Look here, now, what more do you want?"

The challenge was plain. It was the case-hardened Newporter's way of arguing thus: "We have the best of everything in the outdoor line here. Events that would keep any other summer place howling about itself throw themselves at us. We have the best tennis players, the best riders, the best yachtsmen. We're used to them. It's their crude way of giving Newport its due. It's no novelty—hardly amuses us any more."

The orchid wearer stood up. "Come," said he, "let's dress. It isn't at all the thing to sit in the sand on this beach."

I asked him to pause a minute, saying, "Years ago when I was here, lots of people used to go crabbing. Out at the Third Beach on the little bridges over those sandy creeks. You lie flat on your stomach watching the tide go out, lowering into the water a net fastened to a steel barrel hoop with a chunk of raw beef tied in. You wait for Mr. Crab to come elbowing along sideways after the meat. When he pecks at it, you draw up the net, quick, before he scuttles out."

The youth's eyes snapped with excitement. "Yes, those were the old Arcadian days of Newport," sighed he.

Thus we left the golden strand, and the three filmy Mother Hubbard bathing bonnets, one green, one red, one yellow, bouncing between the red huts on Gooseberry Island and the battlemented castle of the eccentric millionaire from Providence.

One felt a past master in knowledge of the Newport view-point not till some days later, toward the end of the tennis, hunts, races and polo. I had learned the faces, at least, of many of the star performers. A big entertainment was given, of the usual Newport sort; electric lights in the shrubbery, tents built out from the villa for dancing and supper, and decorated to give New York newspapers and the *Florists' Gazette* conniption fits. I saw just one tennis player of consequence among the youths present from New York for over Sunday; which recalled that a young girl had lately told me that though some of the visiting tennis players were "nice," not many were ever asked out. "Of course, one saw plenty of youths who had entered the tournament just in order to play on the courts during the matches, which, otherwise, is prohibited. But vainly I looked, even for performers on other fields, for whom the golden latchstring of this household, certainly on this rather general occasion, was hanging free.

Enter my friend of the orchid. It was

Miss Morgan, daughter of E. D. Morgan, sailing her yacht *Echo*.

Carrying the ball down field.

At the float of the New York Yacht Club station.

"The Breakers"—residence of Mrs. Cornelius Vanderbilt, Sr.

to express surprise that none of these faces I had learned to recognize were visible. But that seemed not unnatural to him.

"You see," he smiled, "men like that, you know, generally don't care for this sort of thing." Thus I grasped the distinction between the Newport of tradition and the Newport of outdoors; the gulf between the sporting page and the social column. Newport solicits even the soiled hands of speculation, while the honest democracy of sport for its own sake, it seems, hies itself to bed at 11 P.M., caring not whether it has been patronized by day, but mighty careful that it shall not be by night; entrenched by ponies and yachts, among which no youth with smooth tongue, spreading family tree, or even syndicate profits, may enter unless he has the strenuous spirit and the willing flesh.

Thus enlightened, one feels that, at the Polo grounds, he looks across a great gulf, from the beings in the clubhouse to the players on the field. And the new grounds near Bateman's are a quilt of green for any man to gaze upon and be happy, elevated there like a satin dais over the surf booming upon all sides. Villas perched on the granite eminences all about, if built in better taste, or surrounded with a few olive trees, would fulfill for one who had never been there his idea of the Riviera. In the distance, the roof balcony of the Marble Palace, as appropriate on its tiny lot as Windsor Castle might be on a Bensonhurst 20 x 20, and so porous that it has kept every fog for fifteen years on storage inside, gives the touch of footlessness you expect at Newport; while the stucco imitation of the Old Stone Mill, and the elderly alpaca maidens in the yard of Bateman's boarding house, add the hint of age with which Newport still pursues you.

At little tea tables, on the veranda, sit the most indifferent set of onlookers I have ever seen, backs to the field. Polo at Newport, one is told, has always been of less account than anywhere else in the country. That is disappointing for one who knows little about the game but has rather classed it between football and ice hockey—the two superlative things to see or play. Yet little is more pleasing than to watch ten men on so breezy and aerial a champaign dash about with the staccato, marionettish gait of the excellent pony,

crowding together, windmilling the jackstraw mallet in their arms. But the tables not once stop their talk, turn their heads, or even clatter spoons, when a charge to one corner of the field ends in a straggling retreat of half the company to the middle, as a higher figure is chalked on half the score board. Sometimes the intermittent line of chairs close to the fence, where sit a few enthusiasts either of the generation past or that coming, emit a faint chitter of applause, as if they hated to betray so simple-minded a quality as enthusiasm.

And the Casino of a National Tournament morning cannot be very inspiring, either, to the ardent devotee from Longwood or Southampton. The lawns are not half-filled. Who ever saw the Newport Casino, restaurant, theater, or club, crowded? Compared with the convention hall that once boomed the Pier, and was a proper summer-resort casino, the Newport affair has always gone down in the town's annals, like its hotels, as a failure. Who ever saw any place at Newport crowded, except Easton's Beach with "hated excursionists," and the avenue with motor cars jockeying from side to side? The gilded clock in its egg-shaped tower, over the Casino entrance, looks down upon the empty circular lawn, till well near eleven of each foggy morning. Soon, at intervals, a few of the other sex you read about tack across it, with the broker and real-estate young men entraining, and straggling after the upper circles of Jimburg, Saunderston East Greenwich and the Pier. They aim for the tennis courts *via* the right-hand steps across the piazza horseshoe, and in doing so they pass the only two really absorbed persons you will see at the Casino, excepting the players, or in Newport at all, perhaps. These are the fat, villainous-looking Greek with long-flowing mustaches, who used to run a cellar store on Fifth Avenue, and having now got the concession, spreads his silk rugs on the stirp of lawn under the barber shop. The other ardent onlooker is the "lady reporter," peering from the circular lattice of the horseshoe, the sole permanent audience of the merry little orchestra, noting ecru insertions and empire tulles.

Years ago, before the championship court was moved to the southeast corner of the grounds, and that baby grand stand

THE COURT ON WHICH THE LAWN TENNIS CHAMPIONSHIPS ARE DECIDED

Photograph by Jas. Burton.

was reared under the high fence that insulates you from *hoi polloi* of Freebody Park, every one used to squat in chairs or on the grass three deep around the court, and it was fun to watch their heads following the ball from one side the net to the other, as if all hung upon a single pivot. People used to shack their own chairs in those days, and weren't held up, as soon as they approached the courts, to hire them from a band of ragged banditti in red jerseys. In the midst now of the most exciting plays, every head within ten yards of the court is moving on its own pivot; whoso is sitting with whom to-day, and how that woman dares to dress so gorgeously with her husband just dead! and the extraordinary hats on those new people from Denver, keep neck muscles a-pulling all independently. Any one can now get to the front row around the Court, when in the old days you came early to hold down a chair. It is considered a bore to seat yourself for two hours behind a lot of, perhaps the townspeople's, knees, so the outlying grass teems more or less with the foyer crowd of the Metropolitan opera house in winter—not from the boxes, but the parterre.

Enthusiasts there are, of course, who remain rooted to their seats. Many are young girls, with their chins in their hands, their elbows on their knees, rigid through the whole performance, while parents, having asked how the first set is going, retreat to the lawn and lesser mental efforts than keeping score.

But in tennis week, Newport is not itself. Then, it more or less assumes its reputation in the provinces as a sort of disguise. Lanterns and marquees are built out upon the frowning terraces, and whoever has been lurking covetously in the trenches, and possesses the catapult of an acquaintance with an orderly upon the ramparts, may go up there to feast and "knock." From being the least spectacular place in the world, it becomes almost diverting to the eye. And, indeed, all the worldly world is there.

If you are looking for variety, then cross Conanicut and the two arms of the bay to Narragansett Pier, which should be proud to call itself a suburb of Newport. You hear outlanders speak of Narragansett *and* Newport, as if the two places had interests in common. As well speak of Newport *and* Atlantic City. The Pier is a sort of castle-in-Spain place. Jamestown, with its sunburned girls in sneakers and sailor necks, its match-box hotels with drugstores along the verandas, is far more substantial. Newport is opposite Jamestown, which admits, at least, an assured dependence. The Pier is still too proud and remote to acknowledge hers, though the decadence of the summer hotel the country over has hit her badly, and she still rests upon the laurels of tradition which always had their root in the city across the Bay. Yet never will she fade altogether, as long as she keeps neat and bright, as a sort of secondary base in advancing socially upon Newport. What you have done at the Pier, and how you did it, counts a good deal, though it may get a rather acid credit. But what can you expect of a place (so a Newport maiden once confided) where light blue gloves are worn on the beach in the morning! Surely no resort could ever rival Newport, where, as at the Pier, so many of its feudal clans may still be identified by very name with the trade in which they acquired their omnipotence. Newport has a way of rubbing the registered trademark off its folks, whether in South Dakota or by even less formal routes.

But Narragansett's public appointments are far more Roman. Its now burned casino, compared with Newport's, is as the gilt saloon of a Fall River boat to a dingy private yacht. You pay half a dollar simply to get into a restaurant, to pass over a scarlet Wilton carpet, through polished brass rails, and past a couple of proud men in that chain armor kind of livery, *à la* Dreamland. A famous caterer has lent his name to the place, but neither his cooks nor his cutlery. They bring you specks in a cocktail, and the knives are black where the silver is worn off. Sitting about, are the same faces and the same clothes you have seen at Palm Beach in February, at Hot Springs in May—and you think of the tiny one-horse eating place of Newport, crowded in back of shops and garages, but where the waiters serve, the food is edible, and the attendants are not dethroned emperors hypnotizing you for a tip.

With all its new blood no place is really more conservative than Newport. At

The lawns of the Casino grounds are the feature of tennis week.

least there's no fake about its atmosphere. It doesn't want you to take it for what it doesn't flatly appear to be. It wears its futility on its sleeve, and either thinks it no shame, or a distinction quite divine. After all, it *is* the real thing—as real as any community can be that exists solely to amuse itself; and it gratifies the cynic far better than its many imitations up and down the coast, with their pose of a moral superiority. No place changes less in years, is so fixed in its standards, and assimilates newcomers more easily, provided they are willing to make the proper sacrifices, and have the heaven-born genius to buckle to Newport's standards. No place clings more ardently to its old gods. You do not hear of Newport's ups and downs. It has a sort of Chinese civilization. Every season is billeted across the land as the most brilliant ever, and last year's as the deadliest dull. Truth to tell, Newport delights in thinking itself dull, and in telling outsiders so. Newport loves the truth. Casual strangers, any but those who camp

outside this social Port Arthur, preparing for a three-year, do-or-die siege, do not interest the place. But a family of determined Nogis, their money, origin, the cleverness of their social strategy become proper topics of general talk. The more acceptable the family, the more it is "roasted." That is Newport's way of surrendering. The siege finally becomes a sort of glacial movement, and the outposts parley with the enemy, by saying to one another, "They never really tried to get in, you know. Just think, they've been here three years! Next season they'll be all right. The children are the very best, even if the the old folks are quite impossible. Did you see the aigrettes she had on this morning? Like a cook!" And in the allotted three years, the family is over the ramparts and sitting gorgeously in the market place. But changed, so changed, that to see and hear its members talk, you would imagine that they had always camped upon Ochre Point, that they had ordered the forty steps built, or fed the first sack of corn into the Old Stone Mill.

What is the basis of this mellow despotism? What makes possible Newport as such, and inhibits rivalry? Grant that a social freak must arise in a country developing an exponent caste—neither aristocracy nor plutocracy are words to fit the case—what fate picked upon this plain little town at the tip end of a minor state, for Newport is the most out-of-the-way, annoying place to reach in the East? It is hard to tell. Yet first, almost treeless though it is, nowhere else on the Atlantic Coast are land and salt water so enchantingly wedded. Neither the sands of Jersey nor the Cape yield the circumambient perfection of Newport's slate cliffs, her surf-combed reefs pointing tropicward between three beaches. The soft damp air is the breath of luxury and a nectar to idleness.

But the history of Newport has made her, as well. Through the Revolution and before, Newport was another New York or Philadelphia; but the War of 1812 destroyed her shipping and decay began.

Rantankerous Boston, and New York, being a natural gateway to the West, supplanted the whaler with factory and grain barge. Newport, by her geographical position, could fall back upon no such industries. But her repute survived. The captains of early industry, seeking ease and contrast, turned first to Newport from the growing, barbarous cities, to where wealth and idleness had created the first native aristocracy in the North. In the strenuous times around the Rebellion. young Southerners went there to be educated, and their families followed to avoid the plantation summers. Indiscriminate Northern merchants followed in the seventies, feeling the need of culture, and with that—and the absence of material resource—the native aristocracy expired. But the modern kings of railways and tobacco did not grace the town till the eighties. And bringing all the pleasant evils of a civilization too fast a-ripening, they have revolutionized it—as far as a place which has arisen and lived through the vanity of imitation, and some of the oldest traditions in our country, may be overturned.

18
Old Beverly

SUMMER HOME OF PRESIDENT TAFT, BEVERLY, MASS.

NEW ENGLAND MAGAZINE

VOL. XL.   AUGUST, 1909   NUMBER 6

OLD BEVERLY

By REV. B. R. BULKELEY

THE city of Beverly, has come, of late, into a prominence which, in some of its expressions, is not altogether to the liking of citizens of discrimination in matters of taste. That the President of the United States should spend a season of rest within our borders, may easily be a matter of congratulation on the part of all inhabitants of the staid old town—for it is difficult in fifteen years of municipal life to get quite wonted to being a city, especially when one thinks of the admitted advantages of the earlier form of government. Yes, Beverly was pleased to have the privilege of saying the President would make his residence here for the summer. But why so much cheap ado over it? On the whole it is quite as agreeable to the genius of a self-respecting old community to be called plain Beverly as "The Summer Capital,"

By the way, as to the pertinence of

FIRST PARISH CHURCH, UNITARIAN,
REV. B. R. BULKELEY, PASTOR

names, many will recall Dr. Holmes' Beverly-by-the-Depot," as a bit of a take-off, which he sent to one who found pride in "Manchester-by-the-Sea," instead of the unadorned name of the town. And, speaking by and large, a good percentage of the names which, through conceit or fastidiousness, have been put forth as substitutes for, or appendages to, good old names, might as well be left out of the account as undesirable.

From the far off time in the 1630's, when our little community was known as the "Bass River Side" of Salem, of which it was a part, until this day we have had a good old English name, and while, for convenience, other names must be used for special designations of parts of the growing city, we seek for no new name for the community as a whole, not even Garden City-by-the-Sea.

The account of the beginning of the town is highly interesting and attended

JOANNA REVERE HOUSE   BIRTHPLACE OF   POWDER HOUSE   HALE HOUSE,
FIRST SCHOOL   LUCY LARCOM   BANCROFT

by quaint features of fact and tradition. Originally part of Salem, which connection takes us back to 1629, the first settlers had to go, in many cases, two miles or more to worship with that society which claims to be the first one established in New England *de novo*, for Plymouth Church (be it said) was founded across the seas and *imported*— all praise to its distinctive record. Now, when the community over on this side of the tide-river became of considerable size, then, getting restless over the necessity of walking so far, as well as the need of taking a ferry-boat, for the attendance at divine service, they presented this petition to the old church: "We, whose names are hereunder written, the brethren and sisters on Bass River side, do present our desires to the rest of the church in Salem, that with their consent, we and our children may be a church of ourselves, which we also present unto Mr. Hale, desiring him to form with us and be our pastor with the approbation of the rest of the church." This was signed by Roger Conant, a leading spirit in his day, who, with forty-eight other members, made up the first parish in Beverly under the charge of John Hale, who, by the way, is one of the ancestors of the late venerable Edward Everett Hale. The unanimous consent of the mother church was given on July 4, 1667, the ordination of Mr. Hale taking place in September, of the same year.

It gives a touch of quaint interest to read that the salary of the minister was to be £70 a year with 30 cords of firewood and he should have the use of a new house, two acres of land to be fenced in, as much meadow as would bear about four loads of hay, and the benefit of pasturing during the time he remained with them in the ministry. Under his pastorate, the famous Salem witchcraft delusion came to an end when his wife was accused and he was led to recognize the absurdity of the superstition.

Thus much has been said about the old first parish, as its life made the beginning of the town; the latter, at first, paying the minister's salary, as we have seen. It may be added that two of the successors of Hale in the large history of the church have become presidents of colleges, Joseph Willard going to Harvard in 1781, and Joseph McKean to Bowdoin in 1802; also that the first Sunday School established in America began in a house still preserved on Davis Street, in 1810, under the lead of Joanna Prince and Hannah Lunt, of the First Parish, so that the One Hundredth Anniversary of the event will be celebrated next year.

Since the early days the town has had much set down to its credit on the pages of history. Sharing, with other towns, in its response to demands upon men and treasure in the time of war, and now and again having some special distinction. It had a large part in the "Flower of Essex," sacrificed at the Deerfield Massacre. It is recorded with pride that the first cotton mill built in the United States stood out in sufficient prominence, having been built in 1789, to atttract the attention of the world and receive a visit from Gen. Washington, who visited the Norwood on Cabot, where, also, La Fayette was entertained.

Again, the first vessel put into commission in the War of the Revolution, embarked from the harbor of Beverly under the name Hannah, and four other vessels were put into commission by Washington soon after taking command of the Continental Army under the famous elm at Cambridge, and earlier than any other man-of-war. Hard by the Norwood house, mentioned above, is the house of the Beverly Historical Society. This society is of comparatively recent origin, but it is steadily accumulating a rich store of historical works, manuscripts, relics and curios of all sorts. Among the valuable

autographs which belong to its collection may be mentioned those by Henry VIII., Napoleon Bonaparte, Sir Henry Vane, George Washington, Cornwallis and Queen Elizabeth. Among rare volumes may be seen: First Edition of Northumberland Household Book, volumes belonging to the second minister, Thomas Blowers; Revolutionary rustic rolls and orderly books, Old Beverly documents, and records of Kings of England and France. Two fine bronze tablets give the names of those who went from Beverly to the engagements with the English at the famous battle of Concord and that at Trenton.

Within the memory of many who are still living, the land along the beautiful North Shore began, increasingly, to attract the attention of the residents of Boston as being most desirable for Summer homes, and very interesting stories are told of sales of farms for

ROAD TO FARMS, BEVERLY, MASS.

HISTORICAL SOCIETY BUILDING, BEVERLY

good prices as they seemed in the early days, before the "shore" development was fairly begun, but which now, compared with the values that attach per acre in the possessions of millionaires, can appear but insignificant, indeed. The development, however, has been characterized by a somewhat uniform type of estate, set in spacious grounds and commanding broad views on wooded vistas towards the ocean. Many of the finest families in Boston, whether from the point of view of inheritance or atmosphere of culture or literary accomplishment, have made Summer homes within the limits of Beverly and became a valuable acquisition as furthering the development of its best interests. From the proximity to Boston the families thus located could easily spend a long Summer on the beautiful North Shore, some staying very late into the Fall, as, indeed, many come in the Spring, while a few make visits to their fine estates in the Winter time.

The development of a city even in the direction of culture and high spiritual interests must wait, more or less, on the extension of resources and the accumulation of material power. These alone cannot, indeed, make a literary atmosphere; in fact, they seem often to shut out such, as the smokiness of a thriving metropolis may obliterate the beauty of sky and deprive the longing eye of the view of mountains and sea—otherwise, the privilege of the community. But granted a tendency to the higher accomplishments of life, granted an ancestry of the right sort, in the case of a good minority of the families making up a town, then there will be helpful connection between commercial welfare and the refinement and culture which now and again must furnish the environment of writers and benefactors in the higher realms. Sometimes the higher interests are postponed with a dangerous insistence on the worldly success which characterizes a growing city; but the best people do not account such as an end to abide in, but hope sooner or later to make some record in matters of refinement and belles-lettres as well. Touching this matter, we recall the remark of a Chicagoan (it is said) who, when reminded of some short-coming of the great metropolis in the more aesthetic attainments, said: "We don't boast much yet of culture, but when we take it up we will make culture *hum*."

The growth of Beverly in the early days was, of course, based on agriculture; in the last century the manufacture of shoes became the chief element, with still, as now, a large interest in market gardens and green-house products. Since the beginning of the twentieth century much of her pros-

perity has been due to the remarkable growth of the enterprise known lately as the United Shoe Machinery Company. Its magnificent plant was at the time of its erecting the largest in the world of the particular type of construction known as the reinforced concrete; while its product of many millions' worth goes far around the world.

Within a hundred years there has been a growth in literary atmosphere in the region hereabout which is worth recording. Whittier lived not far away at Amesbury and Oakknoll, Mary Abigail Dodge, "Gail Hamilton," found her home in the adjoining town of Hamilton and had close connections here, where her visits were frequent. Her friendship with Whittier was a marked one and many tokens of it have been preserved. Dr. Andrew P. Peabody, most beloved by Harvard students, whose cheers for the venerable preacher to the University re-

THE OLIVER WENDELL HOLMES HOUSE, BEVERLY FARMS, MASS.

HOSPITAL POINT, BEVERLY

sounded in the "Yard" less heartily than for none other, was born in Beverly and used often to repair hither for the Summer season.

Lucy Larcom Beverly claims as its own, as she was born here and spent most of her life in the town. The peculiar association of her, whose "Wild Roses of Cape Ann" was issued in the full flush of her powers, with the very regions she describes, is reflected in the comment of Dr. Holmes that "she was as true a product of Essex County soil as the bayberry." "A New England Girlhood," is a choice picture of her own tender years modestly set forth, while the sequel to that period is contained in the life of Lucy Larcom, written by Daniel Delaney Addison, once rector of St. Peter's church here, giving also, as he does, extracts from her letters and diary.

Mrs. Larcom was well acquainted with Whittier, having lent him considerable assistance in the shaping of the collections entitled, "Child Life" and "Child Life in Prose," and more conspicuously in the valuable "Songs of Three Centuries," published by Whittier.

Sensitive to the charms of Nature and in touch with humanity in high circumstance and humble, it was the privilege of this singer to give helpful utterance to that which came sweetened from her spirit, to help many to come under the spell and harmony of the heavenly life which she knew. As the kaliedoscopic changes of life's experiences are brought quickly to view in the passing crowd and the question of the purpose of all may press to the front for the on-looker, she gives a helpful tune to the thought:

"But think! No jewel out of setting
   shows
As in its own fit work. So let us learn
To look upon these various lives that
   turn
To one illumming centre. Lo! Each
   glows
In the full brotherhood of Christ's dear
   face,
And is by that relationship divine—
The bond that glorifies your life and
   mine—
Forever lifted out of commonplace!"

And now mention must be made of
one, whose paternal ancestry goes
back to the original settlers of Beverly,
and who, born at the homestead to
which he now and again returns, has
made large appreciative mention of
Beverly in his verses, while he has
valued the setting of nature among his
native scenes and caught the spirit of
its history. The life of George E.
Woodberry has been given to letters,
while for about twelve years he was
professor of comparative literature in
Columbia College. His literary
product is considerable, and he is in
the full measure of creative power.
Various volumes of essays on literary
men and periods, poems in several issues, with, more recently, a collection
giving the published and hitherto un-
published material until 1903, "The
Torch," a book on comparative literature; "Appreciation of Literature," a
critical book on Emerson, besides lives
and estimates of Poe and Shelley in
more exhaustive form,—these items
tell of literary activity, of a mind clear
in insight, suggestive in ideas, sensitive
to Nature, non-traditional in spiritual
tendencies, and while entertaining confessed prejudices, yet open to the
poetic interpretating of the thought
and life of men, which befits the seer,
whose qualities he, in part, exempli-
fies. Surely we have here the most
significant literary product of the community which makes up old Beverly,
and, withal, the most original thinker
that has come from its soil. A man
of letters, he appeals rather to the
world of thinkers—not thus necessarily

to the world of readers. His output is
not for popular consumption, but
rather fit food for those who have had
some fondness for ambrosial viands in
their training and development. "The
Torch" and "Appreciation of Literature," may be taken as marked ex-
amples of his originality. His estimate
of Emerson will give evidence of his
keen analysis and insight with some
glimpses of an acknowledged prejudice—indeed one to which he refers in
the volume.

In "The North Shore Watch," which
celebrates his attachment to an intimate friend, taken away by death in
1878, we get a blending of the human
element as seen in true friendship and
a marked sensitiveness of Nature, making the descriptions, though strikingly
subjective, still impressive and beautiful. Note the following stanza which,
in form, is the type of all the forty-
seven composing the elegy:

"Still planet, making beautiful the
   West,
   Bright bringer of the stars and shel-
      tered sleep,
Calling our hearts as some beloved
   guest,
   Whom for a little while our eyes
      may keep,
   And through long years shall weep;
O, eloquent with flowers to the soul,
   Even as his eyes beneath thy pure
      empire
Beamed the mute music of the heart's
   desire,
   Thee, too, doth Fate control:
And brief as this, thy hour of light
   must be—
To Earth her starry hush, thy solitude
   to me."

Beverly inhabitants who have valued
the literary associations of the community must recall with grateful memories the many Summers during which
Dr. Oliver Wendell Holmes repaired
to his residence at Beverly Farms. The
genial presence of the "Autocrat"
must have a place in the choice recol-
lections both of those who find here a
home only in the Summer and those

whose continuous residence is in Beverly. Many well recall his driving about through the beautiful scenes of the North Shore, while some will have special memories of incidents or pleasantries of conversation which they treasure. The writer heard only recently of one who as a little girl having lost her way as she wandered a bit from the house where she was visiting, was accosted by the good doctor who, upon finding the cause of her tears, led her back to the place she was seeking.

Affable and humorous as he was, leaving to the world so much to charm away care and weariness as one comes under the spell of his musings and comments on human traits and tendencies, sometimes his criticisms were more to be enjoyed by a third party than by the one to whom they were made, as on the occasion which Dame Rumor has handed down, in which the Doctor, having repeatedly attended a country church, suggested to the minister that his services would be improved if he put more work on them.

It is pleasant to record that while no one takes the place of our gentle humorist, the house where he last lived in Beverly, the old Marshall place, is occupied by his son, who inherits the father's full name, one of the justices of the Supreme Court of the United States.

Of course, from its proximity to Boston, though other considerations would be necessary, Beverly has been visited by many literary men and women, who have stayed here for a longer or shorter sojourn. Some will recall that years ago the historian, Prescott, lived here for a season or two.

James Russell Lowell and Edward Everett Hale once boarded together in a little house not far from Mingo Beach, which this present season is the residence of Bishop McVickar and family, and a little beyond, for a season, lived O. B. Frothingham, the writer of New England Transcendentalism.

The atmosphere of the town, in the way of such associations, is touched also by neighboring communities, and so Salem with its Hawthorne and Manchester with Mr. and Mrs James T. Fields, who found there for years a retreat from their busy Boston life, have helped to maintain the spirit and suggestiveness of a life of letters. Mrs. Field, as a literary hostess, has, of course, done much in the way of stimulating intercourse on a higher plane, while it is recalled especially that Sarah M. Jewett, only recently withdrawn by death, spent many a period in enjoyment of Mrs. Field's hospitality, and thus was brought near to many who had found a charm in her stories.

No doubt the coming of President Taft has suddenly increased the prominence of Beverly in the minds of thousands and revealed the fact of its existence to possibly a greater number in far off regions. But before this unsought, though welcome, emphasis on

PRESIDENT'S PIER, BERGEN POINT

MINGO BEACH

its desirableness as a place of residence established by the choice of the President of the United States, it had been to thousands a spot favored by Nature, gathering to itself an interesting history and an increasing store of literary associations to blend with patriotic annals, and altogether a community which, happily, combining city and country, hill and shore, furnishes a habitation and environment for fine achievement in the humanities of social life, but also in the realm of art and letters.

May the inspiration that inheres in the prominence which comes this season to Beverly, tersely expressed by the alternative name, "The Nation's Summer Capital," find an issue and resultant in such larger life, as its future unfolds itself to the widening acquaintance of the world.

19
The Fish Ponds
of Cape Cod

THE FISH PONDS OF CAPE COD

BY JOHN MURDOCK

PHOTOGRAPHS BY THE AUTHOR

TO most people, the name Cape Cod brings up the idea of salt-water fishing—the codfish, of course, mackerel, pollock, bass, tautog, scup and squeteague, not to mention the ubiquitous quahaug, prized in his early youth as the "Little Neck clams," substitute for the oyster at summer dinner-parties.

There are plenty of all these, to be sure, but in addition, the numerous ponds furnish pickerel fishing, which is certainly not surpassed, if equaled, anywhere in New England. Of late years, too, many of these ponds have been stocked with small-mouthed black bass, which have thriven and furnish excellent sport. The common eastern pickerel, *Esox reticulatus*, however, is pre-eminently *the* fresh-water fish of the Cape, and in some of the ponds grows to a remarkable size.

The pleasant old town of Orleans is essentially a region of ponds, and if one chose to go far afield, with Orleans as a base, he might fish a fresh pond every day of the season.

The largest neighboring bit of water, Linnell's Pond, is no longer what it was thirty-odd years ago, when the writer visited Orleans on college vacations. In those days the western shore was a clean sand beach, with only a sparse line of lily-pads at the edge of the deep water, where the shelving beach suddenly dips down. Here the big fish used to lie, and by wading out, and throwing—casting is hardly the word—a big spoon with the long heavy pickerel-rod of those days, one could easily reach them, while the clean sandy beach made an ideal place to land your fish without gaff or landing net. The fish were greedy, too, and an hour's work along that little stretch of beach, not over an eighth of a mile, was sure to give at least one good fish, and usually more.

But the pond is changed now. The once clean beach is foul with a thick growth of rushes and sedge, and in place of the sparse line of lily-pads at the edge of deep water, a dense bed of lilies and floating-heart makes fishing impossible except at occasional breaks in the barrier. Along the western shore the big fish still lurk in the old place, but they have changed too. Whether from excessive fishing, or because the pond is so full of feed, especially of young herrings, the fish have grown sophisticated and fastidious. A plain bare spoon no longer tempts them—it must be baited, and even then often fails. Sometimes live minnows or angleworms will do the trick, but nothing is sure.

A surer find is "Aunt Sally Mayo's" Pond, a little gem nestling among the hills close to the salt water of Pleasant Bay. This is a longer walk, nearly two miles, down past the post office and across the hills, but one never grudges it, for he is always reasonably sure of a good basket. It is the only available one of a chain of three lovely little ponds, for of the other two, one is private property and preserved, and the other so thickly beset with lilies that fishing from the shore is impossible. There is no boat on "Aunt Sally's Pond," so we must wade along the shore, often mid-thigh deep. But much of it is clean beach, and the water plants are not thick enough to interfere seriously with fishing, while the fish, though not extremely plenty, run to a good size, and take the bait with a rush that often brings them clean out of water after they have seized it.

In the other direction, going toward the

Where Walton might have been happy, among the Cape Cod hills.

A try at Percival's Pond.

Forcing a way through the rushes.

railway station, and about a mile from home, lies Percival's Pond. In old times this was famous, but when the writer came back to the Cape, five or six years ago, people said: "It is no use fishing there—the fish have all been killed out." One wonders how such beliefs originate. The first time we tried the pond out of curiosity, last season, we took nine fine fish. After that we went there several times, and never got less than two fish, running to two pounds weight and better; the shore is clean, the deep water easily reached by wading, and the fish are easily handled.

But after all, our favorite stand-by is the little pond, a few minutes' walk from the house, which we call "Frank Gould's," though Frank Gould, the butcher, has been long dead; on him, in old times, before the days of Chicago beef, and butcher-carts driving by two or three times a week, we used to depend for our only taste of fresh meat. Many a happy hour we spend there every season. The fish are small—one of a pound weight counts for a big fish—but there are lots of them, and they are hungry for anything—spoon, live minnow, frog's leg, pickerel throat, or even a bit of pork rind. Curiously enough, hungry as they are, these fish never take the bait with a rush, like "Aunt Sally's" pickerel. A slight check as your bait is drawn through the water, the eclipse of your gleaming spoon by a dark body, is often your only warning of a strike, and it is always necessary to wait for your fish leisurely to turn the bait round and take it wholly into his mouth before you hook him.

But what, after all, makes it a sporting pond, is the difficulty of fishing it. The cedar trees and the bushes grow close down to the water's edge, and one has to wade along the shore, forcing his way through the rushes and flags, casting into accessible holes among the lily-pads, where one can often see the fish poised motionless in the crystal-clear water, and when once hooked, must be coaxed hurriedly through open holes, lest he twist the line around the rushes. Indeed, he must often be lifted clear of the tops of the rushes, and swung dexterously inshore before he has time to drop from the hook, and must be handled and basketed while you stand up to mid-thigh in water. What with rushes, lily-pads and bushes, nearly as many fish find

their way back to the water as get into the basket. It is a delightful little pond, and possesses one great advantage. The fish bite as well in sunshine as in cloudy weather.

The chain of big ponds, Great Cliff, Middle Cliff, or Little Long Pond, and Lower Cliff, or Higgins' Pond, back in the woods across the Brewster line, have a great reputation for big fish, but it is a long rough walk to the nearest, and they do not often lure us away from our favorite near-by haunts. Beside, they are all closely wooded to the water's edge, and have so little beach that fishing from the shore is practically impossible, especially when the ponds are high, and the only available boats are on Great Cliff Pond. This pond has given us good sport with game little bass, running from half a pound to two pounds, and very large yellow perch; but in four trips we have only taken two small pickerel, though, to be sure, we were devoting ourselves particularly to the bass fishing. Middle Cliff we tried once, but the lilies were so thick that we did nothing, while in Lower Cliff in seasons of low water we have found a few fair fish.

Hidden in the woods, not far west of the Cliff ponds lies the little Ralph's Pond (pronounced "Rafe's" in the true old English fashion). It takes its name from old Micah Ralph, the Indian, who in old colony times owned unnumbered acres of woodland around it; Little Ralph's is famous for its winter fishing through the ice. We went there once last season, and found it surprisingly like our favorite "Frank Gould's," except that the rushes are not so bad, the woods not so near the water, and the fish, if anything, thicker and greedier. I never saw pickerel so hungry. In less than two hours, going once around the pond, two of us had basketed twenty-seven fish, all of them small.

Over in Harwich, an hour's drive from our base, lies another chain of ponds, of which the largest, Long Pond, or Pleasant Lake, lying partly in Harwich and partly in Brewster, is nearly three miles long. They say there are plenty of fish in this pond, but it is so big that it is hard to find them, and the fishermen, a good many of whom come down from the city, devote themselves to the string of round ponds, each some twenty or thirty acres in area,

Linnell's Pond, the largest of these bits of fresh water.

and separated from one another only by narrow sand bars, which stretch away from the eastern end of the lake, evidently the remnants of a larger lake of earlier times. We did very little fishing here, for we could get no boat, and the lily-pads—or "bubbly stuff," as the old sea-captain we talked with called it—prevented fishing from the shore, but we saw a fine string of pickerel, among them a four-pounder, which had just been caught in Greenland Pond, the first of these small ponds, where bass also abound.

Then, in the afternoon, we turned south, and drove four or five miles through East Harwich just over the line into Chatham, where we found another cluster of ponds among the bare grassy hills, which reminded us strongly of "Aunt Sally Mayo's" Pond, though most of them were larger. There are pickerel in all of them, but our time was getting short, and we only tried one, which yielded seven small fish in a short time. Some day we mean to fish them thoroughly, for they look promising.

Another day we went exploring over in Eastham. Here, close to the railroad station, we found another cluster of ponds, one of which, Cole's Pond, is said to be very good, though in the short time we had, we caught only a few small fish. This pond is best fished by trolling a spoon from a boat, for the deep water is not easily reached from the shore. The yellow perch, too, are very abundant and large, and the little Depot Pond, just over the hill, is said to be full of white perch. One of these days we mean to make a trip down to Wellfleet, where there is another cluster of ponds, from which we hear great stories of eight-pound pickerel.

East of the Cliff ponds, on the line between Brewster and Orleans, is Baker's Pond, a beautiful bit of water, and always a favorite with the fishermen who stay in Orleans village, but to fish it you must cart a boat in, for none are kept there, and fishing from the shore is of no use. At present fishing is allowed there three days only in the week, for the State Fish Commission has just stocked the pond with trout.

In East Orleans, almost over at Nauset Harbor, is still another pickerel pond, called Thatcher's, where some very good fish have been taken, but it is right in the midst of a colony of "summer folks," and consequently is fished very hard.

As to baits, we use a variety—live minnows, when it isn't too much trouble to catch them. The fish take them well, but more often we use cut baits of some kind—perch bellies with the red fins, pickerel throats—remember Dr. Holmes' lines:

There's a slice near the pickerel's pectoral fins,
Where the *thorax* leaves off and the *venter* begins;
Which his brother, survivor of fish-hooks and lines,
Though fond of his family, never declines—

or, best of all, perhaps, a frog's leg, skinned. We have found all of these cut baits far more killing when fished on a little casting spoon. Whether fishing with a spoon or not, we use a rather light fly rod, casting and fishing with a "sink and draw."

Trolling a spoon from a boat has given us a few fish in Linnell's Pond, but phantom minnows and such apparatus do no good at all. On the whole, the fresh-water fish of Cape Cod are simple in their tastes, with few cultivated eccentricities.

20
Yarmouth
A Typical Cape Cod Town

SANDY NECK LIGHT.

Yarmouth--A Typical Cape Cod Town

By Ella Matthews Bangs

"THIS is a glorious sunset," a visitor in Yarmouth once remarked to a native of the place. The man addressed gave a grudging glance toward the panorama of the heavens, radiant in violet, rose, and amber, and returned succinctly, "Don't think much o' *em*, seen too many of 'em."

But while this lack of appreciation is by no means common among the natives of Cape Cod, they perhaps by reason of lifelong association fail to see the quaint and picturesque charm in the towns and villages around them, which to visitors from other parts of the country is as distinctly characteristic as are the beautiful sunsets. Much might be written of Provincetown, so many of whose inhabitants are of foreign birth or parentage; of Hyannis with its fine harbor and attractive streets and the claim of being the only Cape town which now shows a steady growth; or of picturesque little Wellfleet, made famous by Marconi and his wireless telegraphy.

But each of these is, in a sense, an exception.

A town more nearly typical of Cape Cod villages as a whole, in past enterprise and present passivity, is Yarmouth; which, like the grandmother she is, after having sent her offspring out into all parts of the world, has settled down to the enjoyment of a serene old age. The earliest mention of this vicinity in history comes under the date of 1622 when, there being a dearth of food at Plymouth, Governor Bradford with a company of men sailed around the Cape and after stops at other places, bought at Nauset and Mattachiest (Yarmouth) twenty-eight hogsheads of beans and corn. The following year Miles Standish came to Mattachiest or Mattacheese to buy corn of the natives, and being forced to lodge in the Indian houses became convinced that there was a desire to kill him on the part of the Indians. Here also "some trifles were missed." These were only a few beads, but the little captain

317

with his usual intrepidity demanded restitution, which the sachem caused to be made, and then ordered more corn to be given the visitors by way of recompense.

In 1637 liberty was granted Mr. Stephen Hopkins to erect a house at Mattacheese and cut hay there to winter his cattle, provided that he should not withdraw from the town of Plymouth. Others soon followed in his footsteps and the permanent settlement of Yarmouth was made in 1639, and by October of that year so well established was the town that the court ordered "a pair of stocks and a pound to be erected."

Among the most prominent men of this period were Anthony Thacher, John Crow (Crowell), and Thomas Howes; descendants of whom, bearing the same names, may still be found within a few miles of this early settlement. The first of these, Antony Thacher (as he spelled his own name), was a man of education and refinement, for in records still in existence he is mentioned as curate for his brother, the Rev. Peter Thacher, rector of St. Edmunds, Salisbury, England, from 1631 to 1634. He had been with the colony at Leyden, and is said to have had almost as many adventures by land and sea as the hero of the Odyssey. In the "Swan Song of Parson Avery," the poet Whittier had told of the shipwreck off Cape Ann on the night of August 14, 1635, when twenty-one out of twenty-three persons were drovned, the two escaping being Anthony Thacher and his wife. Mr. Thacher's letter to his brother Peter, written a few days after the wreck; is remarkable for unaffected pathos and Christian faith. It begins:

"I must turn my drowned pen and shaking hand to indite the story of such sad news as never before this happened in New England. There was a league of perpetual friendship between my cousin Avery and myself, never to forsake each other to the death, but to be partakers of each other's misery or welfare, as also of habitation in the same place. Now upon our arrival in New England, there was an offer made unto us. My cousin Avery was invited to *Marblehead* to be their pastor in due time; there being no church planted there as yet, but a town appointed to set up the trade of fishing. Because many there (the most being fishermen) were something loose and remiss in their behavior, my cousin Avery was unwilling to go thither, and so refusing, we went to *Newbury,* intending there to sit down. But being solicited so often, both by the men of the place and by the magistrates, and by Mr. Cotton, and most of the ministers, who alleged what a benefit we might be to the people there, and also to the country and commonwealth, at length we embraced it, and thither conserted to go. They of *Marblehead* forthwith sent a pinnace for us and our goods. We embarked at *Ipswich,* August 11, 1635, with our families and substance, bound for *Marblehead,* we being in all twenty-three souls, vis: eleven in my cousin's family, seven in mine, and one Mr. William Elliot sometime of *New Sarum,* and four mariners."

After a vivid description of the storm and shipwreck, and the casting ashore of himself and wife upon an island, where provisions and articles of clothing were also washed ashore, Mr. Thacher's letter thus concludes:

"Thus the Lord sent us some clothes to put on, and food to sustain our new lives, which we had lately given unto us, and means also to make a fire for in an hour I had some gunpowder, which to mine own (and since to other men's) admiration was dry. So taking a piece of my wife's neckcloth, which I dried in the sun, I struck a fire, and so dried and warmed our wet bodies, and then skinned the goat, and having found a small brass pot we boiled some of her. Our drink was brackish water. Bread we had none. There we remained until Monday following, when about three of the clock in the afternoon, in a boat that came that way, we went off that desolate island which I named after my name 'Thacher's Woe,' and the rock 'Avery, his fall,' to the end that their fall and loss and mine own, might be had in perpetual remembrance. In the isle lieth buried the body of my cousin's eldest daughter, whom I found dead on the shore. On the Tuesday following, in the afternoon, we arrived at *Marblehead*."

In the Massachusetts Colonial Records, under date of September 3, 1635, is the following:

"It is ordered that there shall be fforty marks given to Mr. Thacher out of the treasury towards his greate losses."

And under date of March 9, 1636-7:

"Mr. Anthony Thacher had granted him the small iland at the head of Cape Ann (vpon wch hee was pserved from shipwrack) as his pp inheritance."

And Thacher's Island still bears his name.

From Marblehead Mr. Thacher went to Mattacheese (Yarmouth) and built a house—in which he died —near the salt marsh on the north shore of the town, and in the vicinity of that built by Stephen Hopkins. For eleven years Mr. Thacher represented the town of Yarmouth in the General Court at Plymouth. John, a son of Anthony, also held several public offices, being for nearly twenty years a member of the Provincial Council. He also held the rank of Colonel, and at his death in Yarmouth was buried with military honors. John Thacher married Rebecca Winslow, a niece of the first Governor Winslow, and the Thacher Genealogy furnishes this interesting anecdote concerning this couple:

"On his return to Yarmouth with his bride and company, they stopped at the house of Colonel Gorham, at Barnstable (town adjoining Yarmouth). In the merry conversation with the newly married couple, an infant was introduced, about three weeks old, and it was observed to Mr. Thacher that it was born on such a night, he replied that it was the very night he was married; and taking the child in his arms, presented her to his bride saying, 'Here, my dear, is a little lady born on the same night that we were married. I wish you would kiss it as I intend to have her for my second wife.' 'I will, my dear,' she replied, 'to please you, but I hope it will be a long time before you have that pleasure.' So taking the babe she pressed it to her lips, and gave it a kiss. This jesting prediction was eventually verified. Mr. Thacher's wife died, and the child, Lydia Gorham, arriving at mature age actually became his wife, January 1, 1684, O. S.

"Tradition also furnishes the following anecdote concerning the manner of obtaining the second wife. After the death of his first wife, John, while riding in Barnstable, saw a horse belonging to his son Peter tied to a tree in front of Colonel Gorham's residence, and as a thoughtful parent is inclined, he went in to see what his son was doing, and found that he had advanced considerably in a suit with Miss Lydia, whom the father had prophetically declared would be his second wife; and whether it was on account of that prophecy, or that he had had his attention called to the girl before, he took Peter aside and offered him ten pounds, old tenor, and a yoke of black steers, if he would resign his claims.

As to whether Peter was satisfied with this transaction, tradition sayeth not; but it was the father and not the son who married Miss Lydia.

Besides Mattacheese, the old township included Hockanom, Nobscusset, and Sursuit, (North and East Dennis); to which latter location Richard Sears of Leyden and Plymouth led a company in 1643, and many sons and daughters of Yarmouth today are proud to trace their ancestry back to "Richard the Pilgrim." In the ancient cemetery, not far from the site of the first dwellings erected. the descendants of Richard Sears have raised a fine granite monument to his memory.

In common with all New England, at this period the church took precedence of the town; indeed no set-

CATHOLIC CHAPEL.

LIBRARY
PRESENTED BY
NATHAN MATTHEWS, SR.

CONGREGATIONAL CHURCH.
Photos by Elmer W. Hallett

tlement was recognized as such until it had its church and minister. So in Yarmouth the church antedated the incorporation of the township by several months. The first church building undoubtedly stood on the spot known as Fort Hill, near the old burying ground—a log house, 30 by 40 feet, with oiled paper in place of window glass—and to this rude little building the faithful were called together on Sabbath morning by beat of drum. And it became all to be faithful in those days, for according to a record of 1655,

"If anyone denied the Scriptures to be a rule of life he was to receive corporal punishment at the hands of the magistrates."

and two men were fined ten shillings each for disturbance at the Yarmouth meeting house, and others five shillings for smoking tobacco "at the end of the meeting house on the Lord's day in time of exercise." The first minister was Mr. Marmaduke Matthews, the eloquent Welshman, who was matriculated at All Souls' College, Oxford, 1623, and came to New England in 1638. Among his successors was the Rev. Timothy Alden, a direct descendant of John Alden, and who for nearly sixty years, from 1769 to 1828, occupied the pulpit. Several years after the building of the first church, a more pretentious place of worship was erected on the main street of the village. This in turn gave place to another and larger structure on nearly the same site; one with a high pulpit, sounding board, and square pews, which in course of time was remodelled to conform to more modern ideas. In 1870, however, the present place of worship was erected on the main street, but farther west than the old one which was sold and for a number of years used as a store and Post

Office, while the second floor, after being put to various uses was fitted up by the C. C. C. Club, (Cape Cod Central,) as their place of meeting. Unfortunately, however, during December, 1902, the old building, a familiar landmark for so many years, was burnt to the ground.

Rev. Timothy Alden has been described as "a little man with his antique wig, small clothes, and three-cornered hat, witty and wise." He lived to complete his ninety-third year. Among his writings is

town were nearly as numerous as the white people." And to the early settlers belongs the honor of fair treatment of these natives. In 1657 Messhatampaine acknowledged that he had been fully paid and satisfied for every parcel of land sold to Anthony Thacher, John Crowell, and Thomas Howes, of Yarmouth. Rev. John W. Dodge, for many years pastor of the first church (congregational), has preserved a number of interesting anecdotes of the native inhabitants. Among these is the

SANDY SIDE (SIMPKINS ESTATE), BUILT BY THE LATE RUTH S. SIMPKINS.
Photo by Elmer W. Hallett

much valuable information concerning the Indians. For many years the southern part of the town of Yarmouth was an Indian reservation, and mission work was at once begun by the church people. During the ministry of Rev. Thomas Thornton, 1667-1693, there were said to have been nearly two hundred praying Indians in town under two native teachers. Writing in 1794 Mr. Alden says, "Within the memory of some the Indians in this

story of Elisha Nauhaught, which Whittier has woven into verse in his poem, "Nauhaught the Deacon." The dwelling of this intrepid hero stood on the shore of what is now known as Long Pond, in South Yarmouth; and near this place a late owner of the grounds, Dr. Azariah Eldridge erected a monument formed of a pile of stone on the upper of which is the inscription:

ON THIS SLOPE LIE BURIED
THE LAST OF THE NATIVE INDIANS
OF YARMOUTH.

The town of Yarmouth extends from shore to shore across what Taureau has called "the bared and bended arm of Massachusetts;" but though incorporated as one township, it has several divisions with a Post Office in each. Thus there are: Yarmouth, Yarmouth Port, West Yarmouth and South Yarmouth; the two latter are villages by themselves, South Yarmouth being formerly known as Quaker Village, and still longer ago as South Sea. Between Yarmouth proper, however, and the Port there is no visible dividing line and both are commonly spoken of as Yarmouth, the two portions designated as "up and down street."

It is a proud tradition of the town that when, in 1776, Captain Joshua Gray had the drum beat to raise volunteers to reinforce Washington at Dorchester Heights, eighty-one men —one half the effective force of the town—were next day on the march. In the same year, when the towns were requested to express their opinion whether, if Congress should declare the Independence of the Colonies, the people would sustain them in the act, the town voted unanimously,

"That the inhabitants of the town of Yarmouth *do declare a state of independence of the King of Great Britain,* agreeable to a late resolve of the General Court, in case the wisdom of Congress should see proper to do it."

Common schools, next in importance to the church in the interests of the early settlers, were well founded here, and today compare favorably with those of New England cities. To the agricultural pursuits of the first white inhabitants was soon added another, that of securing the

THE LATE JOHN SIMPKINS,
*Representative to Congress from the 13th
Massachusetts District*
Photo by James L. Breese, N. Y.

"drift" whales, which in those days were cast upon the shores within the bounds of Yarmouth. Later the business of whaling was originated, and for a hundred years proved vastly profitable. Previous to and immediately after the Revolution, cod fishery was extensively engaged in, and the coasting business to southern and European ports. During the Revolutionary war, owing to the high price of common salt, attention was turned to the question of producing salt from sea water through solar evaporation, and before the end of the eighteenth century a native of this vicinity had invented and perfected a set of contrivances by means of which this end was accomplished. This invention of salt works brought about a business of great profit to the town and vicinity for nearly fifty years and until through the abolition of duties on foreign salt and the development of sources of supply in our own land, the business ceased to be of profit. Until within comparatively a few years, however, the remains of the salt works, with their windmills, formed a picturesque feature of the landscape in the southern part of the town. Between the years 1820 and 1861, when American shipping was at its height, Yarmouth furnished many shipmasters who had no superiors. Contemporary with this engagement in foreign commerce, mackerel fishing and ship-building were carried on nearer home and flourished for a while, but came to an end, practically, with the Civil war.

Between sixty and seventy years ago Henry Hall of Dennis discovered the art of cultivating the cranberry, thus making available the many swamps and marshes throughout the Cape towns. Yarmouth, in common with her neighbors, has found cranberry growing more lucrative than any previous branch of industry, despite the many enemies of the vines and berries in the way of insects and early frosts, and Cape Cod cranberries have acquired a reputation for excellence which extends beyond New England. As is often the case however with other industries, overproduction has of late years interferred somewhat in the way of profit. A ten acre bog in Yarmouth was bought a few years ago by a retired ship-captain for $6,000, though the former owner was for some time reluctant to let it go at so low a figure. From this, in some seasons, four hundred or more barrels of berries have been shipped. When picking begins, the bog is lined off into rows a few feet in width and two pickers placed in each row, while the overseer looks out that no row is left unfinished. Dur-

ing the season, one who is up betimes of a morning may see cart loads of sunbonneted women and broad-brimmed hatted men en route to the cranberry bogs. Merry companies they are too, for there seems to be a fascination about the work difficult to understand by the uninitiated, especially when the pickers come home tired and lame after a day on their knees. They claim, however, that the lameness wears off after a few days—and one must believe it when told that during the noon hour, after the lunches are disposed of, the pickers sometimes repair to the cranberry house, where an accordion or harmonica is brought out and to their enlivening strains the young folks "trip the light fantastic toe" until the one o'clock signal is given, when work must be resumed.

The Yarmouth of to-day presents a long and broad main street, lined on either side by elms which form an arch high overhead as one drives through the Port, falsifying the assertion that nothing can grow from Cape Cod soil; though the early settlers evidently labored under a similar delusion, for in the belief that nothing else would flourish they set out numerous silver-leaved poplars, particularly in the lower (eastern) and older part of the village, and these continue to grow and increase notwithstanding the vigorous attempts to eradicate a second generation. A broad blue sweep of ocean is in sight from the streets of the Port, and glimpses of it may be had all down through the village; while away to the northwest Sandy Neck stretches out its barren length and supports its lonely lighthouse. For two miles or more an unbroken line of buildings extends on either side of the street, ending in the low-

FIREPLACE IN OLD THACHER HOUSE, NOW OCCUPIED BY J. G. HALLETT.
Photo by Elmer W. Hallett

er part of the village near a stream known as White's Brook, named for Jonathan White, a son of the Perigrine White, who was born on board the Mayflower while she lay at anchor in Provincetown harbor. Other reminders of this family may be seen in the old cemetery, where on more than one tombstone one may read, under a coating of moss, the name Perigrine White.

Among the buildings included in these two miles are five churches, a new-comer among these being the little Roman Catholic church of The Sacred Heart, dedicated in 1902. Nearly opposite the Congregational church is a large school house, containing rooms for all grades from Primary to High. A little farther up street is a modern and pretty public hall, a Public Library, Na-

tional Bank, and various offices and stores. Here, too, is a printing office, from which is issued weekly the "Yarmouth Register"; a paper now in its sixty-seventh volume and ably edited for more than half a century by the late Hon. Charles F. Swift, a man closely identified up to the time of his death in May 1903, with the best interests of the town and county. The literary work of Mr. Swift is of lasting value, his "History of Cape Cod" and "History of Old Yarmouth" being recognized as standard authorities. And to the latter the writer is indebted for many facts given in this article.

Leading off from the main street and on a slight eminence, is *Sandy Side*, the residence of the late Congressman John Simpkins, representative from the thirteenth Massachusetts district; a young man whose death in 1898 is still mourned throughout the town in whose public life he was so actively interested. *Sandy Side* is still the summer home of members of the Simpkins family, the house in its setting of green lawns being a prominent object as one nears the railway station. A little farther west is *Mattachese*, the summer residence of Dr. Gorham Bacon of New York, a connection, by marriage, of the same family. Another homestead, attractive in the midst of well kept grounds, was for many years the home of Azariah Eldridge, D. D., a native of Yarmouth, who, after spending the active years of his life elsewhere, came back to pass his declining days in the old town. For several years Dr. Eldridge was pastor of the American Chapel in Paris, France, and he has been honored by a memorial at Yale.

The Yarmouth Institute—a society for literary improvement—has existed with slight interruption since 1829, with a course of lectures or musical entertainments each winter. Later social organizations are the Colonial Club, C. C. C. Club (already referred to), the Woman's Clubs, and Village Improvement Society. About a mile from the village and on the road to Hyannis is the Yarmouth Campground—a fine oak grove covering more than thirty acres—where annual meetings have been held for the last forty-one years. The grounds are attractively laid out, with a small park near the entrance, and though not elaborate the cottages are pleasantly inviting. Near the centre of the grounds is the Tabernacle, with a seating capacity of seventeen hundred; and here some of the ablest preachers of the Methodist Conference may be heard.

Yarmouth was the native place of the twin brothers, Edward and Nathan Matthews; the former the father of Prof. Brander Matthews, the well known writer, while a son of the latter is Nathan Matthews, ex-mayor of Boston. The Public Library of the town was a gift from Nathan Matthews, Sr. Here, also, was the early home of J. Montgomery Sears, the Boston multi-millionaire; and it is to the generosity of the father of this gentleman, Mr. Joshua Sears, that Yarmouth is indebted for her fine system of graded schools. Three Yarmouth ship masters have successively been in command of the missionary brig and steamer, *Morning Star*, namely: Captains Nathaniel Matthews, William Hallet, and Isaiah Bray. Indeed sea captains from this town have found their way into foreign ports the world over. One can tell of a visit to Pitcairn Island, that interesting and rarely visited community with its unique history: while others have romantic tales sufficient to make a volume in themselves; stories of travels in the Holy Land; of adventures in Chinese ports; of shipwrecks, of pirates and mutinies, thrilling indeed when heard at first hand. Few Yarmouth young men are now following a sea-faring life, but many of an earlier generation, now retired, contribute immeasurably to the air of prosperous content, which is as distinctly a part of the old town as that salt breath of the sea which is ever present. By far, the greater number of sea captains, however, have many years since gone out on a last Long Voyage.

In the lower part of the village stands a milestone still bearing in distinct characters the date of its erection in 1720. For many years a touch of the picturesque was given by an old windmill standing a short distance back from the main street, but unfortunately its unappreciative owner allowed it to fall into decay; one by one its lofty arms weakened and fell, till now only the tower remains—a sombre reminder of other days. In September 1889, Yarmouth celebrated her quarter millennial, and, as was fitting from the fact that the church antedated the

Indeed, a small proportion of them have been built within the last fifty years. One of these old houses, which however does not show its age, is the Thacher homestead built in 1680; a large two story house on the main street. Another, nearer the northern shore, dates back from a hundred and fifty to two hundred years, though the exact time of its erection is not known. It is supposed to have been built by Judah Thacher, a grandson of Anthony,

CHANDLER GRAY HOUSE. TAKEN DOWN IN 1899.

organization of the township, the exercises were opened on Sunday, September 1, by union services at the First Church; on which occasion the pastor, Rev. Mr. Dodge, was assisted by Rev. Jeremiah Taylor, D. D., of Boston, a grandson of Rev. Timothy Alden. On the third of September, the anniversary of the town was celebrated by her sons and daughters from all over the country. Many of the residences on the long main street are very old.

and upon the death of its builder passed to his son, Hon. David Thacher. This house is today the home of Mr. James G. Hallet, and one of its rooms remains as it was left by Mr. Thacher upon his death in 1802, and as it is said to have been fitted up by him for the entertainment of his grand company. In this old parlor the woodwork extends to the ceiling, that over the fireplace being of polished mahogany and embellished with paintings of considerable pretention. The work is said to have been done by a French artist. The scene on one side represents the lights at the mouth of Boston harbor as they were at that time, and the other is a view of Fort Warren. The tiles around the fireplace are of porcelain, probably from Holland, and very quaint and curious. The painting on the fireboard itself shows an old fashioned house, (supposed to be the one of which this room is a part) with fish-flakes near by, and in the background Sandy Neck and the harbor, with several vessels in the curious rig of that day, while in the centre is an elaborate portrait of George Washington, and beneath it the words, "The President of the United States." This fact seems to show that the work was done during Washington's administration. Hon. David Thacher, whose taste was thus displayed, was a man of prominence during the Revolution, and one of wealth and influence. For twenty-seven years he represented Yarmouth in the state Legislature and was for two years senator for this county. At the election in 1798 he was re-elected Representative but declined, whereupon the following vote was passed:

"Voted, gratitude and thanks to David Thacher Esq. for the good service done the town for the number of years past, he being aged and declined the service any longer."

As the "Yarmouth Register" has remarked: "This is rather a contrast to the way ex-Representatives are treated in these days."

Another old house, in the upper part of the village, with a two story front and lean-to back, known to the present generation as the Chandler Gray house, is supposed to have been built about two hundred years ago by Jonathan Hallett; passing from him to his son Thomas, who in turn left it to his adopted son Joshua Gray by whom it was bequeathed to his son Chandler Gray. Captain Joshua has already been referred to as the commander of the company of men who marched to help erect the fortifications at Dorchester Heights, and on the night preceding their march, the loyal mothers and daughters of Yarmouth gathered in one of the front chambers of this old house, bringing their pewter dishes and other articles, which they melted into bullets with which to supply their brave husbands and fathers. It seems unfortunate that so historically interesting a building could not have been preserved indefinitely; but grown feeble with age, the ancient house was torn down in May 1899, at which time workmen found reminders of the olden days in the presence of a few bullets around the capacious chimney.

Many another old house, in common with those all over the Cape, is rich in the product of foreign lands, for long before imported needle-work and bric-a-brac was common in the city stores, the wives, daughters, and sweet-hearts of Cape Cod sea-captains were in possession of rare and beautiful articles which might quite have turned the heads of some of their inland sisters: satins, pine-apple cloths, embroidered pongees and India muslins, as well as elaborate India easy chairs, huge palm-leaf fans, inlaid tables and boxes, and articles of exquisite carvings in rose-wood, ivory, and sandal-wood. One Yarmouth housewife has been seen rolling out her pastry with a rolling pin of polished rose-wood with ivory handles, while the wife

OLD HALL HOMESTEAD, NOW OCCUPIED BY HERBERT LOWELL AND FAMILY.
Photo by Elmer W Hallett

of another sea-captain has a set of gray pearls from the Orient, rare and beautiful; and indeed it seems safe to say that there are today laid carefully away in chests of camphor or sandal-wood, dress patterns in silk, velvet or muslin, which have never known the touch of shears. Indeed some of these old rooms are literal curiosity shops, containing not only the products of lands from "Greenland's icy mountains," to "India's coral strands," but rich in many quaint articles of furniture and household adornment handed down from the early settlers.

Speaking from a more practical standpoint, however, it seems that unless some new industry is started to prevent the younger people from going elsewhere, Yarmouth has seen her best days. To many it has seemed that the much talked of Cape Cod ship canal could not be undertaken at a better location than here, from the fact that a natural waterway extends nearly across the Cape at this point, this waterway being formed by Bass river on the south, and Chase's Garden river on the north; a tributary to the latter being White's brook.

As it is, however, many an old house is today closed and tenantless, or opened only during the summer. Many another has but a single occupant; but whatever her future may be, Yarmouth will ever be rich in memories of by-gone days.

21
Brother Jonathon (Trumbull) and His Home

From the Portrait by John Trumbull.

THE

NEW ENGLAND MAGAZINE.

NEW SERIES.   SEPTEMBER, 1897.   VOL. XVII. No. I.

BROTHER JONATHAN

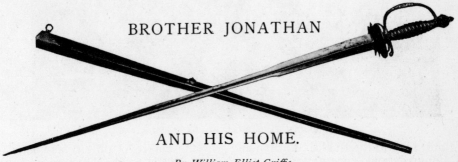

AND HIS HOME.

By William Elliot Griffis.

FROM time to time history shows human characters that incarnate an era, a nation, a civilization. Through inheritance, opportunity and the will and power to interpret and express the attainments and aspirations of their fellows, some men seem able to gather into themselves the forces of an age. Perhaps no one man in American history has more fully embodied the spirit of any one of the thirteen colonies than did Governor Jonathan Trumbull that of Connecticut. So well did he do it that the figure of the Puritan magistrate, transfigured against the Brocken Revolutionary storm-clouds, has become the pictorial embodiment of the United States. The great American republic is personified in him.

We all know the graphic symbols which express the spirit of Connecticut's original settlers and of the men who continued their work. Let us look at these and note the pre-natal life of a noble state in the tried and tempered spirits of those who had for the sake of freedom of conscience endured persecution. Having crossed the seas to maintain their liberty, they took good care to safeguard it when won. The founders of Connecticut were educated Englishmen who, having done noble service for their rights in the home land, had in republican Holland reinforced and enlarged their souls. While tempering their noble contention for religious freedom with tolerance they had also enlarged their conceptions of ecclesiastical and civil government while they were in contact with that democratic spirit that permeated the churches in the Netherlands. Dutch Calvinism, in the sixteenth and early seventeenth century, was the only nurse of freedom of conscience in Europe.

Coming to America from England, but finding the forms of social and political order in the Bay Colony not quite liberal enough, Hooker, Davenport and their co-workers emigrated to a region of broad rivers and streams that empty into Long Island Sound. There they formed a political order of society which, after giving full honor

THE JONATHAN TRUMBULL HOUSE AT LEBANON, CONN.

and credit to the English, Puritan and Congregational inheritance, bears too close a resemblance to the political structure of a Dutch state to be accidental. In details of their political procedure, special features of their town-system, in the liberality of their laws in favor of women, and in their spirit of religious tolerance, Connecticut, though growing much that was original on her own soil, took her precedents from Holland. The founders of Connecticut had lived long enough in the Dutch republic to absorb much of its spirit. Many pages of Ubbo Emmius's history of ultra-democratic Friesland and of the history of colonial Connecticut are wonderfully alike.

With glowing and practical faith in God, these pioneers took as their graphic symbol three fruit-laden vines with the motto, "Qui transtulit, sustinet," fully believing that He who had transplanted the vine of hope and freedom would nourish it in the American wilderness. Led by Hooker and Davenport, they founded a true democracy. They not only believed that, under God, power resided with the people, but they manifested that power

in the choice of officers and magistrates made by the direct vote of the people. Serious, earnest, and nobly infused with that spirit of self-control which makes the true freemen, their colony soon became known as "the land of steady habits."

The geographical nomenclature of a newly settled country reflects truthfully the spirit and tastes of the people, or of their governors, who have the naming of the new "concentrations" and land divisions. It is very interesting to compare the names of Connecticut towns and counties with those, for example, of Massachusetts. On the map of the Bay State we have a panorama of the political history of England. One finds not only the names of English royalty, good and bad, wise and foolish, but also of royalty's favorites, mistresses, places of residence, gentile connections and precedents. From the names of Massachusetts towns, one could write as in an illuminated commentary the story of British kings for a century and a half. On the contrary, in Connecticut, the most democratic of all the thirteen colonies, one will find on the map no name suggesting king, queen or royal favorite, unless perchance it be one like that of Windsor. This, indeed, recalls the seat of a palace; but then it was given by emigrants from Massachusetts. The Connecticut names were born on the soil, transferred from redmen, borrowed from the Bible, Anglicized or, as in the case of Housatonic, *Indianized* from the Dutch, who were the first white explorers, or they are reminiscences of ancestral seats, of historic incidents, or indexes of first impressions.

If we must recognize the "wooden nutmeg" as in any way symbolical of Connecticut, one detects here a tribute to the acknowledged shrewdness and inventiveness of her sons. In making Malay spice grow on New England pine trees, there is probably no more caricature than the keen Connecticut folks have made of their neighbors in New Netherland.

Without controversy or discount, we may say that at the opening of the Revolutionary War the Charter Oak Colony, by its geographical situation, the character of its people, its development in agriculture, industries and trade, its excellent government and sound political and financial methods, was one of the best fitted of all the thirteen colonies to enter into a long war that should try to the uttermost the resources and character of the commonwealth. It was fortunate that in such an hour the chief magistrate was also

the foremost citizen of the commonwealth, incarnating the spirit of its citizens. So thoroughly did Jonathan Trumbull do this, that his name, as familiarly used in council by the Father of his Country, has become the American's title of endearment and the world's term of pleasantry for the great nation now numbering over seventy millions of souls.

The license of caricature has indeed enlarged the Yankee governor's beaver hat to that of the Harrisonian epoch and dimensions; has first lengthened the gubernatorial knee breeches into trousers and then so shrunk their sufficient length as to require straps both taut and elongated under the boots; has borrowed from the fully developed national ensign stripes for the legs and stars for the whig coat, which has sufficiently large brass buttons and wind-swept coattails, to say nothing of an avalanche-like rolling collar. In making out of the Revolutionary "Brother Jonathan" the "Uncle Sam" required for comic caricature, the artist has also grotesquely attenuated his physical frame, sharpened his features and pointed his chin whiskers, so that the ideal personification of the United States, so useful and necessary for the cartoonist, has drifted away somewhat from the original, and from reality. Indirectly the caricature is a compliment to New England, and especially to

ENTRANCE TO THE TRUMBULL HOUSE.

THE OLD WAR OFFICE.

Connecticut, as being "distinctive America." Nevertheless, it seems unreasonable to doubt that the original of Brother Jonathan, as an impersonation of the United States, was the Puritan magistrate of Lebanon and the oft elected governor of Connecticut. As Americans, we may congratulate ourselves that almost as soon as the nation was born a pictorial personification was at hand which, after nearly a century and a quarter, is at once recognized in forty-five states and indeed all over the world.

The name Trumbull comes from an incident that has been symbolized in heraldry. Whether belonging to the same order of legend that ascribes the knightly name of Eyre to the soldier at Hastings who loosened the visor of the stunned and unhorsed William the Conqueror, and gave him air, or

Scudder to the shield bearer (*scutum ecuyer*), or William from gildhelm, or is based on contemporaneous document, we cannot say. The story is told in the reminiscences of Colonel John Trumbull the painter, and is given as history founded on written evidence. In Scotland one of the ancestors of the family saved the life of a royal personage by diverting from the object of its fury an angry bull. In reward for this act of humanity and loyalty, the brave hero was rewarded and allowed to wear as his crest three bulls' heads, because he had turned a

bull away from majesty. In course of time, just as "turkey" on Indian lips became Trukee on one of our western rivers, so turnbull became Trumbull. Until 1766 the family spelled the name Trumble, but after the researches of the artist-son in the Herald's office in London the Governor wrote his name ever afterwards Trumbull.

The first ancestor of the American Trumbulls came from Cumberland county, England, and located at Suffield. This son of John, the immi-

there is one that shows nineteenth century taste and fashion. All around are the eternal hills. Over our heads as we walk along the roadways are grand old elms and maples. One of those once more numerous pine groves, rich in that balsamic perfume which is so gratefully noticeable, especially on a hot day, still remains. The Congregational Church edifice, which is perhaps the first feature to strike the eyes from a distance, pierces the blue sky's expanse with a white spire

INTERIOR OF THE WAR OFFICE, WITH TRUMBULL'S OLD FURNITURE.

grant, had four sons, one of whom, the father of the great Jonathan, settled at Lebanon, Conn., where in 1710 the future Governor was born. At his environment, in the midst of which he grew up, let us now look.

Lebanon is a typical New England village. The spacious green is a mile long, having a double roadway marked by stately trees. The collection of a hundred or less houses is rich in historical interest, though here and

tipped with a flashing gilded vane, while further down on the four faces of the wooden tower are the dials which tell of the passing minutes. The edifice is the third in the course of history. Although the organization of the church is not exactly contemporaneous with the foundation of the town, the history of Lebanon is closely associated with it.

With the wand of imagination or a wave of the hand, like Roderick Dhu's

LEBANON GREEN.

8

in the Highland glen, let us bid church and dwellings, stone walls and well-kept roads, flowering gardens and sober orchards, passing bicycles and baby carriage disappear. Coming back to the primeval nature and aboriginal habitations of nearly two centuries and a half ago, we find that this hill slope and place of goodly cedars was part of the hunting grounds of the Mohegans under Uncas. Its first white settler was Major John Mason, who, like every one of the military leaders of the seventeenth century English colonists in America, had served in the Dutch War of Independence under the orange, white and blue flag. When Mason, in 1637, had given the Pequots proof that the spirit of the ancient "war-man, guerre-man or German" had not been lost in his descendants, but that these could fight in new America as in primeval European forests, Uncas was mightily impressed. He believed the friendship of the English would be an invincible shield against all enemies. He gradually ceded his lands to the Connecticut colony, and they became the property of the General Assembly, which in 1663, to reward Major Mason, allowed him to choose five hundred acres of unoccupied soil and locate his claim where he pleased. The swamp-fighter was not long in making up his mind, for his eye had already rested upon the southwestern slope of Poquechanneeg. He had the surveyors come at once to measure and stake out the land, which by due legal conveyance became his in 1665. His son-in-law, Rev. James Fitch, received the next year from the General Assembly one hundred and twenty acres adjoining Mason's tract, to which the son of Uncas further added a strip five miles long and one mile wide. When to this handsome patch on the earth's surface another tract called "the five mile square purchase" and three

smaller sections were added, the proprietors, seven in number, decided that there was space sufficient for a plantation. "In order that ye Worshippe of goode bee there sett up, ye Kingdom of Christ enlarged," they marked out streets and apportioned to each house-lot forty-two acres.

The golden fleece which we see upon the autumn landscape was not then grown, nor was the living emerald of the mile-long green as yet set, but instead was a dense alder swamp vocal with cat-birds and frogs and having slopes extending back on each side. Soon, however, the Creator and his creatures made greater beauty. With an ax and plow, unceasing industry and toil, having God and time on their side, each reared his "house and home," as old Teutonic phrase describes dwelling and land-lot, and all made a stockaded log fort into which to run in time of danger. From the first there was a well organized social order.

The Indian name of the place was early changed to Lebanon, though it was not until 1697 that "ye new Plantation too ye westward of Norwich bounds" was so called in the records of the General Assembly. This name, so sweet to the ear, so redolent of

THE OLD WAR OFFICE IN TRUMBULL'S TIME.

Biblical associations, suggesting dignity, strength and permanency, was given by the Rev. James Fitch, who was happily impressed with certain superb cedars in this new Land of Promise.

The town is centrally located in eastern Connecticut between Norwich and Hartford, eleven miles north of the head waters of the Thames River. Haddam and New London were its ports of entry, where teams brought to and distributed from this centre the products of the four continents. Lebanon crowns a small elevation which slopes gradually westward to Pease Creek Valley and eastward to the vale of the lively Susquetamscott brook. Hills, vales and fertile fields abound in the neighborhood, and the scenery is delightful.

In those years approaching the Revolution Lebanon was a town of considerable size and importance, numbering 3,960 souls. Being but the fourteenth town in the order of population in 1774, it was the eleventh in valuation in the colony in 1775. That it became the centre of importance in the state and almost the na-

TRUMBULL AND HIS WIFE.
From an early painting by John Trumbull, now in the Wadsworth Athenæum, at Hartford.

tional centre of the American colonies, so that its fame in Europe exceeded that of any place in America except Boston, Philadelphia and New York, was owing to the residence there of the Trumbull family, and especially of "the

only rebel Governor." In the awards for service in the Lexington Alarm but two towns in the state, Windham and Woodstock, were granted larger sums of money as their compensation. Connecticut was the only state that, from 1775 to 1783, was an organic unit in legalized resistance.

To condense a life-story which may be found concisely stated in all the encyclopedias and elaborated in the special biography of Stuart and the Reminiscences of his son, Jonathan Trumbull went to Harvard College when but thirteen years old, becoming well versed in the classics and Hebrew. He graduated at the age of seventeen. He studied theology under the "fighting parson," Rev. Solomon Williams, who was pastor in Lebanon during fifty-four years. In those days there were no theological seminaries. Young Jonathan was actually licensed, preached sermons and expected to enter the active pastorate at Colchester, but Providence had fore-ordained him to be true to his ancestral name and turn John Bull from tossing American law and order to the winds. The Trumbulls, father and sons, were not only men actively interested in farming and village activities, but in domestic and foreign commerce. By the time young Jonathan had nearly reached his majority they were doing a thriving trade, importing from England and Holland in ships chartered by themselves the products of the Old World, and sending back the fish, grain and raw material produced in the colony, besides trading directly with the West Indies. The correspondents of "Trumble, Fitch & Trumble," as the firm then wrote its name, style and title, were at Boston, Halifax, Amsterdam, London and Bristol, St. Eustacius and other West

Indian ports. In Bristol, whence the English sailors sailed out first to discover Antilia, and then under Cabot to make unlocated land-fall in America, their negotiations were especially active.

The loss of an older brother at sea compelled Jonathan's father to call his educated son into the office; and there the young man trained for his state and national usefulness, studying law also in the meantime. There were not many lawyers in the colony at this time, nor was the public opinion in the Puritan colonies, and especially in Connecticut, which had adopted the laws of Moses as its code, favorable to such a profession. Nevertheless young Jonathan Trumbull already foresaw what he afterwards told his son, the painter, when urging him to adopt law "as the profession which in the republic leads to all emolument and distinction." The republic had not yet come, but nevertheless Jonathan found law the straight path to fame, usefulness and profit. When but twenty-three he began his half century of public service. He was elected to the General Assembly, serving several terms, becoming the speaker in 1739, and in 1740 member of the Council and judge.

We need not picture the old training days, when the spirit of West India molasses in the form of rum sometimes befuddled the Puritan patriots, and abundance of cider and various sorts of domestic and imported extracts corroded the interior economy of the Indians and made both the red and white man rather vibratory in his motions toward the end of the day. There were temperate as well as intemperate men in those days, and these conquered themselves. There being

no West Point and militia armory halls for luxury as well as exercise, training days and the French and In-

MADAM FAITH TRUMBULL CONTRIBUTING HER CLOAK
FOR THE SOLDIERS.

dian wars served just as well to make heroes. Jonathan, the Puritan magistrate, became in 1739 Lieutenant Colonel of Militia, though he never took the active field or went to Louisburg. In the Seven Years' War, during which the rolls of Connecticut show 32,000 separate enlistments, he was again quite active in drilling and equipping. He mastered also the secrets of finance, supply and commissary. He was twice asked to go to London as colonial agent, but declined.

During his multifarious occupations as merchant, military trainer, legislator, judge, chief justice, lieutenant-governor and finally governor, which last he became in 1769, he was constantly assiduous in self-culture. He made himself familiar with the course and phenomena of history in the American colonies and in Europe, especially in France, the Netherlands chief executive there was one building in Lebanon, still standing, which became henceforth as closely associated with the councils of the state and

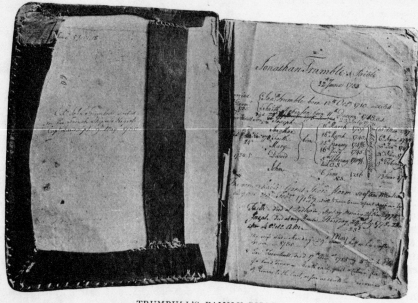

TRUMBULL'S FAMILY BIBLE.
In the Connecticut Historical Society's Rooms at Hartford.*

and England.   He also acquainted himself with the story of ancient history, the causes of national movements and of revolution.   In 1766 the winds of destiny swept his ships from the sea, and the firm became bankrupt; yet this wind, as we now see, boded good to the cause of American freedom, for it served only to develop the sympathies, enlarge the foresight and concentrate the mind of Jonathan Trumbull on public affairs.   As the Revolutionary War approached, he was just the man fitted by constant official training and by minute acquaintance with all parts of the colonies to know what ought to be done and to see that it could be done.   "To difficulties, through difficulties."   In Connecticut the governor was elected directly by the people, and this was the only colony in which this method of choosing the chief magistrate prevailed.

From the moment of his election as later with the councils of the nation, as are the State House in Philadelphia and Faneuil Hall in Boston with American Independence.   This was the storehouse and office of the Trumbulls.   Here the meetings of citizens were held as early as April, 1770, when, because of the Boston Massacre, a committee "met and voted and passed a draft of resolve or Declaration of the rights and liberties which we look upon as infringed by Parliament."   In August of the same year a meeting voted unanimously to send two delegates to New Haven concerning the "non-importation agreement," as well as to form a committee to inspect the conduct of all persons in the town respecting their violation of the true intent and meaning of such agreement.   In a word, the patriots of Lebanon made it too hot a place for

* Trumbull's sword, of which a picture is given at the head of this article, is also in the collection of the Connecticut Historical Society, by whose kind permission these illustrations are given.

tories and half-hearted patriots. Connecticut was the one thoroughly united commonwealth of the thirteen. In it the war movement was one "not of revolution, but of conservatism." It was the whole state itself, under its constitutional and lawful officers, arming in its own defense against a threat of revolution to be enforced upon it from without. The people and the state were one. When the Boston Port Bill took effect, in June, 1774, the Lebanon bells were muffled and tolled from sunrise to sunset. The Town House door was hung with black, on which was nailed a copy of the infamous act. Shops were shut and their windows covered with crape. Governor Trumbull's proclamation announcing a fast, in this year 1774, breathed a spirit of unconquerable tenacity to the cause of law and freedom. Already in this state, where there were few tories, were many who foresaw with Governor Trumbull that the revolution was a foregone conclusion, but they believed that right was on the American side. On the Sunday morning succeeding the battle of Lexington, a messenger, leaving his steaming horse at the church door,

TRUMBULL'S SILVER PITCHER.
In the Historical Society's Collection, Hartford.

strode inside during the services, which were at once suspended. After he had told the story, volunteers for freedom hurried from the church and at beat of the drum enrolled to take up arms for their country. From this time forth Jonathan Trumbull's store became the War Office, the base of supplies for soldiers to be sent to Boston and wherever necessity called during the next seven years.

The term "revolutionist," a mongrel but very convenient word, is not always, because of its associations, accurately applied to good men and opposers of revolution from without. Especially when the political movement fails of success, this term conveys ideas that are more suggestive of the gallows than redolent of olive and laurel. Governor Trumbull and his sons entered solemnly into war as into a holy work, as in conscience bound, and in the belief that they were maintaining the ancestral rights

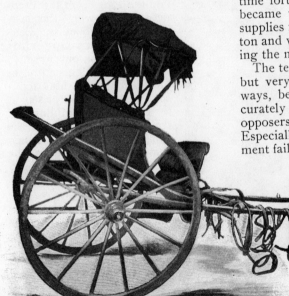

TRUMBULL'S CHAISE.
In the Museum at Bristol, Conn.

of Englishmen. When Joseph Trumbull, the Governor's eldest son, was Commissary General in the Continental Army, and Jonathan, Jr., his second son, Paymaster General of the National Army, private secretary and first aide-de-camp of General Washington, and John, the second son (and painter), was Adjutant-General in Gates's army, and the Governor was by virtue of his office Commander-in-Chief of all the marine and land forces of Connecticut, Hancock sneeringly remarked, at seeing father and sons in office, that *"that* family is well provided for." He seemed to forget that all four would wear halters around their necks if success should not crown the American arms, for the quartette had doubtless agreed to "hang together, lest they hang separately."

Indeed Trumbull was the only col-

JOHAN VAN DER CAPELLEN.
From an old print.

onies the royal governors thwarted the will of the people and were obedient to their master, King George. Most of them, like Tryon, well called "Bloody Billy," Dinsmore and Franklin, Campbell, Wanton and Hutchinson, Brother Jonathan's classmate, were able to retard somewhat the cause of liberty. Trumbull, on the contrary, as an unselfish patriot and a God-fearing man, embodied the spirit of the whole people in the most conservative of the colonies. On the news from Lexington, Israel Putnam, without changing his check shirt, mounted, rode all night, reaching Cambridge at sunrise. The young men from Wethersfield took their fire-locks and at once moved toward the Charles River. Within forty-eight hours of battle tidings five thousand Connecticut troops were on their way northward. Their flags and drums were wreathed with the grape-vine emblems and the motto which uttered their faith that the God who had brought over the fathers would sustain the sons. On the Wednesday, following the lawless British volley on Lexington Green, Governor Trumbull sent out writs to convene the Legislature at Hartford. The Massachusetts men were surprised at the regularity and fullness of the supplies voted by the Connecticut towns, which came so promptly for the army around Boston. Thirty barrels of gunpowder, previously stored ready by Governor Trumbull, arrived in time to fill the powder-horns that were emptied in fire on Bunker Hill. When Washington, under the old elm at Cambridge, drew his sword of command, "promises of mutual reliance, which were never broken, were exchanged with Trumbull, Governor of Connecticut."

onial governor who was also a state's chief magistrate during the war called the Revolution. In all the other col-

In the dark hour when the Ameri-

THE HOME OF GOV. JONATHAN TRUMBULL, JR.
THE BIRTHPLACE OF GOV. JOSEPH TRUMBULL.

THE WELLES HOUSE.
THE BUCKINGHAM PLACE.

can militia, not yet transmuted into an army by the German Steuben, had been defeated on Long Island, the spirit of Jonathan Trumbull rose to the occasion. He wrote: "Knowing our cause righteous, I do not greatly dread what our numerous enemies can do against us." When Washington wrote him a letter revealing the utter weakness of his forces, Trumbull at once summoned the Council again. Though five regiments from the counties of Connecticut nearest the seat of war were already under Washington's orders, Trumbull called out nine regiments more. This was in midsummer, the harvests not yet gathered, nor the time certain when the sowers for next year's crops might return. Yet Trumbull sent word all over the state to those not enrolled in any trained band: "Join yourselves to one of the companies now ordered to New York, or form yourselves into distinct companies and choose captains forthwith. March on: This shall be your warrant. May the God of the armies of Israel be your leader!" The nine regiments, self-equipped, marched to New York.

From this time forth Trumbull became the "guide, philosopher and friend" of Washington, who, as good tradition declares, used a formula in council: "Let us hear what Brother Jonathan says." The man whom God Almighty had raised up and given the capacity to stand repeated defeat and out of disaster to organize victory needed human sympathy, and this he received always from the imperturbable "Brother Jonathan" of Lebanon. Sheltered as Connecticut was from the line of the sea coast, from the great waterway between New York and Canada and from navigable rivers, all of which were paths for the enemy, the state was comparatively free from invasion during the war, except when Bloody Billy Tryon and Arnold attempted their raids. Yet because no large hostile army ever camped on her soil, Connecticut was not less but all the more forward and zealous in maintaining the patriot cause. Only twice did the British wayfarers tarry over night, and "never did they wait long enough to be whipped." Unlike New York, richest in Revolutionary monuments, or Pennsylvania and New Jersey with bloody fields, or Massachusetts, with her famous shaft, Connecticut is "poor in battlefields and monuments of that period," but honorably so.

Her well ordered system of finance, as carefully looked after as Trumbull looked after his own private affairs, enabled the state to maintain credit and furnish its quotas promptly and liberally. Connecticut did indeed see a considerable army, yes, two armies, on her own soil. These exhibited in their contrast the homespun economy

that in the home of the recently married Sarah Backus of Norwich, true daughter of the Revolution, wife of David, the Governor's son, the couple vacated their home and with their little baby went elsewhere to live. Such was the thrift and hospitality of a state whose military headquarters were in a room in a country store.

With practical political sagacity, Trumbull had labored from the first to win for his country friends in Europe. He knew full well that the overwhelmingly superior resources of Great Brit-

THE TRUMBULL TOMB AT LEBANON.

of republican patriots and the gorgeous equipment of imperial warriors. She saw her own sons marching by thousands under the grape-vine flag and the stars and stripes — the only emblem which Trumbull considered more sacred than her own; and she also saw the soldiers of France, who in the white and red uniform of the Bourbons, with martial music and bright uniforms, under the golden lilies on the white silken banners of France, camped at Lebanon. When in the whole village of Lebanon there was but one carpet on the floor, and

ain would enable that country to keep up the war for many years and that it would be necessary for colonists to draw supplies, especially of manufactured war material, from lands beyond the sea. "Brother Jonathan" is to be credited with a goodly share of the influence brought to bear upon the house of Bourbon for its generous aid to America (given, however, as must never be forgotten, with the legitimately selfish purpose of winning back Canada, directly in the interests of French politics and as a part of the European program). Trumbull's wide acquaintance with naval and European men gave him a reputation and standing in Europe which very few of the American statesmen possessed. Very naturally Trumbull looked toward the Dutch republic for sympathy and aid, notwithstanding that British influence was at this particular epoch powerful beyond that in any period known in the history of the Dutch United States. Not only had the stadtholder or hereditary president become closely allied by marriage to the reigning house of Great Britain, not only had he made himself dangerously powerful by abusing his position, which was not elective and impeachable (as the American constitutional fathers, in 1787, took good care to make their presidency), but the able and unscrupulous British minister, Sir Joseph Yorke, had for twenty-five years manipulated Dutch politics and especially the great moneyed power of the Netherlands in the interests of his Hanoverian sovereign. Nevertheless, Trumbull believed that the heart of the Dutch people, who two centuries before had gone through the identical experience of revolting against unjust taxation and despotism and resisting revolution from without, had formed a union of states and had issued a Declaration of Independence, would beat in sympathy with the American brethren. The Dutch republicans in the days when religious toleration was next to unknown had generously harbored his forefathers. As John Adams said:

"If ever there was among nations a natural alliance, one may be formed between the two republics. The first planters of the four northern states found in this country [Holland] an asylum. . . . . . They ever entertained and have transmitted to posterity a grateful remembrance of that protection and hospitality, and especially of that religious liberty they found here, having sought it in vain in England."

Governor Trumbull knew that the pamphlet of the Englishman, Rev. Dr. Price, exposing the villainy of the corrupt Parliamentary party which had forced the war with America, had been translated into Dutch and widely circulated in the republic, and that Dr. Price's second work, printed early in 1776, entitled "Observations on the Nature of Civil Liberty, the Principles of Government, and the Justice and Policy of the War with America," had also been done into Dutch and read by Dutchmen wherever their red, white and blue flag floated; and that, furthermore, when King George III. had in an autograph letter applied to the Congress at the Hague to have them detach the famous Scotch Brigade, which had been for over a century in the Dutch service, to join the British army in America, the proposition was strenuously opposed by Baron Johan Derck van der Capellen, the translator of Dr. Price's pamphlets. Still further, Trumbull knew that some of the first and best supplies for Washington's army (continued throughout the entire war, until the British Admiral Rodney captured the place) had been furnished through the Dutch at St. Eustacius. It was there, on the 16th of November, 1776, that the first salute ever fired by a foreign magistrate in honor of the American flag was rendered by the Dutch Governor Johannes de Graff (whose portrait hangs in the New Hampshire State House at Concord), who had read the American Declaration of Independence. This document had been brought (along with the as yet unstarred banner of the colonial Congress, consisting of thirteen red and white stripes) by the United States man-of-war *Andrea Doria.*

There were two Dutchmen in America at this time whose names deserve to be better known. One of these, Col. Romaine, was a gentleman of great scientific and literary attainments, who had recently been in the service of the British government, surveying, making maps and writing a book on Florida, which is still a standard work. Romaine knowing his own country's history so well was struck, as all students are, with the close resemblance between the Dutch and American resistance of *revolution*

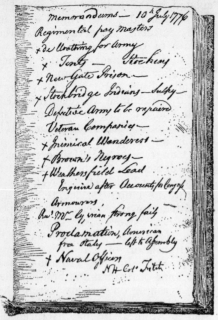

A PAGE OF TRUMBULL'S MEMORANDUM
BOOK.

In the collection of the Connecticut Historical Society.

from without, so that, as John Adams said, "the originals of the one seem to be a transcript of the other." Resigning his office in the British service, Romaine entered the service of the Continental Congress, served honorably in the war, built forts at West Point, and wrote a book (now very rare and the first ever printed in Hartford and under Trumbull's governorship), which shows in detail that the Americans in their revolt from Great Britain were but following in the footsteps of the sixteenth century law-loving Dutchman; or as Governor Livingston of New Jersey wrote to Van der Capellen, "in imitation sir. of your illustrious ancestors." Another Hollander, with whom "Brother Jonathan" was well acquainted, was Gosuinus Erkelens, who, arriving in America in 1774, lived first in New York, then in Philadelphia, and afterwards in Connecticut, interesting himself from the first most energetically in behalf of American freedom. He was a young man, whose mother lived in the well known Leidsche Gracht, or Leyden Waterway, in Amsterdam. Erkelens became a warm friend of Governor Trumbull, and got him to correspond with Baron Van der Capellen, the leader of the patriot or anti-stadtholder party in the republic. Dutch officers of skill and influence came over to fight in the American army, one of whom, Colonel Dircks, after serving in the artillery regiment of Proctor, returned home in 1778. He took back the news of the surrender of Burgoyne, the evacuation of Philadelphia and the battle of Monmouth, giving such clear and detailed information that when circulated in the Dutch newspapers, especially in Professor Luzac's international journal published in French at Leyden, it went all over Europe, powerfully influencing French and European opinion in favor of our cause.

Both in the biography of Baron Van der Capellen, written by my Dutch friend, Mr. J. Sillem, and in his Letters, edited by Mr. W. H. De Beaufort, and published by the Historical Society of Utrecht, we have numerous references to Governor Jonathan Trumbull (as well as other revolutionary fathers) and several of his letters. Trumbull first wrote to Van der Capellen, June 27, 1777. As British cruisers were everywhere along the coast in those days, letters were usually sent in triplicate, — one with the dispatches of Congress, one by any private opportunity that offered itself through trading ship or privateer, and third, which proved to be the safest of all, through the Dutch at St. Eustacius, where through the entire Revolutionary war were usually to be found American ships loading with supplies for the Continental army. When Rodney with his mighty fleet captured the place in 1781, there were fifty American vessels loaded with tobacco to be exchanged for munitions of war, two armed vessels of the United States navy, and two thousand American seamen and officers.

Van der Capellen applied to Governor Trumbull, from Zwolle, September 6, 1778, writing also to Dr. Franklin, then in Paris. Erkelens' first letter had given a pretty full account of the situation and resources of the American colonies. He also enclosed a long and interesting letter from Governor Trumbull to Lord Hillsborough, dated Lebanon, March, 1775, and Lord Hillsborough's reply, besides a paper from Thomas Cushing, dated Boston, September 30, 1768, giving a considerable sketch of the political and financial history of the American colonies, especially those in New England.

gotten that our French allies were carrying out their own schemes, while the Dutch had very little to gain and very much to lose in helping us.

Van der Capellen was kept busy in corresponding with his fellow countrymen of prominence who were warm friends of America. These of course belonged to the Anti-Orange or patriot party and had a common bond of union. Their headquarters were at Amsterdam, then strongly pro-American. Among them were E. F. Van

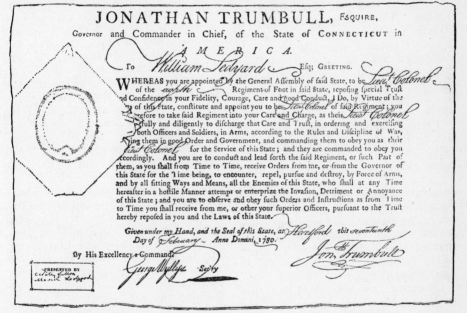

FAC-SIMILE OF TRUMBULL'S COMMISSION TO COL. LEDYARD.
In the collection of the Connecticut Historical Society.

cal and financial history of the American colonies, especially those in New England. These and other papers were translated and circulated in Holland, together with an excellent Dutch account written in America. In the Boston Athenæum there is a collection of fifty or more Dutch books, pamphlets, songs, dramas, etc., which, though but as a few leaves remaining from a forest, show how clearly the Dutch understood the American controversy and why they helped us so unselfishly. For it must never be for-

Berckel, the pensionary of Amsterdam; P. J. Van Berckel, first minister from the Dutch to the American republic, and C. W. Vischer, pensionary of Haarlem. Meanwhile Erkelens was living at Chatham, near Middletown, Conn., while supplies not only in powder and ball, stockings and blankets came through St. Eustacius to the Continental army, but even the very paper on which Thomas Payne wrote his soul-stirring tracts. Toward the end of the war Colonel John Trumbull, son of the Governor, having escaped possible death in England on account of alleged treason, reached Holland. There he was handsomely entertained by the Van Staphorsts, bankers. He also met the Willincks of another Amsterdam banking firm, who, though originally under the influence of the British party, which was led financially by the great house of Hope et Cie, had come out in favor of the Americans. The Willincks negotiated most of the subsequent loans to the Continental Congress, which when paid in 1825 amounted, principal and interest, to nearly fifteen millions of dollars. The Dutch money came in excellent season to pay off the troops who lay inactive after the Yorktown campaign, but who had to be paid and kept proof against monarchy-loving intriguers while waiting at Newburg, N. Y., before the long-delayed peace came.

I remember vividly making my way among hen-roosts and cobwebs in the cellar of an Irish washerwoman's house back of Cornwall, — to such base uses and neglect had the elegant colonial mansion and headquarters of Lafayette come, — to the place where, under the fireplace and reaching down to the bottom of the cellar, was the first of the United States Treasury brick vaults, in which the Dutch money was stored.

Governor Trumbull, like Livingston of New Jersey from this side of the water and Dr. Franklin and John Adams on the other side, kept Van der Capellen and Van der Kemp (who afterwards came to America, founded the town of Barneveldt, now Trenton, New York, and was the pioneer and proposer of the Erie Canal) and other friends of America well informed, until public opinion in the Netherlands was ripened. In due time the Independence of the United States was recognized, whereat the British government at once declared war against the Dutch. These went to war on our behalf, only to lose tremendously in prestige and possessions, with nothing to compensate them. Young Hogen-

dorp, destined to be "the father of the Dutch Constitution," visited America in company with Van Berckel, the first minister of the United Netherlands to our country, and had pleasing interviews with Washington and Jefferson.

In one of the darkest days, when Connecticut seemed to lie bleeding at every pore, Brother Jonathan Trumbull endeavored to get the Amsterdam bankers to lend money to the State of Connecticut. It must be confessed that this looked a little like what we call now-a-days "hard cheek," for Connecticut was but one of the thirteen colonies, and only two, Delaware and Rhode Island, were smaller. To lend money to a separate colony beyond the Atlantic, when no state of the seven in the republic nor the States-General had yet so much as recognized the United States of America, would have been "magnificent, but not finance." Connecticut did not get her loan. Yet even Governor Trumbull, as he wrote to Van der Capellen, was no advocate either of internal or foreign loans. Necessity alone compelled him to this last resort. As Van der Capellen quotes "Brother Jonathan's" opinion, in his letter to Governor Livingston: "It is like cold water in a fever, which allays the disease for a moment, but soon causes it to rage with redoubled violence."

It is now time to recross the ocean and return to Lebanon. The white-haired old hero did not long survive the strain of the war, though he lived to see the triumphs of peace. In our day, and in 1896, there has been appropriate and deserved renewal of his fame in the renovation, rather the reconsecration, of "the Old War Office." To-day, rich in the halo of Revolutionary memories, re-cased in a new coat of preservative timber, put in perfect order inside and out by the grateful Sons of the American Revolution, transformed as to use into a public library, adorned with a bronze tablet certifying its history, and recalling the illustrious names of great leaders whose voices have been heard within its walls, the edifice is an object of pride, not only to the village and state, but to every true American. Having passed its century and a half, it may weather the storms of another century or two. It certainly bids fair to outlast Solomon's House of the Forest of Lebanon. Over its threshold and within its walls have met in council the Americans, Washington, Knox, Putnam, Sullivan, Parsons, Spencer, Sam Adams, John Adams, Benjamin Franklin, and our generous allies, Lafayette, Count Rochambeau, the Marquis de Chastellux, Baron de Montesquieu, the Duke of Lauzun, and Admiral Tiernay. Tories have been here too, including the governor of New Jersey, Benjamin Franklin's renegade son, — but as prisoners. Here have been stored equipments and munitions of war, not only of home production, but also from France and especially from the Netherlands. Among the latter were not a few English products which came to the Continental army by way of St. Eustacius; for all through the Revolutionary war British merchants who wanted tobacco supplied through the Dutch what Americans needed. Some handsome English fortunes were made by selling what in the invoices were described as "hardware" and "grain," but when delivered proved to be cannon and guns, powder and ball.

Connecticut now observes Constitution Day, September 17, in honor of the organic law of the Union adopted on that day, 1787, and Flag Day, June 14, on which date, in 1777, the sacred symbol of our national life was chosen by Congress. Old Lebanon smiled again as gaily as in the days of the French occupation on Flag Day, 1891, when the aged owner, Mrs. Wattles, on whose head the snows of ninety-one years had descended, handed over the ownership of the Old War Office, with a suitable portion of land on and around it, to the Sons of the Revolution. With new sills, partitions, windows and doors, the original oak frame-work being still sound, a new stone foundation and a new colonial chimney fireplace and andirons substituted for the narrow smoke pipe in brick, a new soul seemed put into the old ribs. From beneath the upper flooring a mass of paper, mostly in scraps and often used or rejected by rats and squirrels during their nest building of a century or so ago, was recovered to delight the antiquary. While the members of the Israel Putnam Branch of the Sons of the Revolution, the Connecticut Historical Society and the other guests sat down to dinner and listened to poems and addresses and music, all the town was gay with decoration. Thousands of visitors who had made holiday sauntered about to study the historic sites.

There was, first of all, Brother Jonathan's old home, originally located upon the corner of Town Street and the Colchester road, right alongside the old storehouse. Now, however, it stands midway between the original site and the Trumbull Public Library or renovated War Office. But little changed from the original structure, it dates back to those colonial days when Trumbull was a prosperous merchant, before public duties and honors had come to him. It was here that he and his wife — who was none other than Faith Robinson, a great-granddaughter of the noble prophet-leader and self-effacing pastor of the Pilgrims in Leyden — kept open house. Here the officers of the allied armies enjoyed the bounty of host and hostess; and here the illustrious children of the family were born. The house of Jonathan Trumbull, Jr., the second son of the war governor, is on the opposite side of the village green. Then there are the homes of America's great historical painter, Colonel John Trumbull, and of Governor Jonathan Trumbull, Jr. Since Lebanon furnished five governors to the state, three from the Trumbull family and two others, Clark Bissell, who served during the time of the Mexican war, 1847-49, and William A. Buckingham, for eight years, including the Civil war, the people's boast is still: "We supply Norwich with butter and cheese, and the State with governors, especially when they want good ones." Governor Bissell's residence, however, is in Goshen, three miles from Lebanon centre.

Few visitors fail to visit the home of the dead, — the Trumbull family tomb, half a mile from the centre of the town, on the Windham road, just across the babbling brook. Here are the graves of the forefathers besides many of the Trumbull, the Backus, the Williams and other families. It was Calhoun, we believe, who once looking over Congress said that the graduates of Yale College and men from Connecticut came within five of a majority. So, while lingering in this little God's acre, one wonders whether there is any other small enclosure between the Atlantic and Pacific which contains the dust of so many men whose names are on America's shield of fame.

There is another mound called the Deserter's Grave, but it is on the village green. An insignificant pile of stones mark the resting place of one of those French hussars who deserted their camp, fearing detection because of their depredations upon the neighboring sheepfolds and poultry yards. Arrested and convicted, this one was shot the following day at sunrise. Feminine pity for the unfortunate man has taken the form of touching romance, according to which this private was a titled French nobleman and absent from camp only because he would tell his love to a pretty Yankee maiden beyond the town limits. His false accusation of desertion may have been the trumped-up charge of a rival. So said the story in the New York *Sun*, of twenty or more years ago. Alas, for such a delightful explanation, which lacks historic basis!

It was about the first of December, 1780, when the Duke Lauzun and his legion of five hundred mounted hussars, with their fine horses and finer uniforms of white faced with red, rode into the town. They were quar-

tered here until June 23, 1781, when they moved off to Yorktown. Still more magnificent was the spectacle when Count Rochambeau came, in the same leafy and perfumed month of June, with six regiments of the finest infantry of Louis XV., on their way from Newport to join the American army on the Hudson. For three weeks their bands of music were heard and their silken-lilied banners seen on the village green. The inspections and dress parades drew all the people from the surrounding country to see and hear. To-day a little mound marks the site of the brick camp oven, where that light and toothsome bread in which the French excel was baked. Stacked up on end, carried in arms or wheeled off like bundles of fagots, these staves of life, club-like in form, so different in shape from the loaves sliced on New England tables, must have drawn forth many a Yankee joke about the "staff," which Swift first introduced into our language in his "Tale of a Tub." On Flag Day, French ensigns marked the spots where life was nourished and taken. It was in the Old War Office that the counsels were initiated which led Bourbonnier and Continental, the white and red and buff and blue, to march to Yorktown and there end the war.

One of the oldest houses in town, dating from 1712, is interesting, because when erected it was undoubtedly one of the finest residences in the colony. It was built by the Rev. Samuel Welles to please his wife, who was an English lady of rank, who found it hard to content herself with the simplicity of the little settlements in the woods. One room has been preserved with its original paneled walls, on which are paintings, and not a little of the original clapboarding on the outside is still excellently preserved. In this same house afterwards lived Rev. Solomon Williams, D. D., of a family famous in Deerfield and Hartford. In 1759 he declared in a sermon that the conquest of Quebec was the most important the English had ever made since becoming a nation. Here also was born his son Colonel William, signer of the Declaration of Independence, who in 1775 roused the people by his oratory, collected cloth, pork and gold for the army, and in 1777 sent beef, cattle and money to Valley Forge. He kept up his exertions even when $200 (in Continental money) would not buy one bowl of flip.

It is a little curious that our general histories give so little credit to the work and personality of Jonathan Trumbull. The local and town histories of Connecticut do of course deal justly and with some sense of literary proportion with the matter, but it is strange that historians devote so much more space to the things showy, dramatic and sensational, and so little to the spirit and work that was fundamental to success in the Revolution. Connecticut, having neither dissensions within or hostile troops upon her soil, was able to do probably what no other of the thirteen colonies could do so fully, — that is, to devote her entire resources of men and material to the general good. Furthermore, while General Warren and Sargent Jasper, falling in the smoke of battle, and Nathan Hale, dying on the scaffold, have their names "writ large" on the page of history and their enduring monuments in bronze, we must not forget the ceaseless and exhausting labors of Brother Jonathan. His oldest son, Joseph, illustrating the proverb "Like father, like son," died from overwork in patriotism, as truly a martyr as he who hung by rope or fell by bullet for American freedom.

Think of the twelve hundred meetings held in Lebanon of the Council of Safety, of which eleven hundred and forty-five were held in the Old War Office. Think of the riding in and out of the village of horsemen bearing dispatches to and from Congress, from commander-in-chief and from generals in the field and captains on deck; the fitting out of provision trains and supplies of beef upon the hoof, the re-

ception and distribution from and by the teams of European munitions of war brought by the ships. Hear again the drumbeat and the commands of the drill officers, as recruits for the Revolutionary army moved in and out of this village now so quiet. From this Old War Office went out the orders to regiments to move to the relief of other states or to threatened points on its own frontier. Connecticut had an adventurous little navy during the war, and most of the business of equipping, commissioning and commanding the ships was done in this office. There were many cloudy days when the noblest patriots were discouraged. It was in the darkest of these dark days, when the sons of Connecticut were scattered over the land for freedom's cause, that — to use the sentence on the headstones of so many victims in southeastern Connecticut — the "traitor Arnold and his murthering crew" invaded the state.

"The Governor's face grew sad,
　In 'his store on Lebanon Hill;
He reckoned the men he had;
　He counted the forts to fill;
He traced on the map the ground
　By river, and harbor, and coast;—
'Ah, where shall the men and the guns be found,
　Lest the State be lost?'

"The brave State's sons were gone;
　On many a field they lay;
They were following Washington,
　Afar down Yorktown way;
The men and the weapons failed,
　They were gone with our free good will;
But Jonathan Trumbull never quailed
　In his store on Lebanon Hill."

One is tempted to draw a contrast, as he sees this Puritan magistrate, never too busy amid the direst toils and cares to have morning and evening prayer, to ask deliberately a blessing upon each meal, to read the noblest book of history, religion and devotions daily, with the other figures contemporaneous in history, — Arnold, Jefferson and the Duke of Lauzun.

Think of "Benedict Arnold: general and traitor; b. at Norwich, Conn. Jan. 14, 1741." Though a neighboring townsman of the governor, neither Connecticut nor its chief magistrate ever trusted him or gave him a commission. Whatever honors or opportunity he had to do good or evil came from the other states or from Congress. "It is to the honor of his native state that she rejected him and that he hated her in return with a malignant hatred."

Governor Trumbull's proclamation of June 18, 1776, which has been locally called "the Connecticut declaration of independence," and which has only lately been unearthed and published, is in cast of philosophy and in its phrasing exactly the sort of document of which we find many instances in the writings of Puritan magistrates among the French, the Dutch and the English Puritans or close Bible students. Its rhetoric and vocabulary are founded on the Holy Scriptures. It breathes throughout sublime faith in God. Now if, as tradition assumes, but of which there is no evidence in writing or probability in fact, the Connecticut Puritan and the Virginian disciple of Rousseau, Thomas Jefferson, ever did meet together over the hospitable board in Lebanon, we might, without much strain of the imagination, — imitating Walter Savage Landor, — reproduce an "imaginary conversation." It is safe to say, however, that in the history that has been made since the Declaration of Independence, the spirit of the American people, moving between the two parallel lines marked down in the two state papers we have mentioned, keeps nearer the soul of the Connecticut document.

What strange bedfellows did the revolutionary politics of our fathers make! Who can help the antithesis, as he pictures in imagination the six sparkling regiments of Bourbonniers in camp under the sylvan shadows of Lebanon, and the village Puritans? The trees which had echoed only with the note of Psalms resounded with blare of trumpets and the gay and flimsy strains of opera and waltz. As

the grave magistrate and the gay duke sat down to dinner, the former would taste no food till he first thanked the Father of all mercies. The author of "Reveries of a Bachelor" which we delighted in when, as college lads, we dreamed of future cheeks of rose and home of delight—and now of "American Letters, from the Mayflower to Rip Van Winkle," thus paints the picture—a very Rembrandt in words:

"And what a contrast it is — this gay nobleman, carved out, as it were, from the dissolute age of Louis XV., who had sauntered under the colonnades of the Trianon and had kissed the hand of the Pompadour, now strutting among the staid dames of Norwich and of Lebanon! How they must have looked at him and his fine troopers from under their knitted hoods! You know, I suppose, his after history, how he went back to Paris, and among the wits there was wont to mimic the way in which the stiff old Connecticut governor had said grace at his table. Ah! he did not know that in Governor Trumbull and all such men is the material to found an enduring state; and in himself and all such men, only the inflammable material to burn one down. There is a little life written of Governor Trumbull, and there is a life written of the Marquis (duke of) Lauzun. The first is full of deeds of quiet heroism, ending with a tranquil and triumphant death; the other is full of the rankest gallantries, and ends with a little spurt of blood under the knife of the guillotine upon the gay Place de la Concorde."

Both the Hebrew and the Greek originals of the Bible make clear distinction between labor and work. With the former are associated the ideas of toil and sweat, weariness and waste; with the latter, triumph, value, beauty and permanence. In the fullest sense of the words, Jonathan Trumbull rested from his labors and his works followed him. His fame will grow as a tree — a cedar of Lebanon — planted by the river of waters, with the flow of years.

22
A Connecticut
River Ferry

A CONNECTICUT RIVER FERRY.

By Max Bennett Thrasher.

A RUSTY tin dinner horn hung on a post in front of me, and at my feet, flowing softly past the sandy bank into which the post was driven, was the Connecticut River. On the other side, shaded by huge buttonwood trees, was the ferryman's house; and the tin horn was his telephone.

My railway train had dropped me at one of the little brown wooden stations which dot the valley of the Connecticut River. This particular station was in Vermont, and I wanted to get over into New Hampshire. There was no bridge for several miles either way, up or down the river; but a sign-board beside the sandy road, pointing down toward the fringe of trees which hid the river from sight, said, "To the Ferry." I had picked up my bag and walked down through the leafy tunnel until I had come out upon the river bank, where the horn hung.

A long blast on the horn brought out from the back door of the ferry-man's house a stout young man, bare-headed, whose sinewy arms, bared by the rolling of his shirt sleeves to the elbow, were as brown as his face. He stepped into a flat-bottomed blue skiff and came over after me. The river at this point is between four and five hundred feet wide, and in the low water of summer has little current.

Before the blue skiff had brought me over, a man in a buggy drove down the steep sandy road which leads to the river on the New Hampshire side. The ferryman came down from the house to meet him, passed the time of day, and stepped on board the big, shallow scow in which teams are ferried across. The traveller drove his team on to the boat. The ferryman, standing at the end of the boat farthest from the shore, took firm hold of the stout wire rope to which the big craft hung, through pulleys raised at its side, and, walking slowly from that end of the boat to the other, started it and its load across the stream. When he had walked the length of the boat he went back, took a new hold, and walked again. Midway in the stream my skiff ferry met them. The passenger was sitting calmly in his buggy, talking crops, the horse quite heedless of the fact that the waters of the Connecticut were rippling within a few inches of him on every side,—for the ferryboat at its deepest place is only twenty inches deep. The ferryman, with his gray hair and patriarchal beard, might have been Charon, except for his genial blue eyes.

For pulling the heavy boat and its load across the river and then pulling it back again to his interrupted work, the ferryman is paid ten cents. The legal fee which he might charge is fifteen cents. The charges at a country ferry are more complicated than one would think at first, and a regular legal scale of charges is fixed by the commissioners of the county in which the ferry is located. A ferryman cannot charge more than the legal fee, but he may carry passengers for less, if he chooses. I think the common charge is generally a little under the legal rate. At the ferry of which I write the charges, in addition to those which I have quoted, are fifteen cents for a double team, twenty cents for a heavily loaded team, and five cents extra for every horse, if more than two are carried at a time. Between the hours of 9 P. M. and 4 A. M. during spring, summer and fall, the law allows double fees,—and this for all hours between November 15 and the fifteenth of the next May. This is because crossing in the winter is so much more arduous on account of the river frequently being filled with floating ice or "snow-broth." Cattle are carried over for five cents a head. Eight cows are a load, not because the boat would not carry more, but because the cows are apt to get frightened and push one another overboard, or crowd to one end of the boat and sink her. Back in the days before western beef had driven cattle raising from New England, many a herd of fifty or a hundred head have been driven down to the crossing. Sometimes one load would be ferried over for leaders, and the remainder of the herd urged into the river and swum across. Sheep are to be carried for one cent each; and a boat of ordinary size will carry a hundred head.

"But sheep," said the ferryman, "are the meanest things to take over. They'll jest as likely as not git scairt and jump overboard,—and then it's nigh impossible to catch 'em. Then when you do catch 'em, they'll be so heavy, with a fleece full of water, that you can't lift 'em into a skiff,—and about all you can do is to run 'em ashore somewhere and start over. Why, I've chased a lot of sheep around in the river here with a skiff, and when I got the last of 'em, landed 'em a good mile down the river."

An ordinary ferryboat, like the one of which I write, is forty feet long, eleven feet wide and twenty inches deep. She is made of good hard-pine planks, and will last twenty years. There is no wharf or landing. The square end of the boat is run against the sandy bank. The bottom of the boat slopes up at each end, and a movable "apron" three feet wide serves as a gangway from the boat to the bank. The boat is pulled from one shore to the other by means of a stout steel rope anchored securely at each end by winding it around successive posts and trees. Six hundred feet of rope are needed for a crossing where, like this one, the breadth of the river itself at low water is a little over four hundred feet. The wire used is the best Bessemer steel, about three-eighths of an inch in diameter. When the rope is not in use it lies out of sight beneath the water. The life of a rope is about four years.

The ferry of which I am writing leads from Westmoreland, in New Hampshire, to East Putney, in Vermont. It is typical of all those on the river, and more picturesque than most of them. It has been established there for very many years. The ferryman of to-day has been there since 1858. Twice, early in this century, corporations built a toll bridge across the river at or near this point, and the ferry was discontinued; but each bridge was carried away by ice and high water after a short life, and now for many years the ferryboat has had no rival to its claims. The next nearest places where the river can be crossed are eight miles to the north, at Walpole, by a bridge to Westminster, Vermont, and four miles to the south, where there is another ferry.

In summer, even now, the foundations for the stone piers of the old bridge which was swept away, may be seen as the ferryboat crosses the river, coming almost to the surface in low water; and the massive stone abutments which supported the ends of the bridge still stand among the trees which have grown up on both banks, time-blackened ruins overgrown with tangled masses of wild grape vines.

About the ruins of the old bridge lingers the ghost of a strange tragedy. Nearly a hundred years ago the farm-

THE FERRY AND FERRYMAN'S HOME.

ers' boys of all this region were thrilled by the announcement that "positively the only live elephant ever exhibited in New England" was making a triumphal "tour" from town to town, and could be seen at certain advertised times and places for a fee of "ridiculously small proportions." On account of the fact that the elephant was the whole circus, and that he was far too heavy to be carried about in a wagon, he was taken from town to town at night, that the curiosity of the people might not be appeased by seeing him pass along the highway, and thus the fee of "ridiculously small proportions" be diverted from its proposed destination.

Apropos of this "triumphal tour" a story is told of two boys living near this ferry, who were unable for some reason to go to town to see the elephant, and so, learning by what road he was to make his next midnight march, determined to make him come to them. They had heard from some one who had been to see him that the big animal was greedily fond of sweet apples, which, fortunately for them, are common in the Connecticut valley. The boys provided a bushel of sweet apples beside the road, and waited in the darkness. When, far on in the night, a heavy tread and various unusual noises announced the approach of the strange beast and his attendants, the boys strewed the apples across the road. The elephant's long trunk, swinging vaguely in the darkness, could not help but find the fruit, and after that forty keepers could not have driven him past it. When the boys found they had hooked their strange fish, they lighted a big pile of dry wood which they had built up beside the road, and by the brilliant firelight proceeded to satisfy at leisure their curiosity as to what an elephant looked like. The animal's attendant, advertised as "a native Asiatic, brought at great expense from the elephant's Indian home," prodded the beast vigorously, and is said to have indulged in profanity which had a strangely familiar sound; but the procession did not move on until the last sweet apple was eaten and the light of the fire was growing dim.

It was not long after this that the route of the "tour" brought the aggregation to the bridge, at this place, to cross. The elephant turned back from the bridge repeatedly, and for a long time refused to go on to it. Finally, prodded and scolded by his keeper, he ventured slowly out upon the structure. He had crossed almost to the farther end, when the timbers broke beneath him, and beast and keeper fell to the rocks, which low water had left bare beneath the end of the bridge. Both were killed. For the next few days the people from far and near came to see the broken bridge and the dead animal. Eventually the skeleton of the elephant was taken to Boston, where for many years it has been on exhibition among the curiosities displayed in the foyer of the old Boston Museum. The bridge was repaired, but was carried away by the ice not long afterward and was never rebuilt.

THE FERRYMAN AND HIS WIFE.

I have crossed the ferry of which I am writing very many times, at all seasons of the year, and under almost every possible condition of water and weather. Only one who has summered and wintered with New England's noblest river can understand how many these conditions may be. In summer the Connecticut is a beautiful picture of brown water between green banks. During the almost half a century that the present ferryman has watched it, there has been one winter when the river at this point did not freeze over so as to interrupt crossing with the boats; but usually its surface forms a natural bridge of ice for three or four months every winter. With the coming of spring, the rise and fall of the water and the warm sun on the banks weaken the ice at each side, and there are open places to be crossed with care, and sometimes danger, on temporary bridges of planks. When the weather eye of the ferryman sees the final "freeze-up" coming, the big boat is drawn out of the water and hauled up the bank to a point where it will be above high water,—no small distance on the banks of a river which rises, as the Connecticut sometimes does here, to a height of thirty feet above low-water mark. Years ago this annual drawing out of the heavy boat meant an all day's "bee," at which the help of ten yoke of oxen and as many drivers was required; but now a "tackle block" and one pair of horses do the work in a few hours.

Before the final closing of the river, and after the solid ice goes out in the spring, floating ice and "snow-broth" make crossing difficult. The last named obstacle is saturated snow, filling the water of the river on the surface to a depth of from six inches to two feet, and almost impossible to make progress through. Blocks of floating ice must be dodged or pushed away from the boat's path. Even then the ice will sometimes block suddenly below the boat's crossing and set back so suddenly that the boat will be caught amidstream. Once, in 1864, an ice gorge formed below the ferry so massive that it dammed the river, and the water, setting back, rose so rapidly that it flooded the ferryman's

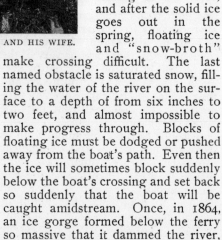

house and drove him and his wife to take their two little children at one o'clock in the morning and flee to safer quarters on higher ground.

"When I start out to go across, when the ice is running," said the boatman, "I never know when I am going to get back." Then he told of one winter experience, when a passenger blew the horn before breakfast. "I went over after him. We got caught in the ice and the rope broke, letting the boat be carried down the stream, but not out of sight of the house. We couldn't get anywhere, and it was noon before we landed. The worst of it was that every little while some of the folks would come out and shout to me that breakfast was ready."

"Yes," said his daughter, who was listening to the story, "seems as if any trouble was sure to come just at meal time, so as to make us women here in the house all the more work."

How much work does fall to the wife and daughters of a ferryman, one

must live with them to really understand. At many crossings they help to run the boats. Here they have not often had to do that, since a family of stout boys has grown up, one after the other, to be the father's helpers; but many is the meal of victuals the women have set for belated and hungry travellers, many the drunken man they have taken in and cared for until he was sober enough so that it was safe for him to go over in the boat. Time and again they have left their work to go out and reassure some nervous woman who is afraid to cross; while more than once they have sheltered and dried, cleaned, brushed and

A SUMMER TIME CROSSING.

THE FERRYMAN'S SEVEN SONS.

ironed out people whom carelessness or accident has plunged into the water. Most accidents occur from people taking chances when the ice is breaking up at the edge of the river in the spring. Sometimes a horse is nervous, and prudence requires that he be unhitched from the wagon before he is taken on to the 'boat, and the wagon be drawn on and off the boat by hand. Once in a great while a horse is found with such an unconquerable aversion to the boat that he can never be made to cross in it. Some men cover a nervous horse's head with a blanket. The ferryman says that more trouble comes from the nervousness of the driver than that of the horse. Only one horse ever plunged off amidstream here during the life of this ferryman,—and he was a blind horse ill managed by a careless driver.

"Once I was taking over a couple who were going to get married," the ferryman said. "The woman stayed in the wagon. The man stood by the horse's head. When the boat came up to the bank on the side where they were to land, the horse snorted and backed a little. The woman screamed, and the man yanked the horse's head and shouted at him. That frightened the horse more, and he backed again, so quickly this time that he sent the hind wheels of the buggy over the side of the boat. Of course, the wagon tipped up, and the woman went out backwards into the water. 'Save her! Save her!' the man cried to me. 'I'll give you a thousand dollars if you'll save her!' I told him to hold his noise and help me get the horse out before he did any more damage. I saw the woman was hanging on to the back of the wagon all right. As soon as we got the horse unhitched and off the boat, I went out and got the woman and brought her ashore. We took them back to the house and dried them up and ironed out their clothes, put the team together and sent them along. The man never said anything more about the thousand dollars,—and much as ever he paid me the regular fee for taking them over."

BELOW THE FERRY.

"Tell him about the woman from ——," the mother of the family suggested.

The ferryman laughed. "One day a woman drove down to the ferry alone. I did not know her, but I recognized the horse as one which I had taken across a number of times, and knew to be perfectly safe. As soon as the woman saw the boat she gave a screech and cried, 'My land! I never can cross there! I'd rather have driven a hundred miles than done it.'

boat herself. 'I'd rather swim across,' says she, 'than go on board that thing!' 'Well, swim, then,' says I, 'if you want to. I'll take the team across and carry your clothes for you too, so they needn't get wet.' I was beginning to get mad, for we had wasted as much as an hour of time on her then. Finally wife and I got her on board, and the whole lot, horse, wagon and woman, went over as quiet as kittens. 'There!' said she, when she drove off the boat on the other side, 'my hus-

A FAMILY GROUP.

I reasoned with her, and told her it was perfectly safe,—and wife came out and told her so too; but she stuck to she'd rather have driven a hundred miles than crossed there. Finally I told her she needn't go anywhere near that far; all she need do would be to drive to Walpole, eight miles up the river, and cross by the bridge there. Then she took another tack, and said she'd go across if I'd unhitch the horse and take the wagon on the boat by hand. So I did that; but after I'd got the horse and wagon on board, and one of the boys to hold the horse, she wouldn't step foot on the

band told me, before I come away from home not to make a fool of myself at the ferry.' Says I, 'You tell your husband I can't say you followed out his instructions.'"

In early summer the boat's passage is obstructed for weeks by the floating logs which are the forerunners of the lumberman's big drive coming down from the forests near the river's source. Sometimes they get so thick that the wire rope cannot be safely used above the water, and a stout man lying flat in the bottom of the boat reaches an arm's length down into the cold water and works the wire there, while other men keep the logs out of the path. No wonder the boatmen have sinewy arms. When the drive itself comes down, the river is sometimes solid full of logs; but the logmen themselves, who walk the logs as steadily as other men do dry land, lend a hand to help pull and push the boat among the obstacles which they have brought with them.

The melting of the snow in the spring and the fall rains swell the river to far above its normal level, and send it sweeping down in a flood too strong for the boat to venture out upon. The force of such a current as that would snap the cable like a bit of wood and send the boat whirling down the stream. Sometimes the boat does break adrift, and then must be guided by a long oar into some eddy from which those on board can reach the bank, along which the boat will be dragged later to its accustomed place. A great freshet brings the river to a height where it overflows its banks and sweeps the broad meadow farms of everything upon them which is movable. I saw it once like that, in the autumn of 1869, when the swirling current from bank to bank was covered with shooks of stalks of Indian corn, among which, here and there, a glistening yellow pumpkin bobbed about. Thousands of bushels of corn were lost or ruined that year, and at the ferry they gathered in with a skiff so much corn floating in an eddy over their garden that they husked from it forty bushels of ears. At that time the water, according to the ferryman's story, nearly came up to his house, but not into it. In 1862 the water drove the family out of the house, which stands twenty-eight feet above the river's normal level, and at its deepest stood sixteen inches deep in the living rooms.

At this place in the ferryman's story the tin horn blew again. Another passenger waited to be brought across the river.

23
Old Summer Street, Boston

SUMMER STREET.
After N. Vautin, from a pencil sketch by Sarah Hodges in 1846.

OLD SUMMER STREET, BOSTON.

By Henry F. Bond.

A WORK of great magnitude and interest is going on at the foot of Summer street in Boston, employing an army of men and attracting a multitude of spectators. There are very frequent inquiries as to what Summer street was and is and is to be.

The foundations are being laid for an enormous union railroad station, perhaps the largest in the world, estimated to cost about $12,000,000. Hundreds of thousands of people await with personal interest the completion of this great enterprise. The

THE GARDNER MANSION, ON THE SITE OF C. F.
HOVEY & CO.'S STORE.

and not a street had been graded, and there was only here and there a very humble cabin. What has been the evolution of Summer street and its neighborhood; what has this district been to Boston; what men of public service or of private virtues have spent their best years of maturity there or laid there the foundations of their characters?

According to Drake, Sir William Pepperell owned an estate on what is now Summer street. This must have been in the early part of the 18th century. He and his heirs were royalists, and the property was confiscated, as was also that of Leonard Vassal, where Hovey's store now stands. Otis place, now Otis street, was laid out through the Pepperell estate about 1815. The grandfather, the first Sir William Pepperell, was extensively known throughout New England, was largely interested in the

imagination is exercised picturing the great building, type of modern ingenuity and audacity, and the vast crowd passing up and down this street which, within the memory of middle-aged men, was admired for its glory of trees and aristocratic residences. We think of the hacks, the cabs, the drays, the express and mail wagons, the private carriages, striving to dodge each other, and the electric cars which cannot dodge but must be dodged. This once quiet and restful street, now a convenient and comfortable location for business, is in our picture of the future a continuous jam. It must become more important as a street of business, of retail rather than wholesale business. The corner of Summer and Washington streets will become trebly perilous for the passing crowds.

To make the contrast stronger we go back in our minds to the time, a little more than a century ago, when Boston was but a provincial town, and this neighborhood was pasture and High street was called Cow lane. Or our minds may revert back two and a half centuries, when the Puritans had but lately landed,

C. F. HOVEY'S STORE.

fisheries, a gentleman of engaging manners, very popular and wealthy, and had long held the highest office in the gift of the people, that of president of the Governor's Council. He was appointed chief justice by Governor Belcher in 1730, and held the office till his death in 1759. In 1745 he distinguished himself as commander in the siege and capture of Louisburg.

While General Heath was in command in Boston in 1777, after the evacuation by General Howe, he established his headquarters at the mansion house of Hon. Thomas Russell, back from Summer street, near where Otis street now is. General Heath claimed to have been the projector of the earthworks at Dorchester Heights.

*OTIS PLACE FROM SUMMER STREET.

cane prevented the attack. General Heath wrote memoirs of himself. A copy of the book was the gift of George Ticknor to the Boston Library. On a fly leaf I found the following: "Jan. 5, 1799 Paid for this book (having unadvisedly subscribed for it) the extraordinary sum of 2 dollars. Vegetables in the Boston Markets from the Heath farm, are always dear, so it seems, is the literary produce from the same soil."

On the southerly corner of Summer and Washington streets, where Shuman's store is now, was once the mansion of Thomas English. A hundred years ago this site belonged to the Bethune family and was occupied by Dr. Charles Jarvis. Next to it at the same

He wrote in his memoirs that Mr. Davis, a merchant of Boston, who became a property owner in Winthrop place, suggested that rows of barrels filled with earth should be arranged around the works with the appearance of strengthening, and recommended that when the enemy made an attack they should be rolled down the hill upon them. A hurri-

time were two wooden dwellings of little pretension; the larger was of three stories and owned by one Steadfast Smith. Leonard Vassal owned an estate below on Summer street. He owned a residence in Quincy, which afterwards became the property of John Adams, more lately of his grandson, Charles Francis Adams, and is now occupied by the great grandson, Brooks Adams. Later Samson Reed, Samuel Salisbury and Frederick William

*The pictures for this article, with the exception of several of the portraits, are reproduced from the Bostonian Society's collection in the old State House, Boston, by whose courtesy they are here used.

THE FIRST CHURCH, IN CHAUNCY PLACE.

corner of Summer and Marlboro streets. In the course of time the Gardner house gave place to the large store of Hovey and company. This and the store of John Chandler opposite were the first dry goods stores on the street.

East of the Vassal estate was that of the First Church. Adjoining that was the property of Ebenezer Preble, brother of Commodore Preble. Chauncy place was cut through these two last estates in 1807, and Mr. Preble's house was built on the lower corner of it. Ebenezer Preble was a leading merchant of Boston and was at one time a partner of William Gray.

Nathaniel I. Bowditch, for many years the accurate and almost sole conveyancer in Boston, said in one of his newspaper articles, signed "Gleaner," in 1855: "Richard Hollinghead of Boston, planter, and Ann, his wife, being preserved to a state of old age attended with many weaknesses and infirmities, and for a valuable sum of money secured to be annually paid us and the survivor of us," conveyed to

Geyer lived there; and afterwards Samuel P. Gardner occupied the house that had been Geyer's, the conficated property of Vassal. The estates of Salisbury and Gardner, about opposite Trinity Church, with their capacious gardens and shady trees, were in my boyhood and for many years afterwards homes such as, with a few brick blocks set well back and adorned with trees in front of them, were the glory of Summer street. They presented such a vista of rural beauty and restfulness as could only now be found miles beyond the limits of old Boston peninsula and can rarely be seen anywhere. The change in Summer street is so great that not a tree now remains there.

Samuel Salisbury for a while owned and occupied with Stephen Salisbury a large three-story store on the north

REV. WILLIAM EMERSON.

Henry Alline and Robert Sanderson, deacons of the First Church of Christ in Boston aforesaid, "whereof we are members," "all that our dwelling house and housing with the land whereon they stand, yards, garden, orchard, barn and land unto us belonging situate on the southerly end of the town of Boston and butted and bounded" (description is omitted), "reserving during their lives the use of the old house, so called, and the little garden, to have and to hold to them, their successors in said office, or assigns, to the only proper use and behoof of said church or society forever," by warranty deed dated De-

ROBERT C. WINTHROP.

five years or more before the First Church moved from the old brick meeting-house on Cornhill (now the northerly portion of Washington street) to Chauncy place. The house stood back from the street, with elms and Lombardy poplars in front. When the church was built in 1808 and the old house was razed, a block of four houses was erected on Summer street, one of which was reserved for the home of the minister. Rev. William Emerson, father of Ralph

DR. NATHANIEL FROTHINGHAM.

cember 17, 1680. Bowditch adds: "Though a quarter of an acre is appropriated as a highway, it conveniently (1855) accommodates two public edifices and four private ones; so that the first occupant had ample room for swinging a cat whenever he felt so inclined." He continues: "There is probably no land in Boston except that on which Chauncy Place Church stands, which is held under a direct conveyance from the first possessor, and of which no subsequent conveyance has ever been made."

In the Hollinghead house, which had become the parsonage, Ralph Waldo Emerson was born in 1803,

REV. RUFUS ELLIS.

CHAUNCY STREET FROM EXETER PLACE.

of the Massachusetts Historical Society, and until his death trustee of the Peabody fund for education in the South.

Dr. Jacob Bigelow has been well known by his popular book on the plants in Boston and vicinity. He had a large practice, and was professor of *materia medica* in the Harvard Medical School. The son, Henry J. Bigelow, was born and brought up on Summer street. The elder Dr. Bigelow's square top chaise and the plated circle of good size on the blinders of his harness designated him afar off and helped those who were in search of him.

Dr. Daniel Harwood was considered at the head of the dental profession, which before the introduction of vulcanized rubber and commercial teeth was a higher honor than it can

Waldo, was minister of the First Church for twelve years, till his death in 1811. Dr. Nathaniel Frothingham and Rufus Ellis are remembered as later ministers. In 1843 the Chauncy place meeting-house was altered, a flat roof of colored panes being substituted for the high ceiling, giving rise to the criticism that Dr. Frothingham was going to try to raise Christians under glass. Within the memory of the living, there dwelt upon the church property and a little above it Robert C. Winthrop, Drs. Harwood and Jacob Bigelow, the Rev. Drs. Frothingham and Kirkland, and Chief Justice Isaac Parker. The distinguished surgeon, Henry J. Bigelow, son of Jacob, lived for a while in Chauncy place.

Robert C. Winthrop, born of a distinguished family, was prominent in the councils of the nation, graceful and distinguished as an orator, for many years Speaker of the national House of Representatives, president

DR. JACOB BIGELOW.

DR. NATHANIEL BOWDITCH.

DR. JAMES JACKSON.

REV. WILLIAM B. O. PEABODY.

JACOB SLEEPER.

behold the sun." Dr. Hedge at his funeral spoke touchingly of the sorrow of such a lover of books and of nature at the loss of sight and said: "The crowning grace of his life was the brave and invincible patience with which he bore the multiplied infirmities of his declining years."

For many years Isaac Parker lived in the First Church block of houses. He was chief justice in Massachusetts, professor of law at Harvard, where he received the degree of LL. D., was president of the Massachusetts Constitutional Convention in 1820, and member of Congress and of the American Academy. He died in 1830.

In 1860 the west corner of Chauncy street became occupied as a post office for a short time.

Chauncy Hall School was established by Gideon F. Thayer, whose methods were in some respects so novel and so systematic that he might be said to have created a new era in Boston education. The public schools with the exception of the high school and Latin school had not then gained great reputation. Mr. Thayer first taught in the rear of Washington street opposite the Old South Meeting House. He erected the building in Chauncy place in 1828. The school was moved into Essex street in 1868, was driven out of its building by fire in 1873, and then occupied the building in Copley square.

Franklin Dexter, a prominent law-

be now. I remember finding him in his native town in Worcester county hunting in the field for suitable quartz for the manufacture of teeth.

Dr. Frothingham was prominent in Boston as a preacher and scholar, many of his sermons, poems and translations being published. He is probably known more generally now by his good hymns. He was the father of Rev. Octavius B. Frothingham, who was more distinguished than himself. The son pays a delightful tribute to the father and mother in his book on the life and work of the father. Dr. Frothingham was totally blind for many years. When he found that an operation to which he had submitted was unsuccessful, his utterance of disappointment was: "Truly the light is sweet and a pleasant thing it is for the eyes to

WILLIAM GRAY.

JUDGE HORACE GRAY.

yer, son of Samuel Dexter, who was distinguished as United States senator from Massachusetts and secretary of war under John Adams, lived in Chauncy place. For a few years Maria Weston Chapman also resided there. She was an earnest and intrepid advocate of abolition in the hottest anti-slavery days. When notified of danger from a mob if the gathering held their meeting in the hall where they were assembled, she replied, "If this is the last bulwark of freedom, we may as well die here as anywhere."

On the lower corner of Summer street and Chauncy place there lived on the Preble estate, as I personally remember, Dr. E. H. Robbins, and with him three young girls, sisters, who were his wards. A daughter of Dr. Robbins, with her own means and such as friends provide her, is now sustaining on Chambers street, an institution for the support and comfort of women. In that same neighborhood in the forties and fifties, Jacob Sleeper resided. He, with Isaac Rich and Lee Claflin, were the founders of Boston

REV. GEORGE E. ELLIS.

University. Jacob Sleeper's benefactions amounted to about $500,000. Mr. Sleeper had served as a state appointed overseer of Harvard University for twelve years and was a member of the Governor's Council. Dr. James Jackson occupied this house at one period, and later a house on the north side of the street between Otis and Winthrop places. He was president of the American Academy and member of several other scientific societies here and abroad. Learned as he was in his profession and skilful in his practice, he would doubtless like best to be remembered as the beloved friend. No kinder, gentler or sweeter dispositioned man was ever called to the sick chamber. His face was a benediction, and the children of his patrons were made very happy by his greeting in the streets. Dr. A. P. Peabody truly says that, "without meaning to do so, he practised the mind cure; his presence was always a power."

Previously, in the second decade of this century, George Cabot dwelt in the Chauncy place side of this house. He

REV. ALEXANDER YOUNG.

Ames, trusted and beloved by Washington." He was the great-grandfather of Henry Cabot Lodge.

Very early in this century David Ellis located just below the Preble house; and this was the birthplace and boyhood home of Drs. George Edward and Rufus Ellis, both well remembered as ministers respectively of the Harvard Church in Charlestown and the First Church in Boston. The former became noted as a historian and was a member of the American Academy and president of the

died in 1823. George Cabot was one of the most prominent public men of his generation. He was master of a ship before he was twenty-one years of age. When twenty-five he was chosen to the Massachusetts Provincial Congress, and in 1779, when twenty-seven years of age, received an honorary degree from Harvard College. He became United States senator, and was president of the Hartford Convention. George Cabot has been represented as tall, over six feet, and well proportioned. Mr. Goodrich wrote of him as "the most imposing man among the members of the Hartford Convention." Webster spoke of him as "the early associate of Hamilton and

NEW SOUTH CHURCH, CHURCH GREEN.

Massachusetts Historical Society. He received from Harvard the degree of D. D. and also that of LL. D. He was one of the most interesting talkers in Boston, and never more interesting than when he talked about old days in Summer street.

Nathaniel Goddard was one of the oldest residents within the memory of those now living. His mansion on the corner of Kingston street faced on Summer street, but his garden extended to Bedford street. On the

REV. W. P. TILDEN.

CHURCH GREEN, SHOWING THE HOMES OF
HENRY GASSETT AND WILLIAM STURGIS.

Pilgrim Fathers of the Colony of Plymouth," and "Chronicles of the First Planters of the Colony of Massachusetts Bay." He was one of the most active members of the Massachusetts Historical Society.

Dr. John Thornton Kirkland, son of a missionary to the Indians, was minister of the New South from 1794 till 1810, when he became president of Harvard College. He lived most of the time on the corner of Summer and Lincoln streets, in the family of Benjamin Fessenden, and briefly in one of the houses belonging to the First Church. He had to a remarkable degree the faculty of remembering those with whom he ever became acquainted. This with his social disposition and his fund of humor made him exceedingly popular with the students. He certainly had very important qualifications for the office, if not the executive ability or the experience in financial affairs of his successor, Josiah Quincy.

lower corner of Kingston street I remember the home of William R. Gray and afterwards of Horace Gray, both sons of William Gray. Horace Gray, son of Horace, one of the present justices of the United States Supreme Court, lived there in his boyhood. John Welles, who became the owner of considerable property on the street, lived next to the house on the corner of Kingston street. Still farther down on the same side was Church Green, the name of the green being given to the property, on account of its fitness, long before the New South Church was built upon it. That church was ministered to in my boyhood by Dr. Alexander Young, who came to the service with a reputation as a scholar, and was a thoughtful preacher. He died in 1854, in the prime of life. Dr. E. J. Young, at one time professor in Harvard Divinity School, is his son. Another son was Alexander, whose entertaining items and comments in the "Taverner" column in the *Boston Post* till the time of his death, a few years ago, are well remembered. Besides Dr. Young's service as minister for twenty-nine years, he edited the "Library of Old English Prose Writers," "Chronicles of the

WINTHROP PLACE, SHOWING THE HOMES
OF GEORGE BOND, HENRY CABOT AND
HENRY CABOT LODGE.

THE HOMES OF NATHANIEL BOWDITCH AND OLIVER ELDREDGE, OTIS PLACE.

or two. Rev. Mr. Tilden was the last minister before the old church was demolished. On the encroachment of business, the worshipers had been driven farther south or out into the suburbs. A new church was built on Tremont street, but that has now been left.

Dr. Jeremy Belknap owned and occupied a house just below Mr. Fessenden's on Lincoln street. He was minister of the Congregational Church in Dover, N. H., nineteen years, and from 1786 till 1798 minister of the Federal Street Church in Boston, over which Dr. William Ellery Channing was settled in 1803, and which is now the Arlington Street Church. Dr. Belknap was the founder of the Massachusetts Historical Society and the author of a "History of New Hampshire" and several other

An anecdote told of him is that a country deacon once called on him for advice about a quarrel in his church concerning the dogma of "the perseverance of the saints," and he said to him: "Here in Boston we have no difficulty on that score; what troubles us here is the perseverance of the sinners." What financial skill he possessed took a philanthropic turn. Dr. Andrew Peabody said of him: "He took a fatherly interest in every member of the college, knew the length of every student's purse, and gave his aid unasked." He suffered in his last years from a stroke of paralysis. He died in 1840. He might have been seen in his last days tottering along Summer street and Otis place, supported by his wife.

Rev. Francis William Pitt Greenwood was settled over the New South Church for a short time. Dr. Orville Dewey preached his grand sermons in the New South for a year

THE HOMES OF JOSHUA BLAKE, SAMUEL CABOT AND GEORGE BANCROFT.

RUFUS CHOATE.

EDWARD EVERETT.

to Harvard University to build Sever Hall. She also bequeathed $100,000 to Harvard and sundry other beneficent institutions.

Colonel Sever's commanding presence when a young man in college, and his discipline as captain of the Harvard Washington Corps saved him from suspension. The president of Harvard, overhearing some professors at a faculty meeting discussing him and his delinquencies, exclaimed: "Sever! turn away Sever! Oh, no, we can't spare Sever!"—and he remained to parade his company before President Monroe and to receive the offer of a cadetship, which his father would not permit him to accept.

William Parsons, brother of Chief Justice Parsons, dwelt on the east corner of Summer and South streets. Nothing is more impressed upon my memory than the rides I occasionally had on the box with the coachman and, what seemed to me cruelty, the use of a goad inserted in the end of the whip-stock. President Quincy lived there a short time. It must have been, I think, about 1825, when William Parsons built his house. He or some other William Parsons had previously occupied a house on the other side of Summer street, about where Webster built.

books. Mr. William C. Bryant gave him the credit of being the first to make American history attractive.

At one time Gorham Parsons owned and occupied the building on the lower corner of Summer and Lincoln streets. Later a brick block was built there and occupied successively by James Carter and Col. James W. Sever. On the west corner of Summer and South streets Jonathan Hunnewell had his residence. Colonel Sever also lived at one time in Chauncy place. Mrs. Sever at her husband's request bequeathed $100,000

DANIEL WEBSTER.

A fourth church in that district was that of the denomination called "Christians" simply, sometimes known as "Christian Baptists." The place of worship was a very modest brick building at the foot of the street, close to the site of the new Union Depot. One of the ministers, Joshua B. Himes, became an Adventist, sympathizing with Miller. He left and built a church on Hanover street. Rev. Edward Edmunds was the much beloved minister from 1843 to 1893, and is now pastor emeritus at 82 years of age. Underneath the church was a saloon. John B. Gough gave one of his first temperance lectures there at the request of Edmunds. The so-

WINTHROP PLACE FROM SUMMER STREET.   HOME OF
RUFUS CHOATE ON THE EXTREME RIGHT.

ciety now worship on the corner of Kneeland and Tyler streets. They occupied the Summer street building for about ten years. Then, perhaps till the great fire, it was a Seamen's Bethel.

I have reached on the south side of

THE HOME OF DANIEL WEBSTER.

THE HOME OF ISRAEL THORNDIKE, EDWARD
EVERETT, GEORGE BLAKE AND DR.
FROTHINGHAM.

Summer street, in my reminiscences, the foot of the street, and I recall the charm of the water view over the wharves. The few houses on the north side up as far as High street were not of special interest, nor am I able to say anything about their inmates; but crossing High street we came in our young days, directly opposite South street, to the home for many years of D a n i e l Webster. The name "Webster" is inscribed on the block which stands upon the spot. Webster might often be seen walking under the shadow of the trees on Summer street. It was not easy to keep one's eyes off him; he was well called "the godlike." The boys of that period were constantly hearing of his successes at the bar and of his orations at Plymouth and

Bunker Hill and Faneuil Hall, and were spouting at school extracts from his great speech against Hayne. The intensity of admiration could only be matched by that of grief when, in 1850, he advocated compromise on the slavery question, reproved those who refused to surrender fugitive slaves, and irreverently scouted the idea of a "higher law." Yet irreverence was by no means characteristic of Webster.

Ex-senator Bradbury of Maine, still living at a very advanced age, tells a story of his effort as a young man to hear and make the acquaintance of Webster. He walked twenty miles to hear him in 1825, when the corner stone of Bunker Hill monument was to be laid, and succeeded in obtaining a position close to him. Hearing that Webster was to give a reception at his house in the evening, he determined to push his way in uninvited. Webster, learning that he was a son of a college classmate, asked him to stop after the company had gone — he wished to talk with

TRINITY CHURCH, SUMMER STREET.

him; and then, finding that the young man had no lodging secured, asked him to spend the night. This was the occasion of the famous reception given to La Fayette, when two houses on Summer street midway between Otis and Winthrop places, Webster's and Israel Thorndike's, were united by cutting a doorway between them.

Nearly opposite Lincoln street, a little above Webster's house, were the residences of Benjamin Loring and James C. Paige. They were erected on the estate once owned by Henry Hill. Rev. Samuel May writes: "I remember perfectly the old Henry Hill house as the most attractive of all the fine houses on the street. It stood about midway between what be-

TRINITY CHURCH AFTER THE GREAT FIRE.

SUMMER STREET, OPPOSITE KINGSTON, AFTER
THE GREAT FIRE OF 1872.

came Winthrop place and High street, — a two-story brick building, painted, I should say, a soft yellow, gambrel roofed, giving spacious attic of course, — a little distance back from the street, with grass and shrubbery between, a high gate, and a substantial wall devised architecturally and ornamental. It faced the south and was rather more artistic in appearance than most of the Boston houses were. I could think then of nothing handsomer or more comfortable. I never was in the grounds; but they ran back to Federal court, at the head of which court my uncle, Colonel Joseph May, father of Rev. Samuel J. May, lived, and

THE HOME OF JOHN TAPPAN, ON THE CORNER
OF ARCH AND SUMMER STREETS.

I often looked through the fence paling into the orchard-like and decidedly country-like space. When Milton place was laid out from Federal street it ran back into the Hill grounds, and the Friends (Quakers) who had been driven out of Congress street, built a meeting-house there." Colonel Loring was an old bachelor of a jovial disposition, a great favorite, well known in the business community, which was very largely supplied from his stationery store. Further up street you would have come in those days to the dwelling of Capt. William Sturgis, next to which on the corner of Winthrop place was the house of Henry Gassett. During my memory of Captain Sturgis he had given up the sea and become a wealthy and generous merchant. As a sea captain he had been on the coast of Washington and Alaska, then known as the "Northwest Coast," and had had intercourse with Indians. His early education had been meagre, but he had learned

much in the school of life. When he was in the Massachusetts legislature, a pedantic member quoted Latin, which Sturgis did not understand, and he replied in the Indian language. In front of Captain Sturgis's house began the extra wide brick sidewalk, measuring at least seventeen feet, and with its densely foliaged trees extending to Otis place.

On the west corner of Summer street and Winthrop place, now Devonshire street, Henry Higginson abode in the third decade of the century. He was followed by Dr. Alexander Young of the New South Church, whose services have already been mentioned. Passing by in those early days the abodes of Capt. Benjamin Rich, Charles Brooks and William Rollins, we came to a house once occupied by Alexander H. Everett. Alexander H. Everett was hardly less

SUMMER STREET, FROM WASHINGTON TO "CHURCH
GREEN," IN 1871.

distinguished as a literary man than his younger brother, Edward, though much less known as an orator. Encyclopedias give his birth as in 1792 and his graduation at Harvard in 1806, his age at graduation therefore fourteen, and he was the first scholar in his class. He studied law with John Quincy Adams and went to Russia with him as secretary of legation, was *chargé d'affaires* at the Hague for nearly six years, was author of treatises on the powers of Europe and on the powers of the Western Continent, was five years editor of the *North American Review,* was commissioner to China, and died there in 1847. Alexander Everett married Lucretia Peabody, sister of the twins, Oliver William Bourne Peabody and Rev. William Bourne Oliver Peabody.

Oliver Peabody lived on Summer street, and assisted his brother-in-law in editing the *North American Review,* was for several years editor of the *Boston Daily Advertiser,* and was a member of the Massachusetts Historical Society. He was licensed as a Unitarian preacher in 1845, but had been a lawyer in all his previous years of maturity. He was settled in Burlington, Vt., and after three years of service there he died. Dr. William Peabody, the brother, was settled at Springfield, Mass. The twin brothers were very much alike in person and I should suppose also in mind and heart. It used to be told that they fell in love with the same young woman. William gained the greater affection, and the brother never married.

In this part of Summer street lived Israel Thorndike, who had owned much property in Summer street and Otis place, and who also had a farm. Back of the house in which he lived there was a little open lot known as Thorndike's pasture. Here and in a stable-yard close by the rear of the Catholic cathedral on Franklin street were often kept temporarily the donkeys which he had imported for his farm. They made the welkin ring

hideously and we wished they were farther off.

On the east corner of Otis place, now Otis street, there lived for a considerable time John C. Gray, one of the sons of William Gray. John C. Gray was a lawyer by education, was in the Massachusetts legislature and one of the Governor's Council, and delivered the Harvard Phi Beta Kappa oration in 1821. He was a fellow of the American Academy. Dr. Nathaniel Langdon Frothingham succeeded George Blake, for many years United States district attorney, on the west corner of Otis place after a few years of home on the First Church property.

Edward Everett, brother-in-law of Dr. Frothingham, lived in the next house, the twin house to Dr. Frothingham's, which had been occupied by Israel Thorndike, and for a short time by Daniel Denny. As he did not die till 1865, his speeches and lectures, his accurate and elegant diction, his clear cut elocution and dignified and graceful bearing are still well remembered throughout the length and breadth of our land; but the full evidence of his industry, the number of his useful and honorable offices and the extent of his charities can hardly be realized even by those who were adults before he passed away. He delivered the Phi Beta Kappa oration at Cambridge in 1824, La Fayette being present on the occasion. He was for many years in Congress, was governor of Massachusetts, president of Harvard College, Secretary of State, United States senator, and minister to England. He received the highest literary honors from Harvard, Yale and Dartmouth, and also from Oxford and Cambridge. He was at one time editor of the *North American Review.* His famous lecture upon Washington, delivered nearly a hundred and fifty times, and his weekly articles for the *New York Ledger* yielded over $100,-000 for the purchase of Mt. Vernon. Only six days before he died he made an address in Faneuil Hall in aid of sending provisions to the suffering people of Savannah. It was a great gratification to his thousands of admirers, who felt that his conservatism had sometimes been a hindrance to noblest influence, to have him live through the Civil War, at its outset to come out grandly with several patriotic addresses, and to be associated with the consecration of the National Cemetery at Gettysburg by delivering the address. It was fitting that he should close his political life as he did, by giving a vote as presidential elector for Abraham Lincoln. William Everett, who has distinguished himself as an educator and been a member of Congress, is his son.

After passing John Tappan's, you came to the Bussey estate on the northwest corner of Arch street. Benjamin Bussey lived for about ten years before 1820 on the west corner of Arch and Summer streets. He was a very successful merchant, and left to Harvard University $350,000, including the Bussey Farm.

The fine mansion with its attractive garden which stood at the corner of Hawley street, well back from Summer street, opposite the side of Trinity Church, John P. Cushing's in my day, was once occupied by Governor Sullivan, afterwards by William Gray, who had been a state senator and lieutenant governor, and next by his son, Francis C. Gray. James Sullivan was born in Berwick, Maine. He was a member of the Provincial Congress of Massachusetts, of which Maine was then a part. He held many responsible positions, was judge, member of the State Constitutional Convention, representative to Congress, member of the Executive Council, state attorney general and governor, and president of the Massachusetts Historical Society. He died in 1808.

William Gray, very generally spoken of as Billy Gray, was said to be owner of more than sixty square-rigged vessels, and was called the richest man in Massachusetts. When

asked how much a man wanted after he had a million dollars, he replied: "A little more." His wife devoted much time to the poor. He died in 1825. I have been told that William Gray employed barber Weiss of Congress street to shave him every day, at six o'clock in winter, at four or five o'clock in summer, and paid him $400 a year — perhaps for the purpose of helping the education of Weiss's son, Rev. John Weiss, who proved so gifted.

Francis C. Gray, like his brother, John C. Gray, studied law, but did not practice it. He was private secretary to John Quincy Adams when he was minister to Russia, was a Massachusetts legislator, a member of the Massachusetts Historical Society, and fellow of the American Academy. He received the degree of LL. D. He left about $95,000 to Harvard College for museum, library and art gallery.

John P. Cushing had come from China with great wealth. He owned quite a large estate in Watertown. Fifty or sixty years ago a porcelain fence brought from China stood in front of his house there. Octavius Frothingham in writing of his father says: "He lived in a delightful street well called 'Summer,' a street of gardens and elm trees that branched over so as almost to meet across the way, with Edward Everett next door and excellent people on either side. An air of Oriental magnificence was imparted by Mr. Cushing's Chinese servants in their native dress."

The site of Trinity Church, on the north corner of Summer and Hawley streets, was previously occupied by the "Seven Star Inn," and as Summer street was then narrow and led towards a mill it was called "Seven Star Lane" or "Ye Milne St." As early as 1735 a very plain wooden building was erected for Trinity Church, for which a noble and substantial stone building was substituted in 1828. Here Phillips Brooks preached when he first came to Boston from Philadelphia. After the stone church was destroyed by the great fire in 1872, the church on Copley Square was built. I used to hear of Dr. John Sylvester Gardiner as rector in the early part of this century, and have some personal recollection of Dr. Jonathan Mayhew Wainwright, who was for a brief time one of his successors. Dr. Gardiner was noted for his eloquence and wit.

Between Trinity Church and the large store of Samuel and Stephen Salisbury on the corner of Washington street I can only recollect some small shops, till the large building was erected which was occupied as a store by John Chandler, the founder of the house of Chandler & Company. William Andrews, bookbinder and bookseller, had lived there twenty or thirty years earlier.

In the early part of this century what is now Washington street was known by five names. From Summer street northward to Water street it was Marlboro; from Water street to Dock square, Cornhill; from Summer street southward to Boylston street, Newbury; from Boylston street to Dover street, Orange; all southward to the Roxbury line, Washington. It has been interesting to notice in an official report of estates as they were in 1798, that nearly all the residences had stables and woodsheds belonging to them, that the number of windows was reported, probably as affecting taxation, that very many of the dwellings were three stories high and were built partly of wood and partly of brick. I can myself remember when house furnaces in Boston were fed with unsawed cord wood and when the cooking was done in open wood fireplaces with tin kitchens and Dutch ovens and sometimes by the aid of turnspits attached to the chimney.

The great fire of 1872 caught from some unknown cause in the granite building on the southeast corner of Summer and Kingston streets, destroyed nearly all Summer street and extended west to Washington street,

east to the water and north almost to State street, an area of nearly seventy acres, and the value of the property destroyed was estimated at more than sixty-one million dollars.

In 1821 Winthrop place was laid out by George Bond, who purchased the land from Gorham Parsons. It had been a pasture, with the exception of a portion occupied by two or three small wooden buildings. The lots were sold to be built upon within two years. It was also a condition of the sales, that the houses should be set back six feet from the street and should be no more than three stories high. These conditions greatly enhanced the attractiveness of the place for residences; but when the land was desired for stores the owners were pleased to have the encumbrances removed. At about this time land was released to the city for the wide sidewalk of Summer street already mentioned. At a little earlier date Israel Thorndike laid out Otis place. Devonshire street was widened and opened through to Summer street by way of "Theatre alley" and Winthrop place about forty years ago; and the large business houses of J. M. Beebe & Company, Parker, Wilder & Company, and Jordan & Marsh were located there by 1861. A natural inlet from the harbor once extended about as far inland as the present corner of Devonshire and Franklin streets, as may be seen on some of the old maps.

In Winthrop place, from forty to seventy years ago, there were (not all at any one date) the homes of Thomas H. Perkins, Jr., William H. Gardiner, Rufus Choate, Isaac MacLellan, Isaac P. Davis, John Davis, Benjamin A. Gould, father of the astronomer of the same name, Isaac Rich, William Reynolds, Samuel Whitwell, George Bond, H. Hollis Hunnewell, Thomas Motley, Henry Cabot, John E. Lodge, George Bancroft, Samuel Cabot, Joshua Blake, Francis Staunton, Thomas Lamb, Josiah P. Cooke, and Samuel Greele. In Otis place I can mention Nathaniel Bowditch,

Bryant P. Tilden, Samuel G. Williams, Oliver Eldredge, Augustus Thorndike, Jeremiah S. Boies, Charles Thorndike, Richard D. Tucker, Eben Rollins and John L. Gardner.

Rufus Choate resided in Winthrop place ten years, till about the time of his death in 1859. He was chosen senator when Webster resigned to accept the appointment of Secretary of State, and after Webster's death was the acknowledged leader of the Massachusetts bar. His cadaverous features, his sallow complexion and the intensity of his facial expression made him a marked personality. No American orator was his equal in appositeness of figures and illustrations, in glowing imagery, and in feeling appeals. Like Webster, he was specially eminent as a jury lawyer, and the court room was crowded whenever there was expectation of hearing him. He was the friend and favorite of the young men of his profession. His advice to young lawyers was: "Never treat a witness as if he were lying unless you are sure he is lying." He was a figure in the community much missed when he died. Like the great Daniel and many other men of genius, he had the reputation of being careless in his own money matters. A Middlesex lawyer calling upon him on business expressed his astonishment at the extent of Choate's library. "Yes," he said, "more books than I can pay for—that's the bookseller's matter, not mine." There is a story that Webster once met him in front of the Merchants Bank and called to him: "Come here, I want $500; I want you to endorse my note." "Make it $1,000," said Choate, "I want $500 too."

The home of Rufus Choate was in somewhat earlier days the residence of Isaac MacLellan. Here La Fayette was entertained, to meet General Hull, the father-in-law of Mr. MacLellan, and met Generals Cable and Huntington, Colonel Putnam and others of his old companions in arms. Isaac MacLellan,

Jr., a son in this family, was a lawyer and had some reputation as a poet.

Benjamin A. Gould passed part of his life as a merchant, but is remembered best as one of the earliest and most successful teachers of the Public Latin School.

The "Gleaner" (Nathaniel I. Bowditch) writes of Isaac P. Davis: "As a trustee of one of our literary institutions, I ever found him to be a man of cultivated intellect, courteous manners and the most genial kindness of heart. Habitually possessing almost unequalled knowledge of passing events, and great vivacity in narrating and commenting on them, he was a universal favorite in society. With him the 'rope-maker' was merged in the 'gentleman.' During the two centuries since our city was founded, that occupation has certainly never had a more popular living representative, nor one whose death, though at quite an advanced age, has been more generally and sincerely regretted." Mrs. Davis was a much respected neighbor; but after all, the greatest interest in that house centered in her mother, a very benevolent old woman, whose declining years were far from useless. She was familiarly known by us as "Grandma Jackson." Children were brought up with the impression that she was decidedly angelic, and now after sixty or seventy years I cannot think of her otherwise. She took delight in visiting the poor, carrying her bag of clothing or other comforts and her purse of money, which were cheerfully replenished out of the abundance of her friends and by freewill offerings of children's earnings.

Our next neighbor, Samuel Whitwell, was off nearly every season, I think, to shoot woodcock down on the Cape, and I remember well that his return was a gustatory satisfaction to us.

Isaac Rich is known as the principal founder of Boston University, leaving for that purpose in his will the bulk of his large estate estimated at nearly one and a half million dollars. His property was almost all invested in Boston real estate, and the great fire of 1872 destroyed nearly all his buildings; but his investments yielded between seven and eight hundred thousand dollars towards establishing the university. A cargo of salt fish had been spoiled on its voyage to a hot climate. Isaac Rich was a fish merchant. He had become very wealthy, but he declared that he could send fish safely if he picked them out himself; and he picked them out, and his cargo arrived at its destination safe and sound.

It would not be becoming for me to write much of the good things I know about George Bond; yet I may justly suppose myself to know and feel more about him than anybody else now living. He had certainly the reputation of strict integrity, of good citizenship, of great interest in public and philanthropic affairs, and of generosity. He is probably best remembered by some old people by the few occasions on which he appeared in public and insisted on the right of free speech or deprecated lawless violence, notably when on a legislative committee at a hearing he rebuked George Lunt, who insulted Dr. Charles Follen, a much respected professor at Harvard, a liberal in both religion and politics and an abolitionist in those exciting times, and when meetings were called condemning the Alton rioters for the murder of Lovejoy, and when in the financial crisis of 1837 orders came from Washington for the demand at the post offices of specie payment when sufficient amount of specie could not be obtained and when the Government itself was paying in paper. Capt. William Sturgis of Summer street and Abbott Lawrence also counseled moderation and delay. The mob spirit had well nigh prevailed; but the storm was averted, the premonitory thunder ceased, and peace prevailed. Benjamin A. Gould of Winthrop place presided at the meeting called on this occasion.

Dr. Nathaniel Bowditch was our next neighbor. Two generations have grown up since his death. His ancestors were shipmasters. Nathaniel was taken from school when ten years old to assist his father, who had become a cooper. After apprenticeship to a ship-chandler, he went to sea as clerk, then as supercargo, then as master and supercargo. After his death, the following resolutions offered by Edward Everett were unanimously adopted by the American Academy:

"Resolved, that the Fellows of the American Academy of Arts and Sciences entertain the liveliest sense of the exalted talents and extraordinary attainments of their late president, who stood prominent among men of science in the United States, and who by universal consent has long been regarded as one of the most distinguished mathematicians and astronomers of the age, ... whose services were of the highest value in the active walks of life, whose entire influence was given to the cause of good principles, whose life was a uniform exhibition of the loftiest virtues, and who with a firmness and energy which nothing could shake or subdue devoted himself to the most arduous and important duties and made the profoundest researches of science subservient to the practical business life."

Bowditch's *Navigator* has been of immense value to seafaring men and owners of vessels. The writer remembers the wonder with which he, a supercargo's clerk, nearly sixty years ago, keeping a log book for his own satisfaction, discovered what an easy matter it was with the logarithms and formulas to determine, by observations of the heavens, the location of the vessel. Certainly no one can estimate the expedition secured and the accidents avoided for thousands of vessels by the indefatigable labor and wonderful accuracy of Doctor Bowditch's work. Much of his success was due to his punctuality. His righteous indignation was likely to be visited upon any one who was regardless of the value of his time and failed to keep an appointment promptly. On returning from a sea voyage in 1802, he found the places of business closed, for it was a holiday in recognition of Commencement at Harvard. It was useless for him to remain in the city, and he joined the great concourse in Cambridge. He was surprised and delighted to hear his own name announced as the recipient of the degree of Master of Arts. Fourteen years afterwards he was honored with that of LL. D. At Mt. Auburn cemetery is an excellent bronze statue of Bowditch erected by his friends. Of his four sons, three were educated at Harvard College, and the fourth received the highest honorary degree.

Nathaniel Ingersoll died in 1861. Jonathan Ingersoll and Dr. Henry Ingersoll did not die until lately, and therefore are better remembered. William Ingersoll still survives. The family record has surely been very honorable. Nathaniel Ingersoll published a history of the Massachusetts General Hospital, issued a memoir of his father, and compiled a unique book of Suffolk names. He gave $70,000 to Harvard University for scholarships.

For many years Samuel Cabot lived in one of the stone houses which he had built opposite Doctor Bowditch and George Bond, in the same house that was afterwards the widow Bliss's, whom George Bancroft married. Bancroft lived there several years. His history of the United States is everywhere recognized as a work of great research and industry and brilliancy of style. He had the honor of being secretary of the navy, and minister to England and to Germany. No name on the Harvard Quinquennial, unless it be that of Edward Everett, has appended to it so long a list of honors. He lived to be over ninety years of age, and had not long ceased to work and to ride horseback.

Samuel Cabot, Jr., was a prominent physician, and became a fellow of the American Academy. His brother,

James Elliot Cabot, is the literary executor and biographer of Ralph Waldo Emerson. He received from Harvard in 1885 the degree of LL. D.

Passing out the door of the Bancroft house, there was a "lion in the way" of entering the Blake house. You could pass around him, however, in safety. You could find in that house in those early days of this century not only a numerous family of children with their parents, but also Uncle Frank and Aunt Mary Staunton, brother and sister of Mrs. Blake. I used to hear from my parents and others special encomiums upon Frank Staunton. The grave of Frank Staunton at Mt. Auburn is designated by a monument erected by the merchants of Boston "in memory of an honest man." Aunt Mary — so she was generally called by the neighbors — had a peculiar defect of speech, poor woman, which naughty boys were fond of imitating; but I never heard anything said against the head and heart from which the speech proceeded. Perhaps I owe my life to her, for I have heard my mother dilate upon her judgment and presence of mind in crossing the street and telling her that I, then a very little fellow, was in danger, instead of sending her loud and startling voice directly up to me, when once I was hanging out of a window.

Thomas Motley was the father of John Lothrop Motley, the historian, and of Thomas, who married Maria Davis, granddaughter of Benjamin Bussey, and lived on the Bussey farm in West Roxbury and was Harvard instructor in farming. Thomas Motley, Sr., was something of a wit. He belonged to a social club that met at the members' houses. I think none of the members can be now living. The breakfast table reports of discussions and *bon mots* of the evening previous made some of the sons resolve that they would some day belong to just such a club. While Thomas Motley was a member of the Massachusetts legislature, he went to France. He told at the club that when he wished on a special occasion to appear at the palace he said to the official at the entrance, "General Court," and was admitted as an army officer.

John Lodge lived in the stone house facing up Winthrop place after 1840. Henry Cabot, his father-in-law, had lived there before. His son, Henry Cabot Lodge, the present Massachusetts senator, was born there. He wrote the biography of his great-grandfather, George Cabot, a book which belongs to the literature of old Summer street.

Josiah Parsons Cooke, father of the late Harvard professor of the same name, was a prominent lawyer and received an honorary degree from Harvard University. Samuel Greele, known very generally as Deacon Greele, — how well I remember him! — was a graduate of Harvard. He was cordial in manner, gleeful, loud in voice, louder in laughter. We would often hear him through our closed windows. "It is one of my gentle smiles," he would say. I think he studied for the ministry, but I do not know that he ever preached. I remember him as a type founder, his place of business being in Congress street. Deacon Greele hustled William Lloyd Garrison into the Old State House to save him from the fury of the mob on the famous occasion when he was in such great danger.

Winthrop place and Otis place were tributary to Summer street and were connected at their lower ends; and, having no outlet into Franklin street except for pedestrians, they formed a sort of double *cul de sac* and, having a continuous brick sidewalk around the block enclosed, provided the boys with a course for their trucks and hoops and sleds and skates. One of our old comrades, James Elliot Cabot, says in his memoir of Emerson: "The Summer street region, even as I remember it twenty years later [than Emerson's day], was a boy's paradise,

and echoed every holiday afternoon and midday recess with 'Coram' and 'Hi-spy,' having just the right admixture of open ground, fences and thoroughfares with intricacies and lurking places of sheds and wood houses and here and there a deserted barn with open doors and a remnant of hay long untouched."

The neighborhood was remarkable for sociability, and the number of children of similar parentage within similar limits could hardly be matched to-day. Nearly every family included from six to eight children. I easily recall thirty-five near enough to my own age to be my comrades. We may have been a little clannish. Probably the "Northenders" and the "Sullivan paddies," with whom we occasionally had pitched battles, may have thought us aristocratic and so conceived an unwarranted dislike to us. There was more play, however, than hostility in our contests. I account it a rare and rich privilege to have lived there. We were near the Common too, which had not ceased to be a common pasture and was a playground all over. I well remember sometimes accompanying the man who took our cow to the Common daily. Not many of our children to-day can have so enjoyed the advantages of both country and city. Some of our playmates have become quite distinguished. I may well mention the late Benjamin Apthorp Gould, the astronomer, and the late Prof. Josiah Parsons Cooke, the chemist, and Rev. Octavius B. Frothingham. "With Octavius Frothingham's death, passed away the most brilliant and interesting figure — excepting one, — of those who were the younger liberal leaders of the last generation," said J. H. Allen.

The land on that part of Devonshire street which was once Winthrop place and that adjoining portion of Summer street on which are now five stores, the whole number of buildings upon the tract being thirty-two, was assessed in 1897, apart from the buildings upon it, on a valuation of $1,668,-

700, very nearly one hundred times its city valuation in 1821. Real estate on Summer street and the adjacent streets must continue to increase in value, all the more on account of the modern innovations of elevators and "sky-scrapers."

One cannot contemplate the great change which has taken place in Summer street and its neighborhood within a century, and mostly within sixty years, without regret, unless he is specially charmed with the victories of mammon; and yet it has been the same change which has made Boston as a whole with its surrounding country so attractive. Summer street has doubtless been an object lesson; so far as it helped to inspire our city workers and traffickers with a love of the rural, it has been the instigator of beautiful suburban villas; and it is now taking its turn in accumulating the wealth so helpful to the beauty, restfulness and healthfulness of the outskirts and environs of Boston.

24
Moose Hunting
in Aroostook

" MOOSE FEEDING ON COARSE GRASSES AND YELLOW WATER LILIES."

FROM A WASH DRAWING BY CLEMENTS,

ENGRAVED BY H. PFLAUM,

OUTING.

VOL. XIV.   AUGUST, 1889.   No. 5.

MOOSE HUNTING IN AROOSTOOK.

BY ARTHUR JAMES SELFRIDGE.

MOOSE are hunted in four ways—first, still hunting in the woods, which means "get a shot, if you can, in any manner you can;" second, still or jack hunting on the water from a canoe in the summer months; third, running them down on snow shoes, when there is a crust, in the spring; fourth, calling in the fall.

The first method is impracticable owing to the dense forest undergrowth and the alertness and shyness of the moose, whose senses of hearing and smell seem to be abnormally developed.

For five falls I have hunted in the Maine woods in the best moose region. During some part of each season I have still hunted with all the patience, caution and craft of which I am possessed. In that time I have succeeded in seeing one moose, although I have started a number. A cracking of brush, a heavy tramping, and all is silent as the grave. Stealing around, I have found a bed or the tracks of some monster, and have always wondered how such a creature could sneak away without giving me at least a chance to shoot. Disappointment comes so often that this, the most scientific, mode of hunting is quickly given over as fruitless.

The second method is the surest, but, owing to existing game laws making the summer months "close season," is unlawful. During June and July the moose seek the water to escape the incessant attacks of the myriads of flies and mosquitoes and gather about the swampy shores of lakes and the boggy banks of the "dead waters," to feed on the coarse grasses and yellow water lilies, of which they are inordinately fond.

Wading into the water until every part of the body except the nose and horns is submerged, they stand through the heat of a summer's day, now and again immersing their heads to drown the ubiquitous fly. This fact, coupled with their wonderful swimming power, may have given rise to the Indian legend and belief that the moose first came from the sea and is amphibious.

So much of natural history will serve to explain the following incident:

As dawn disclosed the contour of the hills about and the islands in the Milmigasset Lake, a hunter was silently sitting in the bow of his canoe, at the leeward of a point behind which the lilies grew in profusion, waiting for advancing day to clear up the landscape. When he distinguished the shape of the loon whose weird, lonesome laugh had filled the woods with echoing sound he signaled to his guide, who noiselessly dipped his paddle into the silvery lake, causing the graceful craft to glide gently onward. The purling ripple of the water set in motion by the cleaving bow and the gentle dripple from the paddle were the only sounds—a muskquash could not have moved more silently. A receding cave with alders and cedars and filled with yellow lily blossoms was revealed as they rounded the point. A blue kingfisher flew from its perch on the single limb of a whitened trunk, uttering his gladsome clack ; save this there was no appearance of life. The guide rested on his paddle. Here and there a fish broke the water, striking some luckless fly skimming too near the surface. Suddenly a mighty splash was heard and the majestic head of an old bull moose rose to view. The stems and leaves of the lilies were dangling from his horns and entwined about his neck. In his capacious mouth was a large root, which he contentedly crunched with the satisfaction of a *gourmet*, little dreaming of the impending danger. The water filled his ears and nostrils, his acute senses were deadened. With thumping hearts and bated breath, with eager expectancy, the hunters sat, not a sound, not a movement. Well they knew that

IN A MOOSE CAMP.

the glisten of the paddle, the slightest "tunk" on the canoe, would rob them of success. Down dove the great head. How quickly the guide plied the paddle! The canoe leaped forward. There was a stir in the water, the guide stopped in the middle of a stroke. The canoe glided on, crunch, scrunch, craunch. Such enjoyment! Again the canoe shot on. The hunter has fitted the butt of his rifle to his shoulder. Up came that unsuspecting creature's head. They were within twenty yards of him. Bang! Splash! The water was thrown into wild commotion. Bang! Bang! Bang! went the repeater. Swash! Splash! Bang! Crash! How the brush snapped. Bang!

"Why didn't you keep the canoe steady?"

"Did all time. You look moose, no see gun," was the Indian's quaint reply.

Next time, Mr. Sportsman, lay aside your rifle, take an eight bore shotgun, load it with six drams of powder and a handful of buckshot, or take a rope and lasso your game.

The following is an incident for which I can vouch. A well-known hunter of the Aroostook region, now dead, returning in his canoe from haying, saw a moose feeding in a "stretch of dead water." His only weapon was an axe. He paddled alongside the moose, while its head was under water. As he raised his axe to

HUNTER BLOWING THE MOOSE CALL.

HEAD OF BULL MOOSE.

Reproduced from OUTING, Vol. XI., page 223.

strike, the moose lifted its head. This capsized the canoe. The hunter caught into the long hair of the moose, still holding his axe. The frightened creature swam across the river. As its fore feet struck the bottom near the opposite bank, the hunter, who had crawled astraddle of its back, with a single blow of his axe severed its spine.

Jack hunting varies from this in that it is done at night, and when a noise in the water proclaims the presence of a moose, the slide of a dark lantern standing behind the bow man is raised, enabling the hunter to aim with greater certainty.

This method of hunting only requires patience in submitting to the attacks of the winged scourges of the forest, skill in paddling and steady nerves.

It always seems cruel to kill a game animal without giving it an even chance of escape. A sportsman ought—a true one does—obtain enjoyment from the escape of his game, if he can only see why and how the senses and alertness of the creature have triumphed over his own skill. The lesson he learns is that he must be able to meet game on its own "stamping ground" and outwit it by his knowledge of its movements and habits. Hunting properly done is only a pleasant, exciting manner of studying natural history.

The third is barbarously cruel. Success depends entirely on deep snow, a crust just strong enough to bear a man's weight, ability to keep running on snow shoes for several hours and a good axe—a gun is usually a useless incumbrance.

Last winter everything combined to make this kind of butchery easy and simple. The yards (portions of territory from one to three miles square, where moose have been feeding during the winter, and within which paths through the snow have been broken, radiating usually from a common centre) were well defined. The snow was six feet deep, the crust

strong enough to bear a man's weight without snow shoes.

One Sunday a couple of men started from a lumber camp on the Munsungun Lake to kill a moose. They knew of a yard containing four cows and two young bulls. Before dawn they were waiting on the edge of the yard for daylight. When it came they started them ; two in their fright bolted in one direction and four in another. The hunters followed the greater number over hills, through swamps and tangled growth for six hours. They came upon three cows, all heavy with calf, in a clump of alders. One of the men gave me the following account : "We come onto them all on a sudden, stretched out on the snow, plum blowed. Their tongues stuck out about a foot, their eyes were closed, their legs all cut and bloody from breaking through the crust. They were panting fearfully,

"THEY MANAGE TO BEND THE TRUNK OVER, STANDING ASTRIDE OF IT."

THE GAME AT HOME.

and groaning and moaning in awful distress.

"My partner says to me: 'Frank, this is what I call luck. Three moose; their skins will fetch $24—better'n a month's work. Come, give it to 'em.'

"I raised my rifle and aimed it at the biggest one, right behind her ear. Just as I was pressing the trigger she opened her eyes as much as to say: 'Murder me.' I dropped my gun, and said to my partner: 'I'm blamed if I'm going to see them poor creatures butchered in this fashion.'

"'Give me your gun. I'll fix 'em,' he snarled. I wouldn't do it. He got mad and cussed me vicious. I couldn't stand it no longer, and I says to him: 'If them moose are going to be killed, you or me is going first. I've got the gun, so just you come away and leave them.'

He added: "I've always felt mighty well that I saved them, and I'll never run another moose on snow shoes. It's a regular dog's trick."

Maine lumber camps are responsible for the unlawful killing of great numbers of moose, deer and caribou. One man boasted to me that his men had fresh meat all winter and he never bought a pound of beef.

The fourth calling is legitimate. It requires the exertion of all the keenest faculties, great endurance, extreme patience, highest skill in imitation, nerve, courage, and not a little genuine suffering.

The calling season begins with rutting in September. It reaches its height about the 1st of October. It continues nearly six weeks, depending somewhat, I am informed, on the changes of the moon. During the early part of this period the cow does not respond to the amorous advances of the bull, which loses some of its extreme caution and goes roaming through the forest in a reckless fashion, seeking everywhere for a mate. Just before the cow begins to give expression to her desire by calling, the bull is on the verge of desperation. This is the time for success in luring him to his death by imitating the cow's call, for, once mated, nothing save the challenge of some intruding bull will separate him from his intimate.

Most of the writers on this subject have called the moose to his end in a manner that required little hardship, which is entirely overlooked in the thrill and excitement of success. Perhaps a better idea of what this sport really is, and what trials may have to be endured, may be had from a description of my latest trip.

On the 10th of September, 1887, we left Presque Isle, the terminus of the New Brunswick Railroad, for Junkins' Farm, the last settlement on the Aroostook River, forty-five miles distant. At this season of the year the Maine rivers are very low and shallow. Oftentimes one of the party will have to wade and pull the canoe, while the others go through the woods. It is a disagreeable and unpleasant way to navigate.

Our guide, an old Frenchman who could speak little or no English, "socked" the canoe up the river, while we tramped fourteen miles through the woods to a point on the river nearest Chandler Brook Lake, our destination, where we made our home camp. We rested here for a day and "cachéd" our valuables, consisting mostly of canned vegetables and onions. Next morning each of us rolled up a pack which contained all the paraphernalia for a week's tramp—blankets, frypan, coffee pot, pork, flour, bread, baking powder, coffee, sugar and a can or two of condensed milk.

Our path to the lake lay over an abominable old "tote" road, mostly corduroy, which was slippery, rotten and treacherous. At one time we would be wading in mud to our knees, at another balancing on a slippery log, trying to avoid some dangerous honey hole. After a five-hours walk we reached an old lumber camp, five miles from the river, which we selected as our abode. Nearly a day was consumed in trying to find the lake. Road after road was followed up, invariably leading to some log yard. It was evident that some of us must climb. Selecting

the tallest spruce on the highest hill, the guide began to climb. For forty feet there was not a branch nor a twig.

After a struggle of ten minutes he reached the top. "Me see de gross mont. Look lake, for sure ; dis way," pointing north. He meant, "I see a large mountain at the foot of which appears to be a lake, the direction from here is north."

The following morning the guide and I started through the woods over hill and through swamp, due north, blazing our trail which led us to the lake, a sheet of water containing about four square miles of surface. The point at which we struck it was "no good for de bull moose, he like de lilly," the guide's expression for "it is an unsuitable place for calling." We followed the shore of the lake, seeking a shallow spot filled with water lilies or "cow lily pads," surrounded by a swamp that gradually rose to a high hill. Our path led us through moss-covered ledges, stunted trees, and over trails that had actually been worn by moose, deer and caribou, traveling up and down the lake. It excites wonder and admiration for these

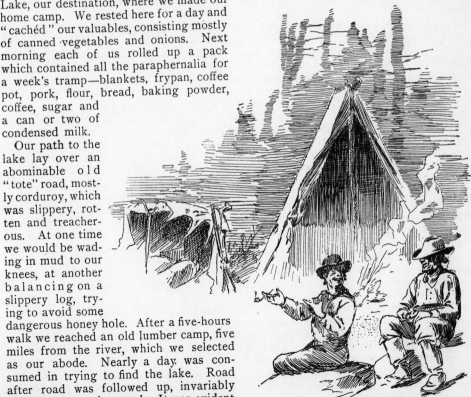

SHELTER FOR THE NIGHT.

wary denizens of the forest to see the places they have selected for their lairs and beats. At one time you are walking lightly over a soft bed of moss ; without any warning you slump through between two great rough boulders that scrape your legs the whole length. Slowly you extricate yourself and select a log to be sure of your footing, when all of a sudden both feet start for the starry sky. Oh, how your head aches ! Our pack, which we took turns in carrying, consisted of one " lit-ly hach " (a belt axe), one rubber blanket, one thin, moth-eaten army blanket, two pounds of salt pork, plenty of hard bread, and a few biscuits. It weighed about ten pounds, and seemed to weigh a hundred. After the first ten minutes of this wretched tramp I drew the cartridge from my rifle to prevent any accident, so frequent were my falls. You may judge of the pleasant paths we trod when I tell you that it took us nearly six hours to do two miles.

We were rewarded, however, by finding an ideal place for calling. An arm of the lake made in between two hills that sloped gradually to a cedar swamp that was, perhaps, a mile across. We chose for our location a little bare spot under the branches of a great leaning cedar, just behind a tuft of alder bushes. Marking the place by a tall pine that stood near we retreated a quarter of a mile to select a camp. We found a level spot underneath two great spruce tops (trees felled the previous winter, from which logs had been cut), which had fallen across each other. With the aid of the belt axe we cut the small limbs that grew downward and soon had a cosey little nest, with at least a foot of soft, fragrant fir spread for a bed. We threw our rubber blanket over the logs and fastened it securely, as we thought, and swung around the hill to be a mile from the calling spot, for a quiet smoke.

We lit our pipes and were dozing off, picturing to ourselves the moose we were going to have. We could almost smell the delicious odor of a broiling steak, when we were brought to our feet by a terrible crash and a terrific peal of thunder, followed immediately by the most vivid lightning I ever witnessed. Quickly I selected a leaning tree, placed my rifle, axe and compass there, so that they would not attract the lightning to me, and rushed for some fallen logs to avoid the pelting rain. For twenty minutes a most frightful thunderstorm, with a terrific rain and wind accompaniment, was passing. Trees were blown down, limbs were falling, and here and there great trees were splintered by the lightning. We were soaked by the torrents of rain. As soon as it cleared off we went out into the bright sun and back to our camp, where we found that the rain had driven underneath our rude tent and drenched our bed.

All the old hunters tell me that if moose smell smoke they will leave its locality. Whether this be true or not I am not sure They have been known to yard for the winter within two or three miles of a lumber camp, where they must have smelt smoke. Once two deliberately walked into my camp when the fire was burning merrily. I have never tried building a fire within three miles of a place selected to call. For this reason we did not dry our bed nor cook our supper. Do not be disgusted—it consisted of raw pork, hard bread and "Old Medford." It was not bad, because every sign indicated a dead moose before morning.

It was growing dusk. We went to our stand, carefully marking our path by bits of birch bark curled about the bushes. Reaching our ground we waited in silence for dark. When it came, my guide wet the horn, which he had carefully made in the afternoon by rolling a piece of birch bark into the shape of a funnel. Fitting the horn to his mouth and holding it to the earth he gently and softly uttered the plaintive, amorous call of the cow moose, given only at this season of the year. Raising his head, so that the end of the horn described the curves of the letter S (beginning at the bottom of it), he gradually increased the volume of sound ; then lowering the horn to its original position, the end having traced a gigantic figure 8, he gradually decreased the volume until near the end of the call, when he suddenly burst out with a plaintive, seductive grunt that went rolling over the swamp and up the hill, bidding any bull moose to come. After a wait of perhaps ten seconds he gave the second of the three parts of the call. This began with an impatient expression of intense eagerness, quickly changing into one long note, which combined quavering complaint, pathetic longing and unrequited affection, and sunk into a confiding appeal. The third followed the second at a shorter interval and commenced with a tone of scolding impatience, which gradually swelled in intensity, approaching fierceness. It closed with an upward toss of the head and a shriek, terminating in a rising inflection, almost a roar, that seemed to say decidedly : " Come, now or never !"

The note is peculiar to the moose and can be compared with nothing in nature. It is made by shaping the mouth as if to pronounce the French u, then forcing the syllable " ehr " through the vocal organs by the use of the abdominal muscles, giving it a decidedly nasal twang. The idea of beginning with the horn held toward the earth is taken from the habit of the cow moose, as is the number of parts of the call.

After waiting until every echo had died away and the oppressive silence had again filled the woods, perhaps half or three-quarters of an hour, a second call was given. It seemed to roll over hill and valley and come echoing back for an interminable length of time. Patiently we waited for the answer, but nothing save the drip, drip, drip, from the wet leaves, the occasional splash of a musk rat, or the lonesome hoot of an owl was heard. Again and again the call was given. The response was the same. For two hours this monotony continued. After a call louder, longer, and more intense than the rest, an answer came in the form of a flash of lightning that illuminated the entire landscape. We could distinguish a flock of ducks on the water within one hundred feet of us. Then followed a peal of thunder and again the rain fell in torrents. We huddled together under the great leaning cedar and held a consultation in whispers.

" Tunner bon for the bull moose. No 'fraid. Come lymly. You try call. No come for me."

We shivered for half an hour before it stopped raining. When it did I began. The guide's voice was a heavy bass, mine a baritone. Putting the horn to my lips I gave the call. Scarcely had the sound died away when the answer came rolling down the opposite mountain to us—clearly and distinctly. A heavy silence of ten minutes followed. Just as I was putting the horn to my mouth for a second call the answer was repeated, this time nearer and more distinct. I replied to it with a plaintive grunt full of satisfactory longing. The response was shorter and quicker. For the next fifteen minutes there was not a sound except the dripping of the leaves and the croaking of the frogs. Raising the horn I gave an

inquiring grunt. The answer came so clear that we judged the moose was within·a quarter of a mile. Taking a dipper I dribbled some water in the edge of the lake. The old bull fairly roared in his eagerness, the brush began to crack and we could hear this majestic creature walk back and forth. Again I poured the water ; an eager answer was the result.

The guide then took my horn and with the power of a ventriloquist gave a furious challenge, that sounded as if it came from another bull far in the opposite direction. Almost before it was finished an angry, smothered roar broke from the now infuriated bull, which dashed into the water. Our flock of ducks took flight and scattered with discordant quacking. " Be ready for shoot. No shake. I trust you," whispered my guide.

Carefully cocking my rifle I stepped out from under the dense shade to be sure of a good light. I thought I could distinguish the moose crossing the space between us and the other shore. For a better light I took another step, and down into a honey hole I went above my knees. I pulled one foot out with a pop. The other was deeper in the mire than ever. I had sunk below the alders and could see nothing. I made another frantic effort. The moose was coming. Alas ! I was slowly sinking in the filthy, black mud, utterly unable to extricate myself. " Why no shoot ?" I tried to make him understand, offering my gun. I had settled to my waist. " Moose there—shoot ! "

I spoke loud enough to make him realize my predicament. The faithful fellow, disregarding the coming moose, pulled me out by main strength. The noise we made was frightful. No wonder the moose stopped coming. When I stood on terra firma everything was silent. We resorted to pouring water again. We could hear his retreating steps. We applied the horn, giving every conceivable variation from an angry challenge to a gentle, plaintive moan expressing abject misery. It was useless ; he had departed. After another hour of patient waiting we gave it up. Oh, how bitter cold it was ! It seemed as if I should freeze. There were no spreading horns to carry home in triumph. It was a wet, gloomy, nasty night. I hated myself for my careless stupidity. The old man tried to comfort and encourage me : " Come next day ; no scard I bet ten dollar."

" Where are we ?" I growled. The

wind had blown our markers away and we were lost. It was cold and cheerless enough. Our axe was at camp and everything was reeking with water. What to do, where to turn, was the question. My sense of location was gone. It was so black and dark that we could not see each other at a distance of ten feet. I turned to old Mathias, who, by the by, was sixty-seven years of age, and said: "Old man, we're lost!"

"No care, by jimruslem! Me fex de flambeau. Find tent for sure." He split the birch horn, rolled it up lightly and applied a match. Crack, sputter, hiss and a hazy yellow light flickered out changing the trees and vines into weird hobgoblins and elves. Leading the way I tramped through dense undergrowth, climbed over fallen logs, always going toward dryer ground, up the slope that led away from the lake.

"No git camp quick; stay all night. Flambeau all gone," as he threw the remains from him. Landing on a small tree high above our heads it blazed out brighter than ever. The undergrowth was less dense. We hurried on. It grew darker. We stopped for a moment to see if there was any spot we could recognize. A bright flame shot up. "De big birch. De camp for sure." Sure enough the dying gleam had shown us two great birch trees that were within a hundred feet of our camp. Tearing off a strip of bark we soon had flambeaux to spare. It seemed like reaching home to be at this poor little tent. We started a small fire, heated a tin cup full of rum, swallowed it, pulled our blanket over us, and back to back soon fell asleep.

How long we remained so I do not know. We were awakened by the dropping of gathered rain in our faces. Raising myself I tried to stop this by drawing the rubber blanket around the log. It was my second fluke that night. The water that had gathered in the hollow of the blanket poured down my sleeve and over the poor old man. We both shivered, and, I am afraid, wished for home. We did not stop to discuss the question, but filled our pipes, smoked, had a pull at the bottle and again lay down and were soon sound asleep. I was suddenly aroused by an agonizing shriek, "De crank, de crank!" My poor guide lay writhing in intense pain. The calf of his leg was drawn into a knot by a terrific cramp. I rubbed and chafed it with rum until it passed away.

"Crank hugly, like a dev. No fix de botte de mashin (machine) come. Make booly now." Taking his boots, which had been his pillow, he stuck them sole upward, each on an upright limb of one of the trees that made our camp.

I have since learned that it is the firm belief of many of the lumber men that if they hang their boots sole upward they will not be troubled with cramps. On large drives of logs as many as twenty pair of boots may be seen at night in this position.

Morning came at length. It was clear, but bitter cold. Our blanket was frozen in places where it had been wet. We turned out cold and stiff. Taking my gun I went to the lake and found fresh moose tracks within a short distance of our calling stand. The creature had returned after we had given him up. We were disgusted and ready to wear dunce caps.

"Let us build a fire and have breakfast, old man."

"No, no! Come back to-day night yesterday (day after to-morrow), get moose, yes! Smoke, moose run. Pork no cook, bon medceen!"

That phantom of hope, that one possibility in a thousand, made me yield, and we sat down on a log to our morning repast. Cold raw pork—ugh! hard bread crushed fine, and two biscuits harder than baseballs, a bill of fare that was almost unswallowable; but hunger triumphed. Our tramp back to the old lumber camp was slow and tedious. It was so late in the day when we arrived that we concluded to rest that night, and to cook something for the next hunt.

We were sitting before our cabin door enjoying a quiet after-supper smoke and the fascinating effect of a brilliant sunset. The forest gleamed with the rich warm colors of autumn, which seemed to reflect the red and gold of the sky. The after glow was slowly fading away when our reverie was broken by a deep-drawn sigh from the guide, who laconically remarked: "Me bed, next day moose." Rising, he went into the cabin.

My genial companion, reclining on a "deacon seat," was watching the flickering blue flame of a sulphur match, waiting to relight his pipe. As it grew into a steadier white blaze it revealed the manly, sunburned features of his face, in which were mingled courage, determination, kindness and good fellowship; a beautiful Gordon setter, curled up at his feet asleep, and, leaning against the cabin, a finely-modeled double gun. The flame died out, leaving only the glowing coal in the pipe. As the fragrant smoke curled upward he said, "I wish you would tell me what you know of the habits of the moose and show me how to call."

I assured him that my knowledge was limited, but I would try to answer any question he might suggest.

"Is it true that a bull moose, with his immense spread of horn, can pick his way through the thickest wood and make little or no noise?"

"You probably know," I replied, "that the moose has a most delicate sense of smell and of hearing. It does not take alarm at ordinary noises or odors, but the slightest unusual sound or smell is a warning of impending danger. A mighty tree may fall with a thundering crash, a skunk may emit a noisome stench, neither of which will affect the equanimity of the moose, but the snapping of a twig, the grinding of the snow under a man's foot, the delicately-perfumed presence of a fastidious human being, will cause him to seek safety in flight.

"It does not, at the approach of danger, break into a run as does the deer, but sneaks away in a rapid stealthy walk that does not rustle a leaf nor crack a twig. An Indian in moccasined feet could not glide through the woods more silently than does the largest bull moose when alarmed. It makes noise enough, however, when feeding or traveling through the woods when there seems to be no danger near. It strikes and rubs its horns against the brush and trunks of trees, often uttering, especially during the rutting season, a short guttural grunt."

"What is their food? I have heard that they dig for moss with their broad antlers."

"Yes, that is a common notion, but I do not credit it. In the first place, they cannot get their horns to the ground without dropping on their knees. They cannot eat grass from the ground without sprawling out their legs or falling in that position. Besides, they do not eat moss in the summer time. They eat the twigs and bark of all deciduous trees; moose wood (mountain ash) is a delicacy. You may have noticed how the young white birches were bent over and pealed in the old moose yard through which we passed yesterday. When they want the bark and

twigs higher than they can reach they manage to bend the trunk over, standing astride of it while they feed. This is called 'riding down.' In the summer time they feed about the shores of the lakes on the long grasses and lily pads. They do not graze as does a cow, cutting the grass to the ground, but merely nip off the tops."

"The track the old man showed me yesterday was pointed at the toe like a deer's, only very much larger, while the caribou's was round shaped, more like that of a horse. Was he right?"

"Yes."

"Now about calling, why do you begin the call by carrying your head to the left and then to the right, slowly raising the horn until it is pointed at an angle of sixty degrees, and then move your head to the left and then to the right as you lower it? Why do you always imitate the cow moose?"

"It is the habit of the animal. I once heard a cow calling. The sound seemed at first to come rolling along the ground, then to rise slowly until it seemed to strike the top of the highest hill, and then gradually to fall. It is a curious sound, and I can only give you an idea of what it is like by making the sounds without a horn. The cow is imitated to lure the bull, which makes only an answer, consisting of short grunts, and a challenge which is indescribable."

I then began a series of illustrative grunts, which my companion repeated, trying to imitate all the different variations of expression that a cow moose makes in a call, stopping after each change in tone to explain why it was necessary "to hold, as 'twere, the mirror up to nature."

The dog seemed to be a little restive, and now and then uttered a smothered whine.

"There is something around here," said my friend. "That dog does not act in that manner unless there is something moving."

"Oh, it's nothing more than a hedgehog, I'll warrant, if it's"—crash, bang! a terrific snort, bow, wow, wow! a tearing and a snapping of brush.

"What's that?" whispered my friend, peering into the darkness, gun in hand.

Bow, wow, wow! "Charge, Jim!" and all was quiet.

"What zat, de moose?" came from the depths of the cabin.

Seizing my rifle I dashed behind the

camp and gave several calls, but with no avail. In another quarter of the woods a fierce challenge sounded. I answered it with all my power. The brush cracked. I cocked my rifle. "No shoot, me not the moose." It was the guide.

We made a flambeau, went down the trail a little way, and there where a small birch tree had fallen across the path were the tracks of an immense bull moose. Then we remembered having heard a few grunts at the edge of the woods (our cabin was in a clearing) which we had supposed were echoes. We did not dream of the presence of a moose, because our camp fire was burning brightly. This fact adds to my suspicion that smoke is not particularly terrifying to them.

The next day the guide selected for a calling stand the top of a dilapidated old lumber camp, around which there were quantities of moose "sign." As they were starting out that evening the guide said to me in his inimitable way : " No hausé (answer) for two hour. Big Blox cold like a dev'. You whoop de moose. Listen de bull one, two time. No cold, stay all night."

My companion had a gun case about three feet in length. The old man could not remember his name. To distinguish him from " Mistur," myself, he called him " Big B(l)ox."

Away they went in high spirits. " Moose for sure ! " When night had spread its intense gloom over the silent forest I heard the gentle seductive notes from the guide's horn, and instinctively reached for my gun, so natural were they. For two hours, at intervals, while keeping the fire alive, I heard the muffled sounds coming through the camp windows. It was growing intensely cold. Slipping on my frock I stepped out under the starlit sky and watched the rising three-quartered moon that was streaking the forest with yellow light. A long, loud call was in progress. As its echo died away I raised my horn to give the requested encouragement. There was no need of it. Within a few hundred feet of my own camp I heard the living answer of a bull, so close, indeed, that I could hear him as he carelessly crashed through the undergrowth and bounded over fallen logs. My impulse was to use the water and gently lure him into my own lair. I bethought me of the dog and the pleasure my friend would take in killing his first moose. On he went, answering at short intervals. He was going straight toward them. Now they hear him. The old man is working him nearer. I can hear him no more. I begin to run over the form I shall use in congratulating my friend on his good fortune, when I am startled with, "By jimruslem ! no fool, Mathias," roaring through the guide's horn, and the stentorian shout of my friend, "You can't keep me out here in the cold any longer with that bloat."

Picking up my horn I gave an answer All is silent. The acute ear of my guide detects the difference between the real call and the imitation. Alas, so does the moose ! How disgusted they are, the old man in particular. " Me call forty year, kill three hundred sixty five moose. Call hundred. Fool some bebé, no till de moose."

Our hunt ended after another week. That phantom, the bull moose, haunted us and kept continually luring us to disappointment. We broke camp and sorrowfully bade our *ignis fatuus* adieu.

25
An Isle of the Sea
(Nantucket)

An Isle of the Sea

By GRACE LE BARON

"It's a snug little Island
A right little, tight little Island."—*Dibdin*.

SEMI-ANNUALLY, at least, the Island of Nantucket, *our* "beautiful Isle of the sea," is foremost in the public eye. It first attracts us when the ice embargo shuts it away from the outside world, when its harbor is filled with enormous cakes of floating ice which imperil navigation, when Winter literally holds it in its icy grasp; and again, when in summer dress, it woos the "stranger" to visit its shores and to listen to its surf, beating on the sandy beach.

FRONT VIEW OF HOUSE OF HENRY M. UPHAM
OF BOSTON, SHOWING ITS ANTIQUITY

Despite all the talk about its "freeze ups" of later days, the one of 1779 must go down into history as unequalled, commencing, so tradition says, in December, and closing the harbor without intermission all winter. To-day, there is the telegraph and the Marconi wireless to mitigate, and the stories of deprivations of Nantucket folk, as now so often told, only subject the fairy-story tellers to jest; for the people of Nantucket prepare for winter, just as a traveller prepares for his journey, and news from the absent is the only thing actually missed by them. Indeed the inhabitants go so far as to say, that it is these winter days, when they are thus shut in together, which are the pleasantest, for then they have time "to get acquainted" as they call it.

But to the "stranger" (the only word which should be eliminated from a Nantucket dictionary, as being, to say the least, uncomplimentary to those who visit its shores year in and year out) the glorious summer time presents it at its best. Its atmosphere is then unequalled, unless it be by the winter air of those farther away Islands of the Bermudas. There is a balminess in its breezes,—a healing balminess,—which brings convalescence to the invalid. Nature seems to have taken from its winds the harshness of many seashore resorts and given to them a healing power.

* * * * * *

The island has its history, as have

FRONT VIEW OF MRS. DAVID NEVINS' RESIDENCE

we all; and history says that the ever-enterprising Bartholomew Gosnold, in 1602, did sight the highest point of the Island where Sankaty Lighthouse now sheds its warning light for the mariner; and that later, one Thomas Mayhew and others were given its ownership, and still later, that this same Thomas Mayhew did transfer his right to those whose descendants still inhabit the Island,—one Thomas Macy being the first settler—for, as tradition tells it, "thirty pounds current and two beaver hats,"—one for himself and one for his good wife;" but alas! rumor does not say the style chosen for Mrs. Mayhew, whether trimmed with birds of plumage as the sea gull or the plover, or the floating seaweeds for which the Island is noted.

A bargain it certainly was, which has thus secured for "generations yet unborn" such a home, and were Mr. Fields living to-day, he would never venture to say "Nantucket's sunk," and "old Ma'am Hacket's garden" would share the honors

with a very live Island town and suburbs, which, year by year, beckons to its children from the North, South, East and West.

Geography tells us that it is an Island thirty miles out at sea; and it is this latter fact, the fact that it *is* out at sea, which has been one of its greatest attractions, and which has, despite its spasmodic isolations, called from all points of the compass, those who visit its shores, and troll, summer after summer, for the blue-fish and who walk its moors and gather its flora. But the Island is a public benefactor, as well as a playground, when the warning of the bell buoy off the bar is heeded:—

"Ship ahoy! it cries in danger,
And so be thou art a stranger
To this coast, be still a ranger.
Fill thy white sails—
Death claims these shoals!"

Still another messenger meets the mariner at Great Point Light, while Sankaty still again adds its final word of warning and of blessing:—

'Aye, Aye!' the sailor cries, as from afar
  Thy warning comes; 'Unwind the cable
    chain!
Stand by the anchor, lads. See! shoal and
    bar.'
  And by thy light, the morning breaks
    again,
    O light o' Sankaty.

'Cross Sconset's plains to Monomoy's
    calm height,
  The balmy breezes do thy praises tell;
And fair Wauwinet, shrouded for the night,
  Calls to Coatue in thy care—'All is well,'
    O light o' Sankaty.

One careless glance—a thousand souls are
    lost;
  One careless thought and Death thy
    Kingdom claims.
This thou dost ken—and ships when tem-
    pest tossed
  Cry unto thee, above all other names,—
    O light o' Sankaty.

. . . .

Praise God for thee whose light is always
    trimmed
    O light o' Sankaty.

Thus can it be said that its coast, though surrounded by danger, is prepared for danger as well, although disasters happen nevertheless.

Time was when Nantucket was foremost in the whaling industry, and there are still those left who compare its past with its present, calling to mind that in 1841 alone, twenty-nine ships were fitted out; but prosperity comes not always in the same general line, and the town has little need of living on its past, for the present makes it the cynosure of all eyes. Nor can it live upon its present alone; but it can and does look forward to a future equally ennobling, and, if statistics tell aright of the past—that future will be as lucrative.

To-day, venerable, white-haired sea captains sit around in what is called the "Captain's room," and revel in telling,—shall we say—"fish stories?" True there may be romance in some, but facts prevail; and facts tell of the loaded vessels entering outside the harbor where now the sail-boat and the steam-yacht signal their coming into port. Indeed, some there are to-day on the Island who treasure the silver dollar which was, in their boyhood

REAR PIAZZA OF MRS. DAVID NEVINS' RESIDENCE

days, their reward for announcing the incoming of some whale-ship, loaded with its barrels of sperm oil, and which was given them by the waiting wife on the housewalk, who had watched for days, ay, for weeks, for the absent husband, *her* Captain, whose "absence had made the heart grow fonder."

Nantucket wives of old well deserve to be called heroines, for oftentimes, voyages counted not only two long years, but twice two years, and, as an inheritance, these

lowering flag shows that another kind of life is led in Nantucket than of yore, and that "the tackling of a sperm whale" has had to give way to the pleasure-seekers after blue-fish and sharks.

There is one word which Nantucketers, "as to the manner born," resent, and that is the word "quaint"; and yet the little Island would lose much of its interest without this very word, for what would it be without its "Stone Alley," its "Plumb lane," and its quaintest of

HOUSE OF WILLIAM BARNES, JR., OVERLOOKING THE SEA

women have handed down to their children nobleness of character, even though the sentimental has had to give way to the practical, and good housewives have had to prevail amongst its women.

Gradually, the whale industry decreased, and now all is changed, for such leviathans no more enter its port, but pretty sail-boats, filled with their merry crews, or some pretentious steam-yacht drops anchor, and the sunset gun with its

all villages, the suburbs of the town itself, Siasconset, or more familiarly spoken of, as "Sconset." Even there fashion has intruded, but there are still left some of the li tle, low houses where one has to crawl up to bed, much as one has to climb a ship's ladder. And quaint customs prevail; such as the curfew ringing, the town crier's call of the "meat auction," or the sale of household goods. But its quaint people are fast dying out (more's the pity!)

and Nantucket people of to-day, who follow the newer ways, are in the majority.

To see Nantucket at her best, visitors must follow the sound of the bell buoy off the bar, round Brant Point on a summer day, and it is an easy matter to believe that a city and not a town welcomes their waiting eyes. The surf beats upon the white, sandy beach and tosses itself playfully across the jetty. Merry bathers dip themselves in the

comers choose the Cliff overlooking the ocean, where they can "see their ships come in," but the town has everywhere some representative of wealth and fashion. Yes, and like Boston, it has its "water side," for Orange Street overlooking the harbor, counts much wealth and solid aristocracy. From here across the harbor, one looks over at Wauwinet's peaceful beach, and Sankaty flashes its revolving light. Monomoy, another settled district of the

HOUSE OF SIDNEY CHASE, OF CHASE AND BARSTOW, BANKERS, BOSTON

waters, which are ten degrees warmer than on the North or South shore. The moors, or more properly called "commons," show every color of the rainbow in their varied flora, and the air seems to breathe new life to all.

It would be difficult to say where was the real aristocratic part of the town; and even the annual summer visitor is disposed to disclaim making it a fashionable resort, although desirous of welcoming only the better element. Some of the newer

town, shows its sun-lit roofs in the distance, and Coatue's long stretch of sand calls to the idle visitor.

Pass up the main street with its avenue of trees, and one passes pretentious houses even of the olden times. Side by side are the three brick dwelling houses once tenanted by the three Starbuck brothers, still talked of, wealthy ship owners of those days, when the men used the harpoon and the women used the distaff.

The Old Mill on a side street beyond is shown to the visitor as a relic of olden times—built in 1746— and was recently bought and presented by a Bostonian to the Historical Society. The Soldiers' monument in the open square records

KENSINGTON COTTAGE, SHOWING ITS WREATH OF ENGLISH IVY. OWNED BY MR. EDWARD ISOM OF CLEVELAND

the names of those who died for their country with that same bravery, inherited from those same mothers of old who cared for their families and paced the housewalk

in patient waiting for the absent captain, who, as the song goes, was "striking a sperm whale." It is said that twenty-nine Nantucket boys served under Paul Jones on the Bon Homme Richard.

As before said, there is no true aristocratic part of the town. Wealth is represented everywhere, when the moors, or "commons" put on their summer dress of flora. Boston boasts its complement of residents, for within a stone's throw, one might almost say, are three Boston "boys," so to speak. One, Mr. Sydney Chase of the banking house of Chase & Barstow, has chosen his home on Main Street and preserved the antiquity of the old houses which he has thrown into one, and, in dull red garb, it stands as an example of old-time days. Mr. Richard Elkins of the brokers' firm of George C. Brooks & Co., occupies his family homestead, and Mr. Henry M. Upham, for almost forty years identified with the Old Corner Book Store, occupies his house on Orange Street, which, like all the houses on this street, has the harbor view before spoken of. In keeping with the houses about, he has preserved the old-time fashion at the front and modernized the back of it only. There are still to be seen the old-fashioned steps, with the wooden railings; the steps themselves running far across the sidewalk; and the beams within the rooms tell that the house has long passed the century mark.

On this same street is the house of Judge Sloane of Sandusky, Ohio; for the West is largely represented amongst the summer colony. Then follows the house of the millionaire Willards of Washington, simple and unobtrusive; and just below, is one of the most pretentious estates of Nantucket, that of Mr. William Barnes, Jr., grandson of the late Hon. Thurlow Weed of Albany.

It is said that the terraces overlooking the sea cost far into the thousands, and it is easily believed when one considers that each terrace is a marvel of masonry, and the green velvety grass which covers them is equally marvellous and beautiful. This, then, is one of the three most pretentious and elegant

It would be difficult to make comparisons, with so many estates to attract the eye, but if one wishes to mount the Cliff and sight land and water from its height, one can readily do so from the broad piazza of Mrs. David Nevins, who once lived in Boston.

A bijou of a house is that of Dr. William Boone of New York, appropriately named Overvine, for the house itself is hidden by a wealth of ivy and vines. To see it

MOORS END, HOUSE OF H. BIGELOW WILLIAMS OF BOSTON

estates of the town; and Boston again shares the honors of the other two; for one would hardly believe it, but there is to be found in Mr. H. Bigelow Williams's estate, "Moor's End," a reproduction of an Italian villa. Its high wall may shut out its beauties from the chance passer-by, but once within the gate, the peristyle and the flowered garden and statuary suggest a villa of beautiful Florence.

at its best is to see it in festal array, with the trees which have long ago over-reached the century mark, and its lawn awaiting a garden party.

The English ivy upon the Island is a surprise to all, who come expecting to see little else but eel grass; but all this is a mistake, though eels and eel grass exist on the Island, but flowers are to be found there, too, and the accompanying illustration of a nook in the garden of Kensington Villa so-called, owned by Mr. Edward Isom, a wealthy summer visitor from Cleveland, Ohio, verifies the words.

Yes, Nantucket has its "freeze ups," but it also has its summer gardens, and its summer folk look with respect upon a people of ster-

of the American Revolution.

To know Nantucket is to love it. To know its people is to respect them. Isolated they may be, but from the time Admiral Sir Isaac Coffin of English fame founded the Coffin school in 1827, the doors of Vassar and of Smith have swung wide open to its students, showing

THE OLD MILL

ling qualities and of sturdy character. It has sent out to the world celebrities such as Lucretia Mott, and Maria Mitchell, the astronomer; and the birthplace of Benjamin Franklin's mother is marked in a befitting manner by the Abiah Folger Franklin Chapter Daughters

that educational advantages have helped to add their glory and made of its people a people of culture and learning, and from the Atlantic to the Pacific are to be found teachers who first learned their A B C's in the modest schoolhouse of this island town.

26
Canoeing Down the West Branch of the Penobscot

CANOEING DOWN THE WEST BRANCH OF THE PENOBSCOT.

BY WILLIAM AUSTIN BROOKS.

IN OUTING for July I had the pleasure of telling how William and I, with our two guides, Francis and Dennis, paddled from the North East Carry at the head of Moosehead Lake to Chesuncook, and how we camped on the shores of that fine lake. For the benefit of all lovers of canoeing, and with the hope that some of my readers may be tempted to follow our pleasant route, I shall describe our further journey from Chesuncook to and across the arduous Ripogenus Carry.

Thus far we had seen no black flies nor mosquitoes, but we knew that this indemnity was our good fortune ; their ravenous hordes would find us sooner or later. At just four o'clock in the morning I threw off my blankets and stepped outside the tent. The sky above the opposite shore was ablaze with crimson and gold and purple clouds. The smooth water of Chesuncook was tinged with the same colors, unruffled by a breath of wind.

Very gradually the red streak in the east expanded into a blaze of light which threw a long, dazzling bridge across the water. Everything seemed propitious for a fine day, but out on the lake two loons were screaming.

As we listened to their wild, quavering notes, Francis said : "Hear that loon yell ; I'm afraid we have wind, perhaps big storm."

While we were getting breakfast clouds commenced to gather and the sky looked like rain. Before we were packed up and the canoes loaded there was a patter on the dead leaves, and by the time we started it was raining hard; but we spread rubber blankets over the luggage and kept on down the lake past the desolate shores, which are bordered with dead trees and driftwood, the result of the flowage from the dam at the outlet. The loons kept up a constant screaming, and as we approached them disappeared under the water only to reappear at a surprising distance. As soon as their heads came above the surface their weird cry again echoed from one to the other as if they reveled in the storm.

We paddled steadily, for between us and the carry were twelve long, monotonous miles.

The rain continued to fall and the lake

remained calm. There was no diverting incident except that, when about half the distance was accomplished, we suddenly heard a faint tinkle like a cowbell, which seemed to come from the woods on the eastern shore, which we were nearest to. We stopped to listen, but not hearing it we started on. In a little while we heard it again, a faint, distant tinkle, and Dennis said that some one must have put a cow-bell on a deer and turned it loose, for we knew there were no domestic cattle within miles of where we were. It was strange, though, that the sound did not change as we went on, and our curiosity was fully aroused, for it was the exact note of a cow-bell heard at a distance.

It was William who solved the mystery. "I think if we look under this blanket we'll find your deer here in the canoe," said he suddenly, and investigation proved that our two frying-pans, one inside the other, moved just enough with the motion of the canoe to produce the sound as they lightly chinked together, while the note, being muffled under the rubber blanket, seemed to come from a distance.

At last we saw Ring Bolt Rock and the outlet dam. The carry, which is three-quarters of a mile long, is on the right bank, and we took a wide circle around to the taking-out place to avoid the suck of the dam.

We were soon standing on dry land again, and not so very dry either, for the rain still fell, though very gently. At the landing the ground was swampy and the purple iris grew in great profusion and was in full bloom. As we stepped ashore the air seemed full of small black insects and we did not need to look twice to tell what they saw.

"Here they are, William," said I, "and glad to see us." "I know 'em; you needn't introduce me; where's that fly oil?" answered William, all in one breath, as he proceeded to anoint his face, neck and hands with the odoriferous tar oil which he had brought for the purpose.

After we had all performed this ceremony and thereby made ourselves obnoxious to our enemies of old, the black flies, we carried canoes and wangan up the path to the high ground, where the pests were less troublesome. We then went down a trail through the woods to the dam, and climbed onto the great log

structure which holds backs the waters of Chesuncook. The scene here was superb. The gates were up and the impatient flood, freed from restraint, leaped through the barrier and rushed down the wild gorge below, a roaring, frothing torrent. There were great rocks on either hand, a wild and angry sky above, the great lake on one side and a tumult of boiling, foam-covered water on the other, while the endless forest surrounded all. We stood a long time, our eyes drinking in the scene, for it was not one on which to bestow a casual glance.

While we were on the dam the rain ceased and the mountains were again visible, though their tops remained hidden in the clouds.

The rain held up just long enough for us to take several photographs and cook and eat our dinner, after which we made the carry through the wet woods. We put in at the foot of the rapids just as the sky cleared again, and, after paddling a few rods down the stream, glided out upon beautiful Ripogenus Lake.

No words of mine are adequate to describe the vision of loveliness which burst upon our view and opened up before us.

We dropped the paddles and gazed enraptured. Ripogenus was as peaceful as if winds never blew nor storms came howling from the mountains, which rise abruptly from it on all sides. Straight ahead, the center of the picture was the group of Nesowadnehunk peaks, with grand old Ktaadn towering proudly above them all.

But the attractions of Ripogenus are not all above the surface, and we knew that other forms of beauty were beneath the wave. We directed our course to the mouth of Frost Brook, but found it completely choked with old logs and drift, so that we could not get to the pool, but we caught a few small trout nevertheless.

The big ones, which must have been under the raft, we could not raise.

At the foot of Ripogenus, near the outlet, is a log camp used by the river drivers in the spring, but deserted the rest of the year, and toward this haven we now pointed our light craft. Though the rain had ceased the sky had not cleared, and we were thankful for a more substantial shelter than one thickness of canvas.

Before morning we had cause to be more thankful still. We carried all the luggage to the camp, and left the canoes bottom up on the shore.

Behind the cabin rose a steep hill covered with white birches, and on the opposite shore we were confronted with a precipitous mountain wall. We had just time before supper to take our rods to the dam, and the white waves below it gave us our first genuine sport with the spangled denizens of the northern waters.

William had his tackle rigged first, and while I was selecting a cast from my fly-book he whipped his leader out to the edge of the foam, where the eddy drew back under the dam. I was just attaching a scarlet ibis—a favorite fly in Penobscot waters—to my leader, when I saw him strike sharply and brace himself for a struggle. The fish was not visible from where I was, but the sight of the rod with its tip bent in a graceful curve, so that it seemed incredible that the slender fabric should stand the strain, caused me to suspend my own preparations and go to his side with the landing net.

The line disappeared beneath the surface out in mid-stream, where the water was white and swift after its plunge. Suddenly from the caldron leaped a shining form, which gleamed in the air for an instant before falling with a splash back to its element. A few feet of line were recovered only to be allowed to run out again.

Again there was a mighty splash, a broad tail churned the water and the jeweled sides sparkled in the air. Then the struggle commenced anew, though it began to be more unequal; the line was reeled in gradually, though several times the pressure on the reel had to be relaxed. The pliant split bamboo did its work nobly, and I, kneeling on the slippery rocks, waited with the net in the water for the almost vanquished warrior.

Carefully William led him toward the bank; just as cautiously I drew the net under him, and a moment later we were both admiring a brook trout which lowered the scales to two and a half pounds.

We caught six fish, though the first was the largest, and then, as darkness was coming on, we retraced our steps toward camp.

We had provided for our evening meal and preferred that our breakfast should remain fresh in the cold storage under the dam.

The night was intensely dark and the door of the old log shanty opened out into a region of Egyptian blackness.

The interior was illumined with a couple of candles whose flickering flames only intensified the shadows which lurked in the corners. The floor was of hewn logs and there was one small window opposite the door. The roof was low, not much higher than a man's head; in the center was the smoke-hole and under it the fireplace. A long bunk ran the length of each side with the deacon seats in front of them.

They were bedded down with fir boughs, to which we had added a fresh supply, and the air was redolent with the aroma of the balsam; a healthful atmosphere, surely, in which to sleep.

Some time in the night we were awakened by the crash of thunder and the fierce pelting of rain on the roof. We could hear it running off the low eaves and splashing on the ground. I soon became aware that the roof immediately over my head was not impervious to water, and that a man's neck constitutes an excellent channel, and his ear a good receptacle for stray drops. Fortunately, however, there were places where the roof was tight, and I moved my blankets to a dryer locality. At frequent intervals the celestial batteries illumined the interior of the camp and the thunder rolled and echoed back and forth from mountain to mountain in deafening reverberations.

How it rained! The storm at the North East Carry was a gentle shower in comparison. Pomola must have been in an angry mood that night, for his revels with the thunder bird lasted a long time; but at last the rain ceased and the rumbling became fainter as the storm passed away over the mountains.

We again rolled ourselves in the warm folds of the blankets, and the next I knew it was broad daylight and the morning sun was streaming through the open door. William's blankets were empty and I hastily performed my toilet, for I suspected that he had stolen a march on me and was probably at that moment fishing. I seized my rod and net and hastened down the path through the wet bushes to the dam. Half there I met, to speak metaphorically, our early bird returning triumphantly to camp with the captured worm. He held up a string of seven beautiful fish ranging from twelve to sixteen inches in length, and in honor of the occasion had adorned his person with a big bouquet of wild roses and a pleasant smile of satisfaction.

As trout for breakfast was an assured fact I restrained my own impulse to skitter the seductive fly above their lair and we walked back together, I, glad of my comrade's success, he, regretting that I had not shared the sport with him.

"But you were snoozing so comfortably that I hadn't the heart to disturb you," said William.

The West Branch before reaching Ripogenus has become a powerful stream. Its waters, reinforced by numerous tributaries, have collected in the great basin of Chesuncook, which gathers, through streams of the same names, the waters of Cuxabexis and Mahneekaybahntie Lakes and various small ponds.

HIS NAME WAS DENNIS.

but irresistible with concentrated power, past the cliff opposite our camp, then bursts through the barrier and leaps wildly down the cañon. Ripogenus Gorge is about two miles long, and the carry around the rapids is three miles.

Three exceedingly long miles they are, too, while weary voyageurs are toting canoes and wangan through the woods and over the hills to the putting-in place. We spent a quiet Sunday at Ripogenus camp, and occupied two days in making the carry. While the guides took over the first canoe, William and I set out for an inspection of the gorge.

The main channel of the stream is by the left bank, but there is another channel to the right, and between them rises a high wooded island with precipitous sides. We crossed to the island by clambering over a wing dam, and then ascended the steep slope through a dense tangle of undergrowth and fallen timber, till we stood on the edge of the overhanging cliff, nearly a hundred feet above the river. We walked along the brink of the precipice for some distance till we saw below us a jam of logs which were wedged between some rocks in chaotic confusion. With rods and camera we slid and scrambled down the almost perpendicular wall, grasping at trees and bushes and digging our heels into the thin layer of soil.

Then, after the tumultuous journey between Chesuncook and Ripogenus, the assembled waters repose peacefully in the shelter of mountains and under the cool shadows of precipice and forest, as if to gain rest and strength for one of the most terrific plunges through a savage and relentless gorge made by any river in its struggles to reach the ocean. The hills which surround Ripogenus close in around the outlet, and the imprisoned flood, impatient of restraint, flows calm and deep,

We climbed out on top of the jam, which jarred and trembled with the constant buffeting of the water, and sat

"THE IMPATIENT FLOOD FREED FROM RESTRAINT." (*p. 474.*) .

down on a quivering log which projected from the interior.

Then we beheld the beauty, the sublimity, the appalling grandeur of Ripogenus. Looking up stream we saw a narrow channel flanked by high, cruel walls of jagged rock, crowned with a dense forest growth of birch and spruce. There was no shore; the crags rose straight up toward the blue sky, and

"THE LOGGERS' DESERTED CAMP."

between their weather-beaten façades, leaping, plunging and surging toward us, dashing us with spray and shaking the jam of logs to its foundation, came a seething, irresistible whirlpool of frothing water, churned into one great mass of foam. In the midst of the torrent a huge boulder, Jenkyn's Rock, splits the current, throwing the water high into the air.

Our ears were stunned by the roar, which seemed to bound and rebound from one side to the other, and a shout was like a whisper.

The rocks in the gorge were waterworn and full of seams and cracks; sharp points, ragged edges and black fissures were everywhere. We sat for a long time on the jam, looking at the scene and experiencing an intense exhilaration, while the blood in our veins throbbed in unison with the titanic pulse of Nature beating beneath our feet. We set up the camera on the trembling logs and made two instantaneous exposures, one up and one down the gorge.

More than one strong man has gone down to death in the merciless waves of Ripogenus. When the West Branch drive goes down in the spring the logs are sluiced through the dam at the outlet and then go on their wild voyage down the rapids, alternately diving and leaping as the freshet hurries them on.

Men are stationed at points on the brink of the precipice, where night and day they watch for the formation of jams; for if a log becomes wedged in the rocks, it stops others, and in a few moments there is a pile of timber thrown together in the most intricate confusion. In this case the watchers signal, one to another, by means of torches, to those at the sluice and no more logs are turned from the boom. Then the jam must be broken and the river drivers are called upon to perform the most dangerous task incidental to their adventurous calling. A log jam is like an enormous stack of gigantic jackstraws and usually one particular stick is the key to the puzzle.

This log must be cut out and started, when the whole mass falls asunder and the river again seizes them.

The men, armed with axes and cant-dogs, swarm out on the jam. When it starts they leap for the shore and safety, jumping from log to log.

They have calks in the soles of their boots and are sure-footed as cats, but death rides the rapids and occasionally some poor fellow finds himself face to face with the grim spectre.

As we toiled back to the summit of the island, we noted that contrast of delicacy and strength, beauty and savageness, which Nature often shows us, for clinging to the rock were ferns, grasses and blue harebells, nodding safely in the wind, where we could scarcely find a foothold.

At the lower end of the island, where the water eddies around in a little cove, we stood in the shadow and cast our flies. One would imagine that even a mountain trout would hesitate before braving the current of Ripogenus, but they were there, and the scarlet ibis and brown hackle proved potent charms.

So the river gave us our dinner and we returned to camp. Near the foot of the gorge there are two islands, isolated masses of precipitous rock, which, from their shape, are known respectively as the big and little heater. They are like flat-irons, with the pointed ends upstream and their flat tops on a level with the cliffs on either side. The water has worn away the rock and soil around them, and they stand there, monuments to the power of the elements. The blue berries which grow on them can be gathered only by the birds. As we walked back the woods were beautiful, though the way was beset with difficulties. The ground was carpeted with thick, soft mosses, and the wild roses and mountain laurel were in bloom. Ledges of rock and thickets of spruce and fir compelled us to deviate from a straight course; old, mossy logs had to be clambered over, and fallen trees crawled under; but the air was sweet with the smell of the woods, the shade of the green above was grateful, and our creels held the treasures of Ket-tegwe-wick.

In the afternoon we crossed the carry, Francis and Dennis with a load suspended from a setting-pole, and William and I with burdens on our shoulders.

The carry path goes up hill and down for three miles through the woods and is very steep in places. On the top of the ridge we paused to rest at a spot, where, from the top of a great rock, we had a grand view of Ktaadn and the valley below.

We went through extensive patches of

tall ferns as high as our heads, and after we descended the farther slope our path led through the bed of what was once an ancient lake.

The floor of the forest was covered with large boulders which were completely clothed with moist green moss, and so thickly were they strewn that we could barely find level ground for our feet between them. Tall trees reared their straight boles and rustled their branches all about, but as far as we could see between them the green rocks were everywhere. We cached our packs under the canoe and retraced our steps through the forest. We returned leisurely, enjoying relief from our burdens, while the shadows lengthened and the cool of the twilight refreshed us.

There are two springs by the way beside which we paused to rest and quaff the cold beverage which they held, and we paused at intervals to gather wild strawberries to add to our evening meal. The delicious little fruit was plentiful, and so were the mosquitoes.

It was dark when we ran down the hill through the grove of white birches back of the camp, but we soon had a fire going and after a late dinner of trout and strawberries, followed by a quiet smoke, we again stretched ourselves on the boughs.

We started early across the carry with our loads, but paused at the end of the first mile to visit Carry Pond, which can be seen from the trail. A mile further on we dropped our packs and turned toward the river, following a narrow path which disappeared in a dense mass of verdure. This led us to a dangerous stretch of water below the gorge proper, where the rapids are hardly less impetuous, but the walls not so high. Great masses of granite, cleft and seamed by some terrible convulsion of Nature in the past, bordered the swift current. This place is called the Arches. As we sat on a mossy ledge watching the water thunder by us in great rolling waves, Francis suddenly exclaimed, "See that duck!"

We looked, and right in mid-stream was a wood duck riding the surges and evidently struggling to keep on the surface. The bird was swept swiftly past and out of sight. On the opposite shore was a woodchuck scurrying about in search of his breakfast, and on the carry we saw several broods of young partridges led by the old hens.

Moose had recently been along, their hoofprints showing in several places; bruin also had left the imprint of his feet in the mud, and we feared that he might have visited the things we had left under the canoe the previous day, but everything was intact when we reached the end of the carry.

Near the camp we found an old snowshoe and a weather-bleached caribou antler, the relics of somebody's hunt during the winter. At the Arches we found a bed of pitcher plants (*Sarra cenia purpurea*) in blossom.

Francis and Dennis left us there to take some pictures, and after exposing several plates we jointed our rods and caught about a dozen fine trout for our supper.

In the meantime our two companions had returned to the log camp for the remaining impediments; we returned to our packs, shouldered them, and only dropped them when we reached the river. Our camp at the lower end of the carry was in a very pretty grassy glade, a few rods from the water.

The tent was pitched, and for bedding we used the giant ferns. When the guides came we had some dinner for them, and after resting a while they went back for the other canoe. We went up to the foot of the rapids and caught some more fish, after which we set about preparing supper, so that when the others came, tired and hungry, as they were sure to be, everything would be ready for them.

William was chief cook and proved himself an able one. While we were busy about the camp a rabbit came out of the bushes and sat up and watched us. He evidently did not know what to make of us, but apparently found us very amusing objects. A smudge was built at the tent door as a gentle hint to the mosquitoes that we were not at home to callers, and by the time our chores were done we heard Francis and Dennis coming. Soon a strange-looking apparition was seen approaching through the bushes, which might have been an elephant, judging from appearances; but as the body disengaged itself from the legs and was deposited on the grass, it divided itself into its component parts—the other canoe and our two companions. Ripogenus Carry was at least behind us, and we were all glad to seek an early bed that night.

27
Soldiers of the Sea

With the exception of one man all the crew of the *Jason* were lost.

SOLDIERS OF THE SEA

BY CLAY EMERY

THE day was drawing to a close on the 23d of December, 1897. There had been squalls of snow until about five o'clock, when the wind veered to the northeast and snow began to fall steadily. The wind increased in violence every minute and by six o'clock it was blowing a gale. Captain Jim of the Orleans Life Saving Station, on the Massachusetts coast, ascended the stairs leading to the tower at the top of the station and gazed out into the night.

"Afraid we'll have trouble," he remarked to the lookout stationed there. "Heaven help any vessel that strikes the shoals to-night!"

The captain descended the ladder to the kitchen of the station where the watch were getting on their boots and reefers preparatory to starting on their lonely beat; and his orders were few and to the point:

"Keep to the water's edge as much as possible to-night and keep a sharp lookout for signals off shore. If you see a light or hear the sound of a gun, report here as quick as you can. If you are nearer the half-way house than the station, make for that and telephone and wait orders from me there."

With a cheery, "All right, sir," the men started out into the night. Not a pleasant trip this, patroling the beach in the teeth of a biting snowstorm and gale of wind.

The captain was uneasy. He seemed to have a foreboding of disaster. He went out into the boat-room, examined all of the equipment carefully and saw that everything was in its place and ready for instant use. He next put on his cap and overcoat, turned the collar up around his ears and went out to the barn where his horse was munching her evening meal. He patted the mare's head affectionately, as he said, "Maria, old girl, I'm afraid you've got to go out into the storm. Sure's you're born we're going to have trouble 'fore morning. I feel it."

Captain Jim left the barn, fastening the door carefully behind him and returned to the station. All was warm and cozy within, the men not on duty were sitting around reading and smoking, apparently as unconcerned as though there were no chance of a wreck.

The telegraph operator at the little railway station sat comfortably installed in her chair near the stove complacently knitting and thinking that within an hour's time she would be able to close the office and go home. Visions of a roaring log fire and a hot supper were suddenly interrupted by the rapid click of the receiver, and she dropped her work to take the message:

SUPERINTENDENT LIFE SAVING SERVICE:

Four masted schooner ashore four miles south of Orleans station. Impossible for us to cross inlet account heavy sea. Send help quick.
(Signed)
DOANE, Keeper.

It was four miles from the telegraph station to the Superintendent's house near the coast and no one could be got to venture with the message, for by this time the snow had drifted in places to the height of a man's head and it was blowing a gale. For a while it looked as though the despatch

The *John S. Parker*, from which the crew were saved by means of the breeches buoy.

would remain undelivered, but finally the young proprietor of a near-by store volunteered to make the attempt.

For the first half hour he made good progress, but the high wind, blinding snow and great drifts he was constantly obliged to push through, soon began to tell on his strength, yet the thought that the delivery of the message might possibly be the means of saving the lives of the crew of the stranded vessel urged him forward. Fiercer and fiercer grew the storm. At times he was obliged to stop altogether and turn his back to the wind to catch his breath. Then after a moment's respite, he would renew his journey, the high drifts often necessitating his making a wide detour from the road through the fields. At the end of two hours' time his strength was almost exhausted. He was chilled to the bone by the biting cold wind and an intense longing to sit down and rest began to come over him. Visions of the wrecked ship with the winter seas breaking over her, the men high up in the rigging, lashed there for safety, slowly freezing to death, constantly came in his mind; and with it the energy.

"Will I never reach there?"

The Superintendent of the Life Saving Service, busily writing in his library, was startled by a heavy weight falling against the hall door. Peering out he could see nothing and was about to close the door when a heavy gust of wind forced it wide open and he beheld for the first time, the apparently lifeless body of a man stretched on the step.

"Good God, it's Henry," he exclaimed, as he dragged into the light the insensible youth, to whom later the Treasury Department sent a most complimentary letter on his exploit.

The Superintendent was well versed in the various methods of reviving people in this condition and hastily set to work, and it was not long before he had the messenger back to consciousness and comfortable, while he got into communication with the Orleans Life Saving Station.

"Just as I expected," said Captain Jim. "Call all hands. Get the beach apparatus ready and harness my horse quick; take extra shovels and torches and a dozen blankets."

In five minutes time the captain and crew were on their way tugging at ropes each side of the wagon to help the horse through the fearful night. Mighty drifts of snow that could not be gone through without shoveling were encountered; and the driving sleet was almost blinding. Gallantly the little band of men struggled forward on their four-mile journey to a point abreast the wreck.

Suddenly one of the men in advance shouted back: "There she is Cap, I can just make out a light. She's well off shore."

In another ten minutes they had arrived opposite the wrecked vessel and halted.

"John, unhitch the horse and take her to that old shanty below the bank, and the rest of you to your stations," said Captain Jim.

Every man sprang to his work. Each one had a certain part to do, each a certain piece of apparatus to unload. Short and quick were the orders the captain gave.

"Snap those torches. Put that sand anchor as high up on the beach as you can get it. Quick there with the lee and weather whip. Get those snatch blocks ready. Place the gun here on this little knoll. Bend on that shot line, *lively.*"

Captain Jim dropped to his knees and shoved the cartridge home, following it with the solid shot to which the long line was attached, and which demands high marksmanship and judgment to shoot over the masts of the stranded vessel.

"Everything ready, sir," came from the "number one" man.

"All right, stand by."

Captain Jim knelt over the sight of the brass cannon, now swinging the carriage from right to left and working his elevating apparatus.

"That ought to fetch her," he said under his breath, and standing erect he waited for a favorable lull in the wind to give the order to fire. He had not long to wait. "Fire!" A sharp report, and the shot and line were speeding on their mission. It was almost daylight and the captain watched the line hum out of the box, following the direction it had taken with his keen eye.

"The line is landed right over the fore stay, Cap'n Jim."

"All right. Now watch for some sign of life aboard of her."

In vain the little crew waited. No sign of life was visible aboard of the doomed vessel.

"We'll fire the gun again," said Captain Jim. "If there's anybody aboard perhaps they'll hear it this time."

The life-savers launching their boat.

The report of the gun died away and still no sign of life was seen.

"She's working inshore all the time, Cap."

"It's no use," said Captain Jim, "the crew have all been washed overboard or frozen to death and we can't do a thing to help them. The lifeboat couldn't live a minute in that sea. Spread out along shore men and keep a sharp lookout for bodies. The ship will break up before we are two hours older."

Suddenly the noise of a terrific crashing reached their ears.

"There goes the foremast, Cap'n."

Sure enough the weather rigging had given way and the foremast had gone by the board. Bits of wreckage soon began to be strewn along the beach. First a hatch and then a section of bulwark, timbers and planking, deck beams, a small piece of the cabin, the topgallant forecastle and bits of wood fairly wrenched to pieces by the tremendous force of the sea, and finally a piece of wreckage with a quarter board bearing part of the name of the wrecked vessel, "Cal——" It was soon daylight now and the wreck, with decks all awash and fast breaking up, was plainly visible.

"Haul the shot line ashore," commanded Captain Jim, "and then spread out to the south."

Soon a dark object was discerned apparently lashed to a small spar. Captain Jim's keen eyes had sighted it as it was washed from the wreck. "If I'm not mistaken," he said huskily, "there's one of the poor devils. Take a couple of heaving lines and a grappling hook and follow me, John."

Nearer and nearer the dark object came, sometimes taking a sudden move in toward shore and again when almost within reach of the line and grappling hook moving away again, carried out by the strong undertow. Captain Jim stood with a heaving line coiled in his left hand and the grappling hook in his right ready to cast it at the first favorable opportunity. Suddenly as a big sea broke, Captain Jim, who had never taken his eyes from the floating

The *Kate Harding* was so light that she came up high and dry on the beach and all her crew were rescued.

The *Elsie M. Smith*, from which thirteen men were saved before she broke up.

body for an instant, dashed into the sea nearly up to his waist, and before the next sea had broken had cast his grappling hook with unerring aim across the body and the spar to which it was lashed. He dashed back to shore before the next sea broke, carefully paying out the line until satisfied that the grappling hook had caught around the spar.

"Steady now, John. Stand by and when that next sea breaks run in and grab him."

Skilfully Captain Jim handled the line, paying it out when the undertow was so strong that it threatened to release the grappling hook.

"Now scoot!" and in a second more the body of a sailor was brought up on the beach out of the reach of the waves.

"Go back to the wagon and bring one of those torches," commanded Captain Jim. "There may be some life in him." He knelt by the body and unbuttoning a heavy pea jacket placed his hand over the sailor's heart. "There's a chance," he muttered and without waiting for the torch he lifted the body in his arms and rushed up the beach to where the gear wagon stood.

"Give me a bottle of whiskey quick and cut open that bundle of blankets."

"He ain't alive, is he Cap?" queried John.

"Don't know, but there might be a chance. I think his heart beats. So now, force his mouth open till I get some of this fire-water down him."

A low moan followed this treatment.

"Call Amos and Bill and tell them to build a fire in the shanty—where the horse is. We ain't got a minute to lose if we're going to save him," and taking the body in his arms he forced his way through the drifts to the shanty.

The shanty was used by gunners in the cold weather as a sort of warming up place, and a fire from a quantity of driftwood stored in it was soon roaring in the stone fireplace. Quickly removing the sailor's wet clothes they forced more whiskey down his throat, rubbed his body with blankets and then wrapped him up in a half dozen of them, constantly slapping his hands and going through the tactics prescribed by the service to revive such cases.

"I must go back," said Captain Jim, "stay here and work over him. We'll save him sure."

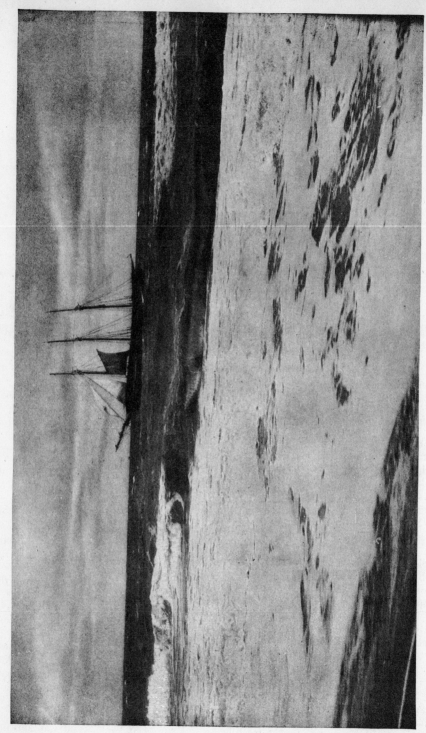

The *Lily* was beached by her captain fifteen miles east of Cape Cod light.

All of the forenoon they worked hauling up bits of wreckage beyond the reach of the sea, keeping a sharp lookout for bodies. Five more were picked up by noon. The others probably drifted out to sea. The first rescued was the only one they succeeded in resuscitating, however. Tenderly and carefully each corpse was wrapped in a blanket and hauled to the station in the beach cart and before that day was done the vessel itself had entirely disappeared. The beach for miles to the south was strewn with wreckage.

It seems almost incredible that a big, four-masted ship, so strongly built, will within a few hours after striking the beach in a heavy storm be entirely demolished. Oftentimes, however, the storm subsides soon after the vessel strikes and the crew is saved and the vessel floated. The four-masted schooner, *Katie J. Barrett*, for instance, which went ashore within a short distance of the Orleans Station, February 16, 1890, is an illustration of how close in a vessel is driven, even when loaded, by the fierce gales which sweep the coast. This wreck was so far up that one could walk dry shod around the vessel at normal low tide. On the morning when she came it was blowing so strong that the surf boat could not be launched from the beach. After two unsuccessful attempts the station men gave up further effort in that direction, and as the vessel was too far off shore to be reached by a line shot from the gun, they hurried to the harbor two miles distant and launched the boat from the Humane Society house and managed to get out over the harbor bar where the seas were not breaking so heavily. The captain and crew of nine men were nearly exhausted from the cold, but were taken ashore safely. The wreck master and his crew were then taken aboard, hoping that if the gale moderated they might be able to hold the vessel where she was with her ground tackle. Two days later, however, a heavy gale drove the schooner high up on the beach and all efforts to get her off at that time were abandoned and she was accordingly stripped. In September of the same year, however, the wreck was sold to Boston parties; and on extremely high-course tides, by means of strong tugs, the vessel was worked off shore, being kept afloat by having her

hold completely filled with empty casks. She was towed to Boston, placed in dry dock and put in repair.

An instance of where the entire crew of ten were saved by the breeches buoy was at the wreck of the schooner *Kate Harding*, which in a heavy gale with an unusually high sea on, came ashore without any cargo in her, November 3, 1892, about a mile north of the Highland Life Saving Station. The vessel was so light that she came up high and dry on the beach and the sailors were landed without great trouble.

One of the most difficult and trying conditions for the life saving men is when it is too rough to launch the surf boat and the vessel is too far off shore to get a line to. They can see the crew in the rigging of the vessel and know that it is but a few hours before these men will die, while they are powerless to save them. The wreck of the British ship *Jason*, which came ashore December 5, 1893, was such a one. She came ashore about half a mile north of the Pamet River Life Saving Station during a violent storm, and the crews of the High Head and Cohoon's Hollow Stations were summoned to the Pamet River Station to give assistance. It was too rough to launch the boat and twenty-four attempts, all of which failed, were made to shoot a line over the wreck. All of the crew were lost with the exception of one man who was washed ashore.

June and July is the inactive season at the life saving stations and during this period no crews are maintained, the captain being required only to sleep at the station and make observations three times during the night. It sometimes happens that even in these months when storms are most unlikely to occur, a vessel is wrecked on account of fog. The wind is usually light and the strong currents which sweep the New England shores carry vessels out of their course. The crews are unable to take any observations and consequently they find it impossible to tell where they are. Under these conditions, the British schooner, *Walter Miller*, was stranded on Nauset Bar during a dense fog, June 10, 1897. There was, of course, no one on duty at the Orleans and Nauset Stations except the captains, but they succeeded, however, with the help of some of the villagers who happened to be on the beach, in shooting a line

The fragments of the *Cal*—— were strewn along the shore.

off to the wreck and bringing the crew, including the captain's wife, to shore safely in the breeches buoy. The assembly flag had been hoisted on the stations as soon as the wreck was sighted and on the arrival of the crew, the sea having moderated somewhat, the surf boat was launched and the wreck boarded. The seas were sweeping over the after-part of the vessel and it was with much difficulty that they managed to save many of the personal effects of the crew. The wreck master and his crew stood by the wreck until the 17th of June, when tugs from Boston succeeded in getting her off on an extremely high tide and towed her to that port.

Vessels are wrecked also on account of their cargo shifting in a heavy gale. This makes the vessels unmanageable to a great extent and starts them leaking. At such times the crew must keep constantly pumping till exhausted or the water in the hold gains on them too fast. Then the captain beaches the vessel. Under such conditions the British schooner *Lily* was put ashore by her captain fifteen miles east of Cape Cod light on the morning of January 3, 1901. The patrol of the Nauset Life Saving Station saw the signals of distress at daylight and the crew immediately tried to launch the life-boat. It was found impossible to do so however and a short time afterward the captain of the schooner hoisted sail and beached his vessel about two and a quarter miles south

of the Nauset Station and the crew left the vessel and reached the shore safely in their own boat.

An instance of where the cargo of a vessel was saved, owing principally, however, to its being lumber, was in the British three-masted schooner, *John S. Parker*. She became unmanageable in a heavy north-east gale and struck the Orleans beach at 2.30 A.M., November 7, 1901, coming in far enough, fortunately, to allow a line to be shot aboard; and the crew of six men were saved by means of the breeches buoy. After the storm was over, the lumber was thrown overboard and hauled ashore by means of an endless line. The vessel itself, however, was a total loss.

The Gloucester fisherman, *Elsie M. Smith*, had made a successful trip to the Banks and was loaded with a full fare of fish homeward bound, when within a day's run of home she was wrecked on February 13, 1902. Proceeding under shortened sail in a northeast gale and driving snow-storm, for two days the crew had not seen the sun, and it was impossible for them to tell where they were. With hardly a moment's warning, the little vessel struck the beach two miles south of the Orleans Life Saving Station and on the instant commenced to break up. They attempted to launch one of their small fishing boats, but when two of the crew had dropped into her, she was forced away from the side of the vessel by a heavy sea which parted the painters, and being unmanageable the boat was swamped and the two men drowned. The seas were now breaking over the schooner's entire length and the remaining thirteen men of the crew were driven to the fore rigging. The vessel was sighted from the beach almost as soon as she struck and in a few moments a line was successfully shot over the forestay, the breeches buoy rigged and the thirteen men saved. The vessel and cargo were a total loss and she broke up in a few hours.

Probably no location on either the Atlantic or Pacific coasts has had so large a number of vessels stranded on its beach as this long stretch of white sand known as Cape Cod, which reaches out into the ocean from eastern Massachusetts, and it is due to the efficient life saving service instituted by the Government that so many lives are saved.

In almost every graveyard in the little villages along this coast are buried the bodies washed ashore from wrecked vessels. Generally the names are not known and no clue is found on the bodies by which they can be identified; but a careful record is kept in the archives of each village of such interments, giving the name of the ship, the date on which it came ashore, and the date the body was picked up.

Every few miles along the beach the Government has life saving stations and a crew on duty at each of them ten months in the year. These stations are connected by telephone and also with the house of the district superintendent. A local physician is appointed for each district and all bodies that come ashore must be inspected by him before interment. The marine underwriters also appoint an agent to each district, known as the wreck master of the coast and he, in their behalf, does what he can to save all property of the vessels and if possible the vessels themselves.

Few people realize the judgment and courage shown by the captains and crews of these stations, or the hardships endured in patroling the beach during the cold and bitter winter storms. They lead a lonely life, the salary is small and the danger great.

All praise to the gallant souls whose lives are devoted to the saving of men who go down to the sea in ships.

The end.

28
Wood-ware in the Rough (logging)

WOOD-WARE IN THE ROUGH

WINTER LOGGING

A SERIES OF PHOTOGRAPHS BY ARTHUR HEWITT

The man with the axe

His winter quarters and the sawmill.

How he goes to camp at the close of the day.

Binding on the great load.

The pathfinder.

Rolling up the logs.

Loaded.

Going to mill.

29
Nashua, The Gate City of the Granite State

BUSINESS SECTION OF MAIN STREET, NASHUA

NASHUA,
THE GATE CITY OF THE GRANITE STATE

By FRANKLIN HULL

IF called upon to choose from among New England's thriving cities, the one combining in a superlative degree beauty of location and surroundings with intense commercial activity and bright promise of golden reward for its spirit of vigorous enterprise and unselfish devotion of its business men to the furtherance of its every interest, Nashua, New Hampshire, must be kept in mind while all her sister cities are challenged to show in what respects they are her superior.

Nashua is the gate city of the grand old Granite State, located in the beautiful valley of the Merrimac River upon the Merrimac Valley State Highway, the main thoroughfare from the State of Massachusetts to the White Mountains, one of the greatest resorts in this country. The dweller here has at his command all the advantages of a big city, enjoying, at the same time, complete freedom from the thousand disadvantages. All modern facilities and conveniences, which usually come under municipal construction and management, are here maintained at the very highest standard.

Nashua possesses public spirit; evidence of this fact abounds on every hand. Her charitable institutions are numerous. Her people whole-heartedly support any project which is generally admitted to redound to her advantage. Wages are fully the average paid in any city in this country. House rent averages less than in any other city of her size in New England.

This is truly a manufacturing city as well as a city of homes. Visitors are at once impressed with her beauty and attractiveness and up-to-dateness meets the eye on every hand. Her streets are paved in the business section, macadamized in the residential, and are so abundantly shaded that from the tops of high buildings the city has the appearance of a vast park.

The population of Nashua is in excess of 30,000 and she is growing fast. Her city valuation is $20,000,000, and she has invested in school and city buildings $798,740, with $142,000 in her fire department, which is one of the finest in the entire East. The valuation of her manufactured products for one year is $20,500,000 and her wage payment $4,000,000 during that period—an exceptionally fine showing, and in no mean measure her enterprising Board of Trade, characterized by a spirit of broad and deep understanding of local requirements and hearty co-operation with other centres from which radiate live wires, is directly responsible for the facts cited.

Her public buildings are of the finest, including a Federal building, Court House, State Armory, Library, Hospitals, etc., and she owns public parks and play-grounds galore, the former embracing over 200 acres.

The school buildings of Nashua are modern in every respect. They are equipped with splendid systems of ventilation, heating and lighting, and the greatest care has been exercised that the sanitary conditions be of the highest order of excellence. The standard of scholarship is unexcelled.

The modern city of Nashua dates from the establishment of the cotton industry, that is from 1823, when the Nashua Manufacturing Company was chartered by the general court.

MASONIC TEMPLE   I. O. O. F. BLOCK   NASHUA M'F'G. COMPANY

Back of that lies the story of the early settlements, which is a matter rather of local and curious interest than of general importance, although, as in most New England communities, it has left its marks that are visible not only in the past, but also in the civic life of to-day. These, however, are rapidly fading before the influx of foreign population and the weightier interests of present day commercial life.

Old Dunstable and its divisions, the boundary dispute that was a source of contention in the British parliament for nearly 80 years, and the contentions that appear to be the universal heritage of the city that is built on both sides of the river, even though the river be but a span wide, are all matters out of which the story teller may glean plots and local color for the setting of his tales of early New England life, but the great stream of working men and women that is the Nashua of to-day know little about them and care less.

The Nashua of to-day is a city of the hardest kind of hard facts. Tariff issues that are mere academic discussions in many other communities are matters of immediate and vital concern. Economic conditions throughout the Nation are immediately reflected in her great industries. Questions of immigration, naturalization, and public education, about which so many things are said from vague and general sentiment, are issues that are being unconsciously met by the churches, the merchants and the educators, the employers and the toilers, themselves, in this great and typical New England manufacturing centre.

Our story must of necessity be a story of hard facts for thinking people. Of Nashua's 30,000 inhabitants, nearly 20,000 are of foreign birth or parentage, who reside in a city of varied industries, the majority of which are in an exceedingly prosperous condition. These two facts belong together, and mean that

WATER WORKS PUMPING STATION   CENTRAL FIRE STATION   NASHUA UNION STATION

this great foreign population has adapted itself to American industrial conditions, has produced skilled labor of sufficient intelligence, sobriety and steadiness to allow of progressive development, and is building in our midst a great city, of whose continuous growth and prosperity no reasonable observer can fabricate a doubt. It is only the most idle and foolish of critics who can turn away from such facts

time, it would be difficult to reassure him as to the fate of his beloved city. Unquestionably, also, Nashua and other cities similarly situated have their political and moral difficulties. But the wonder is not that these exist. They existed, also, in the good old times in another form, perhaps, but no less really. The wonder is in the order, the average morality, social and political decency, and the evidences of civic

SOLDIERS' MONUMENT, NASHNA

with a pessimistic shake of the head. A more statesmanlike view can only result in the highest optimism.

Unquestionably, if some old resident from the first part of the 19th century, who had been accustomed to seeing the sons and daughters of New England farmers coming into the village at early dawn with their lunch pails in their hands for the day's work in the mill, should stand at the gates at closing

pride and patriotism that are building a city that is an American city and a sign of promise.

Our first important fact, then, about the city of Nashua is, that it is the home of an abundant and capable laboring population who may be depended upon in the building up of an industry. They are healthy, industrious, law abiding, and loyal. Nashua is not a city of turbulent strikes or labor diffi-

UNITED STATES FISH HATCHERY   NASHUA BOAT CLUB HOUSE

culties. It passed through the recent trying time without distressing its population and without recourse to soup houses, or any other form of public charity. Families were fed and tradesmen's bills paid, although hours of labor were somewhat shortened. This is a very creditable showing, not duplicated in many large centres during that same period, and it speaks volumes for the excellence of the industrial conditions of the city, and for the thrift and intelligence of the laboring population.

Hard facts do not build upon pretty sentiments, but sentiments have a way of weaving themselves about hard facts and making them beautiful. I think that to a true lover of New England there can be no sweeter or more beautiful picture than that of the growth of the children of the foreigner into our life and institutions. It is a curious truth that the highest genius has rarely sprung from academic shades and surroundings of ease and culture. And who knows what element of salvation, what added intellectual grace these foreigners may graft upon our somewhat cold New England stock?

Be all that as it may, this is the first point that we wish to make,—that the city of Nashua possesses a splendid industrial population.

Another fact of the utmost important-

ance is that here is an important railroad centre. Transportation facilities unsurpassed in New England are at the service of the producers. Nashua has no equal in this section in railroad centering, being located upon two divisions of the Boston and Maine system, i.e., the Worcester, Nashua, and Portland and the Southern, the headquarters of the former being in Nashua. This makes Nashua the centre of six different radiating lines of steam railroads. The frog and switch shops of the entire system are here located. There are eight local freight trains and forty-two through freight trains starting from or passing through Nashua daily. There are forty-five passenger trains leaving Nashua daily, twenty-two from the East and South, twenty-three from the West and North. Nashua is only one hour's ride from Boston and six hours' from New York. The city is also a centre for electric railways, which have direct lines to Lowell, Boston, Manchester, Concord. Haverhill, Lawrence, and about fifteen miles of local system operated by the Boston and Northern Street Railway Company. With all the advantages named here, Nashua can well claim to be one of the best shipping points in New England, which is a fact of great importance to manufacturers. Nashua

ENTRANCE TO GREELEY PARK

is in immediate touch with the widest possible markets.

Whatever we may think, politically, about railroad combinations, the fact that all these railroads centre in Nashua and are, practically, under one system, simply makes for prompt and efficient service as far as the industrial world is concerned. Whether or not the abundant trolley lines centering in the city are of immediate benefit, may be a point for fair difference of opinion, but unquestionably as the city expands, they will play a very important part in the homing problems. That day of expansion cannot be very far off. I think that almost every one feels that New England is now on the verge of a great upward movement. It is said on competent authority, for example, that over $50,000,000 will be expended within the next two years for new construction in the textile in-

dustries alone, Nashua is going to share in that expansion, and in view of that fact, the abundant electrical equipment must be included among transportation facilities as an asset of value.

But the most important fact of all is that the industries at present located in the city are prosperous. Prosperity depends upon too many and too complicated conditions for any man to logically deduce it as the necessary result of any set of facts he might put together. We might analyze correctly or incorrectly the conditions that have produced the present prosperity of the city. But vastly more important than our analysis is the fact itself of prosperity.

The Pennichuck Water Works, incorporated 1853, furnishes the city of Nashua with an abundant supply of wholesome water, as pure as that sup-

COL. W. D. SWART
L. E. THURBER
GEN. J. E. TOLLES

RESIDENCES OF

F. E. ANDERSON
DR. C. S. COLLINS
MRS. DR. COLBURN

plied to any American city. The springs and flowing wells are known and famed for their quality and purity. Chemical analysis and bacteriological tests rightly enable the company to place the pure water label on its product.

For industrial and manufacturing purposes the water is equal to any. In addition to the supply from springs and wells this company has large storage reservoirs of extra fine quality water that can be used for power and fire purposes. The ponds of the company are surrounded by forests and woodlands, owned and controlled by the company, which conserve the water and protect the supply from polution.

The average daily pumpage is 2,730,000 gallons. In case of possible conflagration the company has a reserve pumping capacity of 14,000 gallons per minute, or about sixty first-class fire streams.

The supply and distribution systems are so arranged that during large fires the normal water pressures can be raised to 100 pounds per square inch.

The rates of the Pennichuck Water Works are less than most cities of the Merrimack Valley and elsewhere; and for industrial and manufacturing purposes, the lowest meter price is at the unusual rate of five cents per thousand gallons.

The Nashua Light, Heat and Power Company has a station capacity of 2250 H.P. It lights the streets with 272 arc lights and 80 incandescent on an all night and every night schedule of about 4000 hours per year. Carbon lamps are furnished and renewed free, and no charge is made for service wires or setting meters.

The company furnishes power at a maximum rate of nine cents, graded down to two cents per K.W., according to quantity.

PLANT OF THE MAINE MANUFACTURING COMPANY

HIGHLAND SPRING SANITARIUM
POST OFFICE
HILLSBORO COUNTY COURT HOUSE
NEW HIGH SCHOOL

PUBLIC LIBRARY
ST. JOSEPH'S HOSPITAL
THE ARMORY
THE INTERMEDIATE SCHOOL

The Nashua Manufacturing Company, capitalized at one million dollars, has averaged to pay seven per cent dividends for many years and this concern possesses quick assets in the shape of raw cotton, manufactured goods, and tenement property sufficient to cover the full value of the capital stock, without including the great mills and their equipment, or making a single dollar's allowance for dividend-paying power, upon which so many mushroom industries base their entire capitalization. The stock is widely distributed throughout New England, a good deal of it being locally owned.

The Jackson Manufacturing Company is capitalized at $600,000 and is in about the same situation as the Nashua Manufacturing Company.

There are five banking institutions in Nashua, two national, two savings and one trust company, having a total deposit of more than $4,000,000. The oldest is the Indian Head National Bank, organized in 1851. Its new quarters in the Telegraph Block are among the most attractive and convenient in the state. The officers are: President, David A. Gregg; Vice-president, William H. Beasom; Cashier, Ira F. Harris; Asst. Cashier, J. B. Tillotson. The bank's surplus exceeds the capitalization and it has passed through every financial panic serene and untroubled. Its newly equipped safe deposit vault is one of the best in the state.

The Second National Bank, with which the First, chartered in 1863, has recently been united, was established in 1875, and was the United States Government depositary during the time of its separate existence, and it ranks as one of the strongest financial

STARK SQUARE, NASHUA

institutions of the city. The present officers are: President, F. W. Estabrook; Vice-presidents, S. D. Chandler and W. E. Spalding; Cashier, F. A. Eaton.

The Nashua Trust Company is very strong, handling all the large variety of banking business that has come to be included in the work of trust companies, such as accounts subject to check, savings deposit, trust funds, guardianships, and acts as transfer and fiscal agents for municipalities and corporations. This company has a finely equipped safe deposit vault for use of renters. Its officers are: George W. Currier, President; W. D. Swart, Vice-president; Joseph L. Clough, Cashier.

The City Guaranty Savings Bank, organized in 1891, has grown with great rapidity.

The bank has deposits of $1,250,000 and a guaranty fund of about 20 per cent. It is purely a savings bank. Lester J. Thurber, President; H. W. Ramsdell, Treasurer.

The Citizens Institution for Savings was incorporated by the Legislature of New Hampshire in 1899 and opened for business April 2nd, 1900. The Bank was chartered as a Mutual Savings Bank, the earnings being equitably apportioned to the depositors. The laws of New Hampshire governing Savings Banks are considered as strict and conservative as those of any state in New England. From the start it has been the purpose of the Trustees to make this Institution a strictly safe place for deposits. By its charter it receives deposits of Trustees, Executors, Administrators and Guardians. Interest at three and one-half per cent is paid on all deposits, reckoning from the third day of each month. The deposits are invested in New Hampshire securities and largely in real estate mortgages, making the bank a strictly home institution, one in which the working people can safely place their money. The wisdom of the policy of the Trustees has been vindicated, as is shown by the healthy growth of the institution, indisputable evidence of the confidence and unqualified approval of the people. The banking rooms are pleasantly located in the McQuesten Block, with large vaults and safety deposit boxes.

New England's second great industry, the manufacture of boots and shoes, is also strongly represented in Nashua, which has the distinction of having the largest shoe shop under one roof in the United States. This is the Estabrook-Anderson Shoe Company. More than twelve hundred resident employees carry on the work of this great plant, which has a capacity of 15,000 pairs of shoes a day. The company was organized in 1879, and the present factory was erected in 1885. The President of the firm is Frank E. Anderson, and the Treasurer, Fred W. Estabrook.

A new factory, now in process of building, will be some over five hundred feet long, fifty feet wide, and five stories high.

It will be devoted to the manufacture of Goodyear welt shoes which will be an entirely new line for the Company.

The new factory will have an output of 600 dozen per day, and will be equipped in every particular in the most modern way, with every facility for turning out this line of goods in competition with any manufacturer in the country.

This will give the Company a capacity in both factories of 20,000 pairs of shoes per day, which, with possibly one or two exceptions, will be the largest output of any shoe manufacturing concern in this country, and will add a very large number to Nashua's resident employees.

In 1888 the W. D. Brackett and Company Factory, now operated by the W. L. Douglas Company, was brought to Nashua by inducements held out by the city government and by the citizens. Since the original plant was erected the firm has twice remodeled and enlarged its quarters. its production has constantly increased, together with the number of employees. This is a signal instance of what may wisely be done in the way of inducing industries to locate in particular communities, the faith of those who labored to bring the Brackett Company to Nashua having been fully justified by its prosperity and its value to the city.

One of the oldest establishments in the city is the Nashua Card Gummed & Coated Paper Company. A few years ago they moved into their new factory on Franklin Street. In this substantial brick building, equipped with the most modern machinery, they are doing a constantly increasing business in the manufacture of gummed, coated and glazed papers. Organized sixty years ago, it is to-day considered one of Nashua's most thriving industries.

And here is located that old-established concern, The Maine Manufacturing Company. The fact that they make the "White Mountain" refrigerators endears them not only to New England, but to the strong dealer and to the good house-wife, all over the United States. And not a town of importance but knows the cold breath of the "White Mountain." This great industry, owned, controlled and operated by John E. Cotton and I. Frank Stevens, represents a production of 50,000, and upwards, refrigerators year in, year out, in the largest refrigerator factory in the world. The "White Mountain," famous as "The Chest with the Chill in it," adds greatly to the city's wealth.

The largest and most complete factory in the world devoted to the manufacture of ice-cream freezers is another of the industries which have been drawn to Nashua by solid advantages.

An industry that has done as much as any other to carry the name of Nashua to all parts of the civilized world is the White Mountain Freezer Company. This concern was established in Nashua in 1880 and its factory is the largest and most complete of any of its kind in the country. The White Mountain Freezer is a Nashua product, of which the people of the Gate City are enthusiastically and justly proud.

Several branches of the lumber business are located in Nashua, among the largest of which is that of Gregg & Son, manufacturers of doors, sash and blinds; Proctor Brothers and Company manufacturers of barrels, kegs and pails; Roby and Swart Mfg. Co., and J. H. Tolles & Co., manufacturers of boxes and box shooks and producers of mouldings and cabinet work.

The Roby & Swart Manufacturing Company, whose principal output is boxes and box shooks, are the largest concern in their line in New England, with an annual cut of from 24,000,000 to 26,000,000 feet per year. Advantageously located on the main line of the B. & M. R. R., they use their own water power. Their property includes 30 acres, upon which are erected several fine buildings admirably equipped for their business, in which they employ 200 people. This firm supplies the Nashua Manufacturing Company and the Joelson Company with packing boxes, the remainder of the output going largely to the middle States.

The Roby & Swart Manufacturing Company is owned by the American Box and Lumber Company.

Among the metal workers of Nashua is the William Highton & Sons Company, manufacturers of hot air registers and ventilators, who moved to Nashua from Boston in 1889; and the Rollins Engine Company, which is a product of Nashua enterprise and inventive skill. The first Rollins engine was built in 1878, and installed in the old plant of the Nashua Card and Glazed Paper Company. It is an automatic engine, designed for mill and factory use. The company employs highly-skilled labor, and in its long history has never had a strike nor any serious difficulties with its employees. The Nashua Saddlery Hardware Company was organized in 1889, the stock having been subscribed by Nashua citizens. The concern has always prospered, and it possesses to-day one of the best-equipped plants of its kind, with a market throughout the United States and extending to South America and the Phillipines.

PILGRIM CONGREGATIONAL CHURCH   FIRST CONGREGATIONAL CHURCH
M. E. CHURCH   CROWN HILL BAPTIST CHURCH   EPISCOPAL CHURCH
ST. FRANCIS XAVIER CHURCH

An old and well-known Nashua enterprise is the Londonderry Lithia Water Company. Londonderry Lithia Water was first introduced as a medicinal water, but lately has been carbonated in bottles and sold as a table water throughout the length and breadth of the land. The water comes from a spring in the town of Londonderry, located in the centre of the large tract of land owned by the company. The flow of water is very abundant, even in the dryest seasons, and the bottling is conducted with the greatest care. Probably no concern in the city gives a wider publicity to the name of Nashua.

This list by no means covers the entire field of Nashua's industries, but it serves to illustrate the wide diversity and the fact that their prosperity must depend upon broader grounds than any small local advantage which might give rise to some one successful line of production. Nashua turns out a line of goods ranging from shoes to steam engines, and from cotton blankets to Londonderry Lithia Water, and all this business prospers exceedingly, compelling us to find some reason in the location and transportation facilities, for there is always a reason: Things do not simply happen.

Citizens of the city, under the guidance of the Board of Trade, very rationally look forward to growth through an inflow of varied industries. The experience of the city with new enterprises that have been induced to locate there, is of the happiest kind, affording strong encouragement to further undertakings in the same line. It is a lesson, also, to other New England communities that have often been too backward and conservative in their hospitality toward new business combinations. No such spirit exists in Nashua and any prospective manufacturer will find in this city not only exceptional advantages, but a hearty welcome and every rational inducement.

Withall, the city of Nashua is an attractive one. It was not laid out in the beginning by a landscape gardener, and the local bickerings that seem to be an inseparable element in early New England history did not always result in the happiest kind of location of highways and public buildings. But it is an old saying that time and Nature are kindly friends and very charitable toward human failings. Nature, the great adapter, softens the hard outlines and fits herself to our human idiosyncracies with the most surprising and happy results. There is many a picturesque glimpse in the old city of belfries, between treetops, and even the mills, vine-clad, rising from the water's edge, are not devoid of beauty. Nashua has a unique and beautiful library building, some very fine churches and beautiful residences, and is in line with the forward movement of our age in the matter of substantial and attractive school buildings. And there are some undeveloped possibilities. The banks of the river and its bridging, and the inevitable civic requirements of a growing city, afford opportunities for the expression of beauty in architecture and parkways that are certain to be utilized by the patriotism and civic pride of her citizens.

30
Trout and Philosophy
on a
Vermont Stream

TROUT AND PHILOSOPHY ON A VERMONT STREAM

By HOWARD C. HOLLISTER

IF any serious subject is touched upon in what is here written it will be but an incidental circumstance. Consider not your books and pens, my friends; for a little while, put away anxious thoughts and the cares which corrode the soul, the responsibilities of life and all concern therein; forget the money machine, the office and the workshop, the schoolroom and the daily task, whatever it may be, and go with me to the woods and the murmuring streams.

No thundering cataracts are here, nor will be heard the booming of raging surf upon a rocky shore. These suggest crises in men's lives, the tumult of deep emotions, and passions scarcely controlled. Nor shall great mountains with beetling crags and awful precipices tower above us. There is nothing heroic in my tale. But if you love to hear the summer breeze whisper through the pine-tree tops, if you can detect a song in the sound of running waters, if bird notes give you thoughts of joy and hope, then you can feel, if you cannot see, the scenes which indeed no brush can adequately portray, yet which my rash pen will strive to depict.

Do these things please thee or art thou he of whom it is written: "Of these, if thou be a severe, sour-complexioned man, then I here disallow thee to be a competent judge?"

The appointed day has come! The old Angler and his Friend are to start early in the morning for the upper reaches of the river and, fishing down all day, will end it at the old house. Down the country road he swings, a quaint and venerable man, the famous trout fisherman of Vermont. Henry P. Wells must have had the old man in mind when he wrote his definition: "Angler! The term is to me a title of nobility, an order of knighthood open to personal merit alone. Not to every one who casts the fly is it given to belong to this brotherhood. He who would claim admission must be gentle, kindly, courteous, temperate, unselfish, a lover of nature, a pleasant companion and a true friend; and let us be thankful there are many such." His seventy years have but bent his shoulders a little and whitened his beard and hair. An old straw hat set well on the back of his head frames a face of winning sweetness; the forehead is high, the eyes blue and keen, the nose aquiline. He has a soft mouth about which a kindly smile often plays; it is a thoughtful face, with no sternness in it. It shows the calmness of the soul that has found peace. It is like "Fishin' Jimmie's" face. What! Have you not read "Fishin' Jimmie"? Get it at once! It will bring wholesome tears.

"Good morning, Friend," comes the cheery voice; "this is just the day for us; the wind is in the south, and there will be a fine ripple on the brook; the still, glassy water is the worst to fish in; the trout see you and even the slender leader; and it will be cool and clear, with an occasional cloud to cast a shadow now and then. Come, let us start. How is your tackle?"

"Here it is, Angler, exactly as you have advised—a split-bamboo rod of eight ounces, ten feet long; a reel holding about fifty yards of tapered silk line of medium weight; flies and hooks, not forgetting a perforated tin box with close-fitting cover for the grasshoppers I caught in the upland pasture last evening just after the sun went over the western mountain. The quickly generating dew and the cool air had quite taken the hop out of them and they were easily collected, as you said they would be."

"Truly you are an apt pupil. Let me see your tackle. Yes, the rod is right for our purpose and well rigged with rings. Of course, for lake fishing or on a large stream, where in both cases a boat is used, one should have a lighter rod, five or six ounces; they are often made a fraction over four ounces and shorter. Nine feet is a good length. There the fish may run safely in the deep water and you may play them long and bring them in with a landing net. Here we shall frequently fish over bushes and through them, where we can find apertures for our rods. In such places the fish cannot safely be played. The trout when struck must be held firmly. This rod is strong enough. Let the fish fight it, the line being always taut. No trout under three pounds can overcome its spring, and in these waters we shall not find such large fish. The great ones have been too eagerly sought for many years, but we may catch some fine trout of a pound in weight, or something more. These will test your tackle well and are not secured without much care. Nor will you lose in sport for the larger fish are more sluggish. They rise to the surface deliberately as become their proportions, and take the lure slowly as the long tug on the line indicates; but the smaller trout come with a rush, and often leap clear of the water before taking the cheat, or at the time of doing so, and besides, the delicacy of their flesh is in the inverse ratio of their greatness."

Talking together, they trudged along, rods in hand, the fish baskets well stored with a lunch to be eaten at the famous spring at the foot of the maple tree in the meadow, where the noonday sun beats down hot and the fishing is not so good as in the earlier and later hours. Past the schoolhouse they go, and the old brick tavern with its wide front yard now grassgrown, where in bygone days the stage and four drew up with a flourish and discharged the tired passengers eager for a Yankee breakfast after an all-night's ride over the mountains from Boston.

The old hen scratches about the stoop, clucking to her brood, oblivious of the fact that Webster, too, stood there on the day he met the committee of citizens at the mountain top, whom he addressed in the wonderful speech beginning: "Fellow citizens, I greet you among the clouds." And the Angler told how he was there and the impression the statesman made on his youthful mind, and how at the village church the next day, it being the Sabbath,

" Talking together they trudged along."

the hymn book, Watts', was handed the great American, who waived the courtesy aside, saying he knew it all by heart. And then they talked of the Webster celebration at Dartmouth and the discussion there of the question whether or not Webster was a religious man.

The old Angler, whose knowledge of the world and of men is not circumscribed by the narrow limits of his physical horizon, to whom grief and sorrow are not unknown, whose simple life gives time for thinking deeply, and to whom doctrines and dogmas are but stumbling blocks in man's pathway in his search for truth and righteousness, said seriously, yet kindly: "Yes, it is said he did those things, but, as a man thinks in his heart, so he is. No man could speak as Webster did unless his soul was great. No great soul ever dwelt in a sordid body. He was very human; hence very weak. It is the erring whose hearts are right, who are the most joyfully received into the Kingdom.

"And now," said he, "put on a coachman, a No. 8 is best to-day. If the water were higher I should use a No. 6, and on a clear, still day a No. 10. Your leader is right for these waters, six feet long without any intermediate loops. One fly is all you can manage where there are brush and bushes. That will get caught often enough. Yes, the selection of the proper fly is a difficult matter, as different waters or streams or stages of water or time of season or time of day or the changes in the weather call for different flies; but for general use the coachman is the best. Why, I cannot tell, as it does not imitate anything that I ever saw or have heard of; then come the caddis, the black fly and gnats, the white miller, the brown hockle, the stone fly, the professor, and several of the miller species of dark brown to light brown. The fact is that while, generally speaking, it is well to imitate as nearly as possible the particular fly the trout are feeding on at the time, yet they will often strike vigorously at flies which have no resemblance to anything in the heavens above or the earth beneath or the waters under the earth. They probably regard any fly when properly handled as something alive and hence good for food. They eat other fish and each other, insects, frogs, crawfish, snails, field mice; many a

young duckling has furnished a meal to a large trout and I have seen them rise to a small brown leaf which the wind is blowing over the top of the water. But in some waters a bright fly is best and in others the more sober hued."

And now they have reached the stream. The banks, heavily wooded on either side, presenting no opportunity to cast from the shore, there is no help for it; into the water they must go. No rubber boots, if you please, but heavy hobnailed shoes and long woolen stockings. Cold? It is the essence of millions of icicles, and no degree of self-restraint can prevent the yell one emits as the water creeps up his legs.

"Angler," says the Friend, the swift, icy water swishing about his knees, "why does stepping into this water resemble the entrance into sin?"

"Give it up."

"Because it is the first step that hurts the most."

"Not so bad for so early in the morning, but please do not make such an awful noise, and stop plunging about so or we won't find a trout in the pool."

"Wh-r-r-r-r-r-r" goes the alarm rattle of a kingfisher, as he flies up the stream, frightened by this abrupt intrusion into his ancient preserves. He is our old friend who fishes the summer away on the Miami, a quaint bluish bird with long bill and wearing his grandfather's high, white collar. It is a good sign; he is here on business. A muskrat runs along the farther bank and disappears into his hole. A song sparrow pours out his cheerful lay nearby; sprightly little bird who "finds it in his heart to sing, whether in Florida or in the far Aleutian Islands," as some one has said.

And now the Angler's face shines with anticipation. The lengthening line straightens out behind and before until sixty feet of it await the final cast up the stream toward the smooth eddy just below the big rock, around which the water glides swiftly. Up into the air a trout goes, sparkling as a fugitive sunbeam strikes him, and, coming down, fastens himself on the cheat. Then he makes a great rush to one side and then to the other, the line cutting the water audibly. The rod bends to a bow. Now he is jerking and trying to get back whence he came. In vain. Already the Angler, not using the reel at

"'At the beginning of the Revolution,' said the Angler."

all, has drawn in some of the unwilling line, using his left hand, holding the line fast at the rod with the forefinger of his right hand as he gathers it in inch by inch from the reluctant fish. Then the trout makes his last great effort and comes straight at the Angler with a rush. Pull the line in fast now, O, Master Angler, or he is gone! With left hand working like a piston, the old man, breathing fast, and with flashing eyes, draws the line through the rings, still holding the fish on the spring of the rod, until it is nearly at his feet. A short dash to either side and its fight is done. It lies at the surface of the water and the fisherman leads it to the shore. Reaching down his left hand he takes hold of the leader near the hook and lifts his prize to the bank. And there it lies, its dark green, gold, and pink, and its crimson spots gleaming against the turf, the most beautiful of fish.

Then down the stream the Angler and Friend plodded, now along a meadow, through woods again, among willows and alders, casting in here and there with varying success, while the sun is shining hot.

Ah, there is the maple and the spring gushing from about its roots, the water so cold that it pains the hand thrust into it.

In the deep shade of the tree the baskets are laid, and now a fire is started nearby, one of Van Dyke's little "friendship fires," which shall also cook a few trout. "Get two flat stones, Friend—and they'll be hard to find in this boulder country, but they are sometimes worn quite flat—while I gather some sufficient wood." Into the fire the stones go and the wood is heaped about them. Soon the intense glow of live wood embers indicates that the time has come. The trout, a sliver of bacon in each, are placed on one stone, first well dusted of its ashes, and the other stone is laid upon them. Now the hot embers are raked about and over the stones and the lunch is spread on the big rock near the spring. O, ye epicures, who think nothing good unless served by a Delmonico or a Sherry, go ye into the mountains, follow a brook for half a day, get wet and tired and hungry, sit down by an ice-cold spring, and eat brook trout cooked on the spot, and delicious bread and butter liberally spread with clover honey. Not till then have ye dined.

"At the beginning of the Revolution," said the Angler as the pipes were filled, "this was old Colonel Marsh's farm. Colonel Marsh was a famous fighter in the French and Indian war and owned these acres, 1,200 of them. He was rich and loved money and had patriotic impulses, too, and was a good neighbor. In July, 1777, the Continentals were in full retreat after Ticonderoga was surrendered by General St. Clair. The rear guard under Colonel Seth Warner was defeated at Hubbardton, but only after such an obstinate resistance as to check pursuit. The retreating troops united at Fort Edward with General Schuyler's army. Burgoyne was marching southward to meet Howe at Albany and the Colonies were about to be cut in two. Lincoln and Warner were recruiting at the village of Manchester four or five miles to the southwest of us and Stark was coming over the east mountain there. Every able-bodied man must declare for king or country. The outlook for the Colonists was dark. Colonel Marsh was seen to mount his horse and spur to the south, toward Manchester. He turned, came back, rode past his house a distance to the north, then back he came and rode well to the south; again he

turned, and spurred his horse into the north, away from friends and home and honor and duty. In a few days the Battle of Bennington was fought by his neighbors and friends. Now hope came to the Colonists. Recruits poured in and Burgoyne's destruction was only a question of time. Poor Colonel Marsh! If only some friend had met him that morning; the scales were evenly hung; a word would have turned them, so narrow is the margin between success and failure, between glory and ignominy."

The old man sighed, but in a moment his face lighted up. "Speaking of Ticonderoga," he said, "my great-grandfather was at Ethan Allen's side when he demanded from the British officer in charge the surrender of the fort 'By the authority of the Great Jehovah and the Continental Congress.' That is what the histories say he said; what he actually did say was even more forcible, but it would not look so well in print. Ethan was a character. He loved to sit long at the Catamount tavern in Bennington and consume large quantities of 'West India goods.' Returning late one night to his home at Arlington, he was riding his horse along the road through a long stretch of pine trees. In the darkness he saw figures in white standing in the way waving their arms. It was a trick some of his friends were playing on him. His horse refused to go on. Honest Ethan, neither frightened nor sobered by the apparitions, shouted loudly at them:

"'If ye be men, Ethan Allen fears no man. If ye be angels, ye won't harm poor Ethan. If ye be devils, come home with me and I'll show ye a match for the whole of ye.' He was permitted to proceed."

And as they sat by the spring the old man told many a touching story of the simple life among these green hills, of gladness, and of tragedy as deep as falls to the lot of those who abide in the great cities, and of his own life. The death of his wife was the taking of the light of his life. He told how, after she was laid away and the bitterness of his grief and loneliness could not be borne longer, he had taken his rod and soon on the banks of the little river, day by day, in close communion with nature, had found peace, the peace that passeth all understanding, the gift of

God who expresses himself to us all the time in his beautiful works. "Ah, Friend," said he, "whenever you are in the midst of doubts and misunderstandings; if great grief comes to you; or when you are in any way in conflict with yourself, gather up your tackle and go to a little river and talk with it. It will sing to you a soothing song; the trees, the flowers, and the birds will speak to you as they did to me. Do you remember what Robert Louis Stevenson says: 'There is no music like a little river's. It plays the same tune (and that's the favorite) over and over again, and yet does not weary of it like men fiddlers. It takes the mind out of doors; and, though we should be grateful for good houses, there is, after all, no house like God's out-of-doors.'

"And now we must go on, for soon the western mountain will send its shadow even to the middle of the valley and a long stretch of stream awaits our fishing." First gathering up the débris of the lunch and hiding it in the bushes, they started along the stream, now taking a fish where the alders hang over the water; then standing in mid-stream they cast long lines in the deep water penned in by the thick willows on either side, a most likely place for trout and hard to get at. The old mill pond bordered by flags, the yellow lilies with an occasional white one showing where the shallow water deepened, added some luck to their creels; and now a broad meadow lay before them, through which the stream threaded its meandering way. The Angler had gone to fish a hole he knew in a brook nearby and the Friend, putting a fresh grasshopper on his hook, dropped it over a bush, holding his rod at arm's length, at a bend in the stream where the current had dug its way against and under the opposite bank. He could not see his lure struggling on the surface, but he saw the golden gleam of a trout darting from the dark brown depths toward it. "Did he see me?" "Will he take it?" A strong tug on the line. Let him go down with it an instant, then strike sharply. Heavens, what a splash, and rushing to and fro, and leaping and diving, and churning of the water! "Hold fast, Harrison hook. I can't see you, but the rod will break before you will." There is nothing to do but hold hard, and, gradually

as the trout tires himself bring the rod down stream until it is free of the bush. And the old Angler back in the meadow, hopping around with sympathetic excitement, cheers on the struggle and shouts words of encouragement and advice. Now the trout is pulled to the shore, struggling, a *monster* fish. Will he unhook himself and fall back as so many have done? Never, if it can be helped! And the Friend, contrary to all the rules for landing trout, with rod over his shoulder, bended double, shouting: "I've got him! I've got him!" starts at full run away from the stream, dragging the trout twenty feet into the meadow—a shameful thing. And the Angler says solemnly: "Well, I'll be—(H'm-m, how the old habits stick to one), that is to say, I've fished fifty-five years for trout and never saw one caught that way; but never mind, it was perfect until you landed him; and he weighs by my pocket balance here something over a pound and a half. I congratulate you, Friend. It is the largest speckled trout caught this season in the whole valley." A beauty he was indeed; who could describe him? The hole in the top of the basket was too small for him, and he was laid at the bottom of it, his head and tail curving up its sides.

Now the old house shows around the bend; the evening shadows deepen, the Phœbe bird, who from time immemorial has built her nest under the bridge, alarmed, flits away into the gathering darkness; the Angler disappears up the road, and the Friend carries his catch proudly into the house as the children and the grown-ups too crowd about, shouting "What luck? What luck?" And the big fish is held up to an admiring audience, who contemplate it and the smaller ones as they go into the refrigerator with intense satisfaction, having in view to-morrow's breakfast: fried trout, hot biscuit, maple syrup, and other good things.

The bath, the hot supper, the narration of the events of the day to interested auditors, fill up the early evening hours until at last the Friend is left alone, sitting by the great fireplace meditating a little before going to bed. Little gusts of air, drifting the tobacco smoke from the glowing bowl, tell of the rising night wind, always chilly in these mountains. Another log will make that right. The blazing fire paints the rafters and the far corners with pink; the old clock at the top of the stairs almost like a ladder, so steep are they against the central chimney around which the house is built, measures the fleeting seconds with ceaseless beats. How drowsy it makes one feel. Indeed, this has been a famous day, well spent, with no offense to God or man, and much was learned of the gentle art and more from the simple philosophy of the wise old man. Surely this sport is not puerile or trivial. Was not Christopher North a great fisherman? and did not Dr. Paley say to the Bishop of Durham, who inquired of him when an important work of his would be finished: "My lord, I shall work steadily at it when the fly-fishing season is over!" The great Isaac understood well the virtues of the art and its practise. "Nay, let me tell you," says he, "there be many that have forty times our estate that would give the greatest part of it to be healthful and cheerful like us, who, with the expense of a little money, have ate, and drank, and laughed, and angled, and sung, and slept securely; and rose next day, and cast away care, and sung, and laughed, and angled again; which are blessings rich men cannot purchase with all their money."

"Yes, I'll put on another log. The bright warm blaze is very comforting after this long day's tramp. Those old rings and hooks on the swinging crane, what

pendant pots of generous fare they must have held in the bygone days, and the great long oven in the brick work at the side of the fireplace—one can almost see the brown loaves come out, of wheaten bread and rye and *Injun,* and the pies and cakes. What scenes these old houses have witnessed, the weddings, the merry-makings. No diamonds flashing in the light; no priceless glass and plate; no mad endeavor to outdo neighbor in ostentatious display of the trappings of wealth recently acquired in devious ways. Simple souls were they, but their minds were set on lofty things. What they ate and wore came from the farm, and its surplus sent the boys, and girls, too, to the best schools of the day. Yes, and sadness came. Many a time the white-haired preacher told to the neighbors gathered together for the last sad service how the one who lay there so still had led a good life and had gone to the reward. You may count them now among the silent stones at the top of the hill. What are our houses but convenient resting places as the generations pass through them from the cradle to the grave?"

"Ding," "dong," goes the old clock. The Friend jumps up. "What, two o'clock!" A faint blue smoke curls up from the ends of the expiring logs. The cold pipe drops clattering to the floor. "And I was so tired, and was going to bed so early! I—I guess I must—have been—asleep! Good night."

31
Froggin in Maine Waters

FROGGING IN MAINE WATERS.

BY H. J. CRAIG.

NOWHERE else have I seen such mammoth bullfrogs as are to be found around some of the most remote, small lakes in Maine. The party of which I made one went "down in Maine" for fish, but eventually we ate frogs with a relish and considered them every bit as savory as trout. But it was not from lack of fish that we turned to frogs, for we had suffered the tortures of pack-carrying and rough walking in order that we might get to where fishermen were scarce and fish plentiful; and we were not disappointed.

Fried frog was an incidental luxury which we had not anticipated. I had the honor of establishing the toothsome dish on our bill of fare. I was seated on a stranded log that jutted out into the lake on which our camp was situated, leisurely cleaning a string of fine trout, when a dusky water phantom rose without warning close under my hand. It came so suddenly that it startled me for an instant, but it was only a frog, yet the largest frog I had ever seen, and I coveted him immediately just on account of his size—using him for food was an afterthought. And I hardly had him secured when I noticed his mate on the other side of the log. Frog number two cost me a wet leg, but the commotion attending his capture stirred up a third that drifted within grabbing distance and then went the way of his two predecessors.

That was the beginning. Those three frogs went into the frying-pan that night when supper was being prepared; "cook" protested a little, but I carried the point on the plea of variety. They were only samples, though, tried simply for the sake of curiosity, for none of us considered them really wholesome food; but those samples created an unexpected demand for frogs. It was unanimously agreed that the word delicious of all adjectives came the nearest to expressing their qualities, and henceforth frogs took a place of equality with the aristocratic trout.

Catching them was a peculiar sport; it was essentially a game of grab. As near as I could learn, the big frogs scarcely ever set foot on the shore. Small fry and tadpoles swarmed in the shallows, but the big black fellows, with heads nearly as large as your fist, were principally to be found in the accumulation of driftwood that formed one of the remarkable characteristics of our particular lake. There were acres of this drift completely choking up the outlet end of the lake, bleached white as old bones and water-worn with years of drifting and chafing. It was so snarled and packed together that one could with care and dexterity make his way anywhere over it, although the water underneath was from two to five feet deep. And here in this floating tangle of logs and branches, and sometimes whole trees, roots and all, were the haunts of the big bullfrogs.

They were worthy of a rifle bullet, or they could be "paddled" with a stick, as they were remarkably tame, until you touched them; but both of these methods were decidedly objectionable, for no matter how good the aim the frog would make one last convulsive leap overboard and be lost. The only safe way was to select your frog, creep up close to him, extend your hand slowly, at the same time balancing yourself nicely, and then make a mighty grab. Even after the game was fairly caught he sometimes got away, as it was no easy thing to keep both hands on the big slippery frog and both feet on a teetering, half water-logged timber. For safe keeping I used to put them one in each pocket of my old hunting-jacket, and dispose of them later. Strange to say, a frog in a pocket remained as quiet as a mouse until brought out again, but two frogs in one pocket make the liveliest kind of trouble right away. It was not a monotonous sport; sometimes the drift would start to sink under you and you would have to scamper for a better footing; sometimes a log would roll over under your weight, necessitating a frog-like leap for safety. The many sharp snags and stubs of branches that stuck up all over the drift were as hard on trousers as barbwire fence, and every frog hunt had to be supplemented by a visit to the repair kit.

At one place there was a clear space, a little pond of open water in the drift, and in the center of it a point of rock showed a few inches above the surface. Day after day I noticed a big frog enthroned on that bit of rock. Although he may not have been the king frog I considered him the largest one of all, and mourned that he was out of reach and could not be grabbed. But the king frog had troubles of his own as I discovered. One day while I was watching him and wondering if any kind of bait would tempt him to take a hook, a big mud-turtle, as large around as a dinner-plate, came to the surface and skirmished around the rock as if he had half a mind to storm it. In fact that is just what he did. For the space of half a minute there was a lively tussle over that miniature Gibraltar. I imagined they were old acquaintances and had struggled there before, they seemed to have such little respect for each other. The turtle drew his head in out of sight and rammed with all his might, while the frog kicked and scrambled and did

his best to hold his ground, but he was forced off. I closed my eyes for a moment to relieve them from the painful, dazzling reflection of the sun on the water, and when I looked again the two contestants had made a compromise— the king frog sat on the turtle's back as composedly as you please. I tried to steal away to get my camera, but the turtle was wary, and at the first move I made he slid off into the water, taking the frog along on his back.

Six of the big frogs, dressed for the frying-pan, weighed about a pound and three quarters, and furnished all the meat that four of us cared for at a meal. Frog's meat is not to be eaten in large quantities like roast beef. There are a peculiar sweetness and a flavor, almost a fragrance, about it, that invite you to stop often to taste it ; so it comes nearer being a relish than a staple, filling food. As a delicacy it can scarcely be over-estimated. There is a tradition that only the hind legs are fit to eat, but if the frog is big enough to repay the trouble of preparation, the shoulders and trunk are just as desirable as the legs. Frogs are a little troublesome to prepare, for, in common with the proverbial hen with her head off, they have a way of "not knowing when they're killed," as one of our party neatly expressed it ; and even after they are in the frying-pan they exhibit a capacity for post-mortem antics most astonishing to the novice. But this is not caused by even the faintest vestige of life remaining in them ; it seems to result from the action of the heat and the salt on the peculiarly sensitive muscles.

Our frogs were cannibals ; I can state that for a fact. I remember one specimen that had swallowed another frog a third as big as himself ; big enough, I should think to have made a very uncomfortable stomachful, or even, if swallowed alive, as must have been the case, to have kicked a hole in the captor. But in addition to the swallowed frog were half a dozen crawfish with shells and claws like flint, and the crevices were filled with horny-cased water bugs. This goes to show that the frog had an enviable digestion. With good reason one might have expected to find him dancing around with his hands on his stomach, suffering from a bad attack of colic ; but when he fell into my hands he was quietly sunning himself.